The K&W Guide To Colleges For
The Learning Disabled

The K&W Guide To Colleges For The Learning Disabled

A Resource Book for Students, Parents, and Professionals

Marybeth Kravets, M.A.
Imy F. Wax, M.S.

HarperPerennial
A Division of HarperCollins*Publishers*

Let no children be demeaned, nor have their wonder diminished, because of our ignorance or inactivity.
Let no children be deprived of discovery because we lack the resources to discover their problem.
Let no children—ever—doubt themselves or their mind because we are unsure of our commitment.

Foundation for Children
With Learning Disabilities
90 Park Avenue
New York, N.Y. 10016
(212) 687-7211

This publication is designed to provide accurate and authoritative information in regard to the subject matter covered. It is sold with the understanding that the information provided by the authors does not guarantee acceptance of any student to any college. The authors have attempted to ensure that the information in this book is accurate at press time. Statistics, costs, policies, programs, services, and personnel change periodically. Important information should be verified with current data from the various colleges.

All inquiries should be addressed to:

Kravets, Wax and Associates, Inc.
P.O. Box 187
Deerfield, Illinois 60015-0187

HarperCollins books may be purchased for educational, business, or sales promotional use. For information, please call or write: Special Markets Department, HarperCollins Publishers, Inc., 10 East 53rd Street, New York, NY 10022. Telephone: (212) 207-7528; Fax: (212) 207-7222.

FIRST EDITION

Library of Congress Cataloging-in-Publication Data

Kravets, Marybeth.
    The K & W guide to colleges for the learning disabled : a resource book for students,
parents, and professionals / Marybeth Kravets & Imy F. Wax — 1st ed.
        p.   cm.
    Rev. ed. of: The K & W guide, colleges and the learning disabled student. 1991.
    Includes index.
    ISBN: 0-06-271560-7—ISBN 0-06-461042-X (pbk.)
    1. Universities and colleges—United States—Directories.
    2. Learning disabled—Education (Higher)—United States.   I. Wax, Imy F.   II. Kravets,
    Marybeth. K & W guide, colleges and the learning disabled student.   III. Title.   IV. Title:
K and W guide to colleges for the learning disabled.
L901.K73   1991
371.9'0474'02573--dc20   91-40318

92 93 94 95 96 MPC 10 9 8 7 6 5 4 3 2 1

Contents

Acknowledgments

To the families of Marybeth Kravets and Imy F. Wax: Alan, Wendy, Steve, Mark, Sara, Cathy, Dan, Howard, Lisa, Gary, Debrah, and Greg, for their patience and support in this endeavor.

To Deerfield High School and High School District 113 for their on-going support of learning disability programs and services, and their belief in promoting the development of independence for all students and guiding them to make good decisions for life after high school.

To all of the colleges who responded to the questionnaire requesting information and who provide services and programs to promote the educational endeavors and dreams of learning disabled students.

To Daniel Appelbaum, Michael Barron, Alisa Brickman, and Lynne Lava, for their written thoughts on being involved with learning disabilities.

To Stephanie Gordon, Learning Disability specialist, Deerfield High School, Deerfield, Illinois, for her professional assistance.

To Muriel Dompke, Gail Marovitz, Dr. Dorothy Michno, Dr. Lynne Schaeffer, and Kay Severns for editing assistance.

To The Laser Shop, Inc. in Glencoe, Illinois for electronic database, layout, and typesetting.

To Opportunities Incorporated, Highland Park, Illinois, and all of the handicapable men and women, learning disabled, mentally retarded, physically disabled, who provided some assistance for this project.

Introduction

The K & W Guide To Colleges For The Learning Disabled was researched and written for students, parents, and professionals. Our objective was to write a reference resource book that benefits all three of these groups with the common goals of exploring and identifying appropriate colleges and universities. We asked ourselves: What special programs or services would professionals recommend to students with learning differences and limitations? What would professionals need to know about the programs and services at colleges and universities in order to help the students and parents in this search process? What information would be helpful to students and parents as they review descriptions of the various programs, accommodations, admission procedures, and criteria? What other information is important in providing a clearer understanding of the colleges and universities such as student enrollment, cost, and housing information? We pictured the professional and the family meeting to discuss and review various educational options. We also visualized the students and parents at home independently using this reference resource book to learn about the colleges and universities and to determine which ones would provide the necessary services for the student to have a successful experience in college. We strived for a book that would be an easy-to-use reference.

Searching for appropriate college choices is often tedious and tense but can be enjoyable and rewarding. Students with unique learning needs should approach this college search with the hope of identifying colleges which will fill all of their educational, cultural, and social needs. We hope that the *K and W Guide* to colleges with varying learning disability services will be beneficial in this college search.

In the process of compiling important information, a questionnaire was developed and sent to many colleges and universities around the country. Our aim was to be precise, comprehensive and succinct in our soliciting of information. We asked questions that would give us not only facts but also insight. We were interested in special programs and services, as well as the college's sensitivity to the learning disabled student. Some colleges and universities answered the questionnaire in full detail and even added other pamphlets and brochures that we have used in describing their programs and services. Some questionnaires were returned partially finished, and other questionnaires were returned blank, indicating no program or service or a written preference not to be included in this Resource Book.

We elected to exclude colleges that do not provide room and board although many have exemplary programs. Also excluded were colleges that offered minimal services accommodating students needing very little interaction. We have made a conscientious effort to include in this Guide the colleges which fit into our three designated support categories of Structured Program, Coordinated Services, or Services. We have included a "Quick Contact Reference List" in the back of the Guide that provides contact information for all of the colleges described in our Guide. Also included is contact information on additional colleges, community colleges, and two-year colleges not included in the descriptive part of this Guide, which will be useful to you in this search process.

We are especially appreciative of the individuals who have contributed their thoughts in our Comment Section of this Guide. All of these people have been involved with learning disabilities either professionally or personally. We felt their comments would provide a better understanding of the challenges and successes of learning disabled students.

In keeping with our philosophy of trying to make this Guide user-friendly, we have provided a section on "How To Use This Guide". Within this section we have briefly described all of the categories used in our format. We have also included a short section on the definitions of the various testing instruments and assessments required by most colleges requesting auxiliary documentation.

We are of the belief that there is not just one right college for any student, learning abled or learning disabled. Students need to explore options and select several colleges that would provide a successful environment. *The K & W Guide* describes the necessary information about programs and services available to students with a learning disability, and helps to answer questions, give direction, and add a level of comfort to the decision-making process. The authors gratefully acknowledge the time and effort of all the colleges who responded to our request for assistance in gathering current information about their services and programs. It is these colleges and others like them who believe in empowering learning disabled students to articulate their needs and are willing to work closely with these students as they seek to pursue a college education.

. . . A College Consultant

All students have their own individual learning styles. A Learning Style Inventory sometimes given to the freshman class at Deerfield High School provides information about whether students learn better in the afternoon or morning; with background noise or complete silence; from a lecture, a video, written material, or a combination of these; or whether they learn best from group or individual instruction. In addition to these learning styles, students operate on different levels of ability and motivation. Students with learning disabilities are confronted by complications which affect the way in which they receive, retain, and verbalize information.

Students who demonstrate discrepancies between motivation and ability level, and actual achievement in school are usually certified as learning disabled and are eligible to receive accommodations in high school (P.L. 92–142) as well as in college (Section 504 of the Rehabilitation Act of 1973). Documenting disabilities through educational testing and psychological assessment is an important step in helping students and their families understand the areas affected by the disability, such as reading comprehension, written and oral expression, math computation and problem solving, time management, organizational skills, notetaking skills. and social skills. Hopefully these students receive services from their school districts commencing with the identification of the learning problem and continue to be serviced throughout their education, or until it is determined that special services are no longer necessary or desired.

As the College Consultant at a public high school that sends approximately 92% of the graduates on to college, it is my responsibility to counsel all students. Generally, 10% of the graduating class receives some type of special services through the Special Education Department and 90% of these students matriculate to college. How do I help the students (and their parents) assess their individual needs and explore options for their post-secondary education?

The process begins in ninth grade through group meetings, where the general discussion "Understanding Learning Disabilities" is led by social workers and learning disability specialists. Throughout their high school years learning disabled students in the school district are exposed to special college nights which feature panel presentations by past graduates of both high schools (Deerfield and Highland Park) who are learning disabled, as well as directors of college programs with special support services, and discussions of various college programs and services led by the College Consultants and the Learning Disability Specialists. In addition, each year, so they can observe first hand the programs that are being offered, the learning disabled students are supervised on a field trip to regional colleges that offer special support services or programs.

Another important component of this process is the ongoing work between the case manager and the student. Students are given individual time to understand their disability better, to see how it impacts on academics and to determine what will help them overcome or compensate for their limitations. The goal is to assist students to articulate their particular disability, to describe the services they are receiving in high school as well as what help they will need to succeed in college.

Often during junior year, support groups led by social workers and learning disability specialists allow learning disabled students to discuss issues that present problems or concerns. Topics range from social relationships and academic problems to personal concerns about leaving high school and going to college. During the spring of junior year the college consultant and learning disability specialist meet with each learning disabled student and include parents, case manager, and counselor. The meeting concentrates on students' assessments of their disabilities and the services needed to succeed in college. At this time, my expertise becomes very important. I have traveled to over 500 campuses and have met with the directors of support services. As a consultant for the students and an interpreter of the various programs and services offered by the colleges, I act as the facilitator. I have a knowledge of the student's strengths and weaknesses through input from the case manager in the high school as well as from the testing that has been done. I am able to help the family and student sort out information, identify possible college choices, and even provide a description of the campus, the facilities, the dorm rooms and my interpretation of the environment. A list of criteria is developed for each student which matches the student with colleges that might be appropriate. There are several colleges that require early application for special programs and thus the junior year intervention is essential.

Senior year begins with follow-up meetings with each student to be certain that appropriate action is taking place at the right times based on where the student is in this process. Students' continued involvement in this college selection process is extremely important. The student must "own" the process and the "supporting cast" (college consultant; counselor, parent, case manager) needs to provide information and encouragement. Naturally the possibility exists for some disappointments, often in the form of college rejection. Learning disabled students need to be assured that if there is no "room at some inns," there will be acceptances at other colleges. Even the brightest students who are not learning disabled experience rejection from some of their college choices. Learning disabled students need to be prepared for this, and good counseling and active involvement from the student and family will usually result in successful admission to a good college match.

Most colleges will give students the opportunity to identify as learning disabled somewhere on the application. This information and accompanying documentation is useful in helping college admission officers to better understand the learning disabled student and often this data can allow the admission officers to be more flexible in an admission decision. By law, this disclosure of a learning disability cannot be used to discriminate against the student in the admission process. Some colleges will not inquire on their application about learning disabilities. If colleges do not include any question or section that allows the learning disabled students to self-identify, students may attach a letter with information.

I encourage students to base their college choices on many factors, and not solely on their learning disability. They must consider their ability level, interest, career goals, and social needs. Choosing a college is an important decision that has an impact on the life of the student. The team approach at Deerfield High School has been very successful, and the end result has been good decision making based on solid information. Many colleagues encouraged the writing of this Resource Guide to provide a more comprehensive understanding of what is available for learning disabled students. Colleges omitted from this book were either not contacted, did not respond to a request for information, do not offer services, do not fit in to one of our three categories of programs or services, or do not wish to be included in the Guide. Colleges included in the Guide were chosen solely on a collaborative decision by the authors. The factual information is a combination of descriptive information provided by the college through the questionnaire, printed materials, as well as personal interpretations and opinions.

I am very enthused about providing this information to students, parents, and professionals. I encourage you to use this as a base for your search and continue by personally contacting colleges which appear to be appropriate.

I wish you success in your pursuit of the right match and I encourage from the readers comments and suggestions to be considered for a future edition of this Guide.

Marybeth Kravets
College Consultant at Deerfield High School
Co-Author of *The K & W Guide*

. . . A Parent Of A Learning Disabled High School Student

As parents of a high school student with a learning disability, we constantly ask ourselves if we are doing everything possible for our child. We want to be able to give our child the best input and direction based on knowledge we have gained from the "experts". Eventually we must also look to ourselves for the answers.

Over the years, as we have watched our children grow and learn, we have tried to prepare for each stepping-stone they would encounter. Together, as parents and students, we have learned both the limitations and strengths that exist. While the student has been tested, poked, and prodded we have waited on the sidelines cheering. We hope that we are not pushing too much nor too little, and we hope that each time they are tested great increases in capability will be discovered. But the question always remains— how accurate are those tests, and how much can they tell us, as parents, that we don't already know? Many times they fail to reflect strengths about our child that our own observations have revealed.

When our adolescent is ready to progress to the next stepping-stone of life, both of us need to be able to have on hand the necessary instruments to make good choices. This book is for the student who is ready to seek out a higher education and for the parent who wants to be able to feel comfortable supporting this choice.

While my daughter and I were reviewing a variety of reference books on colleges for students with learning disabilities, we were constantly aware of issues and answers not being addressed clearly and concisely. Marybeth Kravets, my co-author of this Guide, and I decided to write a new reference book that would provide essential information about each college so that the student, parent, and professional could have a clearer understanding about what the colleges offered for learning disabled students.

Marybeth has traveled to hundreds of colleges and universities throughout the country, speaking to administrators regarding their interest in working with students who have learning disabilities. She has a great deal of expertise and insight regarding learning disability programs and services in colleges. From information provided by the colleges and universities we have tried to analyze and understand the opportunities offered. We have established three standards: (1) Colleges with structured programs for the learning disabled in which the program director is actively involved in admission decisions; (2) Colleges with coordinated services offering a great deal of assistance and at least one person on staff certified in learning disabilities; and (3) Colleges which offer services and are strong advocates of the learning disabled students, providing a supportive environment but have no learning disability specialist on staff.

As a parent, it was important to me that when I open a resource book to read about a particular college, descriptive information regarding that college's learning disability program would be available. I felt that the first piece of information presented should be comments about the college's overall attitudes, goals, and atmosphere of the program or services offered. These comments should enable me to quickly select some of the more appropriate colleges or universities as possibilities for my student.

In selecting the format for the information included in this Guide, we felt it was most important to describe the learning disability program and services first, followed by general information about the college. *The K & W Guide* will enable you to familiarize or refamiliarize yourself with various colleges and universities. It will help you to develop a sense of understanding regarding the vast amount of opportunities available to your student and will lend a greater degree of comfort to you as a parent.

Imy Falik Wax, M.S.,
Parent and Co-Author of *The K & W Guide*

. . . An Admission Director On Admitting The Learning Disabled To College

Twenty-two years ago when I first became an admission officer at a medium-sized public university in Texas, my mentors and colleagues suggested to me that I would encounter applicants who had not performed very well in high school. I was told to expect that some of those students would "claim" to have a reading problem and others would actually use the term dyslexia. It seems that many of my admission colleagues were somewhat dubious about the true extent of such disability (although the term dyslexia was not in widespread use at the time). It is with horror that I look back on those times when many of us simply discounted such students as just being lazy, dumb, or underprepared.

We are blessed today by greater knowledge about these conditions but, more importantly, also by compassionate understanding of those individuals who cope with one or more of the growing list of what we now call learning disabilities. Often these students exhibit superior intellectual capacity but lack the facility to mark the appropriate bubble or put it on paper in the prescribed time period. They are a resource that cannot be overlooked or swept aside by our application of some of the more odious and inappropriate labels used of the past.

We must take risks along with these students in order to help them develop their potential. We have learned that there are many disorders that impact an individual's ability to learn but do not impair their intellectual capacity. I am pleased to say that now there are many more of my colleagues who understand these needs and, working carefully with disabilities specialists and faculty, are developing ways to provide these students with the opportunity for a higher education.

At Iowa, we have a special relationship with our Office of Services for Persons With Disabilities and have operated a very successful program of alternative admission consideration for such students. We strive to enroll students with excellent academic records who also have displayed personal achievement outside the classroom. Students with learning disabilities who have used the resources available to them to their fullest potential are the ones we seek.

A diverse student body with a variety of talents, interests and backgrounds is necessary to truly deserve the label "University." Iowa welcomes applications from students with documented learning disabilities and/or attention deficit disorder. The staff in the Services for Persons With Disabilities Office as well as those in the Office of Admissions carefully evaluates the overall academic performance of these students for evidence that they will be able to successfully pursue a demanding and rigorous collegiate program. We keep in mind that we are looking for students with the ability to do college work reflected in the strength of the courses that they have taken as well as the compensatory strategies that they have employed during their high school years.

Some students fulfill all of our regular admission requirements despite documented learning disabilities. This does not mean that they no longer need compensatory strategies or a special office to assist them in advising faculty of their special needs. They do. We have had excellent success at Iowa with our special admission process for students with learning disabilities and recent data suggests that with proper attention as many as eight out of ten such students succeed at the University. Faculty are recruited to be partners in this process although we are not always perfect in our efforts and as successful as we might want to be.

We recognize that the decision for students to self identify as learning disabled is a personal choice. A student's decision not to self-identify is respected. However, it has been our experience that learning disabled students who do acknowledge the existence of a disability and seek assistance early are more likely to achieve academic success than those who wait for problems to develop. It was not too long ago that such students probably would never graduate from high school. Even if they did, they could not look forward to a future with very many options for employment. Thankfully we are making breakthroughs for many of these students and now are at the plateau of providing access and opportunities for higher education. While there are programs like Iowa's that are beginning to achieve success, we have by no means provided a paradigm consistently accepted and used throughout the country. That will come only through our making public the successes and failures of those of us who have met the challenge and taken the risk. This book certainly is one of those resources I hope will be widely used in that effort.

While we are working to educate our colleagues, to modify our systems to accommodate these students, and to provide them with the opportunity to obtain the education that they deserve, we also must begin to work as partners with industry. It will not be enough to provide an environment where an individual can complete a university degree and yet fail miserably in the world of work because of its lack of understanding and inappropriate job placement procedures. Our experience at Iowa is that these students desperately want to succeed and they want to stand on the merits of

their own achievements. To deny them the opportunity to be an asset at the highest level of their ability is to squander a valuable human resource, creating an unnecessary and unwanted liability for society. I urge students with learning disabilities and their families to demand the services they need and to be patient with those of us in the education establishment as we seek to understand. I also encourage educators at all levels to be sensitive to and aware of these individuals as a resource not to be wasted and to work diligently to provide educational opportunity to all.

Michael Barron
Director of Admissions
University of Iowa

. . . A Director Of A Learning Disability Program In College

Learning disabled students at DePaul University are successful if they prepare for college while in high school and continue to maintain and develop these skills during their college education. At the high school level, when applying to DePaul University, or other colleges, self-understanding, self-advocacy, and knowing what level of service will be needed in college are a few of the criteria to master. Students who take college preparation courses, when possible, are considered stronger applicants. A grade of "B or B-" in a college preparatory course is looked upon more favorably than a lower level course in which the student has earned an "A." If access to learning disability services began after the first year of high school and there is marked improvement in grades since the onset of services, a letter from a high school counselor or case manager would be beneficial. The letter to the admission office should request that the calculation of the cumulative grade point average exclude the year(s) of grades during which the student had no services. Aside from developing a strong foundation in high school, once accepted to college, the student should continue to refine and maintain self-awareness skills.

The most successful students in the PLuS program at DePaul University continue the maintenance process by persisting in the continued development of self-understanding, self-advocacy, and understanding the type of services and accommodations which will be needed for each course. The same would be true for learning disabled students participating in programs and services in other colleges and universities. The accomplished students are highly motivated and organized, and have realistic goals based on their strong ability. Motivated students ask questions and meet with professors to find out if assignments are "on track." They schedule times to write papers and study

for exams rather than wait until the day before to complete their work. Students in PLuS are mainstreamed in regular college courses, and they often take a reduced course load to make sure they have enough time to prepare for their classes each day. This is all part of being well organized. Students should use date books to schedule class assignments and tests as well as study times. The organized students will meet with their learning disability specialists or seek the extra help needed, and have their own agenda. PLuS offers study sessions that are student directed rather than teacher directed and tend to be the most productive. Finally, realistic goals and expectations are crucial for determining a major which taps the student's strengths instead of weaknesses. For example, if a student's learning disability is primarily in math, the student should probably avoid math related majors.

Successfully choosing a college is a complex process for all students. However, for students with learning disabilities (who plan to attend college), the search is even more complex when the variable of locating appropriate support services is added to the equation. Factors that contribute to the success of learning disabled students in college extend beyond admission requirements. Services provided in colleges and universities range from minimal support to full-blown support programs. *The K & W Guide* by Marybeth Kravets and Imy F. Wax provides crucial information for students with learning disabilities who plan to make the transition from high school to college. This Guide combines current information with vast experience on college programming for the special needs of learning disabled students.

Alisa Brickman, M.A.
Director of Productive Learning Strategies (PLuS)
DePaul University

. . . A Parent Of A Learning Disabled Student In College

As the parent of a learning disabled student, the authors have asked me to give my perspective on the college search process. When we started our "homework" for the right school, there were resources available, often vague and misleading. None gave the depth and wisdom that *The K & W Guide* provides. In this book you will find detailed information about learning disability programs as well as admissions criteria for general admission and learning disability admission, if different. You will also find answers to important questions you may not have thought to ask. You can use these questions and guidelines as you research and make decisions about college selections.

Our children are learning disabled and the first step in selecting the right school is to acknowledge and accept this fact. While being learning disabled can be a broad-based term it signifies that our children do learn differently. I was so very proud of my son Adam when I heard him discuss his learning disability clearly and intelligently with administrators, teachers, and fellow students as we visited campuses. Your child should be able to say what the disability is (decoding, processing, reversal, etc.), how it manifests itself in the learning process, and what services are required to help compensate. Whether your child needs untimed tests, taped text books or frequent tutoring, the goal is to match the student with the college that offers services that will allow for success at the college level. This Guide Book along with a realistic understanding of your child's needs, is almost all you will need to select appropriate schools.

From a parent's point of view, I have some inside tips that might help. When you and your child visit selected campuses, do schedule an interview with the Learning Disability Services Director and ask to meet learning disabled students participating in the program. Ask students how they arrange for the help they need and what kind of academic advisors they have. These students can also be an invaluable source of information about campus life, dorms and activities.

Another suggestion is to prepare your student to be assertive in college. For example, Adam knows that he needs to sit in the front of the classroom to concentrate better and avoid distractions. He has learned that he must introduce himself as a learning disabled student to his professors and make his requests known. In another situation, Adam had to ask his economics professor to rephrase a question so he could understand it. The point I'm trying to make is that our children have to know what kind of learning works best and have the confidence to seek help, use the services offered, and speak up as the need arises. We need our students to learn to compensate and live comfortably with their learning disability. It may be hidden, but it is always there.

Fortunately, the help you need in selecting the right college begins with this Guide. So good reading, and most of all good luck students as you open up a new and very exciting chapter of your life.

Lynne Lava
Parent of Adam
Deerfield, Illinois

. . .A Student With Learning Disabilities Who Has Graduated From College

As a high school student I struggled academically in a competitive environment. I was born with dyslexia, a condition marked by reading, spelling, writing, and language comprehension problems. However, this diagnosis was not clearly made until I was preparing to apply to college in my senior year of high school.

I always found school difficult, but with nurturing teachers, special courses, self-motivation, and a great deal of parental support, I was able to complete high school. It was Robert Nash, Director of Project Success at the University of Wisconsin-Oshkosh, who correctly diagnosed my learning disability as dyslexia. One teacher in high school never felt I would last any longer than six months in college, but Robert Nash and his program provided the vehicle for me to prove that teacher wrong.

Not only did I earn a Bachelor's Degree from the University of Wisconsin-Oshkosh with honors, but I also received a Master's Degree in the University's Business Administration Program. There is no doubt that the assistance I had from Project Success was instrumental in my completion of both degrees. I also reaffirmed that a learning disability need not be an embarrassment, and in addition to parental and faculty support, college friends were very accepting of my disability and interested in learning more about dyslexia.

Some of the courses in college proved to be more challenging for me, especially Accounting and Finance, but willingness to put in extra hours helped me overcome these obstacles. I was also determined to prove that high school teacher dead wrong who claimed I'd only last six months in college. Inner motivation was a key to my academic success, but I knew that I would need the strength and fortitude to look beyond the label of dyslexia and learning disabled and maintain a high degree of determination to succeed in the real working world. To other students out there who are "dealt" a learning disability I say "stick to your goals, have a set of expectations, and believe in yourself."

Daniel Appelbaum
Daniel Appelbaum works for Penguin Frozen Foods and is involved in marketing and overseeing distribution of frozen seafood products throughout the continental United States.

The purpose of *The K & W Guide* is to help students with learning disabilities who are getting ready for the college selection process. The major part of getting ready is for students to understand their strengths and weaknesses, their short term and long term goals, their disability, and what services they have been given in high school to accommodate their learning disabilities. Ultimately students will identify appropriate college choices to match their individual needs. The following are guidelines to use as a checklist to ensure that students consider all of the necessary information to enhance the final decision-making process and selection.

STUDENT SELF-ASSESSMENT: Before a student begins to explore options for post secondary education, it is important to do a self-evaluation.

1. What is the student's level of performance in high school? Is the student enrolled in regular college preparatory courses. modified courses, or individualized courses?

2. What are the student's individual strengths and weaknesses? Is it easier to remember information given during a class lecture or when the material is read to the student from a text book? Does the student perform better on written assignments or oral presentations? How are the student's skills in memorization, time management, test-taking, note-taking, and spelling? Which high school subjects are easier and which are more difficult? Which are the student's most favorite and least favorite courses and why?

3. What are the student's short term and long term goals? Are there academic areas in which the student is trying to improve? Is the student actively utilizing resource assistance and learning compensatory strategies? What does the student plan to study in college? What skills and competencies are required for the career goals being pursued?

ARTICULATION: It is helpful for learning disabled students to clearly understand their learning differences. Not only should they comprehend how the disability impacts on their learning, they should also be able to explain the nature of the disability. Students should meet with their counselor and/or case manager to learn how to describe their particular learning problems. It is helpful for students to be able to identify the assistance they are receiving in high school as well as any curriculum modification.

1. Does the student have difficulty with written language, such as using the appropriate words, organizing thoughts, writing more lengthy compositions, using correct punctuation and sentence structure, or clearly expressing thoughts?

2. Does the student have a hard time with verbal expression: for example retrieving the appropriate words, understanding what others are saying, and using words in the correct context?

3. Does the student have an eye-hand coordination problem such as finding certain information on a page or perfoming tasks which require fine motor coordination?

4. Does the student find that reading is a frustrating task? What happens when the student tries to decode unfamiliar words, understand reading assignments, or complete reading assignments within a reasonable time frame?

5. Does the student find that he or she often misspells words? Does the student mix up the sequence of letters when spelling words or get confused when trying to spell irregular words that are not spelled as they phonetically sound?

6. Does the student experience difficulty doing mathematics? Has it been hard to master the basics such as the multiplication table and how to do fractions? Does the student forget the necessary sequence of steps when answering various mathematical questions?

7. What are the study habits of the student? Does the student pay attention in class for an extended period of time or does the student get easily distracted? Are assignments often not completed or does the student not allow the necessary time to answer all the questions on a test? Are good notes taken in class or is important information left out?

8. Assess the student's handwriting ability. Are assignments difficult to read? Is appropriate capitalization used.? Does the student stay within the lines when writing and is enough space left between words?

EXPLORATION AND TIMELINES: Decision-making is an ongoing process but students who are learning disabled are encouraged to begin their exploration early in their high school years.

1. Although sophomore year is probably too early to apply to most programs in colleges or universities, there are are a few specialized learning disability programs that do require early inquiry and application. Therefore, by sophomore year students and parents should begin exploring various options. Meet with the high school counselor, the case manager, the college counselor, and begin to collect information and write for information.

2. By junior year students and their parents will have a better idea of the achievement level of the student and can begin to match this knowledge to appropriate colleges and universities. Students should try to visit some colleges, register to take the SAT or ACT if

required, and determine if they are eligible for a non-standardized administration of these tests.

3. By fall of the senior year students should be submitting their applications, scheduling required interviews, and releasing current psychological and educational testing to colleges to which they are applying. (Students under the age of eighteen must have their parent's signature to release testing information.)

CAMPUS VISITS: Often distance from home and cost can limit trips to visit colleges or universities that students may be considering as possible choices. If a tour of a few campuses can be arranged, this is an excellent way to assess the college as a possible choice.

1. Often an interview is required prior to any admission decision into special programs for learning disabled students. Interviews are generally scheduled with the director of the program. Students and their parents may also want to meet with someone from the general admissions office.

2. While visiting campus it is very helpful to take a tour of the campus with an official tour guide. Guides can provide an overview of life on campus as well as show many of the campus facilities.

3. Locate the office which services students with disabilities and meet the staff and get information.

4. Try to eat a meal in the student cafeteria, see the dormitory, locate the student center, bookstore and library, and attend one of the classes scheduled during your time on campus.

5. Drive the boundaries of the campus to get an idea of what the surrounding area may be like.

6. Take notes, take pictures, and take time to talk to some students on campus.

INTERVIEW: If an interview is required prior to an admission decision, students and parents should view this interview as an opportunity to help determine the appropriateness of the college as a possible choice. The director of the program or services or the director of admissions will have questions to ask students, and students and their parents should prepare a list of questions they would like answered.

Directors may ask:
1. When was the learning disability first diagnosed?
2. What type of assistance has the student been receiving in high school?
3. What kind of accommodations will the student need in college?
4. Can the student describe the learning difficulties?
5. How has the disability affected the student's learning?

Students and/or parents may ask:
1. What are the admission requirements, and is there any flexibility? For instance, if certain courses or a particular grade point average is required, can these requirements be modified with appropriate documentation of a disability?
2. What is the application procedure and is a special application required?
3. What auxiliary testing is required?
4. Are there extra charges or fees for the special programs?
5. Are there any remedial courses available on campus?
6. Are course waivers available for some of the required courses for graduation?
7. Who is the contact person on campus for learning disabled students?

Guidelines for a successful interview:
1. Develop a list of questions that are usually not covered in the college catalog.
2. Know what accommodations will be needed in college.
3. Students should make a short list of information that may not appear in an application but may be of interest to the director of admissions.
4. Practice interviewing to be able to answer questions clearly and comfortably.
5. Be able to describe strengths and weaknesses.
6. Be prepared to talk about extra-curricular activities.
7. Take notes and write down the name of the interviewer to use for future reference.
8. Try to relax.

RECOMMENDATIONS: Students are often required to include letters of recommendations with their college applications.

1. Students applying to special programs should have descriptive letters from counselors, teachers, or case managers who are familiar with the student's learning style, degree of motivation, and level of achievement.

2. If a particular subject area has been more difficult than others, it is helpful to have a teacher from that discipline describe the student's improvements.

3. Recommendations are often sent to the college directly by the individual who is writing the letter. Be certain the recommender knows which college the letters should be mailed to and when the letter is due.

We have just highlighted some of the areas of importance in getting ready. Now it is time to begin to utilize the information in this Guide that describes the various programs and services in over 150 of the colleges and universities in the United States.

The K & W Guide To Colleges For The Learning Disabled includes information on more than 150 colleges and universities that offer services to learning disabled students. No colleges are identical in the programs or services they provide, but there are some similarities. For the purpose of this Guide, the services and programs at the various colleges have been grouped into three categories.

Structured Programs (SP):

Colleges with structured programs offer the most comprehensive services for learning disabled students. The director and/or staff are certified in learning disabilities or related areas. The director is actively involved in the admission decision and often, the criteria for admission may be more flexible than general admission requirements. Services are highly structured and students are involved in developing plans to meet their particular learning styles and needs. Often students participating in structured programs sign a contract agreeing to actively participate in the program. There is usually an additional fee for the services.

Coordinated Services (CS):

Coordinated services differ from structured programs in that the services are not as comprehensive. These services are provided by at least one certified learning disability specialist. The staff is knowledgeable and trained to provide assistance to students to develop strategies for their individual needs. The director of the program or services may be involved in the admission decision or be in a position to assist the student with an appeal if denied admission to the college. To receive these services generally requires specific documentation of the learning disability and students are encouraged to self-identify prior to entry.

Services (S):

Services is the least comprehensive of the three categories. Colleges offering services generally provide assistance to all students. Most colleges require documentation of the disability in order for the student to receive certain accommodations. Staff and faculty actively support the learning disabled student by providing basic services to meet the needs of the students. Sometimes, just the small size of the student body allows for the necessary personal attention to help the student succeed in college.

Categories Used To Describe The Colleges And Universities/Programs and Services

The following categories will describe the topics of information used in this Guide. Each college in the book is covered on two pages, beginning with pertinent information describing the learning disability program or services. This is followed by special admission procedures, specific information about services offered and concluding with general college information. Names, costs, dates, policies and other information is always subject to change and colleges of particular interest or importance to the reader should be contacted directly for verification of the data.

1. Support:
Categories for the continuum of services
SP -Structured Program
CS -Coordinated Services
S - Services
Refer to "How to use this Guide"

2. Institution:
Type of institution (two-year or four-year public or private)

3. Comments:
A brief description of the program and services, that may include philosophy, goals and objectives

4. Program Name:
Name of special program or services

5. Program Director:
Designated person in charge of program or services
Phone Number: Telephone number for Program Director

6. Contact Person:
Person to write to or call with questions
Phone Number: Telephone number for contact Person if different from Director

7. Admissions:
Description of any special admission procedure or requirements, and/or special applications

8. Interview:
A meeting between the student and the Director of the Program or Admissions

SAMPLE

HOWAL UNIVERSITY
Howal, IL 60001
708-555-1212
IL

① **②**

Support: CS   *Institution:* 4 Yr., Public

LEARNING DISABILITY PROGRAM AND SERVICES

③ *Comments:*
The Office of Student Services at Howal University has attempted to respond to the needs of its learning disabled students by making services and staff available to them. Each student in the program is assigned a counselor who meets with them three times per week. The purpose of the initial sessions with the student is to develop guidelines for their individualized program. Some of the Services provided are: content tutoring, test accommodations and study strategies.

LEARNING DISABILITY ADMISSIONS INFORMATION

④ *Program Name:* Office of Student Services (OSS)   *Telephone*
Program Director: Beth T. Marie Packer **⑤**   708-555-1213
⑥ *Contact Person:* Charles M. Imes   same
⑦ *Admissions:*
All applications are initially reviewed by the Admissions office. If the student has indicated that they have a learning disability, the application is forwarded to the Office of Student Services. An interview may be required by Admissions and the director of OSS. A complete diagnostic evaluation is required with the application form. If the student does not have the required testing the University will administer the appropriate assessments. Some students may qualify through the Window Program, which is a conditional program for borderline admissions applicants.

⑧ *Interview:* Yes   *Diagnostic Tests:* Yes
Documentation: WAIS; WISC-R; W-J
College Entrance Exams Required: Yes   *Untimed Accepted:* Yes
Course Entrance Requirements: Yes
Are Waivers Available: Yes
Additional Information:
Students who are considered for the Window Program may have SAT scores of 600 - 750, or an ACT score of 16 - 20. These students often rank at the bottom 1/4 of their class. They have taken a college prep curriculum and have shown the potential for success.

Individualized high school coursework accepted: Yes
Essay Required: No
Special Application Required: Yes   *Submitted To:* Program Director
Number of Applications Submitted Each Year: 28
Number of Applications Accepted Each Year: 23
Number of Students Served: 69
Application Deadline for Special Admission: September of Senior year
Acceptance into Program means acceptance
into college: No, there is an appeal process

9. **Diagnostic Tests:**
   Psychoeducational evaluation
   (WISC-R WAIS-R; Woodcock-Johnson;
   WPAT; PIAT; SDAT)

10. **Documentation:**
    A summary of the interpretation and
    description of standardized tests and
    IEP (Individualized Educational Plan)

11. **College Entrance Exams
    Required:**
    Standardized tests taken prior to
    admission
    Untimed Accepted:
    Extemded time allowed

12. **Course Entrance
    Requirements:**
    Specific high school courses and other
    requirements for admission

13. **Are Waivers Available:**
    Student may be excused from certain
    high school course requirements or
    take an alternative course

14. **Additional Information:**
    May include alternative options for
    admission

15. **Individuaiized High
    School coursework
    Accepted:**
    Individualized Special Education
    classes

16. **Essay Required:**
    Student's written autobiography or
    answer to specific questions or
    description of disability

17. **Special Application
    Required:**
    Special application for special program
    or services

18. **Submitted to:**
    Application should be submitted to
    program director and/or to the office
    of admissions

19. **Number of Applications
    Submitted Yearly:**
    Number of applications received each
    year for the program or service

HOWAL UNIVERSITY
Howal, IL 60001
708-555-1212

Support: CS   *Institution:* 4 Yr., Public

LEARNING DISABILITY PROGRAM AND SERVICES

Comments:
The Office of Student Services at Howal University has attempted to respond to the needs of its learning disabled students by making services and staff available to them. Each student in the program is assigned a counselor who meets with them three times per week. The purpose of the initial sessions with the student is to develop guidelines for their individualized program. Some of the Services provided are: content tutoring, test accommodations and study strategies.

LEARNING DISABILITY ADMISSIONS INFORMATION

Program Name: Office of Student Services (OSS)   *Telephone*
Program Director: Beth T. Marie Packer   708-555-1213
Contact Person: Charles M. Imes   same
Admissions:
All applications are initially reviewed by the Admissions office. If the student has indicated that they have a learning disability, the application is forwarded to the Office of Student Services. An interview may be required by Admissions and the director of OSS. A complete diagnostic evaluation is required with the application form. If the student does not have the required testing the University will administer the appropriate assessments. Some students may qualify through the Window Program, which is a conditional program for borderline admissions applicants.

Interview: Yes   (9) *Diagnostic Tests:* Yes

(10) *Documentation:* WAIS; WISC-R; W-J

College Entrance Exams Required: Yes ———(11)——— *Untimed Accepted:* Yes

(12) *Course Entrance Requirements:* Yes

Are Waivers Available: Yes (13)

(14) *Additional Information:*
Students who are considered for the Window Program may have SAT scores of 600 - 750, or an ACT score of 16 - 20. These students often rank at the bottom 1/4 of their class. They have taken a college prep curriculum and have shown the potential for success.

(15) *Individualized high school coursework accepted:* Yes

Essay Required: No (16)

(17) *Special Application Required:* Yes   *Submitted To:* Program Director (18)

Number of Applications Submitted Each Year: 28 (19)

Number of Applications Accepted Each Year: 23

Number of Students Served: 69

Application Deadline for Special Admission: September of Senior year

*Acceptance Into Program means acceptance
Into college:* No, there is an appeal process

20. **Number of Applications Accepted Each Year:**

    Number of students admitted to participate in special program or services

21. **Number of Students Served:**

    Total number of students at the college receiving assistance or participating in the program

22. **Application Deadline for Special Admission:**

    In some cases there is a deadline for application for the special program

23. **Acceptance into the program means acceptance into the college:**

    A student's admission into the college or university is offered directly through the special program, or jointly by general admission and special services

HOWAL UNIVERSITY
Howal, IL 60001
708-555-1212

Support: CS   *Institution:* 4 Yr., Public

LEARNING DISABILITY PROGRAM AND SERVICES

Comments:
The Office of Student Services at Howal University has attempted to respond to the needs of its learning disabled students by making services and staff available to them. Each student in the program is assigned a counselor who meets with them three times per week. The purpose of the initial sessions with the student is to develop guidelines for their individualized program. Some of the Services provided are: content tutoring, test accommodations and study strategies.

LEARNING DISABILITY ADMISSIONS INFORMATION

Program Name:	Office of Student Services (OSS)	*Telephone*
Program Director:	Beth T. Marie Packer	708-555-1213
Contact Person:	Charles M. Imes	same

Admissions:
All applications are initially reviewed by the Admissions office. If the student has indicated that they have a learning disability, the application is forwarded to the Office of Student Services. An interview may be required by Admissions and the director of OSS. A complete diagnostic evaluation is required with the application form. If the student does not have the required testing the University will administer the appropriate assessments. Some students may qualify through the Window Program, which is a conditional program for borderline admissions applicants.

Interview: Yes   *Diagnostic Tests:* Yes

Documentation: WAIS; WISC-R; W-J

College Entrance Exams Required: Yes   *Untimed Accepted:* Yes

Course Entrance Requirements: Yes

Are Waivers Available: Yes

Additional Information:
Students who are considered for the Window Program may have SAT scores of 600 - 750, or an ACT score of 16 - 20. These students often rank at the bottom 1/4 of their class. They have taken a college prep curriculum and have shown the potential for success.

Individualized high school coursework accepted: Yes

Essay Required: No

Special Application Required: Yes   *Submitted To:* Program Director

Number of Applications Submitted Each Year: 28

20 *Number of Applications Accepted Each Year:*   23

Number of Students Served: 69 **21**

22 *Application Deadline for Special Admission:*   September of Senior year

Acceptance Into Program means acceptance

Into college: No, there is an appeal process **23**

24. **Learning Resource Room:**
Room or center used for delivery of services

25. **Curriculum Modification Available:**
Required courses that may be altered, waived or substituted with a different course

26. **Kurzweil Personal Reader:**
A computer that reads printed material with an optical scanner and then speaks

27. **Tutorial Help:**
Tutoring available in specific courses and/or specific skill areas

28. **Peer Tutors:**
Tutoring performed by college students with the necessary skills to provide content tutoring in a specific subject

29. **LD Specialists:**
Certified learning disability specialists

30. **Maximum Number of Hours Per Week for Services:**
The number of hours of services/tutoring given to each student each week and for each course

31. **Oral Exams:**
Exams read to the student

32. **Services For LD Only:**
Services are offered to learning disabled students only

33. **Added cost:**
Yearly additional fee for services and/or program

34. **Books on Tape:**
Course books available on tape

35. **Calculator Allowed in Class Exams:**
Professors may allow the use of a calculator in class during exams ("Y/N" used if the decision varies with each professor)

LEARNING DISABILITY SERVICES

(24) *Learning Resource Room:* Yes (25) *Curriculum Modification Available:* Yes
(26) *Kurzweil Personal Reader:* No (27) *Tutorial Help:* Yes (28) *Peer Tutors:* Yes
(29) *LD Specialists:* 3 (30) *Max. Hours/Week for services:* No Maximum
Oral Exams: (31) Yes
(32) *Services for LD Only:* Yes (33) *Added Cost:* $400 per semester
(34) *Books on Tape:* Yes
Calculator allowed in exam: Yes (35) *Taping of books not on tape:* Yes
Tape recording in class: Yes *Dictionary/computer/spellcheck during exam:* Yes
How are professors notified of LD: By the student or Program Director

GENERAL ADMISSIONS INFORMATION

Director of Admissions: Jane O. Bethy *Telephone:* 708-555-1214
Entrance Requirements:
4 yrs. English; 3 yrs. Math; 2 yrs. Science; (1 yr. Lab Science); 2 yrs. Social Studies; 2 yrs. Foreign Language; 6 electives

Test Scores: *SAT:* 920 - 950 *ACT:* 24
G.P.A.: 2.8 (average) *Class Rank:* Top 50%
Application Deadline: 8/1 *Achievement Tests:* No

COLLEGE GRADUATION REQUIREMENTS

Foreign Language: Yes *Waivers:* Depends on major
Math: No *Waivers:*
Minimum Course Load per Term: 12 credits if on financial aid

ADDITIONAL INFORMATION

Location: The University is located on 198 acres of wooded land, 60 miles northeast of Chicago.

Enrollment Information: *Undergraduate:* 12,280 *Women:* 49% *Men:* 51%
In-State Students: 70% *Out of State:* 30%
Cost Information: *In-State Tuition:* $1,500 *Out of State:* $4,230
Room & Board: $3,200 *Additional Costs:* $120
Housing Information: *University Housing:* Yes *Sorority:* 3%
% Living on Campus: 75% *Fraternity:* 10%
Athletics: NCAA Div. II

HOWAL UNIVERSITY

**36. Taping of books
not on Tape:**
A service to tape books not already on tape

37. Tape Recording In Class:
The professor may allow a student to use a tape recorder during class

**38. Dictionary/Computer/
Spellcheck During
Exams:**
The professor may allow learning disabled students to use these items during exams (may be answered by "Y/N" depending on the particular course)

**39. How Are Professors Notified of
Learning Disabilities:**
The person(s) responsible for notifying a professor about a student's disability

40. Director of Admissions:
Person in charge of general admissions
Phone Number: Telephone number for Office of Admissions

41. Entrance Requirements:
High school course requirements for admission and other additional information

42. SAT:
Scholastic Aptitude Test: A college entrance exam

43. ACT:
American College Test: A college entrance exam

44. GPA:
Grade Point Average

45. Class rank:
Student's rank in high school graduating class

46. Application Deadline:
Date application is due to Admissions Office

47. Achievement Tests:
Content-oriented tests required by many selective colleges for admission

---

LEARNING DISABILITY SERVICES

Learning Resource Room:	Yes	Curriculum Modification Available: Yes	
Kurzweil Personal Reader:	No	Tutorial Help: Yes	Peer Tutors: Yes
LD Specialists:	3	Max. Hours/Week for services:	
Oral Exams:	Yes	No Maximum	
Services for LD Only:	Yes	Added	
Books on Tape:	Yes	Cost: $400 per semester	
Calculator allowed in exam:	Yes	36 Taping of books not on tape: Yes	
Tape recording in class: 37	Yes	Dictionary/computer/spellcheck during exam: Yes 38	
How are professors notified of LD:	By the student or Program Director 39		

GENERAL ADMISSIONS INFORMATION

Director of Admissions: Jane O. Bethy 40   Telephone: 708-555-1214

Entrance Requirements:
4 yrs. English; 3 yrs. Math; 2 yrs. Science; (1 yr. Lab Science); 2 yrs. Social Studies; 2 yrs. Foreign Language; 6 electives 41

Test Scores: SAT: 920 - 950 42	ACT: 24 43	
G.P.A.: 2.8 (average) 44		Class Rank: Top 50% 45
Application Deadline: 8/1 46	Achievement Tests: No 47	

COLLEGE GRADUATION REQUIREMENTS

Foreign Language: Yes   Waivers: Depends on major
Math: No   Waivers:
Minimum Course Load per Term: 12 credits if on financial aid

ADDITIONAL INFORMATION

Location: The University is located on 198 acres of wooded land, 60 miles northeast of Chicago.

Enrollment Information:	Undergraduate: 12,280	Women: 49%	Men: 51%
	In-State Students: 70%		Out of State: 30%
Cost Information:	In-State Tuition: $1,500		Out of State: $4,230
	Room & Board: $3,200		Additional Costs: $120
Housing Information:	University Housing: Yes		Sorority: 3%
	% Living on Campus: 75%		Fraternity: 10%

Athletics: NCAA Div. II

HOWAL UNIVERSITY

48. Foreign Language:
The foreign language requirement for graduation from the college

49. Waivers:
Learning disabled students may be excused from taking specific college courses usually required for graduation (may allow a course substitution)

50. Math:
The math requirement for graduation from the college

51. Minimal Course Load Allowed Per Term:
The smallest number of courses allowed each semester

52. Location:
Location of the college

53. Enrollment information:
Total number of undergraduate students at the college

54. Women:
Number of women undergraduates

55. Men:
Number of men undergraduates

56. In-State Students:
Percent of undergraduates who are residents of the state

57. Out-Of-State:
Percent of undergraduates who are not residents of the state

58. Tuition In-State:
Cost to attend college as an in-state student

59. Tuition Out-Of -State:
Cost to attend college as an out-of-state student

60. Room and Board:
Dormitory room and food costs per year

LEARNING DISABILITY SERVICES

Learning Resource Room:	Yes	*Curriculum Modification Available:* Yes	
Kurzwell Personal Reader:	No	*Tutorial Help:* Yes	*Peer Tutors:* Yes
LD Specialists:	3	*Max. Hours/Week for services:*	
Oral Exams:	Yes	No Maximum	
Services for LD Only:	Yes	*Added*	
Books on Tape:	Yes	*Cost:* $400 per semester	
Calculator allowed in exam:	Yes	*Taping of books not on tape:* Yes	
Tape recording in class:	Yes	*Dictionary/computer/spellcheck during exam:* Yes	

How are professors notified of LD: By the student or Program Director

GENERAL ADMISSIONS INFORMATION

Director of Admissions: Jane O. Bethy   *Telephone:* 708-555-1214

Entrance Requirements:

4 yrs. English; 3 yrs. Math; 2 yrs. Science; (1 yr. Lab Science); 2 yrs. Social Studies; 2 yrs. Foreign Language; 6 electives

Test Scores: *SAT:* 920 - 950   *ACT:* 24

G.P.A.: 2.8 (average)   *Class Rank:* Top 50%

Application Deadline: 8/1   *Achievement Tests:* No

COLLEGE GRADUATION REQUIREMENTS

48 *Foreign Language:* Yes   **Waivers:** Depends on major

Math: No **50**   **49** *Waivers:*

51 *Minimum Course Load per Term:* 12 credits if on financial aid

ADDITIONAL INFORMATION

52 *Location:* The University is located on 198 acres of wooded land, 60 miles northeast of Chicago.

53 *Enrollment Information:* *Undergraduate:* 12,280   *Women:* 49% **54** *Men:* 51% **55**

56 *In-State Students:* 70%   **57** *Out of State:* 30%

Cost Information: *In-State Tuition:* $1,500 **58**   *Out of State:* $4,230 **59**

60 *Room & Board:* $3,200   *Additional Costs:* $120

Housing Information: *University Housing:* Yes   *Sorority:* 3%

% Living on Campus: 75%   *Fraternity:* 10%

Athletics: NCAA Div. II

HOWAL UNIVERSITY

61. Additional Costs:
Extra fees

62. University Housing Available:
Dormitories or apartments owned and operated by the university

63. Sorority:
Percent of females who join a sorority

64. Fraternity:
Percent of males who join a fraternity

65. Percent Of Students Living On Campus:
Percent of undergraduates who live in university housing

66. Athletics:
Inter-Collegiate Athletic Association

LEARNING DISABILITY SERVICES

Learning Resource Room:	Yes	*Curriculum Modification Available:* Yes	
Kurzweil Personal Reader:	No	*Tutorial Help:* Yes	*Peer Tutors:* Yes
LD Specialists:	3	*Max. Hours/Week for services:*	
Oral Exams:	Yes	No Maximum	
Services for LD Only:	Yes	*Added*	
Books on Tape:	Yes	*Cost:* $400 per semester	
Calculator allowed in exam:	Yes	*Taping of books not on tape:* Yes	
Tape recording in class:	Yes	*Dictionary/computer/spellcheck during exam:* Yes	

How are professors notified of LD: By the student or Program Director

GENERAL ADMISSIONS INFORMATION

Director of Admissions: Jane O. Bethy   *Telephone:* 708-555-1214

Entrance Requirements:

4 yrs. English; 3 yrs. Math; 2 yrs. Science; (1 yr. Lab Science); 2 yrs. Social Studies; 2 yrs. Foreign Language; 6 electives

Test Scores: *SAT:* 920 - 950   *ACT:* 24

G.P.A.: 2.8 (average)   *Class Rank:* Top 50%

Application Deadline: 8/1   *Achievement Tests:* No

COLLEGE GRADUATION REQUIREMENTS

Foreign Language: Yes   *Walvers:* Depends on major

Math: No   *Walvers:*

Minimum Course Load per Term: 12 credits if on financial aid

ADDITIONAL INFORMATION

Location: The University is located on 198 acres of wooded land, 60 miles northeast of Chicago.

Enrollment Information: *Undergraduate:* 12,280   *Women:* 49%   *Men:* 51%

                          In-State Students: 70%   *Out of State:* 30%

Cost Information: *In-State Tuition:* $1,500   *Out of State:* $4,230

                          Room & Board: $3,200   *Additional Costs:* $120 **61**

Housing Information: *University Housing:* Yes **62**   **63** *Sorority:* 3%

         65 *% Living on Campus:* 75%   *Fraternity:* 10% **64**

Athletics: NCAA Div. II **66**

HOWAL UNIVERSITY

College and University Listings

Support: S   **Institution:** 4 yr. Public

LEARNING DISABILITY PROGRAM AND SERVICES

Comments:

The Office of Student Services assists students with learning disabilities in participating in academic and student life. The primary role of the office is to serve as a referral agent of campus services that are available to learning disabled students. The Learning Skills Center is available to provide all students with reading assistance, writing lab, and support with different academic subjects. Tutoring is provided by work study students on a first-come-first-serve basis.

LEARNING DISABILITY ADMISSIONS INFORMATION

Program Name: Learning Disability Program   **Telephone**

Program Director: Warner Moore   205-348-6796

Contact Person: same

Admissions:

All students must meet regular entrance requirements. Learning Disability students like any other must be admitted to the University prior to seeking accommodations for their disability. To be provided accommodations they must present evidence of a learning disability and have been tested within 3 years from the date of entry to the University.

Interview: No   **Diagnostic Tests:** Yes

Documentation:

College Entrance Exams Required: Yes

Course Entrance Requirements: Yes   **Untimed Accepted:** Yes

Are Waivers Available: No

Additional Information:

Individualized high school coursework accepted: Yes

Essay Required: No

Special Application Required: No   **Submitted To:**

Number of Applications Submitted Each Year:

Number of Applications Accepted Each Year:

Number of Students Served:

Application Deadline for Special Admission:

Acceptance into Program means acceptance into college:

13

LEARNING DISABILITY SERVICES

Learning Resource Room: Yes   **Curriculum Modification Available:** No

Kurzweil Personal Reader: No   **Tutorial Help:** Yes   **Peer Tutors:** Yes

LD Specialists: No   **Max. Hours/Week for services:**

Oral Exams: No   2 hrs. p/w

Services for LD Only: Yes   **Added**

Books on Tape: Yes   **Cost:** None

Calculator allowed in exam: Yes   **Taping of books not on tape:** Yes

Tape recording in class: Yes   **Dictionary/computer/spellcheck during exam:** Yes

How are professors notified of LD: By memo from the Director of the program

GENERAL ADMISSIONS INFORMATION

Director of Admissions: Dr. Roy C. Smith   **Telephone:** 205-348-5666

Entrance Requirements:

4 yrs. English; 3 yrs. Math; 3 yrs. Science; 2 yrs. Social Science; Foreign Language; 2 yrs. History; 6 electives.

Test Scores: **SAT:** 952   **ACT:** 22 minimum

G.P.A.: 2.0 minimum   **Class Rank:**

Application Deadline: 4/15   **Achievement Tests:**

COLLEGE GRADUATION REQUIREMENTS

Foreign Language: Yes   **Waivers:** No

Math: Yes   **Waivers:** No

Minimum Course Load per Term: 12 credits per/semester

ADDITIONAL INFORMATION

Location: The school is located 11/2 hours from the city of Birmingham.

Enrollment Information: **Undergraduate:** 17,000   **Women:** 51%   **Men:** 49%

      In-State Students: 66%   **Out of State:** 34%

Cost Information: **In-State Tuition:** $1,724   **Out of State:** $4,260

      Room & Board: $2,900   **Additional Costs:** $452

Housing Information: **University Housing:** Yes   **Sorority:** 30%

      % Living on Campus: 28%   **Fraternity:** 28%

Athletics: NCAA Div. I

Support: CS   *Institution:* 4 yr. Public

LEARNING DISABILITY PROGRAM AND SERVICES

Comments:

The University of Alaska students with learning disabilities may receive a broad range of support services once admitted. A counselor trained to work with disabled students provides specialized assistance and referral to other service agencies. To allow time for planning and scheduling assistance students are encouraged to contact the Disabled Student Services office several weeks before registration each semester. On-going communication with the counselor throughout the semester is encouraged.

LEARNING DISABILITY ADMISSIONS INFORMATION

		Telephone
Program Name:	Disabled Student Services	
Program Director:	Doran Vaughan, Counselor	907-786-1570
Contact Person:	Doran Vaughan, Katty Weinhold	907-786-1406

Admissions:

Open admissions policy. The Disabled Student Services office is reviewing possible standardization of learning disability testing and assessment. Students who are not eligible for entrance to the 4 year program may be admitted under the Associate of Arts Program or through open door admissions.

Interview: No

Documentation:

College Entrance Exams Required: Yes

Course Entrance Requirements: Yes

Are Waivers Available: Yes

Diagnostic Tests: No

Untimed Accepted: Yes

Additional Information:

Many courses have prerequisites which can be waived based on prior high school coursework or assessment tests.

Individualized high school coursework accepted: Yes (Vocational courses)

Essay Required: No

Special Application Required: No   *Submitted To:*

Number of Applications Submitted Each Year: 70

Number of Applications Accepted Each Year: All who request

Number of Students Served: 40%-60% of school population

Application Deadline for Special Admission: No

Acceptance into Program means acceptance into college:

LEARNING DISABILITY SERVICES

Learning Resource Room: Yes   **Curriculum Modification Available:** No

Kurzweil Personal Reader: No   **Tutorial Help:** Yes   **Peer Tutors:** Yes

LD Specialists: 2   **Max. Hours/Week for services:**

Oral Exams: Yes   No limit

Services for LD Only: No   **Added**

Books on Tape: Yes   **Cost:** None

Calculator allowed in exam: Yes   **Taping of books not on tape:** Yes

Tape recording in class: Yes   **Dictionary/computer/spellcheck during exam:** Y/N

How are professors notified of LD: By the student or the Program Director

GENERAL ADMISSIONS INFORMATION

Director of Admissions: Linda Berg Smith   **Telephone:** 907-786-1525

Entrance Requirements:

Open admissions. High school transcript- recommended: 3 yrs. English; 2 yrs. Math; 1 yr. Social Science; 1 yr. Science; 1 yr. Foreign Language; 1 yr. Science; Computer Science; Art. A student with a GPA below 2.5 may be admitted on a probationary basis.

Test Scores: **SAT:** 851   **ACT:** 21 average

G.P.A.: 2.5   **Class Rank:**

Application Deadline: 7/1   **Achievement Tests:**

COLLEGE GRADUATION REQUIREMENTS

Foreign Language: No   **Waivers:**

Math: Yes   **Waivers:** Case-by-case basis

Minimum Course Load per Term: Students not on financial aid may take as few credits as they want.

ADDITIONAL INFORMATION

Location: The University of Alaska is an urban campus, on 350 acres, 7 miles from downtown Anchorage.

Enrollment Information: **Undergraduate:** 12,860   **Women:** 59%   **Men:** 41%

          In-State Students: 91%   **Out of State:** 9%

Cost Information: **In-State Tuition:** $1,192   **Out of State:** $3,600

          Room & Board: $1,800   **Additional Costs:** $74.

Housing Information: **University Housing:** Yes   **Sorority:** No

          % Living on Campus: 1%   **Fraternity:** 1

Athletics: NCAA Div. II

Support: CS   **Institution:** 4 Yr. Public

LEARNING DISABILITY PROGRAM AND SERVICES

Comments:

Students in the Disabled Student Resources Program are mainstreamed. Support is available but students need to be assertive and have a desire to succeed. The services of the Program are geared to the need of the particular student. The goal of the program is to assist the student in becoming academically and socially independent. Every service is individually based. The Program is integrated into the mainstream programing for all ASU students. Services include individual academic program development, tutoring, test accommodations and support group meetings.

LEARNING DISABILITY ADMISSIONS INFORMATION

Program Name:	Disabled Student Resources Program	**Telephone**
Program Director:	Tedde Scharf	602-965-1234
Contact Person:	Deborah Taska; Susan Frank; Denise Labreque	same

Admissions:

Students apply to ASU and self-identify as learning disabled to be eligible for the Program. Learning disabled students must complete ASU general admission requirements and submit a current diagnosis of their specific learning disability and the WAIS-R. Students also must submit an extensive case history. In general, students accepted into ASU rank in the top 50% of their class.

Interview: Optional

Diagnostic Tests: Yes

Documentation: WAIS-R; Psychometric summary of scores

College Entrance Exams Required: Yes   **Untimed Accepted:** Yes

Course Entrance Requirements: Yes

Are Waivers Available:

Additional Information:

If denied admission an appeal is possible by writing a descriptive letter stating reason for wanting to attend ASU and give examples of ability to be successful. Include examples of motivation and perseverance in high school. The high school transcript should show gradual upward trend in courses and grades. Three letter of recommendation should also be included. SAT and ACT Verbal are used for English placement purposes.

Individualized high school coursework accepted: As appropriate

Essay Required: Part of appeal process

Special Application Required: **Submitted To:**

Number of Applications Submitted Each Year:

Number of Applications Accepted Each Year:

Number of Students Served: No cap at this time

Application Deadline for Special Admission: No

Acceptance into Program means acceptance into college: No

17

LEARNING DISABILITY SERVICES

Learning Resource Room: Yes	**Curriculum Modification Available:** Y/N	
Kurzweil Personal Reader: Yes	**Tutorial Help:** Yes	**Peer Tutors:** Yes
LD Specialists: 3	**Max. Hours/Week for services:**	
Oral Exams: Yes	Individually determined	
Services for LD Only: No	**Added**	
Books on Tape: Yes	**Cost:** None	
Calculator allowed in exam: Yes	**Taping of books not on tape:** Yes	
Tape recording in class: Yes	**Dictionary/computer/spellcheck during exam:** Yes	

How are professors notified of LD: Student self-identifies

GENERAL ADMISSIONS INFORMATION

Director of Admissions: Susan R. Clouse   **Telephone:** 602-965-7788

Entrance Requirements:

11 academic credits including: 4 yrs. English; 2 yrs. Lab Science (biology, chemistry or physics); 2 yrs. Algebra; 1 yr. Geometry; 1 yr. American History; 1 yr. Social Studies. Out-of -state applicants must rank in the top 25% of their class or have a GPA of 3.0, or a 24 ACT or 1010 SAT.

Test Scores: **SAT:** 930/1010 (out-of-state)   **ACT:** 22/24 (out-of-state)

G.P.A.: 2.5/3.0 (out-of-state)   **Class Rank:** top 50%

Application Deadline: Rolling   **Achievement Tests:** No

COLLEGE GRADUATION REQUIREMENTS

Foreign Language: **Waivers:** Major specific

Math: **Waivers:** Major specific

Minimum Course Load per Term: 12 hours to be full time

ADDITIONAL INFORMATION

Location: Arizona State University is a city school about 5 miles from Phoenix.

Enrollment Information:	**Undergraduate:** 32,606	**Women:** 48%		**Men:** 52%
	In-State Students: 79%			**Out of State:** 21%
Cost Information:	**In-State Tuition:** $1,400			**Out of State:** $6,400
	Room & Board: $3,500		**Additional Costs:**	
Housing Information:	**University Housing:** Yes			**Sorority:** 9%
	% Living on Campus: 12%			**Fraternity:** 11%

Athletics: NCAA Div. I

Support: CS   **Institution:** 4 yr. Public

LEARNING DISABILITY PROGRAM AND SERVICES

Comments:

The S.A.L.T. (Strategic Alternative Learning Techniques) Program provides services to help learning disabled University of Arizona students develop their study and life skills. Support services include both academic programs and counseling components. Students receive assistance with academic planning and registration followed by regularly scheduled staff contact to monitor progress. A Drop-In-Center is available for study, tutoring and student/staff interaction.

LEARNING DISABILITY ADMISSIONS INFORMATION

Program Name:	S.A.L.T.	**Telephone**
Program Director:	Eleanor Harner	602-621-1242
Contact Person:	Rose Wilhite	same

Admissions:

When making application to the University, the student should clearly identify as learning disabled. Joint consideration will then be given to the application by the Admissions Office and the S.A.L.T. Staff. Students wishing to enroll in S.A.L.T. must also apply directly to the program in addition to the general University application. Documented identification of the disability must be provided from school, psychologist or clinic. A G.P.A. between 2.0 and 2.5 may be considered under special circumstances as determined by the Admissions Staff.

Interview: Yes   **Diagnostic Tests:** Yes

Documentation: WAIS-R; Woodcock-Johnson

College Entrance Exams Required: Yes   **Untimed Accepted:** Yes

Course Entrance Requirements: Yes

Are Waivers Available: Yes

Additional Information:

There are no minimum ACT or SAT scores required for admission. Each student is evaluated on an individual basis.

Individualized high school coursework accepted: Yes

Essay Required: Yes

Special Application Required: Yes   **Submitted To:**

Number of Applications Submitted Each Year: 350

Number of Applications Accepted Each Year: 85+

Number of Students Served: 85

Application Deadline for Special Admission: One year in advance

Acceptance into Program means acceptance into college: No

LEARNING DISABILITY SERVICES

Learning Resource Room:	No	**Curriculum Modification Available:** No	
Kurzweil Personal Reader:	No	**Tutorial Help:** Yes	**Peer Tutors:** Yes
LD Specialists:	3	**Max. Hours/Week for services:**	
Oral Exams:	Yes	10	
Services for LD Only:	Yes	**Added**	
Books on Tape:	Yes	**Cost:** $2,100.	

Calculator allowed in exam: **Taping of books not on tape:** Yes

Tape recording in class: Yes   **Dictionary/computer/spellcheck during exam:** Yes

How are professors notified of LD: By student

GENERAL ADMISSIONS INFORMATION

Director of Admissions: Jerome A. Lucido   **Telephone:** 602-621-3237

Entrance Requirements:

4 yrs. English; 3 yrs. Math; 2 yrs. Science (Biology, Chemistry or Physics); 2 yr. Social Studies. There may be admission with deficiencies.

Test Scores: **SAT:** 930/1010 (out-of-state)   **ACT:** 22/24 out-of-state

G.P.A.: 2.5/3.0 out-of-state   **Class Rank:** upper 25%

Application Deadline: 4/1   **Achievement Tests:** No

COLLEGE GRADUATION REQUIREMENTS

Foreign Language: **Waivers:** Depends on Program

Math: **Waivers:** Depends on Program

Minimum Course Load per Term:

ADDITIONAL INFORMATION

Location: Situated in downtown Tucson on 325 acres. The University is surrounded by the Santa Catalina Mountain range in the Sonora Desert.

Enrollment Information:	**Undergraduate:**	27,932	**Women:** 49%	**Men:** 51%	
	In-State Students:	62%		**Out of State:** 38%	
Cost Information:	**In-State Tuition:**	$1,374		**Out of State:** $6,484	
	Room & Board:	$2,436		**Additional Costs:** $1,362	
Housing Information:	**University Housing:**	Yes		**Sorority:** 14%	
	% Living on Campus:	83%		**Fraternity:** 13%	

Athletics: NCAA Div. I

HENDERSON STATE UNIVERSITY
Arkadephia, Ar. 71923
501-246-5511

Support: CS   *Institution:* 4 yr. Public

LEARNING DISABILITY PROGRAM AND SERVICES

Comments:

The aim of the Student Support Services is to provide any needed support that the student can use to have a positive experience at the University. Services can include study skills classes, academic counseling, tutoring, print enlarging, assistance with registration, extended testing time, and diagnostic testing.

LEARNING DISABILITY ADMISSIONS INFORMATION

Program Name: Student Support Services   *Telephone*

Program Director: Kathy Muse   501-246-5511

Contact Person:

Admissions:

There is no special admissions procedure except that students must submit a special application. Students meeting general admissions requirements will be eligible for admissions. If a student receives less than a 690 on the SAT, they must take developmental courses.

Interview: Yes   *Diagnostic Tests:* Yes

Documentation: whatever is necessary

College Entrance Exams Required: No   *Untimed Accepted:*

Course Entrance Requirements: Yes

Are Waivers Available:

Additional Information:

High School diploma or GED. Below 690 SAT or 19 ACT requires extra course-work.

Individualized high school coursework accepted: Yes

Essay Required: No

Special Application Required: Yes   *Submitted To:*

Number of Applications Submitted Each Year: 550

Number of Applications Accepted Each Year: 300

Number of Students Served: 300

Application Deadline for Special Admission: 3 months before college starts

Acceptance into Program means acceptance

into college: No, there is an appeal process

21

LEARNING DISABILITY SERVICES

Learning Resource Room: No   **Curriculum Modification Available:** No

Kurzweil Personal Reader: **Tutorial Help:** Yes   **Peer Tutors:** Yes

LD Specialists: 1   **Max. Hours/Week for services:**

Oral Exams: Yes   As needed

Services for LD Only: No   **Added**

Books on Tape: Yes   **Cost:** None

Calculator allowed in exam: Yes   **Taping of books not on tape:** Yes

Tape recording in class: Yes   **Dictionary/computer/spellcheck during exam:** Yes

How are professors notified of LD: By student and Program Director

GENERAL ADMISSIONS INFORMATION

Director of Admissions: Tom Gattin   **Telephone:** 501-246-5511

Entrance Requirements:

15 units including: 4 yrs. English; 3 yrs. History; 2 Natural Science; 2 yrs. Math; 2 yrs. Foreign Language; 1/2 yr. of Computer Science. Open admission for in-state-residents.

Test Scores: **SAT:**   **ACT:** 17

G.P.A.: 1.5 conditional admit/2.0 out of state   **Class Rank:** Top 50% out of state

Application Deadline: Rolling   **Achievement Tests:**

COLLEGE GRADUATION REQUIREMENTS

Foreign Language: **Waivers:** Some degrees require a Foreign Language

Math: Yes   **Waivers:** Must appeal

Minimum Course Load per Term: 12 hours-full time; Below 12 hours, part time

ADDITIONAL INFORMATION

Location: The University is located on 132 acres in a small town 60 miles SW of Little Rock.

Enrollment Information: Undergraduate: 3,066   **Women:** 55%   **Men:** 45%

In-State Students: 92%   **Out of State:** 8%

Cost Information: In-State Tuition: $1,220   **Out of State:** $2,400

Room & Board: $1,850   **Additional Costs:** $20.

Housing Information: University Housing: Yes   **Sorority:** 10%

% Living on Campus: 50%   **Fraternity:** 15%

Athletics: NAIA

UNIVERSITY OF THE OZARKS
Clarksville, Ar. 72830
501-754-3839

Support: SP   **Institution:** 4 yr. Private

LEARNING DISABILITY PROGRAM AND SERVICES

Comments:

The Learning Center program emphasizes a total learning environment. Instruction is individualized and personalized. Ideas, instructional materials and activities are presented on a variety of different levels commensurate with the educational needs of the individual student. This program is very comprehensive in every area. Admitted students participate in a system of phases of services. The quality of services received is a function of the particular phase level. Students receive maximum services in Phase I and progressively lesser amounts in Phase II, III, and IV.

LEARNING DISABILITY ADMISSIONS INFORMATION

Program Name: Ben D. Caudle Program   **Telephone**

Program Director: Dale Jordan, Ph.D   501-754-3839

Contact Person: Susan Hurley   same

Admissions:

There is a special application to fill out as well as the regular application. The high school transcript and the psychological reports are also required. The Learning Center Program requires that the student be at least 17, score at or above average range on WAIS-R, have a personal interview (including the parents). Admitted students participate in a system of phases of services. The student must be listed at the Learning Center. The ACT is required by the University but not by the program.

Interview: Yes   **Diagnostic Tests:** Yes

Documentation: MMPI; WAIS-R; W-J

College Entrance Exams Required: Yes   **Untimed Accepted:** Yes

Course Entrance Requirements: No

Are Waivers Available:

Additional Information:

This program has a waiting list. Apply in Junior year. There is a 2 day testing battery required for all learning disabled students.

Individualized high school coursework accepted: Yes

Essay Required: No

Special Application Required: Yes   **Submitted To:**

Number of Applications Submitted Each Year: 108

Number of Applications Accepted Each Year: 15-20

Number of Students Served: Limit of 90

Application Deadline for Special Admission: Junior year of high school (Waiting list)

Acceptance into Program means acceptance into college: Yes

LEARNING DISABILITY SERVICES

Learning Resource Room: Yes   **Curriculum Modification Available:** No

Kurzweil Personal Reader: **Tutorial Help:** Yes   **Peer Tutors:** Yes

LD Specialists: 29   **Max. Hours/Week for services:**

Oral Exams: Yes   36 hours per week

Services for LD Only: Yes   **Added**

Books on Tape: Yes   **Cost:** $1,415 per/semester

Calculator allowed in exam: Yes   **Taping of books not on tape:** Yes

Tape recording in class: Yes   **Dictionary/computer/spellcheck during exam:** Yes

How are professors notified of LD: By student and Program Director

GENERAL ADMISSIONS INFORMATION

Director of Admissions: Francis Pitts   **Telephone:** 501-754-3839

Entrance Requirements:

15 units with the following high school curriculum recommended: 3 yrs. English; 2 yrs. Math; 1 yr. Social Studies, test scores, recommendations, class rank and essay are also used in making the admission decision. Talent or special ability is also considered. The secondary school record is the most important criteria for admissions.

Test Scores: **SAT:** 800 (minimum)   **ACT:** 15 (minimum)

G.P.A.: 2.5   **Class Rank:**

Application Deadline: Rolling   **Achievement Tests:** No

COLLEGE GRADUATION REQUIREMENTS

Foreign Language: **Waivers:** Depends on major

Math: Yes   **Waivers:** Yes

Minimum Course Load per Term: Case-by-case basis

ADDITIONAL INFORMATION

Location: The University is located on 56 acres, 100 miles northwest of Little Rock. Clarksville is a town of 5,000 residents in the Arkansas River Valley.

Enrollment Information: **Undergraduate:** 796   **Women:** 53%   **Men:** 47%

In-State Students: 71%   **Out of State:** 29%

Cost Information: **In-State Tuition:** $2,900   **Out of State:** same

Room & Board: $2160   **Additional Costs:**

Housing Information: **University Housing:** Yes   **Sorority:** No

% Living on Campus: 75%   **Fraternity:** No

Athletics: NAIA

BAKERSFIELD COLLEGE
Bakersfield, Ca. 93305

805-395-4301

Support: CS   **Institution:** 2 yr. Public

LEARNING DISABILITY PROGRAM AND SERVICES

Comments:

The Supportive Services Center provides services for students with learning difficulties. There are no special classes, and students attend regular classes and are expected to compete on that level. Services include counseling, tutoring, test accommodations, readers, study skills classes and individualized instructional materials. Bakersfield offers a variety of services designed to maximize success for students in their college courses.

LEARNING DISABILITY ADMISSIONS INFORMATION

		Telephone
Program Name:	Supportive Services Center	
Program Director:	Dr. Donald Johnson	805-395-4434
Contact Person:	Debbie Shinn	805-395-4364

Admissions:

There is no special application for admission. The College has an open-door policy. The program gives each student the Woodcock-Johnson assessment to determine the existence of a learning disability. However, if the student has a recent score from their high school it may be submitted. They also require each student to take a College designed test called "Assest" which is similar to an ACT and helps the College obtain curricular information used in placement. This test test is given timed and untimed, however they will administer a different assessment at a later date untimed, if necessary.

Interview: Yes   **Diagnostic Tests:** Yes

Documentation:

College Entrance Exams Required: Yes   **Untimed Accepted:** Yes

Course Entrance Requirements: Yes

Are Waivers Available:

Additional Information:

All courses have reading level requirements and some have prerequisites which must be met before entrance. It is recommended that students be able to read at least at 6th grade level in order to be successful in the College courses. Often students reading below 6th grade level are unable to find courses that are appropriate.

Individualized high school coursework accepted: Yes

Essay Required: Yes

Special Application Required: No   **Submitted To:**

Number of Applications Submitted Each Year: Unlimited

Number of Applications Accepted Each Year: All who apply

Number of Students Served: 200

Application Deadline for Special Admission: No

Acceptance into Program means acceptance into college:

25

LEARNING DISABILITY SERVICES

Learning Resource Room:	Yes	**Curriculum Modification Available:**	
Kurzweil Personal Reader:	No	**Tutorial Help:** Yes	**Peer Tutors:**
LD Specialists:	3	**Max. Hours/Week for services:**	
Oral Exams:	Yes	4 hours	
Services for LD Only:	No	**Added**	
Books on Tape:	Yes	**Cost:** None	
Calculator allowed in exam:	Yes	**Taping of books not on tape:** Yes	
Tape recording in class:	Yes	**Dictionary/computer/spellcheck during exam:** Yes	

How are professors notified of LD: By student

GENERAL ADMISSIONS INFORMATION

Director of Admissions: Nancy Haines   **Telephone:** 805-395-4301

Entrance Requirements:

High school transcript. Open admission except for Nursing and Radiologic Technology programs. The college administers its own assessment test called "Assest." This test is similar to the ACT but is geared toward College curriculum used for placement.

Test Scores: **SAT:**   **ACT:**

G.P.A.:   **Class Rank:**

Application Deadline: Rolling   **Achievement Tests:**

COLLEGE GRADUATION REQUIREMENTS

Foreign Language: **Waivers:**

Math: **Waivers:**

Minimum Course Load per Term: Need permission of Counselor

ADDITIONAL INFORMATION

Location: The College is located on a 175 acre campus 100 miles north of Los Angeles.

Enrollment Information:	**Undergraduate:**	12,473	**Women:** 55%	**Men:** 45%
	In-State Students:	99%		**Out of State:** 1%
Cost Information:	**In-State Tuition:**	$ 0		**Out of State:** $2,880
	Room & Board:	$3,500		**Additional Costs:** $120
Housing Information:	**University Housing:**	Yes		**Sorority:**
	% Living on Campus:	1%		**Fraternity:**

Athletics: Intercollegiate sports

CALIFORNIA POLYTECHNIC STATE UNIV.
San Luis Obispo, Ca. 93407
805-756-2311

Support: CS   *Institution:* 4 Yr. Public

LEARNING DISABILITY PROGRAM AND SERVICES

Comments:

The Disabled Student Services program is very involved in the school both with the faculty and the student population. They print a newsletter, have open house for the staff and generally keep the school population aware of who they are and what they do. For consideration for special admissions through the DSS, the application must be reviewed during the regular application filing periods.

LEARNING DISABILITY ADMISSIONS INFORMATION

Program Name:	Disabled Student Services	*Telephone*
Program Director:	Harriet Clendenen	805-756-1395
Contact Person:	Ann Fryer	same

Admissions:

The following steps should be followed: complete the California State University application; contact the Cal Poly DSS office to set up an appointment; secure 2 letters of reference; request unofficial high school transcript. Each application is reviewed individually.

Interview: Yes   *Diagnostic Tests:* Yes

Documentation: WAIS-R; WISC-R; W-J

College Entrance Exams Required: Yes   *Untimed Accepted:* Yes

Course Entrance Requirements: Yes

Are Waivers Available: Substitutions

Additional Information:

The state requires English Placement Test and Entry Level Math Test

Individualized high school coursework accepted: Evaluated

Essay Required: Yes

Special Application Required: No   *Submitted To:*

Number of Applications Submitted Each Year: 130

Number of Applications Accepted Each Year: 65

Number of Students Served: 350

Application Deadline for Special Admission: Fall of Senior year

Acceptance into Program means acceptance into college: No

27

LEARNING DISABILITY SERVICES

Learning Resource Room: Yes   **Curriculum Modification Available:** Yes

Kurzweil Personal Reader: No   **Tutorial Help:** Yes   **Peer Tutors:** Yes

LD Specialists: 2   **Max. Hours/Week for services:**

Oral Exams: Yes   3-5 hours per/week,per/course

Services for LD Only: No   **Added**

Books on Tape: Yes   **Cost:** None

Calculator allowed in exam: Yes   **Taping of books not on tape:** Yes

Tape recording in class: Yes   **Dictionary/computer/spellcheck during exam:** Yes

How are professors notified of LD: By student

GENERAL ADMISSIONS INFORMATION

Director of Admissions: Dave Snyder   **Telephone:** 805-756-2311

Entrance Requirements:

4 yrs. English; 3 yrs. Math; 2 yrs. Foreign Language; 1 yr. History; 1 yr. Science; 1 yr. the Arts. The University will not admit a student who has a GPA below 2.0.

Test Scores: **SAT:** 1075   **ACT:**

G.P.A.: 2.0 (3.1 is automatic)   **Class Rank:**

Application Deadline: 11/30   **Achievement Tests:**

COLLEGE GRADUATION REQUIREMENTS

Foreign Language: No   **Waivers:**

Math: Yes   **Waivers:** Possible course substitution

Minimum Course Load per Term: No

ADDITIONAL INFORMATION

Location: The campus is located 100 miles north of Santa Barbara.

Enrollment Information: **Undergraduate:** 16,453   **Women:** 43%   **Men:** 57%

In-State Students: 98%   **Out of State:** 2%

Cost Information: **In-State Tuition:** $900   **Out of State:** $5,670

Room & Board: $3,500   **Additional Costs:** $1,005

Housing Information: **University Housing:** Yes   **Sorority:** 10%

% Living on Campus: 18%   **Fraternity:** 10%

Athletics: NCAA Div. II

SAN DIEGO STATE UNIVERSITY
San Diego, Ca. 92182-0579

619-594-5384

Support: CS   *Institution:* 4 yr. Public

LEARNING DISABILITY PROGRAM AND SERVICES

Comments:

The Learning Disabilities Program provides assistance with computer skills, readers, tutors, notetakers, test accommodations and registration advising. There is a student organization for students with learning disabilities. There are LD specialists on the staff. The University believes that a student with learning disabilities can be successful at SDS and will try to provide the appropriate services to foster their success.

LEARNING DISABILITY ADMISSIONS INFORMATION

Program Name: Disabled Student Services

Program Director: Elizabeth Bacon

Contact Person: Joan Kilbourne

Telephone

619-594-6473

same

Admissions:

There is a special admission process. The SAT score range varies according to the students GPA. For example, with a 3.0 GPA a student can have an SAT of 410; a GPA of 2.2 requires an SAT score of 1000+. If students do not meet University requirements, they are asked to send a letter describing their disabilities, and 3 letters from teachers/counselors along with copies of documentation to the Disabled Student Services.

Interview: If possible

Documentation: W-J: WAIS-R with WRAT-R

College Entrance Exams Required: No

Course Entrance Requirements: Yes

Are Waivers Available: Yes

Diagnostic Tests: Yes

Untimed Accepted: Yes

Additional Information:

If Foreign Language classes are waived in high school then they are also waived as an entrance requirement to the University.

Individualized high school coursework accepted: Yes

Essay Required: No

Special Application Required: No   *Submitted To:*

Number of Applications Submitted Each Year:

Number of Applications Accepted Each Year:

Number of Students Served: 550

Application Deadline for Special Admission: No

Acceptance into Program means acceptance

into college: No, there is an appeal process

29

LEARNING DISABILITY SERVICES

Learning Resource Room: No

Kurzweil Personal Reader: Yes

LD Specialists: 3

Oral Exams: Y/N

Services for LD Only: No

Books on Tape: Yes

Calculator allowed in exam:

Tape recording in class: Yes

How are professors notified of LD: By the student

Curriculum Modification Available: Yes

Tutorial Help: Yes   **Peer Tutors:** Yes

Max. Hours/Week for services:

   3 hours per/ course

Added Cost: None

Taping of books not on tape: Yes

Dictionary/computer/spellcheck during exam:

GENERAL ADMISSIONS INFORMATION

Director of Admissions: Nancy C. Sprotte   **Telephone:** 619-594-5384

Entrance Requirements:

4 yrs. English; 3 yrs. Math; 2 yrs. Foreign Language; 1 yr. American History; 1 yr. Lab Science; 1 yr. Visual and Performing Arts.

Test Scores: **SAT:** 880   **ACT:** 20

G.P.A.: 2.0/2.4 (out-of-state)   **Class Rank:**

Application Deadline: 11/30   **Achievement Tests:**

COLLEGE GRADUATION REQUIREMENTS

Foreign Language: Yes   **Waivers:** Depends on major

Math: Yes   **Waivers:** Yes, Substitutions available

Minimum Course Load per Term: 12 credits for financial aid

ADDITIONAL INFORMATION

Location: San Diego State is located within close proximity to beaches, south of Los Angeles.

Enrollment Information: **Undergraduate:** 28,712   **Women:** 52%   **Men:** 48%

   In-State Students: 90%   **Out of State:** 10%

Cost Information: **In-State Tuition:** $0   **Out of State:** $5,382

   Room & Board: $3,968   **Additional Costs:** $926

Housing Information: **University Housing:** Yes   **Sorority:** 2%

   % Living on Campus: 10%   **Fraternity:** 2%

Athletics: NCAA Div. I

SAN FRANCISCO STATE UNIVERSITY
San Francisco, Ca. 94132

415-338-2017

Support: CS   **Institution:** 4 yr. Public

LEARNING DISABILITY PROGRAM AND SERVICES

Comments:

The Director of DSS has a role in the admissions process. The DSS offers a drop-in-center with tutorial services. The Director can also arrange for test accommodations and notetakers and will advocate for the student. The staff is very involved and offers comprehensive services through a team approach.

LEARNING DISABILITY ADMISSIONS INFORMATION

Program Name:	Disabled Student Services (DSS)	**Telephone**
Program Director:	Molly Brodie	415-338-2472
Contact Person:	Terry Smith	same

Admissions:

Students with learning disabilities who do not meet admissions requirements can send documentation verifying their learning disability to the DSS office, and address a letter to the Director of Admissions in the Admissions Office indicating documentation has been submitted. There is some flexibility in admissions. Students may request assistance with their applications from the DSS office. The Director of DSS can also seek permission for substitutions of high school courses in math and foreign language. High school case-managers may write summaries and provide a clinical judgment. DSS wants information about achievement deficits.

Interview: No   **Diagnostic Tests:** Yes

Documentation: Those which give information about IQ, Processing deficits, academic ability.

College Entrance Exams Required: **Untimed Accepted:**

Course Entrance Requirements: Yes

Are Waivers Available: Yes

Additional Information:

Students with learning disabilities can request a substitution of entrance requirements. The high school counselor needs to contact the DSS Director to arrange the substitutions.

Individualized high school coursework accepted:

Essay Required:

Special Application Required: **Submitted To:**

Number of Applications Submitted Each Year:

Number of Applications Accepted Each Year:

Number of Students Served: 250

Application Deadline for Special Admission: No

Acceptance into Program means acceptance into college:

31

LEARNING DISABILITY SERVICES

Learning Resource Room: Yes   **Curriculum Modification Available:** Yes

Kurzweil Personal Reader: Yes   **Tutorial Help:** Yes   **Peer Tutors:** Yes

LD Specialists: 1   **Max. Hours/Week for services:**

Oral Exams: Yes   No limit

Services for LD Only: Yes   **Added**

Books on Tape: Yes   **Cost:** None

Calculator allowed in exam: Y/N   **Taping of books not on tape:** Yes

Tape recording in class: Y/N   **Dictionary/computer/spellcheck during exam:** Y/N

How are professors notified of LD: By the student

GENERAL ADMISSIONS INFORMATION

Director of Admissions: Laura Ware   **Telephone:**

Entrance Requirements:

15 units including: 4 yrs. English; 3 yrs. Math; 1 yr. U.S. History or Government; 1 yr. Science; 1 yr. Visual and Performing Arts; 2 yrs. Foreign Language; 3 yrs. electives. Eligibility index used: GPA x 800 plus SAT or GPA x 200 plus ACT x 10: No one is admitted with a GPA below 2.45.

Test Scores: **SAT:**   **ACT:** 11-34/depends on GPA

G.P.A.: 2.45/3.6 (automatic)   **Class Rank:** top 33%

Application Deadline: 3/2   **Achievement Tests:** No

COLLEGE GRADUATION REQUIREMENTS

Foreign Language: **Waivers:**

Math: Yes   **Waivers:** Depends on major

Minimum Course Load per Term: No

ADDITIONAL INFORMATION

Location: The school is located in downtown San Francisco on 130 acre campus.

Enrollment Information: **Undergraduate:** 28,120   **Women:** 58%   **Men:** 42%

     In-State Students: 78%   **Out of State:** 22%

Cost Information: **In-State Tuition:** $0   **Out of State:** $5,859

     Room & Board: $3,524   **Additional Costs:** $828

Housing Information: **University Housing:** Yes   **Sorority:** Yes

     % Living on Campus: 5%   **Fraternity:** Yes

Athletics: NCAA Div. II

Support: S   **Institution:** 4 yr. Private

LEARNING DISABILITY PROGRAM AND SERVICES

Comments:

The Teaching and Learning Center is part of the Student Learning Resources. The Center provides academic support for students outside the classroom. The goal is to help students"learning to be better learners." A letter is sent to each learning disabled student encouraging the use of the Center for extra help.

LEARNING DISABILITY ADMISSIONS INFORMATION

Program Name: Disabled Student Resources   **Telephone**

Program Director: Christine McIntyre   408-554-4111

Contact Person: same

Admissions:

If the student is not admitted through the regular application process, the student may appeal the decision.

Interview: No   **Diagnostic Tests:** Yes

Documentation:

College Entrance Exams Required: Yes   **Untimed Accepted:** Yes

Course Entrance Requirements: Yes

Are Waivers Available: No

Additional Information:

Recommended SAT between 970-1240.

Individualized high school coursework accepted: No

Essay Required: Yes

Special Application Required: No   **Submitted To:**

Number of Applications Submitted Each Year: 4

Number of Applications Accepted Each Year: 4

Number of Students Served: 4

Application Deadline for Special Admission: No

Acceptance into Program means acceptance

into college: No

LEARNING DISABILITY SERVICES

Learning Resource Room: No   **Curriculum Modification Available:** Yes

Kurzweil Personal Reader: No   **Tutorial Help:** Yes   **Peer Tutors:** Yes

LD Specialists: No   **Max. Hours/Week for services:**

Oral Exams: Yes   27 per/week; 7 per/course

Services for LD Only: No   **Added**

Books on Tape: Yes   **Cost:** None

Calculator allowed in exam: Yes   **Taping of books not on tape:** Yes

Tape recording in class: Yes   **Dictionary/computer/spellcheck during exam:**

How are professors notified of LD: Letter from the student and the Program Director

GENERAL ADMISSIONS INFORMATION

Director of Admissions: Daniel J. Saracino   **Telephone:** 408-554-4700

Entrance Requirements:

4 yrs. English; 3 yrs. Math, (4 yrs. Math for Business or Engineering Program); 2 yrs. Foreign Language, (3 yrs. preferred); 2 yrs. Social Science; 2 yrs. Science.

Test Scores: **SAT:** 1105 (mid 50%)   **ACT:** 21

G.P.A.: 2.9 - 4.0 / 3.42 (average)   **Class Rank:**

Application Deadline: 2/1   **Achievement Tests:**

COLLEGE GRADUATION REQUIREMENTS

Foreign Language: Yes   **Waivers:** No

Math: Yes   **Waivers:** No

Minimum Course Load per Term: Yes

ADDITIONAL INFORMATION

Location: Located one hour south of San Francisco in "Silicon Valley," 3 miles from San Jose airport and 4 hours from Lake Tahoe.

Enrollment Information: **Undergraduate:** 3,700   **Women:** 47%   **Men:** 53%

   In-State Students: 59%   **Out of State:** 41%

Cost Information: **In-State Tuition:** $10,485   **Out of State:** same

   Room & Board: $5,000   **Additional Costs:**

Housing Information: **University Housing:** Yes   **Sorority:** 14%

   % Living on Campus: 55%   **Fraternity:** 20%

Athletics: NCAA Div. I

SANTA ROSA JUNIOR COLLEGE
Santa Rosa, Ca. 95401

707-527-4509

Support: CS   **Institution:** 2 yr. Public

LEARNING DISABILITY PROGRAM AND SERVICES

Comments:

Santa Rosa Junior College is a state-supported school that accepts all learning disabled students who apply and meet the mandatory state eligibility requirements which verify their learning disability. There is currently a 10 month waiting list to be tested for eligibility into the Learning Service Program. If a student is eligible for the Program, an Individualized Educational Plan is developed and implemented. Students may participate in a combination of special and mainstream college classes with appropriate support services as needed.

LEARNING DISABILITY ADMISSIONS INFORMATION

		Telephone
Program Name:	Learning Services	
Program Director:	Jennifer Mann	707-527-4278
Contact Person:	Carla Stone	707-527-4580

Admissions:

The student must meet the state eligibility requirements verifying their learning disability to receive services. To qualify for LD services, students must demonstrate: average and above average intellectual ability, adequate measured achievement in at least one academic area or employment setting, a severe processing deficit in one or more areas, a severe discrepancy between aptitude and achievement in one or more academic areas, adaptive behavior appropriate to a college setting.

Interview: Yes   **Diagnostic Tests:** Yes

Documentation: Woodcock-Johnson, Parts 1 & 2; WAIS-R

College Entrance Exams Required: No   **Untimed Accepted:** No

Course Entrance Requirements: No

Are Waivers Available:

Additional Information:

Admissions to the College for conditional students without learning disabilities is offered on an open door basis. Students must be 18 years or older or hold a high school diploma or its equivalent. Some high school students may be admitted on an enrichment basis.

Individualized high school coursework accepted: No

Essay Required: No

Special Application Required: Yes   **Submitted To:**

Number of Applications Submitted Each Year:

Number of Applications Accepted Each Year:

Number of Students Served:

Application Deadline for Special Admission:

Acceptance into Program means acceptance

into college: Yes

LEARNING DISABILITY SERVICES

Learning Resource Room: Yes	**Curriculum Modification Available:** No	
Kurzweil Personal Reader: No	**Tutorial Help:** Yes	**Peer Tutors:** No
LD Specialists: 4	**Max. Hours/Week for services:**	
Oral Exams: No	2 hours per week/per course	
Services for LD Only: Yes	**Added**	
Books on Tape: Yes	**Cost:** Registration fee $5/unit	
Calculator allowed in exam: Yes	**Taping of books not on tape:** Yes	
Tape recording in class: Yes	**Dictionary/computer/spellcheck during exam:** Yes	

How are professors notified of LD: By the student and the L.D. Director

GENERAL ADMISSIONS INFORMATION

Director of Admissions: Ricardo Navarrette   **Telephone:** 707-527-4509

Entrance Requirements:

Open admissions except for health program. Students must be 18 or have a high school diploma or equivalent.

Test Scores: SAT: **ACT:**

G.P.A.:   **Class Rank:**

Application Deadline: Rolling   **Achievement Tests:**

COLLEGE GRADUATION REQUIREMENTS

Foreign Language: **Waivers:**

Math: **Waivers:**

Minimum Course Load per Term: N/A

ADDITIONAL INFORMATION

Location: The College is located on 93 acres with easy access to San Francisco.

Enrollment Information:	**Undergraduate:** 32,291	**Women:** 58%	**Men:** 42%
	In-State Students: 90%		**Out of State:** 10%
Cost Information:	**In-State Tuition:** $ 0 (Full time)		**Out of State:** $2,880
	Room & Board: $1,650		**Additional Costs:** $115
Housing Information:	**University Housing:** Yes		**Sorority:**
	% Living on Campus: 1/2%		**Fraternity:**

Athletics: Intercollegiate sports

Support: C S   *Institution:* 2 yr. Public

LEARNING DISABILITY PROGRAM AND SERVICES

Comments:

The Learning Disabilities Program is open to all students who meet regular entrance requirements and who have completed testing and evaluation by the Learning Disabilities Specialist. The goals of the program are; to assist learning disabled students in reaching their academic/vocational goals, and to help the students strengthen and develop their individual learning style.

LEARNING DISABILITY ADMISSIONS INFORMATION

Program Name: Learning Disabilities Program   *Telephone*

Program Director: Dr. James Hirschinger   916-624-3333

Contact Person: Kathleen Fields/Denise Stone

Admissions:

There is no special application for admissions.

Interview: Yes   *Diagnostic Tests:* Yes

Documentation: California Community College mandated model: W-J; WAIS-R

College Entrance Exams Required: No   *Untimed Accepted:* No

Course Entrance Requirements: No

Are Waivers Available: Yes

Additional Information:

Individualized high school coursework accepted: No

Essay Required: No

Special Application Required: No   *Submitted To:*

Number of Applications Submitted Each Year: 200+

Number of Applications Accepted Each Year: 200+

Number of Students Served: 100+

Application Deadline for Special Admission: No

Acceptance into Program means acceptance into college: No

LEARNING DISABILITY SERVICES

Learning Resource Room:		**Curriculum Modification Available:** Yes
Kurzweil Personal Reader: No		**Tutorial Help:** Yes **Peer Tutors:** Yes
LD Specialists: 2		**Max. Hours/Week for services:**
Oral Exams: Yes		2 hours per week
Services for LD Only: No		**Added**
Books on Tape: Yes		**Cost:** $5 per unit to $50 / $99 out-of-state
Calculator allowed in exam: Y/N		**Taping of books not on tape:** Yes
Tape recording in class: Yes		**Dictionary/computer/spellcheck during exam:** Y/N

How are professors notified of LD: By the student and the Program Director

GENERAL ADMISSIONS INFORMATION

Director of Admissions: Paul Mendoza   **Telephone:** 916-781-0525

Entrance Requirements:

High school transcript. Open admission

Test Scores: **SAT:**   **ACT:**

G.P.A.:   **Class Rank:**

Application Deadline: Rolling   **Achievement Tests:**

COLLEGE GRADUATION REQUIREMENTS

Foreign Language: No   **Waivers:**

Math: Yes   **Waivers:** No, not at this time

Minimum Course Load per Term: No

ADDITIONAL INFORMATION

Location: The school is located on a 327 acre campus in a rural setting with easy access to Sacramento.

Enrollment Information:	**Undergraduate:** 12,859	**Women:** 57%	**Men:** 43%
	In-State Students: 98%		**Out of State:** 2%
Cost Information:	**In-State Tuition:** $ 0		**Out of State:** $2,970
	Room & Board: $3,568		**Additional Costs:** $115
Housing Information:	**University Housing:** Yes		**Sorority:**
	% Living on Campus: 1%		**Fraternity:**

Athletics: Intercollegiate

SONOMA STATE UNIVERSITY
Rohnert Park, Ca. 94928
707-664-2326

Support: CS   **Institution:** 4 yr. Public

LEARNING DISABILITY PROGRAM AND SERVICES

Comments:

Services at Sonoma State University are provided primarily through two offices on campus: The Disability Resource Center, which offers support services such as support groups and advocacy, and The Learning Skills Services which provides diagnostic testing as well as academic support and skill development. Both offer one to one sessions and workshops given by specialists in various subject areas. In addition, there is a campus Tutorial Program which offers individual peer tutoring. The Director of the DRC works with students to help them become self-advocates.

LEARNING DISABILITY ADMISSIONS INFORMATION

Program Name:	Disability Resource Center (DRC)	**Telephone**
Program Director:	Anthony Tusler	707-664-2677
Contact Person:	Bill Clopton	707-664-2677

Admissions:

Admission is based on a combination of high school grade point average and test score, and college preparatory classes. Learning Disabled students should apply for regular admission through the Admissions and Records Office. If a limited number of required courses are missing, students can be granted a Conditional Admission. These courses must be made-up in college. If students do not meet either Regular or Conditional Admissions they may request Special Admissions through the Disability Resource Center.

Interview: No

Documentation: Any

College Entrance Exams Required: Yes

Course Entrance Requirements: Yes

Are Waivers Available: Yes

Diagnostic Tests: Yes

Untimed Accepted: Yes

Additional Information:

Students who are denied admission may request a Special Admission through Disability Resource Center. These students initiate the request by writing a letter to the Director of the Disability Resource Center providing information about strengths and weaknesses. LD diagnostic evaluation and 2 letters of recommendations are also required. All special admission applicants are interviewed in person or by phone.

Individualized high school coursework accepted: No

Essay Required: No

Special Application Required: Yes   **Submitted To:**

Number of Applications Submitted Each Year: 40

Number of Applications Accepted Each Year: 40

Number of Students Served: 150

Application Deadline for Special Admission: Eight months or earlier (prior to enrollment)

Acceptance into Program means acceptance into college: No

LEARNING DISABILITY SERVICES

Learning Resource Room: Yes   **Curriculum Modification Available:** No

Kurzweil Personal Reader: Yes   **Tutorial Help:** Yes   **Peer Tutors:** No

LD Specialists: 2   **Max. Hours/Week for services:**

Oral Exams: Yes   3 hrs. per course

Services for LD Only: No   **Added Cost:** None

Books on Tape: Yes

Calculator allowed in exam: Yes   **Taping of books not on tape:** Yes

Tape recording in class: Yes   **Dictionary/computer/spellcheck during exam:** Yes

How are professors notified of LD: Student with written verification

GENERAL ADMISSIONS INFORMATION

Director of Admissions: Dr. Frank Tansey   **Telephone:** 707-664-2326

Entrance Requirements:

4 yrs. English; 3 yrs. Math; 2 yrs. Foreign Language; 1 yr. Science; 1 yr. U.S. History; 3 yrs. Electives; 1 yr. Visual, Performing Arts. Eligibility Index: GPA x 800 Plus SAT=3402 for out-of-state: 3072 for in-state; or GPA x 200 Plus ACT x 10 = 842 out-of-state; or 741 for in-state.

Test Scores: **SAT:** 780-1000 (min 50%)   **ACT:** 21

G.P.A.:   **Class Rank:**

Application Deadline: Nov. for consideration   **Achievement Tests:**

COLLEGE GRADUATION REQUIREMENTS

Foreign Language: No   **Waivers:**

Math: Yes   **Waivers:** Yes, alternate Math course selections offered

Minimum Course Load per Term: No minimum

ADDITIONAL INFORMATION

Location: The school is located on 220 acres with easy access to San Francisco.

Enrollment Information: Undergraduate: 7,084   **Women:** 64%   **Men:** 36%

    In-State Students: 92%   **Out of State:** 8%

Cost Information: **In-State Tuition:** $850   **Out of State:** $4,400

    Room & Board: $3,500   **Additional Costs:** $882

Housing Information: University Housing: Yes   **Sorority:** 1%

    % Living on Campus: 13%   **Fraternity:** 1%

Athletics: NCAA Div. II

Support: CS   *Institution:* 4 yr. Private

LEARNING DISABILITY PROGRAM AND SERVICES

Comments:

Stanford seeks to enroll students with excellent academic records and evidence of personal achievement outside the classroom. Students who have used the resources available to them to their fullest potential. The policy on the admissions of students with learning disabilities makes clear there is no separate academic program. A full range of services are available to each student on a case-by-case basis. Services are tailored to each individual and include diagnostic testing, counseling, tutoring, test accommodations, course waivers and support groups.

LEARNING DISABILITY ADMISSIONS INFORMATION

		Telephone
Program Name:	Disability Resource Center	
Program Director:	James Boriquin	415-723-1039
Contact Person:	Molly Sandperl	415-723-1066

Admissions:

Students with Learning Disabilities are admitted on the same basis as other students.

Interview: No   **Diagnostic Tests:** No

Documentation:

College Entrance Exams Required: Yes   **Untimed Accepted:** Yes

Course Entrance Requirements: Yes

Are Waivers Available: Yes

Additional Information:

Course waivers are judged on an individual bases and depend on the student's situation.

Individualized high school coursework accepted: No

Essay Required: Yes

Special Application Required: No   **Submitted To:**

Number of Applications Submitted Each Year:

Number of Applications Accepted Each Year:

Number of Students Served: 60

Application Deadline for Special Admission:

Acceptance into Program means acceptance into college: No

41

LEARNING DISABILITY SERVICES

Learning Resource Room: Yes   **Curriculum Modification Available:** Yes

Kurzweil Personal Reader: Yes   **Tutorial Help:** Yes   **Peer Tutors:** Yes

LD Specialists: 1   **Max. Hours/Week for services:**

Oral Exams: Yes   varies

Services for LD Only: Yes   **Added**
                                        Cost: None
Books on Tape: Yes

Calculator allowed in exam: Yes   **Taping of books not on tape:** Yes

Tape recording in class: Yes   **Dictionary/computer/spellcheck during exam:** Yes

How are professors notified of LD: Student and/or Director

GENERAL ADMISSIONS INFORMATION

Director of Admissions: Dean James Montoya   **Telephone:** 415-723-2091

Entrance Requirements:

College Prep-as demanding as possible - most students rank in the top 10% of their class.

Test Scores: **SAT:** 1260-1440 (mid 50%)   **ACT:** 30 + (usually)

G.P.A.: 3.9-4.0 (usually)   **Class Rank:** top 5% (usually)

Application Deadline: 12/15   **Achievement Tests:** Recommended

COLLEGE GRADUATION REQUIREMENTS

Foreign Language: Yes   **Waivers:** Depends on major

Math: No   **Waivers:**

Minimum Course Load per Term: 9 units

ADDITIONAL INFORMATION

Location: Stanford is located about 30 minutes south of San Francisco.

Enrollment Information: **Undergraduate:** 6,505   **Women:** 56%   **Men:** 44%

                          In-State Students: 37%   **Out of State:** 63&

Cost Information: **In-State Tuition:** $14,200   **Out of State:** same

                          Room & Board: $5,900   **Additional Costs:**

Housing Information: **University Housing:** Yes   **Sorority:** 10%

                          % Living on Campus: 90%   **Fraternity:** 10%

Athletics: NCAA Div. I

UNIVERSITY OF CALIFORNIA - BERKELEY

Berkeley, Ca. 94720

415-642-0200

Support: CS   **Institution:** 4 yr. Public

LEARNING DISABILITY PROGRAM AND SERVICES

Comments:

The Learning Disabilities component of the Program is a resource to help students find ways to accommodate their learning styles within the University. The Coordinator is available for advising and identifying specific ways to assist learning disabled students with their academic course work. Curriculum planning and study skills are also provided, as well as one-to-one tutoring when necessary.

LEARNING DISABILITY ADMISSIONS INFORMATION

Program Name:	Disabled Student's Program (DSP)	**Telephone**
Program Director:	Susan O'Hara	415-642-0518
Contact Person:	Michael E. Spagna;Deirdre Semoff; Kay Runyan	same

Admissions:

A learning disabilities specialist, as well as an admissions specialist, is available to meet with learning disabled students interested in applying to Berkeley. These specialists will review the applicant's High School or College transcript and give advice on how to proceed with the application. Disabled Student's Program keeps a copy of the application to use in case the original application is misplaced. This office works closely with the Office of Admissions and Records.

Interview: Yes   **Diagnostic Tests:** Yes

Documentation: WAIS-R; Woodcock-Johnson: WRAT

College Entrance Exams Required: Yes   **Untimed Accepted:** Yes

Course Entrance Requirements: Yes

Are Waivers Available: Yes

Additional Information:

Special action review is given to students who would not typically be admitted to the University.

Individualized high school coursework accepted: Possibly

Essay Required: Yes

Special Application Required: No   **Submitted To:** DSP

Number of Applications Submitted Each Year: N/A

Number of Applications Accepted Each Year: N/A

Number of Students Served: 165 LD Students

Application Deadline for Special Admission: No

Acceptance into Program means acceptance into college: No

LEARNING DISABILITY SERVICES

Learning Resource Room: Yes   **Curriculum Modification Available:** Yes

Kurzweil Personal Reader: Yes   **Tutorial Help:** Yes   **Peer Tutors:** Yes

LD Specialists: 3   **Max. Hours/Week for services:**

Oral Exams: Yes   Decided case-by-case

Services for LD Only: No   **Added**

Books on Tape: Yes   **Cost:** None

Calculator allowed in exam: Y/N   **Taping of books not on tape:** Yes

Tape recording in class: Y/N   **Dictionary/computer/spellcheck during exam:** Y/N

How are professors notified of LD: By student and Program Director

GENERAL ADMISSIONS INFORMATION

Director of Admissions: Andre Bell   **Telephone:** 415-642-0200

Entrance Requirements:

4 yrs. English; 2 yrs. Foreign Language; 3 yrs. Math; 1 yr. History/Government; 1 yr. Science; 4 yrs. Art/Music and electives. Admissions is based on an eligibility index using grade point average and test scores. Other factors are also considered, such as talent, minority, or first generation.

Test Scores: **SAT:** 1185   **ACT:** 26

G.P.A.: 3.3/3.4 (out-of-state)   **Class Rank:**

Application Deadline: 11/30   **Achievement Tests:** 3

COLLEGE GRADUATION REQUIREMENTS

Foreign Language: Yes   **Waivers:** Yes

Math: Yes   **Waivers:** Yes

Minimum Course Load per Term:

ADDITIONAL INFORMATION

Location: The 1232 acre campus is in an urban area 10 miles east of San Francisco.

Enrollment Information: **Undergraduate:** 22,671   **Women:** 47%   **Men:** 53%

In-State Students: 86%   **Out of State:** 14%

Cost Information: **In-State Tuition:** $1,672   **Out of State:** $7,470

Room & Board: $4,780   **Additional Costs:** $1,640

Housing Information: **University Housing:** Yes   **Sorority:** 3%

% Living on Campus: 30%   **Fraternity:** 4%

Athletics: NCAA Div. I

UNIVERSITY OF CALIFORNIA - SANTA CRUZ

Santa Cruz, Ca. 95064

408-459-4008

Support: CS   **Institution:** 4 yr. Public

LEARNING DISABILITY PROGRAM AND SERVICES

Comments:

Disabled Student Services is committed to making all programs, services and activities accessible to students with disabilities. Services are free of charge, entirely voluntary and provided at the request of the student. Recent documentation which verifies the disability must state the nature of the disability and what accommodations the disability requires. Service coordinators are available to speak to the student to discuss the disability, goals and solutions, as well as strategies for a successful academic year.

LEARNING DISABILITY ADMISSIONS INFORMATION

Program Name:	Disabled Student Services (DSS)	**Telephone**
Program Director:	Lea Van Meter	408-459-2089
Contact Person:	Sharyn Martin	same

Admissions:

If learning disabled students are not admitted through the regular admission process, they would be considered for special action admission. Admissions would request information from the Director of DSS as well as their recommendation. However, the final decision is made by the Admissions Office. Three achievement tests are required: English composition, Math level I and II, and choice of English literature, foreign language, science or social studies. Students may also submit ACT or SAT (untimed are acceptable).

Interview: Yes   **Diagnostic Tests:** Yes

Documentation: WAIS-R; W-J; WRAT

College Entrance Exams Required: Yes   **Untimed Accepted:** Yes

Course Entrance Requirements: Yes

Are Waivers Available: Yes

Additional Information:

There are limited admissions for students not meeting regular requirements. These students must submit 3 letters of recommendation and an essay.

Individualized high school coursework accepted:

Essay Required: Yes

Special Application Required: **Submitted To:**

Number of Applications Submitted Each Year:

Number of Applications Accepted Each Year:

Number of Students Served: 70 LD students

Application Deadline for Special Admission: No

Acceptance into Program means acceptance into college: No, there is an appeal procedure

LEARNING DISABILITY SERVICES

Learning Resource Room: No   **Curriculum Modification Available:** Yes

Kurzweil Personal Reader: No   **Tutorial Help:** Yes   **Peer Tutors:** Yes

LD Specialists: 1   **Max. Hours/Week for services:**

Oral Exams: Yes   2 hrs. per/class, no max.

Services for LD Only: No   **Added**

Books on Tape: Yes   **Cost:** None

Calculator allowed in exam: Y/N **Taping of books not on tape:** Yes

Tape recording in class: Yes   **Dictionary/computer/spellcheck during exam:**

How are professors notified of LD:

GENERAL ADMISSIONS INFORMATION

Director of Admissions: Joseph P. Allen   **Telephone:** 408-459-2705

Entrance Requirements:

15 academic credits: 4 yrs. English; 3 yrs. Math; 1 yr. History; 1 yr. Laboratory Science; 2 yrs. Foreign Language; 4 electives. Students may be admitted by 3.31 GPA alone, or by exams alone. An SAT of 1100 or ACT of 25 and Achievements of 1650 with no individual achievement score below 500 will result in admission. Out-of-state students must have 3.4 GPA and Achievements of 1730 for automatic acceptance.

Test Scores: **SAT:** 970-1220 (mid 50%)   **ACT:**

G.P.A.: 3.45 (average)   **Class Rank:**

Application Deadline: 11/30   **Achievement Tests:** 3

COLLEGE GRADUATION REQUIREMENTS

Foreign Language: Yes   **Waivers:** Depends on major

Math: Yes   **Waivers:** Yes, there is an appeal process

Minimum Course Load per Term:

ADDITIONAL INFORMATION

Location: The University is located above Monterey Bay and the Pacific Ocean on 2,000 acres of redwood forest.

Enrollment Information: **Undergraduate:** 8,883   **Women:** 51%   **Men:** 49%

In-State Students: 97%   **Out of State:** 3%

Cost Information: **In-State Tuition:** $0   **Out of State:** $5,916

Room & Board: $5,465   **Additional Costs:** $1,733

Housing Information: **University Housing:** Yes   **Sorority:**

% Living on Campus: 46%   **Fraternity:**

Athletics: NCAA Div. III

UNIVERSITY OF SAN FRANCISCO
San Francisco, Ca. 94117

415-666-6563

Support: CS   *Institution:* 4 yr. Private

LEARNING DISABILITY PROGRAM AND SERVICES

Comments:

The University of San Francisco believes that students with learning disabilities are capable of succeeding and of becoming contributing members of the University community and society. To this end, USF provides educational support and assistance to those learning disabled students whose goals are successful completion of college and who take an active participatory role in their own education. Students are given assistance through trained peer tutors, study skills and credited courses in expository writing and structural skills.

LEARNING DISABILITY ADMISSIONS INFORMATION

Program Name: USF Services for the Learning Disabled   *Telephone*

Program Director: Cally Salzman   415-666-6876

Contact Person: same

Admissions:

If a student self-identifies as learning disabled in the regular application, the Director of USF Services reviews documentation and gives an evaluation before a decision is made. The Director has a great deal of involvement in the final decision. After admission, students who have a diagnosed learning disability can report directly to the LD Specialist in the Academic Support Services office. In an interview, the student's educational background will be discussed and needs assessed. Necessary interventions and accommodations are determined at that time and on a continual basis as the year progresses.

Interview: Yes   *Diagnostic Tests:* Yes

Documentation: Yes

College Entrance Exams Required: Yes   *Untimed Accepted:* Yes

Course Entrance Requirements: Yes

Are Waivers Available:

Additional Information:
Recommended 950 SAT or 22 ACT

Individualized high school coursework accepted: Yes

Essay Required: Yes

Special Application Required: No   *Submitted To:*

Number of Applications Submitted Each Year: 15

Number of Applications Accepted Each Year: 15

Number of Students Served: 24

Application Deadline for Special Admission: No

Acceptance into Program means acceptance
into college: No, there is an appeal procedure

LEARNING DISABILITY SERVICES

Learning Resource Room: Yes   **Curriculum Modification Available:** Yes

Kurzweil Personal Reader: No   **Tutorial Help:** Yes   **Peer Tutors:** Yes

LD Specialists: 1   **Max. Hours/Week for services:**

Oral Exams: Yes   5-8 hours

Services for LD Only: No   **Added**

Books on Tape: Yes   **Cost:** None

Calculator allowed in exam: Y/N   **Taping of books not on tape:** Yes

Tape recording in class: Yes   **Dictionary/computer/spellcheck during exam:** Y/N

How are professors notified of LD: By student and Program Director

GENERAL ADMISSIONS INFORMATION

Director of Admissions: William A. Henley   **Telephone:** 415-666-6563

Entrance Requirements:

20 academic units including: 4 yrs. English; 3 yrs. Math; 3 yrs. Social Studies; 2 yrs. Foreign Language; 2 yrs. Science. There is a summer opportunity for students not meeting requirements.

Test Scores: **SAT:** 960   **ACT:** 22 (recommended)

G.P.A.: 2.5   **Class Rank:**

Application Deadline: 2/15   **Achievement Tests:** No

COLLEGE GRADUATION REQUIREMENTS

Foreign Language: Yes   **Waivers:** Yes

Math: No   **Waivers:**

Minimum Course Load per Term:

ADDITIONAL INFORMATION

Location: The University of San Francisco is located on 52 acres in the heart of the city.

Enrollment Information: **Undergraduate:** 2,694   **Women:** 59%   **Men:** 41%

In-State Students: 80%   **Out of State:** 20%

Cost Information: **In-State Tuition:** $10,100   **Out of State:** same

Room & Board: $5,245   **Additional Costs:** $340

Housing Information: **University Housing:** Yes   **Sorority:** 5%

% Living on Campus: 50%   **Fraternity:** 13%

Athletics: NCAA Div. I

UNIVERSITY OF THE PACIFIC
Stockton, Ca. 95211
209-946-2211

Support: CS   **Institution:** 4 yr. Private

LEARNING DISABILITY PROGRAM AND SERVICES

Comments:

There is no special program for learning disabled students but the University does have an Academic Skills Center. This Center offers assistance through tutoring, study skills classes, support groups, and testing accommodations. Students register for services after admission by contacting the academic skills center. The Director, Ellen Weir can be reached at 209-946-2458.

LEARNING DISABILITY ADMISSIONS INFORMATION

Program Name: Learning Disability Support   **Telephone**

Program Director: Howard Houck, Coordinator   209-946-3219

Contact Person:

Admissions:

There is no special admissions for the student with learning disabilities. However, there are two alternative methods for admissions. Probationary admissions for the marginal student: "C/D" student, with no special requirements but the University advisor is notified of status. There is no required test score and no quota regarding the number admitted. Other students may be admitted through Special admissions: This admission requires that the student begins in the summer, prior to freshman year, receive at least a "C" average in 2 courses and 1 study skills class (these courses can be taken at a local community college).

Interview: Yes   **Diagnostic Tests:** Yes

Documentation: WAIS-R; Woodcock-Johnson

College Entrance Exams Required: Yes   **Untimed Accepted:** Yes

Course Entrance Requirements: Yes

Are Waivers Available:

Additional Information:

There is no minimum SAT or ACT required.

Individualized high school coursework accepted: Yes

Essay Required: Yes

Special Application Required: No   **Submitted To:**

Number of Applications Submitted Each Year: 15

Number of Applications Accepted Each Year: 15

Number of Students Served: N/A

Application Deadline for Special Admission: N/A

Acceptance into Program means acceptance into college: No

LEARNING DISABILITY SERVICES

Learning Resource Room: Yes   **Curriculum Modification Available:** Yes

Kurzweil Personal Reader: Yes   **Tutorial Help:** Yes   **Peer Tutors:** Yes

LD Specialists: Yes   **Max. Hours/Week for services:**

Oral Exams: Yes   4 (extra time for L.D.)

Services for LD Only: No   **Added Cost:** None

Books on Tape: Yes

Calculator allowed in exam: Yes   **Taping of books not on tape:** Yes

Tape recording in class: **Dictionary/computer/spellcheck during exam:** Yes

How are professors notified of LD: By the Program Director

GENERAL ADMISSIONS INFORMATION

Director of Admissions: Pat Peters   **Telephone:** 209-946-2211

Entrance Requirements:

College Prep courses including: 4 yrs. English; 3 yrs. Math; 3 yrs. Social Studies; 2 yrs. Foreign Language; 1 yr. Science.

Test Scores: **SAT:** 990   **ACT:**

G.P.A.: 2.5 Regular admit   **Class Rank:**

Application Deadline: 3/1   **Achievement Tests:**

COLLEGE GRADUATION REQUIREMENTS

Foreign Language: No   **Waivers:**

Math: Yes   **Waivers:** Waiver available

Minimum Course Load per Term: By petition after conscientious attempt

ADDITIONAL INFORMATION

Location: The University is located on 150 acres, 90 miles east of San Francisco.

Enrollment Information: **Undergraduate:** 3,765   **Women:** 52%   **Men:** 48%

    In-State Students: 70%   **Out of State:** 30%

Cost Information: **In-State Tuition:** $13,000   **Out of State:** same

    Room & Board: $4,798   **Additional Costs:** $320

Housing Information: **University Housing:** Yes   **Sorority:** 20%

    % Living on Campus: 40%   **Fraternity:** 20%

Athletics: NCAA Div. I

REGIS COLLEGE
Denver, Co. 80221
303-458-4900

Support: CS   **Institution:** 4 yr. Private

LEARNING DISABILITY PROGRAM AND SERVICES

Comments:

The goals of the Commitment Program are: to provide a means for underachieving students to enter college; to provide the support needed to be a successful learner; to help students develop the analytical processes which leads to high achievement. The Commitment Program offers learning support classes in reading skills, writing skills and study skills; special advising; tutoring; diagnostic academic testing; study or testing assistance; and training in word processing. Courses in learning support areas apply toward elective credit at Regis College.

LEARNING DISABILITY ADMISSIONS INFORMATION

Program Name: Commitment Program   **Telephone**

Program Director: Julie Elgin   303-458-4900

Contact Person:

Admissions:

There is no special admission procedure for learning disabled students. Although an interview is not required, the College would prefer that the student visit the school and have a minimum GPA of 2.0, an SAT of 800 or ACT of 15-21. Students need to show sufficient evidence of motivation and ability to succeed in College, even though they may not have the required GPA or test scores. Recommendations from counselors and evidence of extra-curricular activities will be used in their decision-making process.

Interview: No   **Diagnostic Tests:**

Documentation:

College Entrance Exams Required: **Untimed Accepted:** Yes

Course Entrance Requirements: Yes

Are Waivers Available:

Additional Information:

Students remain in the Program for the semester and with successful completion, are officially admitted to the College. They must: pass all required Commitment courses with a "C" or better; not fall below a 1.6 GPA in non-Commitment coursework; and agree not to participate in varsity sports, or other activities which may interfere with class attendance while involved in the Program.

Individualized high school coursework accepted: Yes

Essay Required: Preferred

Special Application Required: No   **Submitted To:**

Number of Applications Submitted Each Year: 100

Number of Applications Accepted Each Year: 75

Number of Students Served: 30 Freshman

Application Deadline for Special Admission: No

Acceptance into Program means acceptance

into college: No, there is an appeal procedure

LEARNING DISABILITY SERVICES

Learning Resource Room:	Yes	**Curriculum Modification Available:** Y/N	
Kurzweil Personal Reader:		**Tutorial Help:** Yes	**Peer Tutors:** Yes
LD Specialists:	4	**Max. Hours/Week for services:**	
Oral Exams:	No	Individual basis	
Services for LD Only:	No	**Added**	
Books on Tape:	No	**Cost:** $800	
Calculator allowed in exam:	Y/N	**Taping of books not on tape:** No	
Tape recording in class:	Yes	**Dictionary/computer/spellcheck during exam:** Y/N	

How are professors notified of LD: By the student and the Program Director

GENERAL ADMISSIONS INFORMATION

Director of Admissions: Domenic N. Teti   **Telephone:** 303-458-4900

Entrance Requirements:

High school transcript. Recommended; 4 yrs. English; 3 yrs. Math; 2 yrs. Science; 2 yrs. Foreign Language; 2 yrs. Social Studies; 1 yr. History. There is a Freshman Success Program that admits borderline students.

Test Scores: **SAT:** 900 (minimum)   **ACT:** 20 (minimum)

G.P.A.: 2.0   **Class Rank:**

Application Deadline: 8/1   **Achievement Tests:**

COLLEGE GRADUATION REQUIREMENTS

Foreign Language: Yes   **Waivers:** Sometimes

Math: Yes   **Waivers:** Sometimes

Minimum Course Load per Term: Yes

ADDITIONAL INFORMATION

Location: The College is on a 90 acre campus in a suburban area of Denver.

Enrollment Information:	**Undergraduate:**	1,015	**Women:** 49%	**Men:** 51%	
	In-State Students:	60%		**Out of State:** 40%	
Cost Information:	**In-State Tuition:**	$9,450		**Out of State:** same	
	Room & Board:	$4,700		**Additional Costs:** $390	
Housing Information:	**University Housing:**	Yes		**Sorority:** No	
	% Living on Campus:	50%		**Fraternity:** No	

Athletics: NCAA Div. II

UNIVERSITY OF COLORADO
Boulder, Co. 80309
303-492-6301

Support: CS　　　**Institution:** 4 yr. Public

LEARNING DISABILITY PROGRAM AND SERVICES

Comments:

The Learning Disabilities Program was developed to advocate and support the needs of the learning disabled student in the college environment. The Program centers around an interactive diagnostic-prescriptive process that utilizes "self- acknowledgment" of the learning disability as a means to assist academic and personal growth. A profile of individual strengths and weaknesses is developed between the student and the diagnostician. This diagnostic information enables the student to understand how learning occurs and how strategies may be developed.

LEARNING DISABILITY ADMISSIONS INFORMATION

Program Name:	Learning Disability Program	**Telephone**
Program Director:	Terri Bodhaine	303-492-5611
Contact Person:	same	

Admissions:

Students with learning disabilities must first submit an application through the regular admissions process. The LD Program and the Office of Admissions work together to process a candidate for admission. Consideration for admission is based on ability, rather than disability. LD applicants who meet the regular admissions criteria will not be assessed by the LD Program but will have access to the services. Those who do not meet the criteria will be given further consideration by a special LD Admission Committee. These applicants will have a diagnostic interview on campus. A final admission decision will be made after this meeting.

Interview: Yes　　　　　　　　　　　　**Diagnostic Tests:** Yes

Documentation: WAIS-R or WISC-R

College Entrance Exams Required: Yes　　　**Untimed Accepted:** Yes

Course Entrance Requirements: Yes

Are Waivers Available: Yes

Additional Information:

The diagnostic documentation should be included with the application form. Students are screened for the following values: SAT/ACT scores; IQ; GPA; "internal statistics"; Minimum Academic Preparation Standards(MAPS); and class rank. The applicant must meet the internal values in 4 out of 5 of these areas for further consideration. Acceptance to the Program is an alternate acceptance to the University of Colorado.

Individualized high school coursework accepted: Up to Admissions Office

Essay Required: No

Special Application Required: No　　　**Submitted To:**

Number of Applications Submitted Each Year: 240+

Number of Applications Accepted Each Year: 100

Number of Students Served: 130+

Application Deadline for Special Admission: No

Acceptance into Program means acceptance into college: Yes

53

LEARNING DISABILITY SERVICES

Learning Resource Room: Yes   **Curriculum Modification Available:** No

Kurzweil Personal Reader: No   **Tutorial Help:** Yes   **Peer Tutors:** No

LD Specialists: 4   **Max. Hours/Week for services:**

Oral Exams: Yes   2 hours is required for Freshman

Services for LD Only: No   **Added**

Books on Tape: No   **Cost:** $150 for diagnostic testing

Calculator allowed in exam: Yes   **Taping of books not on tape:** No

Tape recording in class: Yes   **Dictionary/computer/spellcheck during exam:** Yes

How are professors notified of LD: Student self-identifies

GENERAL ADMISSIONS INFORMATION

Director of Admissions: (Interim Director)   **Telephone:** 303-492-6301

Entrance Requirements:

4 yrs. English; 3-4 yrs. Math; 3 yrs. Science (including 2 yrs. Lab); 2-3 yrs. Social Science (including History and Geography); 2-3 yrs. Foreign Language (3 yrs. for Liberal Arts program);1 elective. Not all Colleges have the same entrance requirements.

Test Scores: **SAT:** 1100 (mid 50%)   **ACT:** 25

G.P.A.:   **Class Rank:** Top 30%

Application Deadline: 2/15   **Achievement Tests:**

COLLEGE GRADUATION REQUIREMENTS

Foreign Language: Yes   **Waivers:** Must take Language Aptitude Test for consideration

Math: Yes   **Waivers:** No

Minimum Course Load per Term: 12 credits

ADDITIONAL INFORMATION

Location: The school is located at the base of the Rocky Mountains, 45 minutes from Denver.

Enrollment Information: **Undergraduate:** 19,862   **Women:** 49%   **Men:** 51%

In-State Students: 66%   **Out of State:** 34%

Cost Information: **In-State Tuition:** $2,068   **Out of State:** $8,226

Room & Board: $3,230   **Additional Costs:** $354

Housing Information: University Housing: Yes   **Sorority:** 5%

% Living on Campus: 40%   **Fraternity:** 10%

Athletics: NCAA Div. I

Support: CS   **Institution:** 4 yr. Private

LEARNING DISABILITY PROGRAM AND SERVICES

Comments:

Students with learning disabilities do not take special classes, and are expected to participate in regular course work.. With the additional individual attention and services provided through the LEP , a motivated, qualified student can participate fully in a college-degree curriculum. One important aspect of the LEP involves reducing anxiety about learning in a college environment. Cognitive strategy development is a basic part of individual sessions with a learning specialist. Students are treated as responsible adults and are expected to participate willingly.

LEARNING DISABILITY ADMISSIONS INFORMATION

		Telephone
Program Name:	Learning Effectiveness Program (LEP)	
Program Director:	Maria Armstrong	303-871-2280
Contact Person:	Sue Hunt	1-800-525-9495

Admissions:

Admissions to the University and LEP is a process carried out through both the Office of Admission and the LEP. Potential learning disabled candidates must submit a general admissions application, essay, recommendations, activity sheet, high school transcript and ACT/SAT scores to general Admissions. Students must also provide: documentation of a learning disability, recent diagnostic tests, and a letter from a counselor, teacher or learning disability specialist outlining the services needed from a college LD program. A campus visit and interview is recommended after submission of all documentation and testing.

Interview: Yes   **Diagnostic Tests:** Yes

Documentation: WAIS-R or WISC-R

College Entrance Exams Required: Yes   **Untimed Accepted:** Yes

Course Entrance Requirements: Yes

Are Waivers Available: No

Additional Information:

College Prep classes only. The student must have at least a "C" average. A foreign language is not required. Recommendation from a LD specialist is critical. Letters should describe the student's learning style and the support services necessary for success. Strengths, weaknesses, maturity level, ability to handle frustration and feelings about limitations should also be included.

Individualized high school coursework accepted: No

Essay Required:

Special Application Required: **Submitted To:**

Number of Applications Submitted Each Year: 200+

Number of Applications Accepted Each Year: 25

Number of Students Served: 50-60

Application Deadline for Special Admission: No

Acceptance into Program means acceptance

into college: No

LEARNING DISABILITY SERVICES

Learning Resource Room: No   **Curriculum Modification Available:** No

Kurzweil Personal Reader: **Tutorial Help:** Yes   **Peer Tutors:** Yes

LD Specialists: 1   **Max. Hours/Week for services:**

Oral Exams: No   2 hours per/course

Services for LD Only: Yes   **Added**
Cost: $600 per/semester

Books on Tape:

Calculator allowed in exam: Yes   **Taping of books not on tape:**

Tape recording in class: Yes   **Dictionary/computer/spellcheck during exam:** Yes

How are professors notified of LD: By student

GENERAL ADMISSIONS INFORMATION

Director of Admissions: Roger Campbell   **Telephone:** 1-800-525-9495

Entrance Requirements:

15-20 credits including: 4 yrs. English; 3-4 yrs. Math; 3-4 yrs. Science; 2 yrs. History; 1-2 yrs. Social Studies; 2-4 yrs. Foreign Language; courses in Art; essay.

Test Scores: **SAT:** 1060   **ACT:** 24 average

G.P.A.: 2.0 minimum   **Class Rank:**

Application Deadline: 3/1   **Achievement Tests:**

COLLEGE GRADUATION REQUIREMENTS

Foreign Language: Yes   **Waivers:** Yes

Math: Yes   **Waivers:**

Minimum Course Load per Term: 12 hours to live in the dorm

ADDITIONAL INFORMATION

Location: 230 acre campus, 7 miles southeast of Denver.

Enrollment Information: **Undergraduate:** 3,219   **Women:** 57%   **Men:** 43%

    In-State Students: 32%   **Out of State:** 68%

Cost Information: **In-State Tuition:** $11,500   **Out of State:** same

    Room & Board: $4,000   **Additional Costs:** $144

Housing Information: **University Housing:** Yes   **Sorority:** 42%

    % Living on Campus: 89%   **Fraternity:** 38%

Athletics: NCAA Div. II

UNIVERSITY OF NORTHERN COLORADO
Greeley, Co. 80639
303-351-2881

Support: S   **Institution:** 4 yr. Public

LEARNING DISABILITY PROGRAM AND SERVICES

Comments:

Although the University does not offer a formal learning disability program, individual assistance is provided whenever possible. The Disabled Student Services program provides tutorial assistance when necessary, alternative testing such as extended time testing or testing in a private area.

LEARNING DISABILITY ADMISSIONS INFORMATION

Program Name:	Disabled Student Services	**Telephone**
Program Director:	James K. Bowen	303-351-2289
Contact Person:	Gary Gullickson	303-351-2881

Admissions:

The Directed Admission Program provides an opportunity for students, who do not meet UNC's freshman admission requirements, to earn full admission into a degree program. Students wishing to participate in this program need to complete the special form and return it to the Admissions Office. These students must take 12 hours of college credit and earn a GPA of 2.0 after one or two semesters. They also have to take study skills classes and a non-credit, non-college math class. Students do not need to be learning disabled to apply for this program.

Interview: No   **Diagnostic Tests:** Yes

Documentation:

College Entrance Exams Required: Yes   **Untimed Accepted:** Yes

Course Entrance Requirements: Yes

Are Waivers Available: No

Additional Information:

Each applicant is judged on an individual basis. Some students may be admitted who do not meet entrance criteria. UNC looks for a SAT of 890 or ACT of 21.

Individualized high school coursework accepted: No

Essay Required: No

Special Application Required: No   **Submitted To:**

Number of Applications Submitted Each Year: N/A

Number of Applications Accepted Each Year:

Number of Students Served: numbers not available

Application Deadline for Special Admission: No

Acceptance into Program means acceptance into college: No

LEARNING DISABILITY SERVICES

Learning Resource Room: No   **Curriculum Modification Available:** No

Kurzweil Personal Reader: Yes   **Tutorial Help:** Yes   **Peer Tutors:** Yes

LD Specialists: No   **Max. Hours/Week for services:**

Oral Exams: No   8 hours per/week

Services for LD Only: No   **Added**

Books on Tape: No   **Cost:** None

Calculator allowed in exam: Y/N   **Taping of books not on tape:** No

Tape recording in class: Y/N   **Dictionary/computer/spellcheck during exam:** Y/N

How are professors notified of LD: By the student and the Program Director

GENERAL ADMISSIONS INFORMATION

Director of Admissions: Gary Gullickson   **Telephone:** 303-351-2881

Entrance Requirements:

15 units; 4 yrs. English; 3 yrs. Math (including 2 yrs. Algebra or 1 yr. Algebra and 1 yr. Geometry); 2 yrs. Science (including 1 yr. of Lab); 2 yrs. Social Studies (including History); 4 yrs. elective. A 2.8 GPA or an ACT of 21 or an SAT of 890 and top 60% of the class.

Test Scores: **SAT:** 890   **ACT:** 21

G.P.A.: 2.8   **Class Rank:** Upper 60%

Application Deadline: Rolling   **Achievement Tests:**

COLLEGE GRADUATION REQUIREMENTS

Foreign Language: No   **Waivers:**

Math: Yes   **Waivers:** No

Minimum Course Load per Term: No

ADDITIONAL INFORMATION

Location: The University is located on 240 acres,in a small town 50 miles north of Denver.

Enrollment Information: **Undergraduate:** 8,107   **Women:** 58%   **Men:** 42%

In-State Students: 92%   **Out of State:** 8%

Cost Information: **In-State Tuition:** $1,490   **Out of State:** $4,360

Room & Board: $3,200   **Additional Costs:** $320

Housing Information: **University Housing:** Yes   **Sorority:** 8%

% Living on Campus: 30%   **Fraternity:** 10%

Athletics: NCAA Div. II

Support: S   **Institution:** 2 yr. Private

LEARNING DISABILITY PROGRAM AND SERVICES

Comments:

Briarwood College is a very small school and provides support as needed on a on-to-one basis between student and professor. The faculty is involved in working with students to provide accommodations related to their learning disability. The Dean of Students coordinates the services and monitors the students progress each semester. The Psychologist on staff interprets all documentation and provides each of the student's professors with a clear understanding of the disability and the accommodations necessary. Plans are under way to hire a learning disability specialist.

LEARNING DISABILITY ADMISSIONS INFORMATION

Program Name: Student Support Services   **Telephone**

Program Director: Barbara Mackay, Dean of Students   203-628-4751

Contact Person:

Admissions:

If the student self-identifies as learning disabled, a meeting is arranged between the prospective student (parents can attend), Dean of Students, Academic Dean, and Program Director (of program prospective student is interested in studying). Briarwood is willing to admit any student with a learning disability and work with the student to offer support and accommodations.

Interview: Yes   **Diagnostic Tests:** Y/N

Documentation: Any reliable testing in high school

College Entrance Exams Required: No   **Untimed Accepted:** Yes

Course Entrance Requirements: Yes

Are Waivers Available: Yes

Additional Information:

Each case is treated individually, with career goals and job placement important to any decisions about waivers.

Individualized high school coursework accepted: Yes

Essay Required: No

Special Application Required: No   **Submitted To:**

Number of Applications Submitted Each Year: Varies

Number of Applications Accepted Each Year: No records yet

Number of Students Served: 6

Application Deadline for Special Admission: No

Acceptance into Program means acceptance into college: Yes

LEARNING DISABILITY SERVICES

Learning Resource Room: No	**Curriculum Modification Available:** Yes
Kurzweil Personal Reader: No	**Tutorial Help:** Yes **Peer Tutors:** Yes
LD Specialists: No	**Max. Hours/Week for services:**
Oral Exams: Yes	No limit
Services for LD Only: No	**Added**
Books on Tape: Yes	**Cost:** None
Calculator allowed in exam: Yes	**Taping of books not on tape:** Yes
Tape recording in class: Yes	**Dictionary/computer/spellcheck during exam:** Yes

How are professors notified of LD: By the Program Director

GENERAL ADMISSIONS INFORMATION

Director of Admissions: Debra LaRoche   **Telephone:** 203-628-4751

Entrance Requirements:

High school transcript. Open door admissions.

Test Scores: **SAT:**   **ACT:**

G.P.A.:   **Class Rank:**

Application Deadline: Rolling   **Achievement Tests:**

COLLEGE GRADUATION REQUIREMENTS

Foreign Language: No   **Waivers:**

Math: Yes   **Waivers:** Yes

Minimum Course Load per Term: Minimum load is 12 credits; however, student can be part-time

ADDITIONAL INFORMATION

Location: The College is located in a small town on 32 acres with easy access to Hartford.

Enrollment Information:	**Undergraduate:** 329	**Women:** 96%	**Men:** 4%
	In-State Students: 96%		**Out of State:** 4%
Cost Information:	**In-State Tuition:** $6,995		**Out of State:** same
	Room & Board: $1,996		**Additional Costs:** $200
Housing Information:	**University Housing:** Yes		**Sorority:**
	% Living on Campus: 50%		**Fraternity:**

Athletics: Intercollegiate sports

MITCHELL COLLEGE
New London, Ct. 06320
203-443-2811

CT

Support: SP   **Institution:** 2 yr. Private

LEARNING DISABILITY PROGRAM AND SERVICES

Comments:

The Learning Resource Center offers intensive academic support for learning disabled college students who are accepted into the program. The primary goal of the program is to stimulate the development of learning skills and strategies that are necessary for successful and independent functioning on the college level. The program is designed for students with at least average intelligence and adequate basic skills who have taken high school classes designed for college preparation and who are adequately motivated.

LEARNING DISABILITY ADMISSIONS INFORMATION

Program Name: Learning Resource Center (LRC)   **Telephone**

Program Director: Susan Duques, Ph.D   203-433-2811

Contact Person: same

Admissions:

Applicants are considered for admission in the order in which the completed applications are received in the LRC. Students must complete an application process which includes submitting high school transcript, background information form, WAIS-R with subtest scores, LD teacher report with current achievement testing results for reading, writing and math, and an informal writing sample sent directly to the LRC office. An interview with the LRC staff may be requested following a review of the completed application.

Interview: Yes   **Diagnostic Tests:** Yes

Documentation: WAIS-R with sub-scores, achievement tests, informal writing sample

College Entrance Exams Required: Yes   **Untimed Accepted:** Yes

Course Entrance Requirements: Yes

Are Waivers Available: Yes

Additional Information:

Academic curriculum should be mainstreamed in high school. Upward trend in grades is helpful. Once accepted into the Program, students participate in a thorough diagnostic procedure. From the information obtained, a learning specialist works with each student to develop a contract outlining skills to be taught in individualized sessions.

Individualized high school coursework accepted: No

Essay Required: Yes

Special Application Required: Yes   **Submitted To:**

Number of Applications Submitted Each Year: 150-200

Number of Applications Accepted Each Year: 30-40

Number of Students Served: 35-45

Application Deadline for Special Admission: Fall semester of Senior year

Acceptance into Program means acceptance

into college: Yes

LEARNING DISABILITY SERVICES

Learning Resource Room: Yes   **Curriculum Modification Available:** No

Kurzweil Personal Reader: No   **Tutorial Help:** Yes   **Peer Tutors:** Yes

LD Specialists: 8-10   **Max. Hours/Week for services:**

Oral Exams: Yes   4-5

Services for LD Only: Yes   **Added**

Books on Tape: Yes   **Cost:** $3,000 per/year

Calculator allowed in exam: No   **Taping of books not on tape:** Yes

Tape recording in class: Yes   **Dictionary/computer/spellcheck during exam:** Yes

How are professors notified of LD: By the student and the Program Director

GENERAL ADMISSIONS INFORMATION

Director of Admissions: Kathleen Crowley   **Telephone:** 203-443-2811

Entrance Requirements:

At least a "C" average is recommended. Written recommendations are also helpful. Test results are not as important in the decision-making.

Test Scores: **SAT:**   **ACT:** Yes

G.P.A.: 2.0   **Class Rank:**

Application Deadline: Rolling   **Achievement Tests:**

COLLEGE GRADUATION REQUIREMENTS

Foreign Language: No   **Waivers:**

Math: **Waivers:** Depends on program of study

Minimum Course Load per Term: Full time required to take 12 credits unless otherwise indicated

ADDITIONAL INFORMATION

Location: The school is located on the banks of the Thames River approximately 1 1/2 hours from Hartford.

Enrollment Information: **Undergraduate:** 601   **Women:** 48%   **Men:** 52%

   In-State Students: 48%   **Out of State:** 52%

Cost Information: **In-State Tuition:** $9,336   **Out of State:** same

   Room & Board: $3,952   **Additional Costs:** $600

Housing Information: **University Housing:** Yes   **Sorority:**

   % Living on Campus: 95%   **Fraternity:**

Athletics: NJCAA

UNIVERSITY OF CONNECTICUT
Storrs, CT. 06268
203-486-3137

Support: S   **Institution:** 4 yr. Public

LEARNING DISABILITY PROGRAM AND SERVICES

Comments:

When a student checks "LD" on the admission's application, a letter is generated from admissions requesting that full documentation and testing be sent to the Director of the LD Program. University of Connecticut is not a good choice for students who deviate greatly from regular campus admissions standards. Classes will be large, services minimal and expectations high. Major compensations cannot be made.

LEARNING DISABILITY ADMISSIONS INFORMATION

Program Name: University Program for Learning Disability Students   **Telephone**

Program Director: Joan M. McGuire, Ph. D   203-486-5035

Contact Person: same

Admissions:

High School class rank is important. They are also looking for competitive, college preparatory coursework, above average intellectual potential and strong personal motivation for college study. In addition to completing the standard admissions application for the University, students also need to submit a completed referral form. The University may accept a student who is in the top one-third of the class and has a 900 SAT with documentation. LD applicants are encouraged to submit additional documentation that describes learning strengths and weaknesses.

Interview: No   **Diagnostic Tests:** Yes

Documentation: WAIS-R;W-J; other achievement tests

College Entrance Exams Required: Yes   **Untimed Accepted:** Yes

Course Entrance Requirements: Yes

Are Waivers Available: Yes

Additional Information:

Regular admissions with possible foreign language waiver.

Individualized high school coursework accepted: depends on coursework

Essay Required: No

Special Application Required: No   **Submitted To:**

Number of Applications Submitted Each Year: 200-300

Number of Applications Accepted Each Year: 60-70

Number of Students Served: 90

Application Deadline for Special Admission: No

Acceptance into Program means acceptance into college: No

LEARNING DISABILITY SERVICES

Learning Resource Room: Yes	**Curriculum Modification Available:** No	
Kurzweil Personal Reader: Yes	**Tutorial Help:** No	**Peer Tutors:** No
LD Specialists: 6-7	**Max. Hours/Week for services:**	
Oral Exams: Yes	3	
Services for LD Only: Yes	**Added**	
Books on Tape: Yes	**Cost:** None	
Calculator allowed in exam: Yes	**Taping of books not on tape:** Yes	
Tape recording in class: Yes	**Dictionary/computer/spellcheck during exam:** Y/N	
How are professors notified of LD: By student		

GENERAL ADMISSIONS INFORMATION

Director of Admissions: Dr. Ann Huckenbeck   **Telephone:** 203-486-3137

Entrance Requirements:

4 yrs. English; 3 yrs. Math; 2 yrs. Foreign Language; 2 yrs. Science; 2 yrs. Social Studies; 2 yrs. History; electives.

Test Scores: **SAT:** 900/1100 (out-of-state)   **ACT:**

G.P.A.: 2.7   **Class Rank:** top 50%

Application Deadline: 3/1   **Achievement Tests:**

COLLEGE GRADUATION REQUIREMENTS

Foreign Language: Yes   **Waivers:** Yes

Math: Yes   **Waivers:** Yes

Minimum Course Load per Term: Yes

ADDITIONAL INFORMATION

Location: University of Connecticut is located in Storrs,Ct., 30 miles northeast of Hartford.

Enrollment Information:	**Undergraduate:** 13,127	**Women:** 52%	**Men:** 48%	
	In-State Students: 87%		**Out of State:** 13%	
Cost Information:	**In-State Tuition:** $1,890		**Out of State:** $6,690	
	Room & Board: $4,258		**Additional Costs:** $1,156	
Housing Information:	**University Housing:** Yes		**Sorority:** 9%	
	% Living on Campus: 75%		**Fraternity:** 4%	

Athletics: NCAA Div. I

Support: CS   **Institution:** 4 yrs. Private

LEARNING DISABILITY PROGRAM AND SERVICES

Comments:

The Learning Plus program is an LD support program which helps learning disabled students throughout the University. Learning Plus services are individualized to accommodate the needs of each student. Learning Plus services include: individual tutoring from professional LD specialists or English tutors, faculty consultation to communicate instructional needs of students, modifications in academic procedures to enable students to compensate for their learning differences, and counseling.

LEARNING DISABILITY ADMISSIONS INFORMATION

Program Name:	Learning Plus	**Telephone**
Program Director:	Patricia Williams	203-243-4522
Contact Person:	same	

Admissions:

Students with learning disabilities do not apply to the Learning Plus program,rather, students apply directly to one of the eight schools and colleges within the University. If admitted, LD students may then elect to receive the support services offered. The Admissions Committee pays particular attention to the student's individual talents and aspirations, especially as they relate to programs available at the University. Once admitted to the University, students are requested to meet with the coordinator of Learning Plus to plan support services. The College of Basic Studies students meet with the director of Student Services.

Interview: Yes   **Diagnostic Tests:** Yes

Documentation: WISC-R or WAIS-R; Achievement tests; IEP

College Entrance Exams Required: Yes   **Untimed Accepted:** Yes

Course Entrance Requirements: Yes

Are Waivers Available: Yes

Additional Information:

Waivers are rare; University of Hartford offers alternatives. The University of Hartford also offers a 2 year program called the College of Basic Studies (CBS). CBS is a developmental program, with flexible admission standards, which offers many services. This program gives the student the opportunity to be in a college atmosphere and, if successful, transfer into the 4 year program for the last two years. CBS is not necessarily for LD students although there are some LD students enrolled in the Program.

Individualized high school coursework accepted: Yes

Essay Required: Yes

Special Application Required: No   **Submitted To:**

Number of Applications Submitted Each Year:

Number of Applications Accepted Each Year:

Number of Students Served: 91

Application Deadline for Special Admission: No

Acceptance into Program means acceptance

into college: No, appeal process

LEARNING DISABILITY SERVICES

Learning Resource Room: Yes	**Curriculum Modification Available:** Yes	
Kurzweil Personal Reader: No	**Tutorial Help:** Yes	**Peer Tutors:** Yes
LD Specialists: 3	**Max. Hours/Week for services:**	
Oral Exams: Yes	Unlimited	
Services for LD Only: Yes	**Added**	
Books on Tape: Yes	**Cost:** None	
Calculator allowed in exam: Yes	**Taping of books not on tape:** Yes	
Tape recording in class: Yes	**Dictionary/computer/spellcheck during exam:** Yes	

How are professors notified of LD: By letter from the Program Director

GENERAL ADMISSIONS INFORMATION

Director of Admissions: Richard A. Zeiser   **Telephone:** 203-243-4296

Entrance Requirements:

4 yrs. English; 3-3.5 yrs. Math; 2 yrs. Foreign Language; 2 yrs. Science; 2 yrs. Social Studies plus academic electives; essay. The College of Basic Studies (CBS), a 2 year program, is less competitive and prepares students to pursue a Bachelor's degree.

Test Scores: **SAT:** 900 (mid 50%)   **ACT:** 21

G.P.A.:   **Class Rank:** top 50%

Application Deadline: Rolling   **Achievement Tests:** Recommended

COLLEGE GRADUATION REQUIREMENTS

Foreign Language: **Waivers:** Depends on College

Math: **Waivers:** Depends on College

Minimum Course Load per Term: LD student can take less than 12 credits

ADDITIONAL INFORMATION

Location: The University is located on a 300 acre campus, in a residential section of West Hartford, 90 minutes from Boston.

Enrollment Information: **Undergraduate:** 5,032   **Women:** 47%   **Men:** 53%

In-State Students: 32%   **Out of State:** 68%

Cost Information: **In-State Tuition:** $10,992   **Out of State:** same

Room & Board: $4,766   **Additional Costs:** $410

Housing Information: **University Housing:** Yes   **Sorority:** 5%

% Living on Campus: 85%   **Fraternity:** 5%

Athletics: NCAA Div. I

BRANDYWINE COLLEGE OF WIDENER UNIV.
Wilmington, De. 19803
302-477-2290

Support: CS   *Institution:* 2 yr. Private

LEARNING DISABILITY PROGRAM AND SERVICES

Comments:

Brandywine's Program for Learning Disabled Students is quite small. Students participating in the Program are enrolled in one of the standard curricular majors. In addition to the usual services offered by the College, students in PLDS are also offered: counseling and advising with LD specialists, learning strategy assistance, individual and small group tutoring, individual and group discussion sessions, and a professional staff that serves as advocates with the College.

LEARNING DISABILITY ADMISSIONS INFORMATION

Program Name: Program for Learning Disabled Students (PLDS)   *Telephone*

Program Director: Linda Baum   302-477-2290

Contact Person:

Admissions:

There is a two-fold admissions process. First there is the standard admissions into the College. Then, after an additional review of academic record and selected test results, a campus visit, and an interview, a decision is made regarding acceptance into PLDS.

Interview: Yes   *Diagnostic Tests:* Yes

Documentation: WAIS-R or WISC-R; Bender-Gestalt

College Entrance Exams Required: No   *Untimed Accepted:*

Course Entrance Requirements: No

Are Waivers Available:

Additional Information:

Individualized high school coursework accepted: Yes

Essay Required: No

Special Application Required: *Submitted To:*

Number of Applications Submitted Each Year: 95

Number of Applications Accepted Each Year: 35-50

Number of Students Served: 50

Application Deadline for Special Admission: September,October of Senior year

Acceptance into Program means acceptance

into college: No, there is an appeal procedure

LEARNING DISABILITY SERVICES

Learning Resource Room: Yes   **Curriculum Modification Available:**

Kurzweil Personal Reader: No   **Tutorial Help:** Yes   **Peer Tutors:** Yes

LD Specialists: 3   **Max. Hours/Week for services:**

Oral Exams: Yes   No Maximum

Services for LD Only: No   **Added**

Books on Tape: Yes   **Cost:**

Calculator allowed in exam: Yes   **Taping of books not on tape:** Yes

Tape recording in class: **Dictionary/computer/spellcheck during exam:** Yes

How are professors notified of LD: By the Program Director

GENERAL ADMISSIONS INFORMATION

Director of Admissions: Daniel N. Bowers   **Telephone:** 302-478-3000

Entrance Requirements:

Grades are the most important critera.

Test Scores: **SAT:**   **ACT:** 17 median

G.P.A.: 2.0   **Class Rank:**

Application Deadline: Rolling   **Achievement Tests:** No

COLLEGE GRADUATION REQUIREMENTS

Foreign Language: No   **Waivers:**

Math: Yes   **Waivers:**

Minimum Course Load per Term: 4 courses per semester

ADDITIONAL INFORMATION

Location: The 40 acre campus is located in a city setting, with easy access to Philadelphia which is 20 miles away.

Enrollment Information: **Undergraduate:** 598   **Women:** 60%   **Men:** 40%

In-State Students: 20%   **Out of State:** 80%

Cost Information: **In-State Tuition:** $6,900   **Out of State:** $6,900

Room & Board: $4,760   **Additional Costs:**

Housing Information: **University Housing:** Yes   **Sorority:** 19%

% Living on Campus: 40%   **Fraternity:** 19%

Athletics: NJCAA

Support: S   **Institution:** 4 yr. Public

LEARNING DISABILITY PROGRAM AND SERVICES

Comments:

The University of Delaware offers a number of services for students with high aptitudes and specific learning disabilities through the Academic Studies Assistance Program (ASAP). ASAP is able to provide "state of the art "assistance as a part of the research and development mission of the program. Many ASAP services are available to all university students who seek to improve their learning. The special services for learning handicapped students are one part of the larger program.

LEARNING DISABILITY ADMISSIONS INFORMATION

Program Name:	Academic Studies Assistance Program (ASAP)	**Telephone**
Program Director:	Dr. S. Farnham-Diggory	302-451-1639
Contact Person:	David Johns	302-451-8167

Admissions:

There is no special application. Services begin as soon as the student is enrolled in the University.

Interview: No

Documentation: WAIS-R;WRAT; W-J

College Entrance Exams Required: Yes

Course Entrance Requirements: Yes

Are Waivers Available:

Diagnostic Tests: Yes

Untimed Accepted: Yes

Additional Information:

Act is not accepted. Achievement tests are recommended. Students participating in the Academic Studies Assistance Program are invited to a Summer Enrichment Program prior to freshman year.

Individualized high school coursework accepted: Possible

Essay Required: No

Special Application Required: No   **Submitted To:**

Number of Applications Submitted Each Year: NA

Number of Applications Accepted Each Year: NA

Number of Students Served:

Application Deadline for Special Admission: No

Acceptance into Program means acceptance
into college:

69

LEARNING DISABILITY SERVICES

Learning Resource Room: Yes   **Curriculum Modification Available:** Y/N

Kurzweil Personal Reader: **Tutorial Help:** Yes   **Peer Tutors:**

LD Specialists: No   **Max. Hours/Week for services:**

Oral Exams: No   5 hrs. per/course

Services for LD Only: No   **Added**

Books on Tape: Yes   **Cost:** None

Calculator allowed in exam: Y/N   **Taping of books not on tape:** Yes

Tape recording in class: Yes   **Dictionary/computer/spellcheck during exam:** Yes

How are professors notified of LD: A letter is sent, a follow-up call is made if necessary.

GENERAL ADMISSIONS INFORMATION

Director of Admissions: N. Bruce Walker   **Telephone:** 302-541-8123

Entrance Requirements:

4 yrs. English; 2 yrs. Math; 2 yrs. Science; 2 yrs. Foreign Language; 1 yr. Social Studies; 2 yrs. History; 3 electives. Language substitution available. SAT required.

Test Scores: **SAT:** 1055 (mid 50%)   **ACT:**

G.P.A.: 3.2 average   **Class Rank:**

Application Deadline: 3/1   **Achievement Tests:** Recommended

COLLEGE GRADUATION REQUIREMENTS

Foreign Language: Yes   **Waivers:** Depends on program

Math: Yes   **Waivers:** No

Minimum Course Load per Term: Full time status necessary for housing, there are exceptions.

ADDITIONAL INFORMATION

Location: The 1100 acre campus is in a small town 12 miles south-west of Wilmington, and mid-way between Philadelphia and Baltimore.

Enrollment Information: **Undergraduate:** 14,546   **Women:** 57%   **Men:** 43%

In-State Students: 41%   **Out of State:** 59%

Cost Information: **In-State Tuition:** $2,990   **Out of State:** $7,200

Room & Board: $2,972   **Additional Costs:**

Housing Information: **University Housing:** Yes   **Sorority:** 6%

% Living on Campus: 50%   **Fraternity:** 6%

Athletics: NCAA Div. I

FLORIDA ATLANTIC UNIVERSITY
Boca Raton, Fl. 33431-0991
407-367-3000

Support: S   *Institution:* 4 yr. Public

LEARNING DISABILITY PROGRAM AND SERVICES

Comments:

The Disabled Student Services offers equal access to a quality education by providing reasonable accommodations to qualified students. Students who have a documented learning disability may receive strategy tutoring from the LD Specialist by appointment. There is a Counseling Center with professionally trained staff to help students with interpersonal conflicts and concerns, test anxiety, poor concentration, and guidance services.

LEARNING DISABILITY ADMISSIONS INFORMATION

Program Name: Disabled Student Services (DSS)   *Telephone*

Program Director: Dee Davis   407-376-3880

Contact Person: same

Admissions:

There is no special application process. The learning disabled student may include a cover letter to explain why SAT/ACT scores and high school GPA may be artificially depressed as a result of a lack of services in their high school.

Interview: No   **Diagnostic Tests:** Yes

Documentation: Various

College Entrance Exams Required: Yes   **Untimed Accepted:** Yes

Course Entrance Requirements: Yes

Are Waivers Available: No

Additional Information:

Students may also be considered for admission on the basis of outstanding abilities or extraordinary circumstances which indicate the potential to benefit from a competitive University curriculum and environment.

Individualized high school coursework accepted: Depends

Essay Required: Yes

Special Application Required: No   **Submitted To:**

Number of Applications Submitted Each Year: Unknown

Number of Applications Accepted Each Year: Unknown

Number of Students Served: 40

Application Deadline for Special Admission: No

Acceptance into Program means acceptance into college: No, there is an appeal procedure

LEARNING DISABILITY SERVICES

Learning Resource Room: No   **Curriculum Modification Available:** Yes

Kurzweil Personal Reader: No   **Tutorial Help:** Yes   **Peer Tutors:** No

LD Specialists: 1   **Max. Hours/Week for services:**

Oral Exams: Yes   Determined at the first meeting

Services for LD Only: No   **Added**

Books on Tape: Yes   **Cost:** None

Calculator allowed in exam: Y/N   **Taping of books not on tape:** Yes

Tape recording in class: Yes   **Dictionary/computer/spellcheck during exam:** Yes

How are professors notified of LD: By the student and through a letter from DSS

GENERAL ADMISSIONS INFORMATION

Director of Admissions: Dr.Brian Levin-Stankevich   **Telephone:** 407-367-3040

Entrance Requirements:

19 units including: 4 yrs. English; 3 yrs. Math; 3 yrs. Science (2 yrs. Lab); 2 yrs. Foreign Language; 3 yrs. Social Studies; 4 yrs. electives. Students who have completed more demanding courses receive added consideration.

Test Scores: **SAT:** 1055   **ACT:** 24

G.P.A.: 3.0   **Class Rank:**

Application Deadline: 6/1   **Achievement Tests:**

COLLEGE GRADUATION REQUIREMENTS

Foreign Language: Yes   **Waivers:** Substitution only, no waivers

Math: Yes   **Waivers:** Substitution only, no waivers

Minimum Course Load per Term: Yes, financial aid and housing may be affected

ADDITIONAL INFORMATION

Location: The University is located on 1,000 acres 1 1/2 miles from the ocean and in proximity to Miami and Ft. Lauderdale.

Enrollment Information: **Undergraduate:** 8,346   **Women:** 60%   **Men:** 40%

In-State Students: 90%   **Out of State:** 10%

Cost Information: **In-State Tuition:** $1,300   **Out of State:** $3,800

Room & Board: $3,345   **Additional Costs:**

Housing Information: **University Housing:** Yes   **Sorority:** 1%

% Living on Campus: 10%   **Fraternity:** 1%

Athletics: NCAA Div. II

UNIVERSITY OF FLORIDA
Gainesville, Fl. 32611
904-392-1365

Support: S   **Institution:** 4 yr. Public

LEARNING DISABILITY PROGRAM AND SERVICES

Comments:

The Student Support Service office at the University of Florida acts as an advocate for students with learning disabilities. Each professor is given a letter describing the accommodations necessary for the student to be successful in the class. There is a drop-in tutorial clinic. The Reading and Writing Center offers a class for 1 credit in study skills and language skills. Students with learning disabilities also receive priority registration.

LEARNING DISABILITY ADMISSIONS INFORMATION

Program Name:	Programs and Services for Students with Disabilities	**Telephone**
Program Director:	Kenneth J. Osfield	904-392-1261
Contact Person:	William Kolb	904-392-1365

Admissions:

The student with learning disabilities applies to the University under the same guidelines as all other students. However, learning disabled students are given a separate review. The required SAT or ACT varies according to the student's GPA.

Interview: **Diagnostic Tests:** Yes

Documentation:

College Entrance Exams Required: Yes   **Untimed Accepted:** Yes

Course Entrance Requirements: Yes

Are Waivers Available: Yes

Additional Information:
Foreign Language and Math

Individualized high school coursework accepted:

Essay Required: To explain learning disability

Special Application Required: **Submitted To:**

Number of Applications Submitted Each Year:

Number of Applications Accepted Each Year:

Number of Students Served: 51 with learning disabilities

Application Deadline for Special Admission: No

Acceptance into Program means acceptance into college: No, there is an appeals process

LEARNING DISABILITY SERVICES

Learning Resource Room: Yes

Kurzweil Personal Reader: Yes

LD Specialists: No

Oral Exams: Yes

Services for LD Only: No

Books on Tape: Yes

Calculator allowed in exam: Yes

Tape recording in class: Yes

Curriculum Modification Available: Y/N

Tutorial Help: Yes   **Peer Tutors:**

Max. Hours/Week for services:

Added Cost: None

Taping of books not on tape: Yes

Dictionary/computer/spellcheck during exam: Yes

How are professors notified of LD: By the student with letter from Program Director

GENERAL ADMISSIONS INFORMATION

Director of Admissions: Corinne Willits   **Telephone:** 904-392-1365

Entrance Requirements:

4 yrs. English; 3 yrs. Math; 3 yrs. Science; 3 yrs. Social Studies; 2 yrs. Foreign Language (may admit with deficiency).

Test Scores: SAT: 1130 (mid 50%)   **ACT:** 25 (out-of-state)

G.P.A.: 3.0   **Class Rank:**

Application Deadline: 2/1   **Achievement Tests:**

COLLEGE GRADUATION REQUIREMENTS

Foreign Language: Yes   **Waivers:** Yes, with petition

Math: Yes   **Waivers:** Yes, with petition

Minimum Course Load per Term:

ADDITIONAL INFORMATION

Location: The University is located on 2,000 acres in a small city 115 miles north of Orlando, Florida, and 20 minutes from the Gainesville airport.

Enrollment Information: Undergraduate: 26,461   **Women:** 48%   **Men:** 52%

In-State Students: 90%   **Out of State:** 10%

Cost Information: In-State Tuition: $1,238   **Out of State:** $3,997

Room & Board: $3,330   **Additional Costs:**

Housing Information: University Housing: Yes   **Sorority:** 20%

% Living on Campus: 30%   **Fraternity:** 20%

Athletics: NCAA Div. I

BRENAU WOMEN'S COLLEGE
Gainesville, Ga. 30501-3697

404-534-6133

Support: CS   **Institution:** 4 yr. Private

LEARNING DISABILITY PROGRAM AND SERVICES

Comments:

The Brenau Learning Disabilities Program is designed for the highly motivated student with above average intelligence and a diagnosed learning disability. The student learns how to compensate for her disability in a mainstreamed college environment. The Program is divided into Levels of need. Initially, the student begins the program with Level I services and moves on to Level II and Level III as she becomes more competent and comfortable with the work and her ability.

LEARNING DISABILITY ADMISSIONS INFORMATION

Program Name: Learning Center   **Telephone**

Program Director: Vincent Yamilkoski, Ed.D   404-534-6134

Contact Person: same

Admissions:

To be admitted to the Learning Disabilities Program, a student must first apply for admission to the College. Admission application, SAT and/or ACT scores, high school transcript, and a counselor recommendation are required in order to determine admission status. Upon acceptance into the Learning Disabilities Program the student, her parent or guardian, the program director, and the Dean of the College sign a contract which states that the student will attend scheduled classes, and tutoring, reading therapy, and academic consultation sessions. Failure to meet these commitments may result in discontinuation in the program.

Interview: Yes   **Diagnostic Tests:** Yes

Documentation: WAIS-R; K-TEA; WRAT; BVMG; Draw-A-Person

College Entrance Exams Required: Yes   **Untimed Accepted:** Yes

Course Entrance Requirements: Yes

Are Waivers Available:

Additional Information:

Placement tests in English and Math

Individualized high school coursework accepted: Yes

Essay Required: No

Special Application Required: Yes   **Submitted To:**

Number of Applications Submitted Each Year: 40

Number of Applications Accepted Each Year: 15

Number of Students Served: 60

Application Deadline for Special Admission: 9 months prior to entrance

Acceptance into Program means acceptance into college: Yes

LEARNING DISABILITY SERVICES

Learning Resource Room: Yes   **Curriculum Modification Available:** No

Kurzweil Personal Reader: No   **Tutorial Help:** Yes   **Peer Tutors:** Yes

LD Specialists: 2   **Max. Hours/Week for services:**

Oral Exams: Yes   8 hrs. per/student   3 hrs. per/course

Services for LD Only: Yes   **Added**

Books on Tape: Yes   **Cost:** $2,600. per/semester

Calculator allowed in exam: Y/N   **Taping of books not on tape:** Yes

Tape recording in class: Yes   **Dictionary/computer/spellcheck during exam:** Yes

How are professors notified of LD: By student and Director

GENERAL ADMISSIONS INFORMATION

Director of Admissions: M. Betsy Hale   **Telephone:** 404-534-6100

Entrance Requirements:

4 yrs. English; 3 yrs. Math; 3 yrs. Science; Foreign Language; 2-3 yrs. Social Studies; 7-9 electives.

Test Scores: **SAT:** Required   **ACT:** Required

G.P.A.: 2.0   **Class Rank:**

Application Deadline: Open   **Achievement Tests:**

COLLEGE GRADUATION REQUIREMENTS

Foreign Language: Yes   **Waivers:** Case-by-case basis

Math: Yes   **Waivers:**

Minimum Course Load per Term: 12-15 hours

ADDITIONAL INFORMATION

Location: Small town setting, 50 miles from Atlanta on 37 acres.

Enrollment Information: **Undergraduate:** 507   **Women:** 100%   **Men:**

In-State Students: 78%   **Out of State:** 22%

Cost Information: **In-State Tuition:** $6,018   **Out of State:** same

Room & Board: $4,982   **Additional Costs:**

Housing Information: **University Housing:** Yes   **Sorority:** 85%

% Living on Campus: 75%   **Fraternity:**

Athletics: NAIA

Support: S   *Institution:* 4 yr. Private

LEARNING DISABILITY PROGRAM AND SERVICES

Comments:

The Handicapped Student Services program has a number of goals for its students including: to coordinate services to provide equal access to programs, services and activities; to reduce competitive disadvantage in academic work; to provide individual counseling and referral; to serve as an advocate for student needs; to provide a variety of support services and to serve as a liaison between students and University officers or community agencies.

LEARNING DISABILITY ADMISSIONS INFORMATION

Program Name:	Handicapped Student Services	*Telephone*
Program Director:	Lelia Crawford	404-727-3300
Contact Person:	same	

Admissions:

Students are required to submit everything requested by the Office of Admission for regular admissions. However, an untimed SAT may be submitted in lieu of the timed test. Teacher and/or counselor recommendations may be weighted more heavily in the admissions process. A professional diagnosis of the disability with recommendations for the accommodations necessary for academic success may be required. Essentially each student with a disability is evaluated individually and admitted based on potential for success in the Emory environment, taking into consideration the necessary accommodations requested.

Interview: No

Documentation: No specific test

College Entrance Exams Required: Yes

Course Entrance Requirements: Yes

Are Waivers Available: Yes

Diagnostic Tests: Yes

Untimed Accepted: Yes

Additional Information:

Achievement tests are recommended.

Individualized high school coursework accepted: Yes

Essay Required: Yes

Special Application Required: No   *Submitted To:*

Number of Applications Submitted Each Year:

Number of Applications Accepted Each Year:

Number of Students Served: 18

Application Deadline for Special Admission: No

Acceptance into Program means acceptance into college:

LEARNING DISABILITY SERVICES

Learning Resource Room: Yes	**Curriculum Modification Available:** Yes
Kurzweil Personal Reader: No	**Tutorial Help:** Yes **Peer Tutors:** Yes
LD Specialists: No	**Max. Hours/Week for services:**
Oral Exams: Yes	3 hours per/course
Services for LD Only: No	**Added**
Books on Tape: Yes	**Cost:** None
Calculator allowed in exam: Yes	**Taping of books not on tape:** Yes
Tape recording in class: Yes	**Dictionary/computer/spellcheck during exam:** Yes

How are professors notified of LD: By student and Program Director

GENERAL ADMISSIONS INFORMATION

Director of Admissions: Daniel C. Walls   **Telephone:** 404-727-6036

Entrance Requirements:

4 yrs. English; 3 yrs. Math; 2 yrs. Social Science; 2 yrs. Science; 2 yrs. Foreign Language; 3 electives. They prefer an additional year of Math.

Test Scores: **SAT:** 1050-1290 (mid 50%)   **ACT:** 25-32 (middle 50%)

G.P.A.: 3.5 (average)   **Class Rank:**

Application Deadline: 2/1   **Achievement Tests:** Recommended

COLLEGE GRADUATION REQUIREMENTS

Foreign Language: No   **Waivers:**

Math: No   **Waivers:**

Minimum Course Load per Term: 12 hours

ADDITIONAL INFORMATION

Location: The 631 acre campus is in a suburban section 5 miles northeast of Atlanta.

Enrollment Information: **Undergraduate:** 5,416   **Women:** 52%   **Men:** 48%

In-State Students: 28%   **Out of State:** 72%

Cost Information: **In-State Tuition:** $13,700   **Out of State:** same

Room & Board: $4,300   **Additional Costs:** $200

Housing Information: University Housing: Yes   **Sorority:** 25%

% Living on Campus: 75%   **Fraternity:** 25%

Athletics: NCAA Div. III

Support: CS   **Institution:** 4 yr. Public

LEARNING DISABILITY PROGRAM AND SERVICES

Comments:

The purpose of the University of Georgia's Learning Disabilities Adult Clinic is to provide diagnostic assessment and direct service to students who demonstrate specific learning disabilities. Once students have been evaluated and determined to have a learning disability they are automatically eligible to receive services from the LDAC Service component. The Academic Therapy program is the only service for which there is a charge. This is a one-to one intensive help program for academic subjects.

LEARNING DISABILITY ADMISSIONS INFORMATION

Program Name:	Learning Disabilities Adult Clinic (LDAC)	**Telephone**
Program Director:	Dr. Noel Gregg *542 4589*	404-542-4597
Contact Person:	Dr. Rosemary Jackson	same

Admissions:

The LDAC does not participate in the admissions procedure except in appeal cases. There is a way for students with learning disabilities to apply for special services. This procedure is still in the process of being finalized. In order to be admitted into the LDAC, students must complete comprehensive testing. The test results are used by the professors to modify the classroom work, and to assist in curriculum decisions. In-state students not meeting admissions criteria may enter through the Developmental Studies Program. Out-of-state students may enter by taking night school and transferring after 1 year (with no dorm privileges).

Interview: Yes   **Diagnostic Tests:** Yes

Documentation: Complete evaluation

College Entrance Exams Required: Yes   **Untimed Accepted:** Yes

Course Entrance Requirements: Yes

Are Waivers Available: Yes

Additional Information:

There is no special admissions at this time. However there is a new procedure being finalized. Essentially, the process requires that the student be evaluated by the LDAC. After verification, a recommendation is made to the President's office. Appeals should be directed to the President.

Individualized high school coursework accepted:

Essay Required: No

Special Application Required: **Submitted To:**

Number of Applications Submitted Each Year:

Number of Applications Accepted Each Year:

Number of Students Served: 162

Application Deadline for Special Admission: No

Acceptance into Program means acceptance into college: No

LEARNING DISABILITY SERVICES

Learning Resource Room:	Yes	
Kurzweil Personal Reader:	Yes	
LD Specialists:	9	
Oral Exams:	Yes	
Services for LD Only:	Yes	
Books on Tape:	Yes	

Curriculum Modification Available: Yes

Tutorial Help: Yes   **Peer Tutors:** No

Max. Hours/Week for services:

    3 hrs. per/week

Added Cost: Academic Therapy: $1,600-$$2,000.

Calculator allowed in exam: Yes   **Taping of books not on tape:** Yes

Tape recording in class: Yes   **Dictionary/computer/spellcheck during exam:** Yes

How are professors notified of LD: By student and by letter from the Program Director

GENERAL ADMISSIONS INFORMATION

Director of Admissions: Dr. Claire Swann   **Telephone:** 404-542-2112

Entrance Requirements:

4 yrs. English; 3 yrs. Math; 3 yrs. Social Science; 3 yrs. Science; 2 yrs. Foreign Language.

Sabrina 542 4589

5551212

Test Scores: **SAT:** 900 (minimum)   **ACT:**

G.P.A.: 3.28 average   **Class Rank:**

Application Deadline: 2/1   **Achievement Tests:**

COLLEGE GRADUATION REQUIREMENTS

Foreign Language: **Waivers:** Depends on major and learning disability documentation

Math: Yes   **Waivers:** Depends on major

Minimum Course Load per Term: 12 hours

ADDITIONAL INFORMATION

Location: A large campus located 80 miles from Atlanta.

Enrollment Information:	**Undergraduate:**	21,494	**Women:** 53%	**Men:**	47%
	In-State Students:	85%		**Out of State:**	15%
Cost Information:	**In-State Tuition:**	$1,917		**Out of State:**	$5,085
	Room & Board:	$2,940		**Additional Costs:**	$333
Housing Information:	**University Housing:**	Yes		**Sorority:**	17%
	% Living on Campus:	25%		**Fraternity:**	11%

Athletics: NCAA Div. I

Support: SP   **Institution:** 4 yr. Private

LEARNING DISABILITY PROGRAM AND SERVICES

Comments:

Barat College offers small classes which provide individual attention for students. Learning Opportunities Program participants take specified courses in writing, reading and math and choose a variety of other courses in their area of interest. Additional instruction, as needed, is provided by the LD specialists on an individual basis. Trained peer tutors are supervised by the LD specialist. All accepted students must attend a summer orientation before freshman year.

LEARNING DISABILITY ADMISSIONS INFORMATION

Program Name: Learning Opportunities Program (LOP)   *Telephone*

Program Director: Dr. Pamela Adelman   708-234-8000

Contact Person: same

Admissions:

Barat will consider for admission those students who have a history or current diagnosis of a specific learning disability. These students should have average or above-average ability, a strong desire to succeed in college, and a willingness to work hard. Stage I for the students is to complete the application, send 2 recommendations, transcripts, SAT or ACT, case history, and LD tests. The teacher in high school or the casemanager should complete a special report. The LOP will notify the student about Stage II of the process which includes past evaluation, reports, health information, and placement tests and interview.

Interview: Yes   **Diagnostic Tests:** Yes

Documentation: WAIS-R or WISC-R

College Entrance Exams Required: Yes   **Untimed Accepted:** Yes

Course Entrance Requirements: Yes

Are Waivers Available:

Additional Information:

SAT 825, ACT 18 (Flexible on either one). Each student is evaluated individually.

Individualized high school coursework accepted: Yes

Essay Required: Yes

Special Application Required: Yes   **Submitted To:**

Number of Applications Submitted Each Year: 60-70

Number of Applications Accepted Each Year: 10-20

Number of Students Served: 20-40

Application Deadline for Special Admission: Fall of senior year

Acceptance into Program means acceptance into college: Yes

LEARNING DISABILITY SERVICES

Learning Resource Room: Yes	**Curriculum Modification Available:** Yes	
Kurzweil Personal Reader:	**Tutorial Help:** Yes	**Peer Tutors:** Yes
LD Specialists: 5	**Max. Hours/Week for services:**	
Oral Exams: Yes	Varies	
Services for LD Only: No	**Added**	
Books on Tape: Yes	**Cost:** $500-1200 per/semester	
Calculator allowed in exam: Y/N	**Taping of books not on tape:** Yes	
Tape recording in class: Yes	**Dictionary/computer/spellcheck during exam:** Y/N	

How are professors notified of LD: By student and Program Director

GENERAL ADMISSIONS INFORMATION

Director of Admissions: Loretta Brickman   **Telephone:** 312-234-3000

Entrance Requirements:

High School transcript, campus visit and interview important.

Test Scores: **SAT:** 825   **ACT:** 19

G.P.A.: 2.0   **Class Rank:**

Application Deadline: Rolling   **Achievement Tests:** No

COLLEGE GRADUATION REQUIREMENTS

Foreign Language: Yes   **Waivers:** No

Math: Yes   **Waivers:** No

Minimum Course Load per Term: Decided on an individual basis (12 for full-time)

ADDITIONAL INFORMATION

Location: The College is located on a 30 acre campus in the suburbs, 25 miles north of Chicago.

Enrollment Information:	**Undergraduate:** 725	**Women:** 75%	**Men:** 27%	
	In-State Students: 17%		**Out of State:** 83%	
Cost Information:	**In-State Tuition:** $7,800		**Out of State:** same	
	Room & Board: $3,000		**Additional Costs:**	
Housing Information:	**University Housing:** Yes		**Sorority:** No	
	% Living on Campus: 52%		**Fraternity:** No	

Athletics: NAIA

Support: CS   **Institution:** 4 yr. Private

LEARNING DISABILITY PROGRAM AND SERVICES

Comments:

PLuS is designed to service learning disabled students who can reason, think cognitively and are motivated to succeed in College. PLuS provides intensive help on a one-to-one or small group basis. It is designed to assist with regular college courses, to improve learning deficits and to help the student learn compensatory skills. Students and learning disability specialists meet for a required 2 hours per week for a least the first year of college.

LEARNING DISABILITY ADMISSIONS INFORMATION

Program Name: Productive Learning Strategies (PLuS)   **Telephone**

Program Director: Alisa Brickman   312-362-6897

Contact Person: same

Admissions:

Students with Learning Disabilities must be accepted to DePaul University before they can be accepted to PLuS. The diagnostic testing that is required, if done within the last three years, will be used in the evaluation. If the student does not have the required testing the University will administer the appropriate assessments. Some students may qualify for admissions through the Bridge Program, which is an enhancement program for incoming freshmen. (This program is not for LD students although some students are learning disabled.)

Interview: Yes   **Diagnostic Tests:** Y/N

Documentation:

College Entrance Exams Required: Yes   **Untimed Accepted:** Yes

Course Entrance Requirements: Yes

Are Waivers Available: Yes

Additional Information:

Students considered for the Bridge Program may have SAT scores of 700-710, or an ACT score of 17-20. These students are often in the bottom 1/3 of their class. They have usually taken a college prep curriculum and shown potential for success. The Bridge Program begins with a required summer session prior to Freshman year.

Individualized high school coursework accepted: Yes

Essay Required: No

Special Application Required: Yes   **Submitted To:**

Number of Applications Submitted Each Year: 42

Number of Applications Accepted Each Year: 21

Number of Students Served: 40

Application Deadline for Special Admission: September/October of Senior year

Acceptance into Program means acceptance into college: No

83

LEARNING DISABILITY SERVICES

Learning Resource Room: No

Kurzweil Personal Reader:

LD Specialists: 8

Oral Exams: Yes

Services for LD Only: Yes

Books on Tape: Yes

Calculator allowed in exam: Yes

Tape recording in class: Yes

How are professors notified of LD: By Student Form Letter and Program Director

Curriculum Modification Available: Yes

Tutorial Help: Yes   **Peer Tutors:** Yes

Max. Hours/Week for services:

   No maximum

Added Cost: Under consideration

Taping of books not on tape: Yes

Dictionary/computer/spellcheck during exam: Yes

GENERAL ADMISSIONS INFORMATION

Director of Admissions: Thomas D. Abrahamson   **Telephone:** 312-341-8300

Entrance Requirements:

Recommended Courses from High School: 4 yrs. English; 2 yrs. Math; 2 yrs. Science w/Labs; 2 yrs. Social Sciences; 1 yr. History; 2 yrs. Foreign Languages; 4 electives. Students not meeting entrance requirements may be admitted through the Bridge Program (these students often are in the bottom half of the class, 17-20 ACT, GPA of 2.0-2.4).

Test Scores: **SAT:** 1000   **ACT:** 23

G.P.A.: 2.5 plus   **Class Rank:** top 50%

Application Deadline: 8/15   **Achievement Tests:** No

COLLEGE GRADUATION REQUIREMENTS

Foreign Language: Yes   **Waivers:** Depends on major

Math: Yes   **Waivers:** Depends on major

Minimum Course Load per Term: Students may take two courses per semester and still qualify

ADDITIONAL INFORMATION

Location: Urban University campus located in Chicago's Lincoln Park area on a 3 acre campus, three miles north of the downtown area.

Enrollment Information: **Undergraduate:** 9,416   **Women:** 56%   **Men:** 44%

   In-State Students: 91%   **Out of State:** 9%

Cost Information: **In-State Tuition:** $8,124   **Out of State:** same

   Room & Board: $4,200   **Additional Costs:** $30

Housing Information: **University Housing:** Yes   **Sorority:** 4%

   % Living on Campus: 25%   **Fraternity:** 6%

Athletics: NCAA Div. I

Support: CS   **Institution:** 4 yr. Private

LEARNING DISABILITY PROGRAM AND SERVICES

Comments:

The philosophy of the College is to provide a complete approach which will prepare a student for success in college as well as for life experiences. Kendall does not have an LD program, but it does offer a term of College Preparatory courses for the under-prepared student. The program offers both academic and psychological support for the entering freshman through individualized instruction, advising, support groups, peer tutoring and assessment. The biggest advantage of the College is the small size of the school itself.

LEARNING DISABILITY ADMISSIONS INFORMATION

Program Name:	Freshman Year Program	**Telephone**
Program Director:	Kathy McCarville	708-866-1370
Contact Person:	Peter Pauletti	708-866-1305

Admissions:

There is no special application or admissions process. If a student does not have a 2.0 GPA, 16 ACT or 800 SAT, then placement tests are required along with an interview. If the student is admitted conditionally , a "C" average is required by the end of freshman year. Students with a learning disability will be reviewed by a learning disability specialist. Kendall also offers a 2 year General Studies degree in which the curriculum includes developmental courses.

Interview: Yes   **Diagnostic Tests:** No

Documentation:

College Entrance Exams Required: Yes   **Untimed Accepted:** Yes

Course Entrance Requirements: Yes

Are Waivers Available: No

Additional Information:

If requirements are not met, a placement test is required along with an interview. They are looking for an SAT of 800 of an ACT of 16.

Individualized high school coursework accepted: No

Essay Required: Yes

Special Application Required: No   **Submitted To:**

Number of Applications Submitted Each Year: 50

Number of Applications Accepted Each Year: 40

Number of Students Served: 226

Application Deadline for Special Admission: No

Acceptance into Program means acceptance

into college: Yes if the students complete the Freshman Program successfully with a "C" average.

85

LEARNING DISABILITY SERVICES

Learning Resource Room: Yes   **Curriculum Modification Available:** No

Kurzweil Personal Reader: **Tutorial Help:** Yes   **Peer Tutors:** Yes

LD Specialists: 1   **Max. Hours/Week for services:**

Oral Exams: No

Services for LD Only: No   **Added**

Books on Tape: Yes   **Cost:** None

Calculator allowed in exam: Y/N   **Taping of books not on tape:** Yes

Tape recording in class: Yes   **Dictionary/computer/spellcheck during exam:** Yes

How are professors notified of LD: By student and Program Director

GENERAL ADMISSIONS INFORMATION

Director of Admissions: Peter Pauletti   **Telephone:** 708-866-1305

Entrance Requirements:

4 yrs. English; 2 yrs. Math; 2 yrs. Science; 1 yr. Foreign Language; 2 yrs. Social Studies; 2 yrs. History; 2 yrs. Electives. Two recommendations and an essay are required for culinary school applicants.

Test Scores: **SAT:** 800 (minimum)   **ACT:** 16 (minimum)

G.P.A.: 2.0   **Class Rank:** Upper 3/4

Application Deadline: Rolling   **Achievement Tests:**

COLLEGE GRADUATION REQUIREMENTS

Foreign Language: No   **Waivers:**

Math: Yes   **Waivers:**

Minimum Course Load per Term: 3 hours

ADDITIONAL INFORMATION

Location: The College is located in the town of Evanston, near the beaches of Lake Michigan, 10 miles north of downtown Chicago.

Enrollment Information: **Undergraduate:** 400   **Women:** 45%   **Men:** 55%

In-State Students: 85%   **Out of State:** 15%

Cost Information: **In-State Tuition:** $6,051   **Out of State:** same

Room & Board: $3,777   **Additional Costs:**

Housing Information: **University Housing:** Yes   **Sorority:** No

% Living on Campus: 50%   **Fraternity:** No

Athletics: Intramural sports

Support: CS   *Institution:* 4 yr. Private

LEARNING DISABILITY PROGRAM AND SERVICES

Comments:

The staff in the Center for Academic Development are highly qualified and are very supportive and successful in working with learning disabled students. There is a great deal of communication between the professional staff in the center and the faculty.

LEARNING DISABILITY ADMISSIONS INFORMATION

		Telephone
Program Name:	Center for Academic Development	
Program Director:	Anna Kim	312-621-9650
Contact Person:	Paul Fawler	708-256-5150

Admissions:

Following the determination that an applicant does not meet standard admission requirements and upon the applicant's identification of a disability, the applicant is asked to submit documentation of the disability. The Coordinator of Counseling and Academic Advising arranges for the student to meet with the appropriate personnel to review the student's potential ability to success at the college level. This interview is required. A sub-committee appointed by the Admission Council meets for the purpose of communicating a recommendation and for proposing an individual instructional program.

Interview: Yes   *Diagnostic Tests:* Yes

Documentation:

College Entrance Exams Required: Yes   *Untimed Accepted:* Yes

Course Entrance Requirements: Yes

Are Waivers Available:

Additional Information:

Students not admissible through regular admissions may be admitted provisionally.

Individualized high school coursework accepted: Yes

Essay Required: No

Special Application Required: No   *Submitted To:*

Number of Applications Submitted Each Year:

Number of Applications Accepted Each Year:

Number of Students Served:

Application Deadline for Special Admission: No

*Acceptance into Program means acceptance
into college:*

LEARNING DISABILITY SERVICES

Learning Resource Room:	Yes	**Curriculum Modification Available:**	
Kurzweil Personal Reader:	No	**Tutorial Help:** Yes	**Peer Tutors:** Yes
LD Specialists:	Yes	**Max. Hours/Week for services:**	
Oral Exams:	Yes	2 +	
Services for LD Only:	No	**Added**	
Books on Tape:	Yes	**Cost:** None	
Calculator allowed in exam:	Yes	**Taping of books not on tape:** Yes	
Tape recording in class:	Yes	**Dictionary/computer/spellcheck during exam:** Yes	

How are professors notified of LD: By student and Program Director

GENERAL ADMISSIONS INFORMATION

Director of Admissions: Gail Strauss   **Telephone:** 708-475-1100

Entrance Requirements:

15 academic credits including: 4 yrs. English; 2 yrs. Math; 3 yrs. Social Studies; 2 yrs. Science.

Test Scores: **SAT:** 800 (minimum)   **ACT:** 17 (minimum)

G.P.A.:   **Class Rank:** Top 50%

Application Deadline: Rolling   **Achievement Tests:**

COLLEGE GRADUATION REQUIREMENTS

Foreign Language: **Waivers:**

Math: **Waivers:**

Minimum Course Load per Term:

ADDITIONAL INFORMATION

Location: Formerly known as National College of Education, the school is located in Evanston, on 12 acres in a suburban neighborhood 12 miles north of Chicago.

Enrollment Information:	**Undergraduate:** 2,910	**Women:** 70%	**Men:** 30%
	In-State Students: 81%		**Out of State:** 19%
Cost Information:	**In-State Tuition:** $6,975		**Out of State:** same
	Room & Board: $4,065		**Additional Costs:**
Housing Information:	**University Housing:** Yes		**Sorority:** 1%
	% Living on Campus: 10%		**Fraternity:**

Athletics: NAIA

NORTHERN ILLINOIS UNIVERSITY
DeKalb, IL. 60115
815-753-0446

Support: CS   **Institution:** 4 yr. Public

LEARNING DISABILITY PROGRAM AND SERVICES

Comments:

Services for Students with Disabilities is staffed by personnel who are supportive and sensitive to students. There are no certified learning disability specialist on staff at this time, but it is hoped that a specialist will be hired in the near future. There is a small support group for learning disabled students. Other services offered include tutoring, test accommodations, computers, and curriculum substitution with documentation.

LEARNING DISABILITY ADMISSIONS INFORMATION

Program Name: Services for Students with Disabilities (SSD)   **Telephone**

Program Director: Sue Reinhardt / Linn Sorge   815-753-1303

Contact Person: same

Admissions:

There is no special admissions for learning disabled students. However, the admissions staff has some flexibility if the applicants are close to meeting entrance requirements. Learning Disabled students should check the box on the application indicating they would like to be contacted by the SSD office. These applications will be reviewed by the SSD staff. If the appropriate documentation is included, the SSD can make a recommendation to the Office of Admissions. Very often this recommendation is an important part of acceptance or denial.

Interview: Yes   **Diagnostic Tests:** Yes

Documentation: I.Q.; Achievement tests; summary by a psychologist within 3 years

College Entrance Exams Required: Yes   **Untimed Accepted:** Yes

Course Entrance Requirements: Yes

Are Waivers Available:

Additional Information:

LD students who are denied admission may appeal the decision. The appeal process requires 3 letters of recommendation (2 from teachers and 1 from the LD specialist). Current testing must also be sent to the University. The office of Admissions will review all information as well as a recommendation from the SSD office. Very often Admissions will abide by the recommendation of the SSD office. There is also a Chance Program for academically or economically disadvantaged

Individualized high school coursework accepted: No, if not "regular class work"

Essay Required: For appeal

Special Application Required: No   **Submitted To:**

Number of Applications Submitted Each Year:

Number of Applications Accepted Each Year:

Number of Students Served:

Application Deadline for Special Admission: Fall of senior year

Acceptance into Program means acceptance

into college: There is an appeal process

LEARNING DISABILITY SERVICES

Learning Resource Room:	Yes	**Curriculum Modification Available:** No	
Kurzweil Personal Reader:	Yes	**Tutorial Help:** Yes	**Peer Tutors:** Yes
LD Specialists:	No	**Max. Hours/Week for services:**	
Oral Exams:	Y/N	As needed basis	
Services for LD Only:	No	**Added**	
Books on Tape:	Yes	**Cost:** No	
Calculator allowed in exam:	Y/N	**Taping of books not on tape:** Yes	
Tape recording in class:	Yes	**Dictionary/computer/spellcheck during exam:** Y/N	

How are professors notified of LD: On a per-need basis

GENERAL ADMISSIONS INFORMATION

Director of Admissions: Daniel Oborn   **Telephone:** 815-753-0446

Entrance Requirements:

3 yrs. English; 2 yrs. Math; 2 yrs. Science; 2 yrs. Social Studies. In addition the student must finish 1 year of Art, Film, a Foreign Language, Music or Theater. Class rank of 50-99% and a 19 ACT; or a class rank of 34-49% with a 23 ACT.

Test Scores: **SAT:**   **ACT:** 17-23

G.P.A.:   **Class Rank:** upper 50%

Application Deadline: 8/1   **Achievement Tests:** No

COLLEGE GRADUATION REQUIREMENTS

Foreign Language: Yes   **Waivers:** Substitutions available (cultural courses)

Math: Yes   **Waivers:** Substitutions available

Minimum Course Load per Term: As needed

ADDITIONAL INFORMATION

Location: The school is located on 460 acres in a small town, 65 miles from Chicago.

Enrollment Information:	**Undergraduate:** 18,029	**Women:** 54%	**Men:** 46%
	In-State Students: 94%		**Out of State:** 6%
Cost Information:	**In-State Tuition:** $1,714		**Out of State:** $5,142.
	Room & Board: $2,640		**Additional Costs:** $670
Housing Information:	**University Housing:** Yes		**Sorority:** 11%
	% Living on Campus: 40%		**Fraternity:** 15%

Athletics: NCAA Div. I

Support: S   **Institution:** 4 yr. Private

LEARNING DISABILITY PROGRAM AND SERVICES

Comments:

Shimer offers an integrated curriculum reading original sources and not textbooks. Students gather to discuss the books in small groups. Shimer has been able to meet the needs of learning disabled students who are motivated to seek this kind of education. Students are responsible for seeking the supportive help they want. The class size varies from 8 to 12 students. Skills courses are available in reading, written language, math learning and study strategies.

LEARNING DISABILITY ADMISSIONS INFORMATION

Program Name:	NA	**Telephone**
Program Director:	NA	
Contact Person:	Ms. Bobbie Groth	708-623-8400

Admissions:

Admissions is based on whether or not the College feels it can provide the services necessary for successful learning. Students are encouraged to have a personal interview, write a personal essay, submit ACT/SAT scores, letters of recommendations, and the psyco-educational reports sent to the admissions office.

Interview: Yes   **Diagnostic Tests:** No

Documentation: writing sample

College Entrance Exams Required: Recommended   **Untimed Accepted:**

Course Entrance Requirements: Yes

Are Waivers Available:

Additional Information:

One letter of recommendation is required. SAT/ACT scores are not used for admission.

Individualized high school coursework accepted: Yes

Essay Required: Yes

Special Application Required: No   **Submitted To:**

Number of Applications Submitted Each Year: NA

Number of Applications Accepted Each Year: NA

Number of Students Served: NA

Application Deadline for Special Admission: NA

Acceptance into Program means acceptance into college: Yes

LEARNING DISABILITY SERVICES

Learning Resource Room:

Kurzweil Personal Reader: No

LD Specialists: No

Oral Exams: Yes

Services for LD Only: No

Books on Tape:

Calculator allowed in exam: Yes

Tape recording in class: Yes

How are professors notified of LD: By student

Curriculum Modification Available:

Tutorial Help: Yes   **Peer Tutors:**

Max. Hours/Week for services:

Unlimited

Added Cost: None

Taping of books not on tape:

Dictionary/computer/spellcheck during exam: Yes

GENERAL ADMISSIONS INFORMATION

Director of Admissions: Ms. Bobbie Groth   **Telephone:** 708-623-8400

Entrance Requirements:

High school transcript; 1 letter of recommendation.

Test Scores: **SAT:** Recommended   **ACT:** Recommended

G.P.A.:   **Class Rank:**

Application Deadline: 8/10   **Achievement Tests:**

COLLEGE GRADUATION REQUIREMENTS

Foreign Language: No   **Waivers:**

Math: Yes   **Waivers:** Theoretical math course required

Minimum Course Load per Term: Students proceed at own pace

ADDITIONAL INFORMATION

Location: The school is located in a city setting 40 miles north of Chicago and 40 miles south of Milwaukee.

Enrollment Information: **Undergraduate:** 100   **Women:** 50%   **Men:** 50%

In-State Students: 65&   **Out of State:** 35%

Cost Information: **In-State Tuition:** $8,150   **Out of State:** same

Room & Board: $1,545   **Additional Costs:**

Housing Information: **University Housing:** Yes   **Sorority:**

% Living on Campus: 40%   **Fraternity:**

Athletics: Intramural sports

Support: SP   *Institution:* 4 yr.   Public

LEARNING DISABILITY PROGRAM AND SERVICES

Comments:

Project Achieve is an academic support program for LD students. Students are accepted on a first come, first serve basis providing they qualify for the program. Students are enrolled in regular college courses and are never restricted from any course offerings. Freshman year students are enrolled as full-time students but are restricted to 12 semester hours. As students become more successful, they may enroll in more semester hours. Students have access to individualized tutoring, taped texts, test accommodations, remedial classes, developmental writing course, test proctoring, and advocacy service.

LEARNING DISABILITY ADMISSIONS INFORMATION

Program Name:	Project Achieve	**Telephone**
Program Director:	Barbara Cordoni, Ed.D	618-453-2595
Contact Person:	Sally DeDecker, M.S.	same

Admissions:

Application to the University and the Program are separate. Applicants to Project Achieve are required to provide the following: Achieve application forms, a $50 application fee, a recent photo, and documentation of the learning disability. There is also a $1000 diagnostic testing fee (some fee waivers available). This testing is required before admissions. If admitted, the student takes tests in 5 subject areas and is assigned specific classes within those course areas. In addition, students will receive tutoring. The Project Achieve application can be submitted any time during high school.

Interview: Yes

Documentation: Scaled IQ scores, achievement tests

College Entrance Exams Required: Yes

Course Entrance Requirements: Yes

Are Waivers Available: No

Diagnostic Tests: Yes

Untimed Accepted: Yes

Additional Information:

Foreign Language may be substituted by Art or Music. The 21 ACT can be waived for Project Achieve applicants. For students not automatically admitted, Southern offers a selected admissions through the Center for Basic Skills. In addition, there is a 2 year Associates Program that will consider admitting students not meeting minimum standards for regular admission.

Individualized high school coursework accepted:

Essay Required: No

Special Application Required: Yes   **Submitted To:**

Number of Applications Submitted Each Year: 100-125

Number of Applications Accepted Each Year: 65

Number of Students Served: 130

Application Deadline for Special Admission: Sophomore/Junior year of high school

Acceptance into Program means acceptance into college: No, can appeal

LEARNING DISABILITY SERVICES

Learning Resource Room: Yes

Curriculum Modification Available: No

Kurzweil Personal Reader: No

Tutorial Help: Yes   **Peer Tutors:** Yes

LD Specialists: 14

Max. Hours/Week for services:

Oral Exams: Yes

Unlimited

Services for LD Only: Yes

Added Cost: $1,850. per/semester/ $950. half-time

Books on Tape: Yes

Calculator allowed in exam: Yes

Taping of books not on tape: Yes

Tape recording in class: Yes

Dictionary/computer/spellcheck during exam: Yes

How are professors notified of LD: By student and Program Director

GENERAL ADMISSIONS INFORMATION

Director of Admissions: Mr. Thomas McGinnis   **Telephone:** 618-536-4405

Entrance Requirements:

3 yrs. English; 2 yrs. Math; 2 yrs. Lab Science; 3 yrs. Social Studies. Foreign Language can be satisfied with Art, Music, etc. Students in the top 50% of their class with a 19 ACT or 700 SAT, or students with any class rank who have a 21 ACT or 810 SAT are automatically admitted. If students meet class rank and test scores but have subject deficiencies, they will be reviewed.

Test Scores: **SAT:**   **ACT:** 21

G.P.A.:   **Class Rank:**

Application Deadline: Rolling admissions   **Achievement Tests:**

COLLEGE GRADUATION REQUIREMENTS

Foreign Language: **Waivers:** Depends on majors

Math: **Waivers:** Depends on majors

Minimum Course Load per Term: 12 credits

ADDITIONAL INFORMATION

Location: The campus lies at the edge of the Shawnee National Forests, 6 hours south of Chicago.

Enrollment Information: **Undergraduate:** 20,429   **Women:** 62%   **Men:** 38%

       In-State Students: 82%   **Out of State:** 18%

Cost Information: **In-State Tuition:** $1,560   **Out of State:** $4,680

       Room & Board: $2,636   **Additional Costs:** $607

Housing Information: **University Housing:** Yes   **Sorority:** 6%

       % Living on Campus: 30%   **Fraternity:** 6%

Athletics: NCAA Div. I

ANDERSON UNIVERSITY
Anderson, In. 46012-3462
317-641-4080

Support: CS   **Institution:** 4 yrs. Private

LEARNING DISABILITY PROGRAM AND SERVICES

Comments:

Students with specific learning disabilities may be integrated into any of the many existing services at the Kissinger Learning Center, or more individual programming may be designed. LD students receive extensive personal contact through the program. The Director of the Program schedules time with each student to evaluate their personal learning style in order to assist in planning for the most appropriate learning environment. One of the most successful programs is the individual or small group tutorial assistance. Students are also provided with social and emotional support.

LEARNING DISABILITY ADMISSIONS INFORMATION

Program Name: Program for Learning Disabilities   **Telephone**

Program Director: Rinda Smith   317-641-4226

Contact Person: same

Admissions:

Minimal requirements, regular application procedure.

Interview: Yes   **Diagnostic Tests:** Yes

Documentation:

College Entrance Exams Required: Yes   **Untimed Accepted:** Yes

Course Entrance Requirements: Yes

Are Waivers Available:

Additional Information:

Individualized high school coursework accepted:

Essay Required: Yes

Special Application Required: **Submitted To:**

Number of Applications Submitted Each Year:

Number of Applications Accepted Each Year:

Number of Students Served: 23

Application Deadline for Special Admission: No

Acceptance into Program means acceptance into college: Decision made jointly

LEARNING DISABILITY SERVICES

Learning Resource Room: Yes   **Curriculum Modification Available:** Yes

Kurzweil Personal Reader: No   **Tutorial Help:** Yes   **Peer Tutors:** Yes

LD Specialists: 1   **Max. Hours/Week for services:**

Oral Exams: Yes   Unlimited

Services for LD Only: No   **Added**

Books on Tape: Yes   **Cost:** None

Calculator allowed in exam: Yes   **Taping of books not on tape:** Yes

Tape recording in class: Yes   **Dictionary/computer/spellcheck during exam:** Yes

How are professors notified of LD: By student and Director of Program

GENERAL ADMISSIONS INFORMATION

Director of Admissions: Phillip M. Fair   **Telephone:** 317-641-4080

Entrance Requirements:

4 yrs. English; 2 yrs. Math; 2 yrs. Science (including Lab); 2 yrs. Foreign Language; 1 yr. Social Studies; Electives (which may be non-academic).

Test Scores: **SAT:** 895   **ACT:** 21

G.P.A.: 2.0   **Class Rank:** Upper 60%

Application Deadline: 9/1   **Achievement Tests:**

COLLEGE GRADUATION REQUIREMENTS

Foreign Language: Yes   **Waivers:** Yes

Math: Yes   **Waivers:** Yes

Minimum Course Load per Term: 12 credits for financial aid students

ADDITIONAL INFORMATION

Location: Anderson University is located on 100 acres 40 miles northeast of Indianapolis.

Enrollment Information: **Undergraduate:** 2,015   **Women:** 55%   **Men:** 47%

In-State Students: 55%   **Out of State:** 45%

Cost Information: **In-State Tuition:** $7,300   **Out of State:** same

Room & Board: $2,370   **Additional Costs:**

Housing Information: **University Housing:** Yes   **Sorority:** No

% Living on Campus: 60%   **Fraternity:** No

Athletics: NAIA

Support: S   **Institution:** 4 yr. Public

LEARNING DISABILITY PROGRAM AND SERVICES

Comments:

Ball State University does not have a formal program for learning disabled students, nor a resource room or LD specialist. The University does offer support services available to all students. Learning disabled students need to assess if the Ball State Learning Center, tutoring programs, taped texts, faculty liaison, test accommodations and special advocacy will meet the specific needs for the students. The Learning Center offers many services to enhance academic skills and help students with course work. The center is staffed with faculty, graduate students and peers.

LEARNING DISABILITY ADMISSIONS INFORMATION

Program Name:	Disabled Student Development	**Telephone**
Program Director:	Richard Harris	317-285-5293

Contact Person:

Admissions:

Requirements are the same for all students. Students may take non-standardized ACT or SAT. Learning Disabled students are encouraged to have an interview with the Program Director to determine the appropriateness of Ball State as a college choice. Students not meeting general admission requirements may be admitted to Guided Studies. Students who are below 50% or below an 18 ACT can be considered. Guided Studies is a University College program for freshman. The program is very structured.

Interview: Yes, (Jr. year)   **Diagnostic Tests:** Yes

Documentation: Yes

College Entrance Exams Required: Yes   **Untimed Accepted:** Yes

Course Entrance Requirements: Yes

Are Waivers Available:

Additional Information:

If admitted through Guided Studies, students are assigned a special advisor who meets with the student 2 times a week.. In addition, each semester selected classes in General Studies curriculum are designed as Supplemental Instructional classes(SI). A trained upper-class student attends these classes, takes notes and conducts a study group session.

Individualized high school coursework accepted:

Essay Required: No

Special Application Required: No   **Submitted To:**

Number of Applications Submitted Each Year:

Number of Applications Accepted Each Year: 400-500 in Guided Studies

Number of Students Served:

Application Deadline for Special Admission:

Acceptance into Program means acceptance into college:

LEARNING DISABILITY SERVICES

Learning Resource Room:	No	**Curriculum Modification Available:** No	
Kurzweil Personal Reader:	Yes	**Tutorial Help:** Yes	**Peer Tutors:** Yes
LD Specialists:	No	**Max. Hours/Week for services:**	
Oral Exams:	Yes	As needed (usually 1-2 times per week/per course)	
Services for LD Only:	No	**Added**	
Books on Tape:	Yes	**Cost:** None	
Calculator allowed in exam:	Yes	**Taping of books not on tape:** Yes	
Tape recording in class:	Yes	**Dictionary/computer/spellcheck during exam:** Yes	

How are professors notified of LD: By the student

GENERAL ADMISSIONS INFORMATION

Director of Admissions: Ruth Vedvik   **Telephone:** 317-285-8300

Entrance Requirements:

No specific course requirements but recommend: 4 yrs. English; 3 yrs. Math; 3 yrs. Social Studies; 2 yrs. Science. Students below 50th % or 18 ACT may be admitted through Guided Studies Program.

Test Scores: **SAT:** 800 (minimum)   **ACT:** 18 (minimum)

G.P.A.:   **Class Rank:** 50%

Application Deadline: 3/1   **Achievement Tests:** No

COLLEGE GRADUATION REQUIREMENTS

Foreign Language: No   **Waivers:**

Math: Yes   **Waivers:** Rarely given

Minimum Course Load per Term: 12 credits per semester for financial aid

ADDITIONAL INFORMATION

Location: The University is located on 950 acres, 55 miles from Indianapolis.

Enrollment Information:	**Undergraduate:** 18,880	**Women:** 57%	**Men:** 43%
	In-State Students: 91%		**Out of State:** 9%
Cost Information:	**In-State Tuition:** $2,100		**Out of State:** $4,800
	Room & Board: $2,800		**Additional Costs:** $480
Housing Information:	**University Housing:** Yes		**Sorority:** 10%
	% Living on Campus: 40%		**Fraternity:** 11%

Athletics: NCAA Div. I

INDIANA WESLEYAN UNIVERSITY
Marion, In. 46953
317-674-6901

Support: S   **Institution:** 4 yr. Private

LEARNING DISABILITY PROGRAM AND SERVICES

Comments:

Student Support Services provides tutoring, counseling, notetaker, and test accommodations. The Learning Center, under the direction of Dr. Ruth Dixon, is available to all students who seek assistance with raising the quality of their academic work. Developmental educational courses are offered in reading improvement, fundamentals of communication and skills for academic success.

LEARNING DISABILITY ADMISSIONS INFORMATION

Program Name: Student Support Services / The Learning Center   **Telephone**

Program Director: Dr. Neil McFarlane / Dr. Ruth Dixon   317-677-2192

Contact Person: 317-677-2192

Admissions:

General admissions seeks students with at least a 2.0 GPA, 840 SAT or 20-21 ACT. Students with a GPA under a 2.0 can be admitted provisionally and there are no cut-off scores for ACT or SAT. In addition, some students may be offered an admission which allows them to take 7-8 credit hours in Bible studies, learning skills and speech. These students may live in the dorm and participate in campus activities. Successful completion of these 7-8 credits lead to regular admission.

Interview: Yes   **Diagnostic Tests:** Yes

Documentation: Yes

College Entrance Exams Required: Yes   **Untimed Accepted:** Yes

Course Entrance Requirements: Yes

Are Waivers Available: Yes

Additional Information:

All admitted students are given the Nelson Denny Reading Test and if they score below 10.7 they are required to take Developmental Reading, writing and study skills. SAT verbal score below 350 or ACT English below 10 will also be indicators that the student should take Developmental Reading and Fundamentals of Communication. If students are enrolled in The Learning Center writing or skills course, they are not permitted to take English Composition.

Individualized high school coursework accepted: Yes

Essay Required: No

Special Application Required: No   **Submitted To:**

Number of Applications Submitted Each Year:

Number of Applications Accepted Each Year:

Number of Students Served: 75-125 in Learning Center, more in Student Support

Application Deadline for Special Admission: No

Acceptance into Program means acceptance
into college: No, Provisional acceptance

LEARNING DISABILITY SERVICES

Learning Resource Room: Yes   **Curriculum Modification Available:** No

Kurzweil Personal Reader: No   **Tutorial Help:** Yes   **Peer Tutors:** Yes

LD Specialists: 0   **Max. Hours/Week for services:**

Oral Exams: Yes   Unlimited/2 hrs. per student per course

Services for LD Only: No   **Added**

Books on Tape: Yes   **Cost:** None

Calculator allowed in exam: Yes   **Taping of books not on tape:** Yes

Tape recording in class: Yes   **Dictionary/computer/spellcheck during exam:** Yes

How are professors notified of LD: By the student and Program Director

GENERAL ADMISSIONS INFORMATION

Director of Admissions: Charles Mealy   **Telephone:** 317-674-6901

Entrance Requirements:

Recommended: English; Math; Science; Foreign Language; Social Studies.

Test Scores: **SAT:** 827   **ACT:** 20-21

G.P.A.: 2.0   **Class Rank:**

Application Deadline: Rolling   **Achievement Tests:** No

COLLEGE GRADUATION REQUIREMENTS

Foreign Language: No   **Waivers:**

Math: Yes   **Waivers:** No (General competency)

Minimum Course Load per Term: Provisional and probational students are limited to 12 hrs. or less.

ADDITIONAL INFORMATION

Location: The University is located on a 50 acre campus in a rural city 65 miles from Indianapolis, and 50 miles south of Fort Wayne.

Enrollment Information: **Undergraduate:** 1340   **Women:** 62%   **Men:** 38%

In-State Students: 80%   **Out of State:** 20%

Cost Information: **In-State Tuition:** $6,420   **Out of State:** same

Room & Board: $2,000   **Additional Costs:** $390

Housing Information: **University Housing:** Yes   **Sorority:** No

% Living on Campus: 40%   **Fraternity:** No

Athletics: NAIA

PURDUE UNIVERSITY
West Lafayette, In. 47807

317-494-1776

Support: S   *Institution:* 4 yr. Public

LEARNING DISABILITY PROGRAM AND SERVICES

Comments:

Purdue University offers support services to students with learning disabilities. There is an LD specialist available to provide on-going counseling, communication with the professors, and referral to other services on campus. A special course in understanding disabilities is offered for College credit.

LEARNING DISABILITY ADMISSIONS INFORMATION

Program Name: Program for Adaptive Learning   *Telephone*

Program Director: Kathy Jones/ Sarah Templin   317-494-1776

Contact Person:

Admissions:

All learning disability students must meet regular University admission requirements. Documentation and letters from an LD specialist will help in making the admission decision. Some majors are more competitive for admission than others. There is a Federally funded "Horizon's Program" which offers admission to high risk students. These students are encouraged to apply early in their Senior year.

Interview: No   *Diagnostic Tests:* Yes

Documentation: Yes

College Entrance Exams Required: Yes   *Untimed Accepted:* Yes

Course Entrance Requirements: Yes

Are Waivers Available:

Additional Information:

There is a PALS organization for learning disabled students. Purdue Adaptive Learning Society provides a supportive network for learning disabled students.

Individualized high school coursework accepted:

Essay Required: No

Special Application Required: No   *Submitted To:*

Number of Applications Submitted Each Year:

Number of Applications Accepted Each Year:

Number of Students Served: 200+

Application Deadline for Special Admission: No

*Acceptance into Program means acceptance
into college:*

LEARNING DISABILITY SERVICES

Learning Resource Room: Yes	**Curriculum Modification Available:** Yes	
Kurzweil Personal Reader: Yes	**Tutorial Help:** Yes	**Peer Tutors:** Yes
LD Specialists: 2	**Max. Hours/Week for services:**	
Oral Exams: Yes	As needed	
Services for LD Only: No	**Added**	
Books on Tape: Yes	**Cost:** None	
Calculator allowed in exam: Yes	**Taping of books not on tape:** Yes	
Tape recording in class: Yes	**Dictionary/computer/spellcheck during exam:** Yes	

How are professors notified of LD: By the student and the Program Director

GENERAL ADMISSIONS INFORMATION

Director of Admissions: William J. Murray   **Telephone:** 314-494-1776

Entrance Requirements:

4 yrs. English; 2-4 yrs. Math; 1-3 yrs. Science; 2 yrs. Foreign Language (depends on major); 2 yrs. Social Studies (recommended). Children of alumni may be admitted based on in-state requirements. Upward trend in grades is helpful.

Test Scores: **SAT:**   **ACT:** 22 (higher for some majors)

G.P.A.:   **Class Rank:** 1/2-1/3

Application Deadline: Rolling (except Engineer   **Achievement Tests:** No

COLLEGE GRADUATION REQUIREMENTS

Foreign Language: Yes   **Waivers:** Yes, Depends on Major

Math: Yes   **Waivers:** No

Minimum Course Load per Term: 12 to be eligible for financial aid

ADDITIONAL INFORMATION

Location: Purdue University is located in West Lafayette on the Wabash River, about 65 miles northwest of Indianapolis.

Enrollment Information:	**Undergraduate:**	29,675	**Women:** 43%		**Men:** 57%
	In-State Students:	71%		**Out of State:** 29%	
Cost Information:	**In-State Tuition:**	$2,150		**Out of State:** $7,150	
	Room & Board:	$3,065		**Additional Costs:** $375	
Housing Information:	**University Housing:**	Yes		**Sorority:** 8%	
	% Living on Campus:	51%		**Fraternity:** 13%	

Athletics: NCAA Div. I

Support: S   **Institution:** 4 yrs. Private

LEARNING DISABILITY PROGRAM AND SERVICES

Comments:

St. Joseph's does not have a special program nor remediation, but offers many services. St. Joseph's offers a very nurturing environment in which the faculty works closely with the students. Students are seen on a steady basis and are encouraged to utilize the available resources.There is a nationally acclaimed core curriculum in the areas of Journalism and Communication that does not require a foreign language, math or science.

LEARNING DISABILITY ADMISSIONS INFORMATION

Program Name: Counseling Services   **Telephone**

Program Director:

Contact Person: Diane Jennings   219-866-6116

Admissions:

Certificate of graduation: require 15 units, 10 must be academic. "Freshman Academic Support Program" accepts 25 students yearly who have a GPA below a 2.0, but these students are not necessarily learning disabled.

Interview: Yes   **Diagnostic Tests:** No

Documentation: Verification of learning disability

College Entrance Exams Required: No   **Untimed Accepted:**

Course Entrance Requirements: Yes

Are Waivers Available:

Additional Information:

Individualized high school coursework accepted: Yes

Essay Required: No

Special Application Required: No   **Submitted To:**

Number of Applications Submitted Each Year: NA

Number of Applications Accepted Each Year: NA

Number of Students Served: 90

Application Deadline for Special Admission: No

Acceptance into Program means acceptance into college: NA

LEARNING DISABILITY SERVICES

Learning Resource Room: Yes   **Curriculum Modification Available:** No

Kurzweil Personal Reader: No   **Tutorial Help:** Yes   **Peer Tutors:** Yes

LD Specialists: No   **Max. Hours/Week for services:**

Oral Exams: Yes   Unlimited

Services for LD Only: No   **Added**

Books on Tape: Yes   **Cost:** None

Calculator allowed in exam: Yes   **Taping of books not on tape:** Yes

Tape recording in class: Yes   **Dictionary/computer/spellcheck during exam:** Yes

How are professors notified of LD: By the Director of Counseling

GENERAL ADMISSIONS INFORMATION

Director of Admissions: Ken R. Rasp   **Telephone:** 219-866-6170

Entrance Requirements:

High school transcript; 10 academic units from English, Math, Science, Social Studies, and Foreign Language. The SAT and ACT are used for admissions only.

Test Scores: **SAT:** 910   **ACT:** 19

G.P.A.: 2.0   **Class Rank:** 50%

Application Deadline: Rolling   **Achievement Tests:**

COLLEGE GRADUATION REQUIREMENTS

Foreign Language: No   **Waivers:** Unless seeking a B.A. degree

Math: No   **Waivers:** Unless major requires it

Minimum Course Load per Term: 12 credit hours

ADDITIONAL INFORMATION

Location: The College is located in a small town, 80 miles from Chicago.

Enrollment Information: **Undergraduate:** 1,001   **Women:** 49%   **Men:** 51%

In-State Students: 63%   **Out of State:** 37%

Cost Information: **In-State Tuition:** $8,300   **Out of State:** same

Room & Board: $3,300   **Additional Costs:** $300

Housing Information: **University Housing:** Yes   **Sorority:** No

% Living on Campus: 95%   **Fraternity:** No

Athletics: NCAA Div. II

UNIVERSITY OF INDIANAPOLIS
Indianapolis, In. 46227
317-788-3216

Support: SP   *Institution:* 4 yr. Private

LEARNING DISABILITY PROGRAM AND SERVICES

Comments:

The University of Indianapolis offers a full support system for learning disabled students called B.U.I.L.D.(Baccalaureate for University of Indianapolis Learning Disabled). There is a special admissions procedure as well as some special courses designed specifically for admitted students. Services are extensive and the staff is very supportive and knowledgeable about learning disabilities. Acceptance into the B.U.I.L.D. program is determined by the Directors of the program.

LEARNING DISABILITY ADMISSIONS INFORMATION

Program Name: B.U.I.L.D.   *Telephone*

Program Director: Patricia A. Cook, Ph.D / Nancy O'Dell,Ph.D   317-788-3369

Contact Person: same

Admissions:

Applicants should meet the regular admission criteria, however there is some flexibility. LD students must submit a regular University application as well as a B.U.I.L.D. application. Letters from LD teachers and counselors are important. The SAT and ACT scores are just one part of the decision process. Current information regarding I.Q. scores, reading and math proficiency levels, primary learning style and major learning difficulty is very important. Applicants will be invited to interview after the Directors have reviewed information and determined if the student meets preliminary requirements.

Interview: Yes   *Diagnostic Tests:* Yes

Documentation: I.Q. tests; Reading and Math tests

College Entrance Exams Required: Yes   *Untimed Accepted:* Yes

Course Entrance Requirements: Yes

Are Waivers Available: Yes

Additional Information:

Some substitutions of courses are allowed if it has been determined that the disability is the cause of the difficulty in the course. If an LD student is denied admission, and has not submitted an application for B.U.I.L.D. the Director of B.U.I.L.D. will automatically send an application to the student. Once this application is on file, the student will be reviewed by the B.U.I.L.D. program Directors to determine admissibility based on new information.

Individualized high school coursework accepted: Yes

Essay Required:

Special Application Required: Yes   *Submitted To:*

Number of Applications Submitted Each Year: New Program

Number of Applications Accepted Each Year: 25

Number of Students Served:

Application Deadline for Special Admission: October of Senior year or sooner

Acceptance into Program means acceptance

into college: If not accepted by Admissions,a committee confers

LEARNING DISABILITY SERVICES

Learning Resource Room: Yes   **Curriculum Modification Available:** No

Kurzweil Personal Reader: No   **Tutorial Help:** Yes   **Peer Tutors:** Yes

LD Specialists: 5   **Max. Hours/Week for services:**

Oral Exams: Yes   No maximum

Services for LD Only: Yes   **Added**

Books on Tape: Yes   **Cost:** $1,500. per/semester

Calculator allowed in exam: Yes   **Taping of books not on tape:** Yes

Tape recording in class: Yes   **Dictionary/computer/spellcheck during exam:** Yes

How are professors notified of LD: By student and Program Director

GENERAL ADMISSIONS INFORMATION

Director of Admissions: Mark T. Weigand   **Telephone:** 317-788-3216

Entrance Requirements:

4 yrs. English and Literature; 2 yrs. Math; 2 yrs. Lab Science; 2 yrs. Social Studies; Academic electives.

Test Scores: **SAT:** 800 (minimum)   **ACT:** 18 (minimum)

G.P.A.: 2.0   **Class Rank:** upper 50%

Application Deadline: 8/15   **Achievement Tests:**

COLLEGE GRADUATION REQUIREMENTS

Foreign Language: Yes   **Waivers:** Alternate course (Depends on major)

Math: Yes   **Waivers:** Alternate course

Minimum Course Load per Term: 12 hours; 9 hours affects financial aid

ADDITIONAL INFORMATION

Location: The 60 acre campus in a suburban neighborhood, 10 miles south of downtown Indianapolis.

Enrollment Information: **Undergraduate:** 1,350   **Women:** 60%   **Men:** 40%

In-State Students: 90%   **Out of State:** 10%

Cost Information: **In-State Tuition:** $8,200   **Out of State:** same

Room & Board: $3,250   **Additional Costs:**

Housing Information: **University Housing:** Yes   **Sorority:** No

% Living on Campus: 60%   **Fraternity:** No

Athletics: NCAA Div. II

VINCENNES UNIVERSITY
Vincennes, In. 47591
812-885-4313

Support: CS   **Institution:** 2 yr. Public

LEARNING DISABILITY PROGRAM AND SERVICES

Comments:

STEP (Students Transition into Education Program) is a newly designed support program for the learning disabled who are mainstreamed students at the University. STEP emphasizes students' strengths rather than weaknesses, compensatory techniques rather than remediation. Services include: individualized educational programs, LD specialists for tutoring, remedial classes, weekly monitoring, and coordination with COPE services. COPE is a federally funded program that provides support services to all students at Vincennes including those with learning disabilities.

LEARNING DISABILITY ADMISSIONS INFORMATION

Program Name:	Cope Student Support Services / S.T.E.P.	**Telephone**
Program Director:	George W. Varns/ Cope	812-885-4515
Contact Person:	Jane Kavanaugh, Susan Laue/ S.T.E.P.	812-885-4209

Admissions:

COPE requires a special application and admission procedure for students with learning disabilities. The student needs to send recent psychological tests as well as complete a special LD Information form. The SAT or ACT are not required, but students need to submit their high school transcript. The STEP students need to submit a general application.

Interview: Yes   **Diagnostic Tests:** Yes

Documentation: WISC-R; Bender Visual-Motor

College Entrance Exams Required: No   **Untimed Accepted:** Yes

Course Entrance Requirements: Yes

Are Waivers Available:

Additional Information:

Institutional testing determines verbal and math skill level. Developmental courses in writing, reading and math are required if those skill levels are low. The STEP program will require the student to take a study skills course, word-processing course, and Coping in College seminar that covers topics in self-help, talking to teachers, and stress.

Individualized high school coursework accepted: Yes

Essay Required: No

Special Application Required: No   **Submitted To:**

Number of Applications Submitted Each Year: 60

Number of Applications Accepted Each Year: 30

Number of Students Served: 60 (200 in COPE)

Application Deadline for Special Admission: October,preceding Fall Semester of entry

Acceptance into Program means acceptance

into college: No, there is an appeals procedure

LEARNING DISABILITY SERVICES

Learning Resource Room: Yes   **Curriculum Modification Available:** No

Kurzweil Personal Reader: Yes   **Tutorial Help:** Yes   **Peer Tutors:** Yes

LD Specialists: 2   **Max. Hours/Week for services:**

Oral Exams: Yes   No limit

Services for LD Only: No   **Added**

Books on Tape: Yes   **Cost:** $500 per year for S.T.E.P.

Calculator allowed in exam: Yes   **Taping of books not on tape:** Yes

Tape recording in class: Yes   **Dictionary/computer/spellcheck during exam:** Yes

How are professors notified of LD: By the student

GENERAL ADMISSIONS INFORMATION

Director of Admissions: Stephen M. Simonds   **Telephone:** 812-885-4313

Entrance Requirements:

Open admissions except for health-related programs.

Test Scores: **SAT:**   **ACT:**

G.P.A.:   **Class Rank:**

Application Deadline: Rolling   **Achievement Tests:**

COLLEGE GRADUATION REQUIREMENTS

Foreign Language: No   **Waivers:**

Math: Yes   **Waivers:** Yes

Minimum Course Load per Term: 12 hours

ADDITIONAL INFORMATION

Location: The school is located on 95 acres 45 minutes south of Terre Haute.

Enrollment Information: **Undergraduate:** 6,139   **Women:** 49%   **Men:** 51%

In-State Students: 91%   **Out of State:** 9%

Cost Information: **In-State Tuition:** $1,470   **Out of State:** $4,110

Room & Board: $2,800   **Additional Costs:** $18

Housing Information: **University Housing:** Yes   **Sorority:** 1%

% Living on Campus: 48%   **Fraternity:** 5%

Athletics: NJCAA

Support: S   **Institution:** 4 yr. Private

LEARNING DISABILITY PROGRAM AND SERVICES

Comments:

The Services for learning disabled students are developed individually, based upon identified needs. The process is only intended after a student self-identifies on the application for admission. There is also a support group during orientation week to facilitate adjustment to college, in general, and to Cornell's One Course At A Time. Cornell College is unusual in that it has what is called a "block system" of study. The student takes one course at a time for a period of 3-1/2 weeks. Students usually take 8 blocks each year.

LEARNING DISABILITY ADMISSIONS INFORMATION

Program Name: Student Services   **Telephone**

Program Director: Connie Rosene   319-895-4292

Contact Person:

Admissions:

The Director of the program works with the Office of Admissions in making admissions decisions. They would like as much information as possible regarding the learning disability to use in making an admission decision. Students who are successful at focusing on one area at a time will probably benefit from the Block System.

Interview: Yes   **Diagnostic Tests:** Yes

Documentation: WAIS-R; all possible documentation

College Entrance Exams Required: Yes   **Untimed Accepted:** Yes

Course Entrance Requirements: Yes

Are Waivers Available:

Additional Information:

Cornell admits 25 high risk students yearly on a conditional basis and not all of them have learning disabilities. These students, upon admission, would be in constant contact with the Director of the Student Services for a period covering 4 Blocks and have to maintain a 2.0 to be fully admitted.

Individualized high school coursework accepted: Yes

Essay Required: Yes

Special Application Required: No   **Submitted To:**

Number of Applications Submitted Each Year: 5-10

Number of Applications Accepted Each Year: same

Number of Students Served: less than 20

Application Deadline for Special Admission: No

Acceptance into Program means acceptance

into college: Student evaluated by Program and College

LEARNING DISABILITY SERVICES

Learning Resource Room: Yes   **Curriculum Modification Available:** Yes

Kurzweil Personal Reader: No   **Tutorial Help:** Yes   **Peer Tutors:** Yes

LD Specialists: No   **Max. Hours/Week for services:**

Oral Exams: Yes   Unlimited

Services for LD Only: Yes   **Added**

Books on Tape: Yes   **Cost:** Yes

Calculator allowed in exam: Yes   **Taping of books not on tape:** Yes

Tape recording in class: Yes   **Dictionary/computer/spellcheck during exam:** Yes

How are professors notified of LD: By student or Program Director

GENERAL ADMISSIONS INFORMATION

Director of Admissions: Peter S. Bryant   **Telephone:** 319-895-4477

Entrance Requirements:

4 yrs. English; 4 yrs. History/Social Studies; 3 yrs. Math; 3 yrs. Science; 2 yrs. Foreign Language.

Test Scores: **SAT:** 850 (recommended)   **ACT:** 20 or above (recommended)

G.P.A.:   **Class Rank:**

Application Deadline: 3/1   **Achievement Tests:**

COLLEGE GRADUATION REQUIREMENTS

Foreign Language: Yes   **Waivers:** Yes, Evaluated on a case-by-case basis

Math: Yes   **Waivers:** Yes, Evaluated on a case-by-case basis

Minimum Course Load per Term: One course at a time, this is a "Block System" College

ADDITIONAL INFORMATION

Location: The school is located on 110 acres in a small town of 2,000 people 15 miles from Cedar Rapids, and 20 miles from Iowa City.

Enrollment Information: **Undergraduate:** 1,147   **Women:** 53%   **Men:** 47%

                       In-State Students: 33%   **Out of State:** 67%

Cost Information: **In-State Tuition:** $11,200   **Out of State:** same

                        Room & Board: $3,700   **Additional Costs:** $240

Housing Information: **University Housing:** Yes   **Sorority:** 26%

                  % Living on Campus: 95%   **Fraternity:** 25%

Athletics: NCAA Div. III

INDIAN HILLS COMMUNITY COLLEGE
Ottumwa, la. 52501
515-683-5155

Support: SP   **Institution:** 2 yr. Public

LEARNING DISABILITY PROGRAM AND SERVICES

Comments:

The Strauss-Kephart Institute (SKI) is a post-secondary educational program for students with learning disabilities. The program is designed to meet the special educational and developmental needs of high school graduates who wish to increase their educational achievement and vocational potential. Because of specific learning disabilities these students are usually unable or unprepared to cope with the demands of traditional college programs. The SKI program is offered in the enriching environment of campus life and Indian Hills Community College.

LEARNING DISABILITY ADMISSIONS INFORMATION

Program Name: Strauss-Kephart Institute   **Telephone**

Program Director: Judy Brickey   515-683-5125

Contact Person: same

Admissions:

Students enroll with widely varying levels of achievement and differing goals, and some discover that they can move ahead more quickly. Many eventually enter one or more of the Indian Hills credit courses. A decision to move into college credit courses is made by staff members, parents, and the student involved. This is a self-paced program.

Interview: Yes   **Diagnostic Tests:** Yes

Documentation:

College Entrance Exams Required: No   **Untimed Accepted:**

Course Entrance Requirements: No

Are Waivers Available:

Additional Information:

Individualized high school coursework accepted: Yes

Essay Required: No

Special Application Required: No   **Submitted To:**

Number of Applications Submitted Each Year: 25

Number of Applications Accepted Each Year: 12-15

Number of Students Served: 30

Application Deadline for Special Admission: January of Senior year

Acceptance into Program means acceptance

into college: Yes

LEARNING DISABILITY SERVICES

Learning Resource Room: Yes	**Curriculum Modification Available:** Yes	
Kurzweil Personal Reader: No	**Tutorial Help:** Yes	**Peer Tutors:** Yes
LD Specialists: 3	**Max. Hours/Week for services:**	
Oral Exams: Yes	Based on need	
Services for LD Only: No	**Added**	
Books on Tape: Yes	**Cost:** No	
Calculator allowed in exam: Y/N	**Taping of books not on tape:** Yes	
Tape recording in class: Yes	**Dictionary/computer/spellcheck during exam:**	

How are professors notified of LD: Depends on the wishes of the student

GENERAL ADMISSIONS INFORMATION

Director of Admissions: Jane Sapp   **Telephone:** 515-683-5155

Entrance Requirements:

Required for some: 3 yrs. Math, ACT and test scores used for counseling/placement. Open admission except for nursing technology programs.

Test Scores: **SAT:**   **ACT:** Yes (used for placement)

G.P.A.:   **Class Rank:**

Application Deadline: Rolling   **Achievement Tests:**

COLLEGE GRADUATION REQUIREMENTS

Foreign Language: **Waivers:**

Math: **Waivers:**

Minimum Course Load per Term: No set requirement

ADDITIONAL INFORMATION

Location: The College is located on 400 acres about 2 hours from Iowa City to the east or Des Moines to the west.

Enrollment Information:	**Undergraduate:** 2,857	**Women:** 58%	**Men:** 42%	
	In-State Students: 94%		**Out of State:** 6%	
Cost Information:	**In-State Tuition:** $1,950		**Out of State:** $2,925	
	Room & Board: $2,091		**Additional Costs:** $135	
Housing Information:	**University Housing:** Yes		**Sorority:**	
	% Living on Campus: 14%		**Fraternity:**	

Athletics: NJCAA

IOWA STATE UNIVERSITY
Ames, Ia. 50011
515-294-5836

Support: S   **Institution:** 4 yr. Public

LEARNING DISABILITY PROGRAM AND SERVICES

Comments:

Iowa State University is committed to providing equal opportunities and to facilitating the personal growth and development of all students. Several departments and organizations within the University cooperate to accomplish these goals. The Coordinator of Student Counseling Services is very knowledgeable about learning disabilities. There is a fee for tutoring. There are high school level courses in math and chemistry.

LEARNING DISABILITY ADMISSIONS INFORMATION

		Telephone
Program Name:	Services for Students with Disabilities	
Program Director:	Dr. James W. Copley	515-294-5056
Contact Person:	same	N

Admissions:

If a student is learning disabled and does not meet minimum requirements, the student can request a review and an interview with the Coordinator of Student Counseling Services. However, this is not a program for students with extreme deficits. They are looking for students who can succeed, and have good verbal skills. They are also looking for an up-ward trend in grades. They will look at the pattern on the ACT, not just the score.

Interview: No   **Diagnostic Tests:** Yes

Documentation: Psychological evaluation

College Entrance Exams Required: Yes   **Untimed Accepted:** Yes

Course Entrance Requirements: Yes

Are Waivers Available: Yes

Additional Information:

There is also a Summer Trial Program for students not regularly admissible. The student needs to take 6 credits and get "C" or better. (Students in the Summer Program are often in the top 3/4 of their class but may have a 25 ACT).

Individualized high school coursework accepted: Yes

Essay Required: No

Special Application Required: No   **Submitted To:**

Number of Applications Submitted Each Year: Varies

Number of Applications Accepted Each Year: Varies

Number of Students Served: Varies

Application Deadline for Special Admission: As soon after regular admission as possible

Acceptance into Program means acceptance

into college: Students not meeting regular course admissions, but who otherwise qualify, may be reviewed.

113

LEARNING DISABILITY SERVICES

Learning Resource Room: Yes   **Curriculum Modification Available:** Yes

Kurzweil Personal Reader: **Tutorial Help:** Yes   **Peer Tutors:**

LD Specialists: No   **Max. Hours/Week for services:**

Oral Exams: Yes   Unlimited

Services for LD Only: Yes   **Added**

Books on Tape: Yes   **Cost:** $6. hr. tutoring, $3/ hr. small group

Calculator allowed in exam: Yes   **Taping of books not on tape:** Yes

Tape recording in class: Yes   **Dictionary/computer/spellcheck during exam:** Yes

How are professors notified of LD: By student

GENERAL ADMISSIONS INFORMATION

Director of Admissions: Phil Caffrey   **Telephone:** 515-294-5836

Entrance Requirements:

4 yrs. English; 3 yrs. Math; 3 yrs. Science; 2 yrs. Social Studies (3 yrs. for Science and Humanities majors, plus 2 yrs. of Foreign Language). Three years of High School Foreign Language satisfies requirement to graduate from Iowa State. Requirements for students from out-of-state may be more difficult.

Test Scores: **SAT:**   **ACT:** 24

G.P.A.:   **Class Rank:** Upper 50%

Application Deadline: 8/24   **Achievement Tests:** No

COLLEGE GRADUATION REQUIREMENTS

Foreign Language: Yes   **Waivers:** Varies with major

Math: **Waivers:** Requirements can be waived if documented

Minimum Course Load per Term: 12 to be considered full time, but less if the student wishes

ADDITIONAL INFORMATION

Location: Iowa State University is located on a 1,000 acre campus about 30 miles north of Des Moines.

Enrollment Information: Undergraduate: 21,412   **Women:** 41%   **Men:** 59%

In-State Students: 79%   **Out of State:** 21%

Cost Information: In-State Tuition: $1,826   **Out of State:** $6,000

Room & Board: $2,600   **Additional Costs:**

Housing Information: University Housing: Yes   **Sorority:** 7%

% Living on Campus: 50%   **Fraternity:** 9%

Athletics: NCAA Div. I

LORAS COLLEGE
Dubuque, Ia. 52201
319-588-7235

IA

Support: SP   **Institution:** 4 yr.

LEARNING DISABILITY PROGRAM AND SERVICES

Comments:

The Director of the Learning Disabilities Program makes all admission decisions for learning disabled students. Once accepted, the services provided are individualized to the student's needs. All Freshmen take remedial courses and meet 2 times per week. The courses include strategies for college reading, written expression, memorization and study skills. Students also discuss career alternatives, college policies and have CPR training. Parents are involved in the process. They visit for a follow-up in the Fall and receive a progress report.

LEARNING DISABILITY ADMISSIONS INFORMATION

Program Name: Learning Disabilities Program   **Telephone**

Program Director: Dianne Gibson   319-588-7134

Contact Person: same

Admissions:

LD students interested in this Program must phone or write the Program Director in the fall of junior year. Students should send documentation and information by spring of junior year. The Director will send information back to the student requesting specific tests. An interview is required, usually fall of senior year. During the interview (which includes parents) the student is asked to discuss courses taken in high school,motivation and interests. Individualized courses are accepted if taken early in high school. However, the student should be enrolled in mainstreamed courses by the end of high school.

Interview: Yes   **Diagnostic Tests:** Yes

Documentation: WAIS-R;W-J; reading inventory

College Entrance Exams Required: Yes   **Untimed Accepted:** Yes

Course Entrance Requirements: Yes

Are Waivers Available: Yes

Additional Information:

There are no set requirements but the school looks for college preparatory coursework, including 2 years of Math and Science. They may accept an ACT of 12-15 (there is no minimum although a better Verbal score is preferred).

Individualized high school coursework accepted: Yes

Essay Required: Yes

Special Application Required: Yes   **Submitted To:**

Number of Applications Submitted Each Year:

Number of Applications Accepted Each Year: 16

Number of Students Served: 45

Application Deadline for Special Admission: Spring, Junior year or, Summer before Senior year

Acceptance into Program means acceptance into college: Yes

115

LEARNING DISABILITY SERVICES

Learning Resource Room: No   **Curriculum Modification Available:**

Kurzweil Personal Reader: **Tutorial Help:** Yes   **Peer Tutors:** Yes

LD Specialists: 1   **Max. Hours/Week for services:**

Oral Exams: Yes   No maximum

Services for LD Only: Yes   **Added**

Books on Tape: Yes   **Cost:** $1,600/ freshman: $1,200 other years

Calculator allowed in exam: **Taping of books not on tape:** Yes

Tape recording in class: Y/N   **Dictionary/computer/spellcheck during exam:** Y/N

How are professors notified of LD: A form letter from the student

GENERAL ADMISSIONS INFORMATION

Director of Admissions: Dan Conry   **Telephone:** 319-588-7235

Entrance Requirements:

4 yrs. English; 3 yrs. Math; 3 yrs. Science; 3 yrs. Social Studies; 2 yrs. History.

Test Scores: **SAT:** 800 (minimum)   **ACT:** 20

G.P.A.: 2.0   **Class Rank:** Upper 50%

Application Deadline: Rolling   **Achievement Tests:**

COLLEGE GRADUATION REQUIREMENTS

Foreign Language: No   **Waivers:** Alternative is a classical studies course

Math: Yes   **Waivers:** Possible (but requirement not impossible)

Minimum Course Load per Term: 12 hours considered full-time; appeal possible

ADDITIONAL INFORMATION

Location: The College is located north of Iowa City and overlooks the Dubuque and Mississippi Rivers.

Enrollment Information: **Undergraduate:** 1,984   **Women:** 44%   **Men:** 56%

In-State Students: 65%   **Out of State:** 45%

Cost Information: **In-State Tuition:** $8,065   **Out of State:** same

Room & Board: $3,000   **Additional Costs:** $240

Housing Information: **University Housing:** Yes   **Sorority:** 5%

% Living on Campus: 50%   **Fraternity:** 15%

Athletics: NCAA Div. III

Support: CS   **Institution:** 4 yr. Public

LEARNING DISABILITY PROGRAM AND SERVICES

Comments:

Students who have learning disabilities are provided with individualized, cooperatively planned program of services. SPD provides support services which are structured yet integrated within the existing University services and requirements. To be eligible to receive support services, the student must provide documentation verifying the learning disability. This information is used in designing a program of support services that reflects individual needs and abilities. Although the staff is not certified in learning disabilities, they provide a great deal of support.

LEARNING DISABILITY ADMISSIONS INFORMATION

Program Name: Services for Persons with Disabilities (SPD)   **Telephone**

Program Director: Donna Chandler   319-335-1462

Contact Person: Donna Chandler, Jeff Carstens, Mary Richard   same

Admissions:

Students with learning disabilities are considered individually for admission to the University and do not have to meet general admissions requirements. SPD works in cooperation with the Office of Admissions to recognize and consider extenuating circumstances that could affect admission. The Director of SPD and Admissions work jointly to determine admission for L.D. students. The student must submit a letter describing their disability, and highlight strengths and weaknesses and services needed. An interview with the Director of SPD is highly recommended. Motivation and willingness to utilize services is very important.

Interview: Yes   **Diagnostic Tests:** Yes

Documentation: WAIS-R

College Entrance Exams Required: Yes   **Untimed Accepted:** Yes

Course Entrance Requirements: Yes

Are Waivers Available: Yes

Additional Information:

There are course requirements, but there is some flexibility for LD students. Test scores are not as important as upward trend in grades, motivation and evidence of success in high school. Recommendations are very important. The University is looking for students capable of doing college level work.

Individualized high school coursework accepted: Yes

Essay Required: Yes, Letter

Special Application Required: Yes   **Submitted To:**

Number of Applications Submitted Each Year: 25-50

Number of Applications Accepted Each Year: Varies

Number of Students Served: 135

Application Deadline for Special Admission: January-March of Senior year

Acceptance into Program means acceptance
into college: They are one and the same; there is an appeal procedure

117

LEARNING DISABILITY SERVICES

Learning Resource Room: No   **Curriculum Modification Available:** Yes

Kurzweil Personal Reader: Yes   **Tutorial Help:** Yes   **Peer Tutors:** Yes

LD Specialists: 0   **Max. Hours/Week for services:**

Oral Exams: Yes   5 hours per/week per/course

Services for LD Only: No   **Added**

Books on Tape: Yes   **Cost:** None

Calculator allowed in exam: Yes   **Taping of books not on tape:** Yes

Tape recording in class: Yes   **Dictionary/computer/spellcheck during exam:** Yes

How are professors notified of LD: By the student and Program Director

GENERAL ADMISSIONS INFORMATION

Director of Admissions: Michael Barron   **Telephone:** 319-335-1548

Entrance Requirements:

4 yrs. English; 3 yrs. Math; 2 yrs. Foreign Language; 3 yrs. Science; 3 yrs. Social Studies. Admission is based on a formula of 2 x ACT plus class rank should equal 90 to 100. There is some flexibility. Summer entrance is also possible for students not meeting general admissions criteria. In-state residents who rank in the top 50% of their class, non-residents who rank in the top 30% are also admissible. Prefer ACT.

Test Scores: **SAT:**   **ACT:** 21

G.P.A.:   **Class Rank:** Top 50%

Application Deadline: Rolling   **Achievement Tests:** No

COLLEGE GRADUATION REQUIREMENTS

Foreign Language: **Waivers:** Depends on major

Math: Yes   **Waivers:** With supporting documentation

Minimum Course Load per Term: 12 credits, lower will affect financial aid

ADDITIONAL INFORMATION

Location: The University is on a 1,900 acre campus in a small city 180 miles east of Des Moines.

Enrollment Information: **Undergraduate:** 20,160% **Women:** 51%   **Men:** 49%

                           In-State Students: 73%   **Out of State:** 27%

Cost Information: **In-State Tuition:** $1,826   **Out of State:** $6,200

                           Room & Board: $2,700   **Additional Costs:**

Housing Information: **University Housing:** Yes   **Sorority:** 18%

                  % Living on Campus: 50%   **Fraternity:** 16%

Athletics: NCAA Div. I

KANSAS STATE UNIVERSITY
Manhattan, Ks. 66506
913-532-6250

Support: S   **Institution:** 4 yr. Public

LEARNING DISABILITY PROGRAM AND SERVICES

Comments:

Kansas State provides a broad range of support services to learning disabled students through Services for Students with Physical Limitations, as well as through numerous other University departments. Faculty and staff are sensitive to the special needs of the student and will work with them in their pursuit of educational goals. Developmental courses are offered in study skills, reading and math. Tutoring is also available along with a broad range of other supportive services.

LEARNING DISABILITY ADMISSIONS INFORMATION

Program Name: Services for Students with Physical Limitations   **Telephone**

Program Director: Gretchen Holden   913-532-6441

Contact Person: same

Admissions:

There is no special admissions process for students with learning disabilities. Kansas State has open-admissions for state residents, others must meet some basic requirements for general admissions to the University. To be eligible for support services the student must provide verification of a learning disability. Application for support services can be made by contacting Services for Student with Physical Limitations. Many services provided take time to arrange so they encourage early applications.

Interview: No   **Diagnostic Tests:** Yes

Documentation: Whatever will verify learning disability

College Entrance Exams Required: Yes   **Untimed Accepted:** Yes

Course Entrance Requirements: Yes

Are Waivers Available:

Additional Information:

For certain languages, proficiency examinations are given.

Individualized high school coursework accepted: Yes

Essay Required: No

Special Application Required: No   **Submitted To:**

Number of Applications Submitted Each Year:

Number of Applications Accepted Each Year:

Number of Students Served:

Application Deadline for Special Admission:

Acceptance into Program means acceptance into college: No

119

LEARNING DISABILITY SERVICES

Learning Resource Room: No	**Curriculum Modification Available:** No	
Kurzweil Personal Reader: Yes	**Tutorial Help:** Yes	**Peer Tutors:** Yes
LD Specialists:	**Max. Hours/Week for services:**	
Oral Exams: Yes	Individually determined	
Services for LD Only: No	**Added**	
Books on Tape: Yes	**Cost:** None	
Calculator allowed in exam:	**Taping of books not on tape:** Yes	
Tape recording in class: Yes	**Dictionary/computer/spellcheck during exam:** Yes	

How are professors notified of LD: With student's permission the Program Director

GENERAL ADMISSIONS INFORMATION

Director of Admissions: Richard Elkins   **Telephone:** 913-532-6250

Entrance Requirements:

KSU admits any Kansas resident who is a graduate of an accredited Kansas high school. Out-of-state applicants should rank high in their class and score well on the ACT. Recommended: 4 yrs. English; 3 yrs. Math; 3 yrs. Science; 2 yrs. Foreign Language; 3 yrs. Social Studies. ACT required.

Test Scores: SAT: **ACT:** 23 average

G.P.A.:   **Class Rank:** Top 50% out of state

Application Deadline: Rolling   **Achievement Tests:**

COLLEGE GRADUATION REQUIREMENTS

Foreign Language: Y/N   **Waivers:** Depends on major

Math: Yes   **Waivers:** No

Minimum Course Load per Term: Student enrolls either as full-time or part-time

ADDITIONAL INFORMATION

Location: The University is located on 664 acres in a suburban area 125 miles west of Kansas City.

Enrollment Information:	**Undergraduate:** 16,610	**Women:** 48%	**Men:** 52%
	In-State Students: 86%		**Out of State:** 14%
Cost Information:	**In-State Tuition:** $1,461		**Out of State:** $4,259
	Room & Board: $2,330		**Additional Costs:**
Housing Information:	**University Housing:** Yes		**Sorority:** 23%
	% Living on Campus: 25%		**Fraternity:** 21%

Athletics: NCAA Div. I

UNIVERSITY OF KANSAS
Lawrence, Ks. 66045
913-864-3911

Support: S   **Institution:** 4 yr. Public

LEARNING DISABILITY PROGRAM AND SERVICES

Comments:

The University tries to accommodate the learning disabled by understanding the student's ability and individualizing the services as much as possible. It is important to meet with one of the Directors at the Student Assistance Center to discuss the individual needs prior to enrolling at the University. Early planning will facilitate accessibility. The Center also serves as a referral agent to other resources at the University and in the Lawrence community. Some of the direct services provided are registration assistance, notetakers and advocacy.

LEARNING DISABILITY ADMISSIONS INFORMATION

Program Name: Student Assistance Center   **Telephone**

Program Director: Lorna Zimmer   913-864-4064

Contact Person:

Admissions:

It is important to include recent documentation or diagnosis. Include, as well, samples of students work and parent and student statements regarding educational history. Students entering the University usually have an average ACT score of 22, and an average high school GPA of 3.01. The school is very concerned that a student with learning disabilities be competitive in this academic environment.

Interview: No   **Diagnostic Tests:** Yes

Documentation: Varies

College Entrance Exams Required: Yes   **Untimed Accepted:** Yes

Course Entrance Requirements: Yes

Are Waivers Available: No

Additional Information:

There are 3 ways to qualify for admission: 1) requires a "C" average and the Board of Regent courses including 4 yrs. English; 3 yrs. of college prep Math; 3 yrs. Natural Science; 3 yrs. Social Science; 2 yrs. Foreign Language. 2) an ACT of 24 and a 2.0 GPA. 3) A 3.0 GPA and no cut-off on the ACT. Sometimes students are admitted with a 2.5 GPA without the Board of Regents Courses.

Individualized high school coursework accepted: Yes

Essay Required: No

Special Application Required: **Submitted To:**

Number of Applications Submitted Each Year:

Number of Applications Accepted Each Year:

Number of Students Served: 60

Application Deadline for Special Admission: No

Acceptance into Program means acceptance

into college: No, there is an appeal process

LEARNING DISABILITY SERVICES

Learning Resource Room:

Kurzweil Personal Reader: Yes

LD Specialists: No

Oral Exams: Yes

Services for LD Only:

Books on Tape: Yes

Calculator allowed in exam: Y/N

Tape recording in class: Yes

Curriculum Modification Available: Y/N

Tutorial Help: Yes   **Peer Tutors:**

Max. Hours/Week for services:

Added Cost: None

Taping of books not on tape: Yes

Dictionary/computer/spellcheck during exam: Y/N

How are professors notified of LD: By student and Program Director

GENERAL ADMISSIONS INFORMATION

Director of Admissions: Debra Castrop   **Telephone:** 913-864-3911

Entrance Requirements:

4 yrs. English; 3 yrs. Math; 2 yrs. Foreign Language; 3 yrs. Science; 3 yrs. Social Studies. Students are admitted with a 2.0 GPA and the Board of Regent courses or a 3.0 GPA; or 2.0 GPA with ACT of 24. Students with a 2.5 GPA may be admitted regardless of high school courses.

Test Scores: SAT: **ACT:** 24

G.P.A.: 3.01   **Class Rank:**

Application Deadline: 4/1   **Achievement Tests:** Not used

COLLEGE GRADUATION REQUIREMENTS

Foreign Language: Yes   **Waivers:** No

Math: Yes   **Waivers:** No

Minimum Course Load per Term: No

ADDITIONAL INFORMATION

Location: The 1000 acre campus is located in a small city 40 miles west of Kansas City.

Enrollment Information: Undergraduate: 19,260   **Women:** 49%   **Men:** 51%

In-State Students: 67%   **Out of State:** 33%

Cost Information: In-State Tuition: $1,450   **Out of State:** $4,248

Room & Board: $2,336   **Additional Costs:** $294

Housing Information: University Housing: Yes   **Sorority:** 24%

% Living on Campus: 25%   **Fraternity:** 18%

Athletics: NCAA Div. I

SOUTHERN MAINE TECHNICAL COLLEGE
South Portland, Me. 04104
207-799-7303

Support: CS   **Institution:** 2 yr.   Public

LEARNING DISABILITY PROGRAM AND SERVICES

Comments:

The Learning Assistance Center Program is designed to offer academic support to students through various individualized services. They also offer the Extended Studies Program which provides a year of basic skills, career awareness, personal development, counseling and study skills before beginning a two year program. Southern Maine Technical College believes that all students have certain strengths or weaknesses, and those who may also lack academic credentials or are underprepared do not lack quality or potential.

LEARNING DISABILITY ADMISSIONS INFORMATION

Program Name: Learning Assistance Center   **Telephone**

Program Director: Gail Christiansen   207-799-7303

Contact Person: same

Admissions:

No special admissions. Students are assessed based on high school transcripts, interview, recommendations, SAT and psycho-educational testing.

Interview: Yes   **Diagnostic Tests:** Yes

Documentation:

College Entrance Exams Required: Yes   **Untimed Accepted:** Yes

Course Entrance Requirements: Yes

Are Waivers Available: No

Additional Information:

Extended Studies allows students to complete a typical two-year academic program in three academic years. Students who successfully complete the Program may continue in the technical program of their choice. (Allied Health and Nursing programs may have additional requirements).

Individualized high school coursework accepted: Yes

Essay Required: Yes

Special Application Required: No   **Submitted To:**

Number of Applications Submitted Each Year:

Number of Applications Accepted Each Year:

Number of Students Served: 20

Application Deadline for Special Admission: No

**Acceptance into Program means acceptance
into college:** Yes

LEARNING DISABILITY SERVICES

Learning Resource Room: Yes   **Curriculum Modification Available:** Yes

Kurzweil Personal Reader: No   **Tutorial Help:** Yes   **Peer Tutors:** Yes

LD Specialists: 1   **Max. Hours/Week for services:**

Oral Exams: Yes   NA

Services for LD Only: No   **Added**

Books on Tape: Yes   **Cost:**

Calculator allowed in exam: Yes   **Taping of books not on tape:** Yes

Tape recording in class: Yes   **Dictionary/computer/spellcheck during exam:** Yes

How are professors notified of LD: By student

GENERAL ADMISSIONS INFORMATION

Director of Admissions: Mr. Robert A. Waimont   **Telephone:** 207-799-7303

Entrance Requirements:

High School transcript, essay, recommendation, interview, SAT.

Test Scores: **SAT:**   **ACT:**

G.P.A.:   **Class Rank:**

Application Deadline: Rolling Admissions   **Achievement Tests:**

COLLEGE GRADUATION REQUIREMENTS

Foreign Language: No   **Waivers:**

Math: Yes   **Waivers:** No

Minimum Course Load per Term: Yes

ADDITIONAL INFORMATION

Location: The College is part of the Maine Vocational Technical Institute located on a 50 acre campus in the city.

Enrollment Information: **Undergraduate:** 1,610   **Women:** 33%   **Men:** 67%

       In-State Students: 90%   **Out of State:** 10%

Cost Information: **In-State Tuition:** $1,000   **Out of State:** $2,000

       Room & Board: $2,150   **Additional Costs:** $130

Housing Information: **University Housing:** Yes   **Sorority:** No

       % Living on Campus: 10%   **Fraternity:** No

Athletics: Intercollegiate sports

Support: CS   *Institution:* 4 yr. Private

LEARNING DISABILITY PROGRAM AND SERVICES

Comments:

Unity College offers services for learning disabled students and encourages them to begin their studies in the summer prior to freshman year. There are learning disability specialists on staff and services include tutoring on a one-to-one basis or small group skills remediation in reading, math, spelling, written language and learning techniques. Special courses, mostly for credit, are offered in composition, math, reading, college survival skills and study skills .

LEARNING DISABILITY ADMISSIONS INFORMATION

Program Name:	Student Support Services	*Telephone*
Program Director:	James Horan	207-948-3131
Contact Person:	Ann Dailey	same

Admissions:

Learning disabled students may request an interview with the Director of Student Support Services. Students are also asked to attend a special Summer Institute. Students should submit diagnostic materials which indicate their level of functioning.

Interview: *Diagnostic Tests:* Yes

Documentation: WAIS

College Entrance Exams Required: No   *Untimed Accepted:* Yes

Course Entrance Requirements: No

Are Waivers Available:

Additional Information:

Interview is recommended. Other factors include special talents, leadership, activities, alumni status, and personality.

Individualized high school coursework accepted: Yes

Essay Required: Yes

Special Application Required: No   *Submitted To:*

Number of Applications Submitted Each Year: N/A

Number of Applications Accepted Each Year: 25

Number of Students Served: 50

Application Deadline for Special Admission: No

Acceptance into Program means acceptance

into college: Yes

LEARNING DISABILITY SERVICES

Learning Resource Room: Yes

Kurzweil Personal Reader:

LD Specialists: 1

Oral Exams: No

Services for LD Only: No

Books on Tape: Yes

Calculator allowed in exam: Yes

Tape recording in class: Yes

Curriculum Modification Available: No

Tutorial Help: Yes   **Peer Tutors:** Yes

Max. Hours/Week for services:

Unlimited

Added Cost:

Taping of books not on tape: Yes

Dictionary/computer/spellcheck during exam: Yes

How are professors notified of LD: By the student and Director

GENERAL ADMISSIONS INFORMATION

Director of Admissions: Dean John M.B. Craig   **Telephone:** 207-948-3131

Entrance Requirements:

8 units required and 18 are recommended: 4 yrs. English; 2-4 yrs. Math; 2 yrs. Biological Sciences; 2 yrs. Physical Science; 2 yrs. Foreign Language; 4 yrs. Social Science. Interview is recommended.

Test Scores: **SAT:** 800-1000 (mid 50%)   **ACT:**

G.P.A.: 2.0 (2.6 preferred)   **Class Rank:** 60%

Application Deadline: Rolling   **Achievement Tests:**

COLLEGE GRADUATION REQUIREMENTS

Foreign Language: No   **Waivers:**

Math: Yes   **Waivers:** No

Minimum Course Load per Term: 12 hours to maintain full-time status.

ADDITIONAL INFORMATION

Location: The College is located on 185 acres in a rural community about 20 miles from Waterville.

Enrollment Information: **Undergraduate:** 455   **Women:** 22%   **Men:** 78%

    In-State Students: 37%   **Out of State:** 63%

Cost Information: **In-State Tuition:** $6,050   **Out of State:** $7,350

    Room & Board: $4,100   **Additional Costs:**

Housing Information: **University Housing:** Yes   **Sorority:** 0

    % Living on Campus: 90%   **Fraternity:** 0

Athletics:

Support: SP   **Institution:** 4 yr. Private

LEARNING DISABILITY PROGRAM AND SERVICES

Comments:

The Individual Learning Program is designed for students with documented learning disabilities. Students receive individually planned, sequenced curricula with support services to meet their particular needs for 4 years, if required. The ILP operates under a Level of Service model. Students sign a contract agreeing to participate in the Program. This format allows the faculty of the ILP to deliver specialized educational services to learning disabled students. All new students entering the ILP begin at Level III for a minimum of one semester. There are progress reports sent to students and their parents.

LEARNING DISABILITY ADMISSIONS INFORMATION

Program Name: Individual Learning Program (ILP)   **Telephone**

Program Director: Dr. Robert E. Manganello, Ed.D   207-283-0171

Contact Person: same

Admissions:

There is a special admissions procedure. The admission's application has a box where student may check "LD." Students must submit the general admission application and psycho-educational evaluation to the admissions office. Copies are given to the ILP Director. An interview with the student is scheduled. The ACT/SAT are not used in the admission process. The Verbal sub-score on the WAIS-R is very important. The admission decision is a joint decision between ILP and Admissions. Interested students may request a pre-screening.

Interview: Yes   **Diagnostic Tests:** Yes

Documentation: WAIS-R; achievement tests (given within 12 months of application)

College Entrance Exams Required: No   **Untimed Accepted:** Yes

Course Entrance Requirements: Yes

Are Waivers Available: No

Additional Information:

In addition to offering the ILP program there is also a First Year Option (FYO) program designed especially for academically high risk learning disabled students. This is considered a transition year. FYO students enroll as non-matriculated students who must attend a number of courses offered through the Department of Learning Assistance and Individual Learning. FYO students are required to petition for entrance into the University at the end of their second semester.

Individualized high school coursework accepted: Y/N, up to Registrar

Essay Required: Yes, as part of a Writing Placement Exam

Special Application Required: No   **Submitted To:**

Number of Applications Submitted Each Year: 75-80

Number of Applications Accepted Each Year: 25

Number of Students Served: 20-30

Application Deadline for Special Admission: No

Acceptance into Program means acceptance

into college: Yes for ILP,not for FYO, there is an appeal procedure, request conference from
          Coordinator

LEARNING DISABILITY SERVICES

Learning Resource Room: Yes **Curriculum Modification Available:** Yes

Kurzweil Personal Reader: No **Tutorial Help:** Yes **Peer Tutors:** Yes

LD Specialists: 3 **Max. Hours/Week for services:**

Oral Exams: Yes individualized

Services for LD Only: No **Added**

Books on Tape: Yes **Cost:** $1,140 -$2,900/depends on level

Calculator allowed in exam: Yes **Taping of books not on tape:** Yes

Tape recording in class: Yes **Dictionary/computer/spellcheck during exam:** Yes

How are professors notified of LD: By the student and Program Director

GENERAL ADMISSIONS INFORMATION

Director of Admissions: Patricia T. Cribby **Telephone:** 207-283-0171

Entrance Requirements:

4 yrs. English; 3 yrs. Math; 3 yrs. Science; 2 yrs. History; 2 yrs. Social Studies.

Test Scores: **SAT:** 900 **ACT:** 22-24 (will consider lower)

G.P.A.: **Class Rank:** top 50%

Application Deadline: Rolling **Achievement Tests:**

COLLEGE GRADUATION REQUIREMENTS

Foreign Language: No **Waivers:**

Math: Yes **Waivers:** No

Minimum Course Load per Term: Yes

ADDITIONAL INFORMATION

Location: 121 acre campus is in rural area 16 miles east of Portland.

Enrollment Information: **Undergraduate:** 755 **Women:** 60% **Men:** 40%

In-State Students: 35% **Out of State:** 65%

Cost Information: **In-State Tuition:** $9,120 **Out of State:** same

Room & Board: $4,200 **Additional Costs:** $420

Housing Information: University Housing: Yes **Sorority:** No

% Living on Campus: 60% **Fraternity:** No

Athletics: NAIA

COLUMBIA UNION COLLEGE
Takoma Park, Md. 20912
301-891-4230

Support: S   **Institution:** 4 yr. Private

LEARNING DISABILITY PROGRAM AND SERVICES

Comments:

The Columbia Union College Summer Start program is designed for students who do not meet college entrance requirements. Summer Start is an intensive 6 week academic program that provides students with a strong review of basic Math and English, as well as reading and study skills. The program also gives students an opportunity to learn employment-seeking skills such as resume writing and interview techniques. Summer Start is designed for students who are willing to invest the time and effort required to become successful college students.

LEARNING DISABILITY ADMISSIONS INFORMATION

Program Name: Summer Start   **Telephone**

Program Director: Betty Howard   301-891-4106

Contact Person:

Admissions:

There is no special application or admissions procedure for learning disabled students.

Interview: Yes   **Diagnostic Tests:** No

Documentation: Evaluation done on site.

College Entrance Exams Required: Yes   **Untimed Accepted:** Yes

Course Entrance Requirements: Yes

Are Waivers Available:

Additional Information:

Summer Start and Learning Assistance Program offers admission to students not usually admitted due to academic or economic disadvantage.

Individualized high school coursework accepted:

Essay Required: Yes, for English placement

Special Application Required: No   **Submitted To:**

Number of Applications Submitted Each Year:

Number of Applications Accepted Each Year:

Number of Students Served: 6-8

Application Deadline for Special Admission: No

Acceptance into Program means acceptance

into college: No, there is an appeal procedure

129

LEARNING DISABILITY SERVICES

Learning Resource Room: Yes   **Curriculum Modification Available:** No

Kurzweil Personal Reader: No   **Tutorial Help:** Yes   **Peer Tutors:** Yes

LD Specialists: Yes   **Max. Hours/Week for services:**

Oral Exams: Yes   4 hours per/week

Services for LD Only: Yes   **Added**

Books on Tape: Yes   **Cost:** $975 for Summer Start

Calculator allowed in exam: Yes   **Taping of books not on tape:** Yes

Tape recording in class: Yes   **Dictionary/computer/spellcheck during exam:** Yes

How are professors notified of LD: By the student and the Program Director

GENERAL ADMISSIONS INFORMATION

Director of Admissions: Shiela D. Burnette   **Telephone:** 301-891-4230

Entrance Requirements:

4 yrs. English; 2 yrs. Math; 2-3 yrs. Social Science; 2 yrs. Science; 2 yrs. Foreign Language. ACT is preferred.

Test Scores: **SAT:** 870 (mid 50%)   **ACT:** 16 minimum (20 average)

G.P.A.: 2.5   **Class Rank:**

Application Deadline: 7/1   **Achievement Tests:**

COLLEGE GRADUATION REQUIREMENTS

Foreign Language: No   **Waivers:**

Math: Yes   **Waivers:**

Minimum Course Load per Term: 12 semester hours with individual advising

ADDITIONAL INFORMATION

Location: The College is located on 19 acres, 7 miles north of Washington, D.C.

Enrollment Information: **Undergraduate:** 1,173   **Women:** 64%   **Men:** 36%

In-State Students: 49%   **Out of State:** 51%

Cost Information: **In-State Tuition:** $7,800   **Out of State:** same

Room & Board: $3,400   **Additional Costs:** $180

Housing Information: **University Housing:** Yes   **Sorority:** No

% Living on Campus: 22%   **Fraternity:** No

Athletics: Intercollegiate sports

FROSTBURG STATE UNIVERSITY
Frostburg, Md. 21532-1099

302-689-4201

Support: S   *Institution:* 4 yr. Public

LEARNING DISABILITY PROGRAM AND SERVICES

Comments:

Frostburg State provides comprehensive support services for LD students to assist them in achieving their potential. To be eligible for the Frostburg State University support services, admitted students must provide records of evaluation not more than three years old. Services include: advising and counseling by a qualified counselor familiar with each students needs; assistance in course selection; guaranteed schedules; liaison with faculty; representation at Academic Standards Committee meetings; tutoring and study skills workshops.

LEARNING DISABILITY ADMISSIONS INFORMATION

Program Name:	Student Support Services/Disabled Student Services	*Telephone*
Program Director:	Carolyn Princes	302-689-4481
Contact Person:	Beth Hoffman	same

Admissions:

There is no special admission procedure. There is a Student Support Services/Disabled Student Services Information Form that must be completed by students to enroll in the support program. Admission to FSU is determined by the Admissions Office which assess an applicants likelihood of success in a regular college program, with Support Service assistance.

Interview: Yes   *Diagnostic Tests:* Yes

Documentation:

College Entrance Exams Required: Yes   *Untimed Accepted:* Yes

Course Entrance Requirements: Yes

Are Waivers Available:

Additional Information:

All students must complete the mainstream program in high school and meet all requirements for the University and the State.

Individualized high school coursework accepted: Yes

Essay Required: Yes

Special Application Required: No   *Submitted To:*

Number of Applications Submitted Each Year: 64

Number of Applications Accepted Each Year: 66

Number of Students Served: 66

Application Deadline for Special Admission: No

Acceptance into Program means acceptance

into college: No, there is an appeal procedure

131

LEARNING DISABILITY SERVICES

Learning Resource Room: Yes	**Curriculum Modification Available:** Yes	
Kurzweil Personal Reader: No	**Tutorial Help:** Yes	**Peer Tutors:** Yes
LD Specialists: No	**Max. Hours/Week for services:**	
Oral Exams: Yes	No limit	
Services for LD Only: No	**Added**	
Books on Tape: Yes	**Cost:** None	
Calculator allowed in exam: Yes	**Taping of books not on tape:** Yes	
Tape recording in class: Yes	**Dictionary/computer/spellcheck during exam:** Yes	

How are professors notified of LD: By the student and the Program Director

GENERAL ADMISSIONS INFORMATION

Director of Admissions: David L. Sanford   **Telephone:** 301-689-4201

Entrance Requirements:

4 yrs. English; 3 yrs. Math; 3 yrs. Social Studies; 2 yrs. Science.

Test Scores: **SAT:** 910   **ACT:**

G.P.A.: 2.5   **Class Rank:**

Application Deadline: **Achievement Tests:** Varies

COLLEGE GRADUATION REQUIREMENTS

Foreign Language: No   **Waivers:**

Math: Yes   **Waivers:** No

Minimum Course Load per Term: 12 credits to be full time

ADDITIONAL INFORMATION

Location: The University in located on 260 acres in a small town 150 west of Baltimore.

Enrollment Information: **Undergraduate:** 4,500	**Women:** 48%	**Men:** 52%	
In-State Students: 85%		**Out of State:** 15%	
Cost Information: **In-State Tuition:** $2,016		**Out of State:** $3,666	
Room & Board: $3,585		**Additional Costs:** $446	
Housing Information: **University Housing:** Yes		**Sorority:** 10%	
% Living on Campus: 65%		**Fraternity:** 8%	

Athletics: NCAA Div. III

TOWSON STATE UNIVERSITY
Towson, Md. 21204

301-830-2112

Support: S   *Institution:* 4 yr. Public

LEARNING DISABILITY PROGRAM AND SERVICES

Comments:

Towson State does not have a separate program for learning disabled students. Staff work individually with each student to circumvent the handicap and to help each student work with their own strongest compensating skills. The University policy is to ask students what their needs are rather than to present them with a "plan" to which they must adapt. There is involvement in class selection. Professors are notified of students disabilities which eliminates the need for students to "explain" or "prove" their disability. Towson also offers all students tutorial services, a reading center and a writing lab.

LEARNING DISABILITY ADMISSIONS INFORMATION

Program Name:	Handicapped Students Services	*Telephone*
Program Director:	Margaret M. Warrington	301-830-2638
Contact Person:	same	

Admissions:

The regular application for Admission is used along with appropriate documentation if the student chooses to identify a learning disability. If the SAT's are below 470, students will be tested on campus. An interview is not required but students are encouraged to interview to determine if available services are adequate for their specific learning disability.

Interview: Yes   *Diagnostic Tests:* Yes

Documentation:

College Entrance Exams Required: Yes   *Untimed Accepted:* Yes

Course Entrance Requirements: Yes

Are Waivers Available:

Additional Information:

As of 1991 students will be required to have a foreign language. The Director is still considering this problem for learning disabled students who have a documented disability in foreign language. The admissions staff has some flexibility in interpreting SAT scores and a high GPA can offset a poor SAT score. In cases where high school grades or test scores are low because of a learning disability, the admissions office asks for an explanation of the learning disability.

Individualized high school coursework accepted:

Essay Required:

Special Application Required: *Submitted To:*

Number of Applications Submitted Each Year: NA

Number of Applications Accepted Each Year: 30

Number of Students Served: 130

Application Deadline for Special Admission: No

Acceptance into Program means acceptance

into college: Yes

133

LEARNING DISABILITY SERVICES

Learning Resource Room: Yes

Kurzweil Personal Reader: Yes

LD Specialists: No

Oral Exams: · Yes

Services for LD Only: No

Books on Tape: Yes

Calculator allowed in exam: Yes

Tape recording in class: Yes

How are professors notified of LD: The service sends a memo

Curriculum Modification Available:

Tutorial Help: Yes   **Peer Tutors:** Yes

Max. Hours/Week for services:
   to be arranged

Added Cost:

Taping of books not on tape: Yes

Dictionary/computer/spellcheck during exam: Yes

GENERAL ADMISSIONS INFORMATION

Director of Admissions: Linda J. Collins   **Telephone:** 301-830-2112

Entrance Requirements:

4 yrs. English; 3 yrs. Math; 3 yrs. Social Science; 2 yrs. Science. Basic criteria includes a C+ average. SAT is preferred. Automatic admissions for students with a 3.0 GPA and 1000 SAT.

Test Scores: **SAT:** 900   **ACT:**

G.P.A.: 2.5 (minimum)   **Class Rank:**

Application Deadline: 2/1   **Achievement Tests:**

COLLEGE GRADUATION REQUIREMENTS

Foreign Language: No   **Waivers:**

Math: Yes   **Waivers:** Yes

Minimum Course Load per Term: Depends on student's needs

ADDITIONAL INFORMATION

Location: The school is located on 306 landscaped and wooded acres minutes from downtown Baltimore.

Enrollment Information: **Undergraduate:** 13,464   **Women:** 60%   **Men:** 40%

   In-State Students: 89%   **Out of State:** 11%

Cost Information: **In-State Tuition:** $1,544   **Out of State:** $3,208

   Room & Board: $4,280   **Additional Costs:** $644

Housing Information: **University Housing:** Yes   **Sorority:** 10%

   % Living on Campus: 30%   **Fraternity:** 10%

Athletics: NCAA Div. I

Support: S   *Institution:* 4 yr. Public

LEARNING DISABILITY PROGRAM AND SERVICES

Comments:

The major goal of DSS is to implement arrangements to meet the needs of certified LD students. Students are expected to make contact with instructors and negotiate any special accommodations. Students may request assistance from the DSS office in handling interactions with instructors. Commonly used services include testing assistance, notetakers, tutoring, counseling and reading.

LEARNING DISABILITY ADMISSIONS INFORMATION

Program Name: Disabled Student Services (DSS)   *Telephone*

Program Director: William Scales   301-454-6460

Contact Person: same

Admissions:

There is no special admissions process for students with learning disabilities.

Interview: Yes   *Diagnostic Tests:* Yes

Documentation: WAIS-R: Woodcock-Johnson: Peabody

College Entrance Exams Required: Yes   *Untimed Accepted:* Yes

Course Entrance Requirements: Yes

Are Waivers Available: No

Additional Information:

They are looking for an SAT score of 900 or more.

Individualized high school coursework accepted:

Essay Required: Yes

Special Application Required: *Submitted To:*

Number of Applications Submitted Each Year: N/A

Number of Applications Accepted Each Year: N/A

Number of Students Served: 110

Application Deadline for Special Admission:

Acceptance into Program means acceptance

into college: No, appeal process available

135

LEARNING DISABILITY SERVICES

Learning Resource Room: Yes	**Curriculum Modification Available:** No	
Kurzweil Personal Reader: Yes	**Tutorial Help:** Yes	**Peer Tutors:** Yes
LD Specialists: No	**Max. Hours/Week for services:**	
Oral Exams: Yes	N/A	
Services for LD Only: No	**Added**	
Books on Tape: Yes	**Cost:** None	
Calculator allowed in exam: Yes	**Taping of books not on tape:** Yes	
Tape recording in class: Yes	**Dictionary/computer/spellcheck during exam:** Yes	

How are professors notified of LD: By student and Program Director

GENERAL ADMISSIONS INFORMATION

Director of Admissions: Linda Clement　　　　　　**Telephone:** 301-454-5550

Entrance Requirements:

4 yrs. English; 2 yrs. Algebra and 1 yr. Plane Geometry; 2 yrs. Lab Science; 3 yrs. History or Social Sciences; 2 yrs. Foreign Language. SAT is required. Higher GPA required for out-of-state applicants.

Test Scores:　**SAT:**　　　　　　　　　**ACT:**

G.P.A.: 3.0 (average)　　　　　　　**Class Rank:**

Application Deadline: 4/30　　　　　**Achievement Tests:**

COLLEGE GRADUATION REQUIREMENTS

Foreign Language: Yes　　**Waivers:** Required in Arts and Humanities College

Math: Yes　　　　　　　　**Waivers:** No

Minimum Course Load per Term: 12 credits to be full time

ADDITIONAL INFORMATION

Location: Small town setting within proximity to Washington,D.C. and Baltimore.

Enrollment Information:	**Undergraduate:**	26,863	**Women:** 47%	**Men:** 53%	
	In-State Students:	76%		**Out of State:** 24%	
Cost Information:	**In-State Tuition:**	$2,270		**Out of State:** $6,300	
	Room & Board:	$4,300		**Additional Costs:** $182	
Housing Information:	**University Housing:**	Yes		**Sorority:** 6%	
	% Living on Campus:	20%		**Fraternity:** 6%	

Athletics: NCAA Div. I

AMERICAN INTERNATIONAL COLLEGE
Springfield, Ma. 01109
413-737-7000

Support: SP   **Institution:** 4 yr. Private

LEARNING DISABILITY PROGRAM AND SERVICES

Comments:

Students must have the intellectual ability necessary to meet the demands of a college curriculum, as well as motivation and commitment. Students are mainstreamed and may receive two hours of tutoring/studying strategies each week. Students create an IEP with their tutor during their freshman year and may take as few as four courses each semester. Students generally stay in the program throughout their college years. AIC is nationally recognized for a decade and a half of formal support service delivery.

LEARNING DISABILITY ADMISSIONS INFORMATION

Program Name: Supportive Learning Services Program (SLS)   **Telephone**

Program Director: Prof. Mary Saltus   413-737-7000

Contact Person: Mrs. Susan Lempke   same

Admissions:

There is a special application and admissions procedure. The applicant must submit a WAIS-R with accompanying report prior to an interview with a SLS admissions counselor. The student should indicate on the regular College application that they have an interest in the SLS Program. The SLS Director is actively involved in the admission decision.

Interview: Yes

Documentation: WAIS-R and report

College Entrance Exams Required: Yes

Course Entrance Requirements: Yes

Are Waivers Available: No

Diagnostic Tests: Yes

Untimed Accepted: Yes

Additional Information:

Looking for students who have a College preparatory background.

Individualized high school coursework accepted: No

Essay Required: No

Special Application Required: No   **Submitted To:**

Number of Applications Submitted Each Year: 275

Number of Applications Accepted Each Year: 35

Number of Students Served: 100

Application Deadline for Special Admission: No

Acceptance into Program means acceptance into college: Admissions & SLS decide together

137

LEARNING DISABILITY SERVICES

Learning Resource Room: Yes   **Curriculum Modification Available:** No

Kurzweil Personal Reader: **Tutorial Help:** Yes   **Peer Tutors:** No

LD Specialists: 15   **Max. Hours/Week for services:**

Oral Exams: Yes   Average 3 hours

Services for LD Only: Yes   **Added**

Books on Tape: Yes   **Cost:** $1,300. p/semester

Calculator allowed in exam: Yes   **Taping of books not on tape:** Yes

Tape recording in class: Yes   **Dictionary/computer/spellcheck during exam:**

How are professors notified of LD: By student and Program Director

GENERAL ADMISSIONS INFORMATION

Director of Admissions: Peter J. Miller   **Telephone:** 413-737-7000

Entrance Requirements:

16 academic credits including: 4 yrs. English; 2 yrs. Math; 2 yrs. History; 2 yrs. Science (1 yr. Lab); 1 yr. Social Studies.

Test Scores: **SAT:** 899   **ACT:**

G.P.A.: 2.0   **Class Rank:**

Application Deadline: Rolling   **Achievement Tests:**

COLLEGE GRADUATION REQUIREMENTS

Foreign Language: No   **Waivers:**

Math: Yes   **Waivers:**

Minimum Course Load per Term: 4 courses

ADDITIONAL INFORMATION

Location: The school is located on 58 acres in Springfield, 75 miles west of Boston and 30 miles north of Hartford.

Enrollment Information: **Undergraduate:** 1,273 **Women:** 44% **Men:** 56%

    In-State Students: 54% **Out of State:** 46%

Cost Information: **In-State Tuition:** $7,968. **Out of State:** same

    Room & Board: $4,1320. **Additional Costs:** $561

Housing Information: **University Housing:** Yes **Sorority:** 7%

    % Living on Campus: 62% **Fraternity:** 4%

Athletics: NCAA Div. II

Support: CS   *Institution:* 4 yr. Private

LEARNING DISABILITY PROGRAM AND SERVICES

Comments:

For more than a decade Boston University has been committed to serving college students with learning disabilities. The ultimate goal of the Learning Disabilities Support Services Office (LDSS) is to ensure that college students with learning disabilities can function independently within the academic, social and recreational atmosphere of a competitive university. A 6 week Summer Transition Program (STP) which costs $1,000. is designed to provide incoming students with the opportunity to develop skills necessary to reach their fullest potential.

LEARNING DISABILITY ADMISSIONS INFORMATION

Program Name:	Learning Disabilities Support Services	**Telephone**
Program Director:	Dr. Loring Brinckerhoff	617-353-6880
Contact Person:	Mr. Kip Opperman	617-353-3658

Admissions:

Students with a learning disability are required to submit the same application as other students. However, supporting documentation of the learning disability should be sent directly to the Office of Admissions.

Interview: Optional   *Diagnostic Tests:* Yes

Documentation: WAIS-R;Woodcock-Johnson

College Entrance Exams Required: Yes   *Untimed Accepted:* Yes

Course Entrance Requirements: Yes

Are Waivers Available:

Additional Information:

When test scores are lower than general admission requirements, students may be admitted to the College of Basic Studies which is a 2 year non-traditional, team taught liberal arts program. Successful completion allows transfer within the University. This program is not for LD students, although some of the students are learning disabled.

Individualized high school coursework accepted: Yes

Essay Required: Yes

Special Application Required: No   *Submitted To:*

Number of Applications Submitted Each Year: 75+

Number of Applications Accepted Each Year:

Number of Students Served: 85

Application Deadline for Special Admission: No

Acceptance into Program means acceptance into college: No

LEARNING DISABILITY SERVICES

Learning Resource Room: Yes   **Curriculum Modification Available:** Yes

Kurzweil Personal Reader: Yes   **Tutorial Help:** Yes   **Peer Tutors:** No

LD Specialists: 7   **Max. Hours/Week for services:**

Oral Exams: Yes   2-3 hours per/week

Services for LD Only: Yes   **Added Cost:** $2,000. per/year

Books on Tape: Yes

Calculator allowed in exam: Yes   **Taping of books not on tape:** Yes

Tape recording in class: Yes   **Dictionary/computer/spellcheck during exam:** Yes

How are professors notified of LD: By the student

GENERAL ADMISSIONS INFORMATION

Director of Admissions: Debra Kocar   **Telephone:** 617-353-2300

Entrance Requirements:

4 yrs. English; 4 yrs. Math; 3 yrs. Foreign Language; 3 yrs. Social Science; 1 yr. Biological Science; 2 yr. Physical Science.

Test Scores: **SAT:** 1130   **ACT:**

G.P.A.:   **Class Rank:** Upper 25%

Application Deadline: 1/15   **Achievement Tests:** 3

COLLEGE GRADUATION REQUIREMENTS

Foreign Language: **Waivers:** Course substitutions may be provided

Math: **Waivers:**

Minimum Course Load per Term: 9 credits

ADDITIONAL INFORMATION

Location: The 99 acre campus of Boston University is located on the Charles River in Boston's Back Bay.

Enrollment Information: **Undergraduate:** 14,530   **Women:** 53%   **Men:** 47%

In-State Students: 25%   **Out of State:** 75%

Cost Information: **In-State Tuition:** $14,900   **Out of State:** same

Room & Board: $5,940   **Additional Costs:** $195

Housing Information: **University Housing:** Yes   **Sorority:** 12%

% Living on Campus: 55%   **Fraternity:** 11%

Athletics: NCAA Div. I

Support: CS   *Institution:* 4 yr. Private

LEARNING DISABILITY PROGRAM AND SERVICES

Comments:

The Learning Disabilities program at Clark University, based within the Academic Advising Center, was developed to advocate and support the needs of the learning disabled student in a college environment. When a learning disabled student enters Clark, strategies are developed to help the student cope with the increased demands of the college curriculum. Resources are available to students who experience difficulties, and who may require some support or wish to learn more about their own learning styles.

LEARNING DISABILITY ADMISSIONS INFORMATION

Program Name:	Academic Advising Center	*Telephone*
Program Director:	Martin Patwell	508-793-7468
Contact Person:	same	

Admissions:

The LD Program and the Office of Undergraduate Admissions work together in considering a LD student for admission. Admission is based on ability, rather than disability. All LD applicants must meet usual admissions criteria. An interview with members of Clark's LD support program is highly recommended. In addition, if a student requires any classroom accommodations or support services, a diagnostic assessment must be submitted, completed within the last year, documenting the learning disability. This documentation is needed to evaluate whether the applicant's needs can be met by the support services of the University.

Interview: Yes   *Diagnostic Tests:* Yes

Documentation: WAIS-R;W-J; Psychoeducational battery-R; Cognitive Achievement

College Entrance Exams Required: Yes   *Untimed Accepted:* Yes

Course Entrance Requirements: Yes

Are Waivers Available: No

Additional Information:

Placement tests required in English, Math, and Foreign Language.

Individualized high school coursework accepted: At times

Essay Required: Yes

Special Application Required: No   *Submitted To:*

Number of Applications Submitted Each Year: 125

Number of Applications Accepted Each Year: 65

Number of Students Served: 75

Application Deadline for Special Admission: No

Acceptance into Program means acceptance into college: NA

141

LEARNING DISABILITY SERVICES

Learning Resource Room: Yes

Kurzweil Personal Reader:

LD Specialists: 1

Oral Exams:

Services for LD Only: No

Books on Tape: Yes

Calculator allowed in exam: Y/N

Tape recording in class: Yes

Curriculum Modification Available: No

Tutorial Help: Yes **Peer Tutors:** Yes

Max. Hours/Week for services:
   1 hour per course

Added Cost: None

Taping of books not on tape: Yes

Dictionary/computer/spellcheck during exam: Y/N

How are professors notified of LD: By student and Program Director

GENERAL ADMISSIONS INFORMATION

Director of Admissions: Richard Pierson **Telephone:** 508-793-7431

Entrance Requirements:

16 units including: 4 yrs. English; 3 yrs. Math; 3 yrs. Science; 2 yrs. Foreign Language; 2 yrs. History; 2 yrs. Social Studies; Achievement tests in English Composition.

Test Scores: **SAT:** 1105 (mid 50%) **ACT:**

G.P.A.: **Class Rank:**

Application Deadline: 2/15 **Achievement Tests:** English

COLLEGE GRADUATION REQUIREMENTS

Foreign Language: No **Waivers:**

Math: Yes **Waivers:** No

Minimum Course Load per Term: 3 courses per semester

ADDITIONAL INFORMATION

Location: The University is located on 45 acres in a small city 38 miles west of Boston.

Enrollment Information: **Undergraduate:** 2,220 **Women:** 54% **Men:** 46%

In-State Students: 29% **Out of State:** 71%

Cost Information: **In-State Tuition:** $14,000 **Out of State:** same

Room & Board: $4,700 **Additional Costs:** $270

Housing Information: **University Housing:** Yes **Sorority:** No

% Living on Campus: 68% **Fraternity:** No

Athletics: NCAA Div. III

Support: SP   **Institution:** 4 yr. Private

LEARNING DISABILITY PROGRAM AND SERVICES

Comments:

The Program for Advancement in Learning (PAL) at Curry College is a supportive program for language/learning disabled students. Students who are accepted into the Learning Center and receive services, are Curry College students participating fully in coursework and extra curricular activities. The goal of PAL is to facilitate students' understanding of their individual learning styles and to achieve independence as learners. A PAL summer orientation session is recommended and an additional fee is required for this summer experience.

LEARNING DISABILITY ADMISSIONS INFORMATION

Program Name: Program for Advancement in Learning (PAL)   **Telephone**

Program Director: Dr. Gertrude M. Webb   617-333-0500

Contact Person: same

Admissions:

Applicants must submit the regular application and fee, an official secondary school transcript, scores on the SAT or ACT (recommended), a counselor or teacher recommendation, and, the results of a WAIS-R test. Admissions to the PAL program is made by the Admissions Committee once all credentials are complete. Acceptance into PAL is based on evidence of better-than-average compensational ability, of sound emotional health, and of a strong desire for a college education. Appropriate applicants will receive a questionaire requesting educational and personal history, and an untimed, orginal writing sample.

Interview: **Diagnostic Tests:** Yes

Documentation: WAIS-R; diagnostic testing

College Entrance Exams Required: Recommended   **Untimed Accepted:** Yes

Course Entrance Requirements: Yes

Are Waivers Available:

Additional Information:

Students admitted to the PAL Program must commit to the program for at least 1 year. Subject content tutoring is used to help develop strategies.

Individualized high school coursework accepted:

Essay Required:

Special Application Required: No   **Submitted To:**

Number of Applications Submitted Each Year:

Number of Applications Accepted Each Year: 108

Number of Students Served:

Application Deadline for Special Admission: No

Acceptance into Program means acceptance
into college:

LEARNING DISABILITY SERVICES

Learning Resource Room: Yes

Kurzweil Personal Reader:

LD Specialists: Yes

Oral Exams: Yes

Services for LD Only: Yes

Books on Tape: Yes

Calculator allowed in exam: Yes

Tape recording in class: Yes

How are professors notified of LD:

Curriculum Modification Available: Yes

Tutorial Help: Yes   **Peer Tutors:** No

Max. Hours/Week for services:

Added Cost: $3,000

Taping of books not on tape: Yes

Dictionary/computer/spellcheck during exam: Yes

GENERAL ADMISSIONS INFORMATION

Director of Admissions: Mr. Dana K. Denault   **Telephone:** 617-333-0500

Entrance Requirements:

High school transcript; SAT or ACT; 4 yrs. English; 3 yrs. Math; 2 yrs. Science; 2 yrs. Foreign Language; 2 yrs. History.

Test Scores: **SAT:** 788   **ACT:** 18

G.P.A.: "C" average   **Class Rank:** top 50%

Application Deadline: 4/1   **Achievement Tests:**

COLLEGE GRADUATION REQUIREMENTS

Foreign Language: **Waivers:**

Math: **Waivers:**

Minimum Course Load per Term:

ADDITIONAL INFORMATION

Location: Curry's 120 acre campus in Milton, Massachusetts is minutes from metropolitan Boston.

Enrollment Information: **Undergraduate:** 1,001   **Women:** 52%   **Men:** 48%

In-State Students: 55%   **Out of State:** 45%

Cost Information: **In-State Tuition:** $10,750   **Out of State:** same

Room & Board: $5,500   **Additional Costs:** $325

Housing Information: **University Housing:** Yes   **Sorority:** No

% Living on Campus: 77%   **Fraternity:** No

Athletics: NCAA Div. III

MOUNT IDA COLLEGE
Newton Centre, Ma. 02159
617-969-7000

Support: CS   **Institution:** 4 yr. Private

LEARNING DISABILITY PROGRAM AND SERVICES

Comments:

The Learning Opportunities Program provides services and accommodations for students with learning disabilities and other special needs. In the Learning Skills Laboratory students have an opportunity to work with Mount Ida faculty and students to improve study skills. Services include tutoring, reduced course load, enrollment in Basic English if needed, extended time testing, notetaking, diagnostic testing and course substitutions.

LEARNING DISABILITY ADMISSIONS INFORMATION

Program Name: Learning Opportunities Program   **Telephone**

Program Director: Richard Goldhammer   617-969-7000

Contact Person: Dr. Chris Chase   same

Admissions:

There is no special admissions process for students with learning disabilities. However, an interview is strongly recommended. They would also like the WAIS-R and a test indicating appropriate reading grade level.

Interview: Recommended   **Diagnostic Tests:** Yes

Documentation: WAIS-R;W-J

College Entrance Exams Required: No   **Untimed Accepted:** Yes

Course Entrance Requirements: No

Are Waivers Available:

Additional Information:

Individualized high school coursework accepted: Yes

Essay Required: No

Special Application Required: No   **Submitted To:**

Number of Applications Submitted Each Year:

Number of Applications Accepted Each Year:

Number of Students Served: 60+(This is a new program)

Application Deadline for Special Admission: No

Acceptance into Program means acceptance into college: Yes

145

LEARNING DISABILITY SERVICES

Learning Resource Room: Yes   **Curriculum Modification Available:** No

Kurzweil Personal Reader: **Tutorial Help:** Yes   **Peer Tutors:** Yes

LD Specialists: Yes   **Max. Hours/Week for services:**

Oral Exams: Yes   No limit

Services for LD Only: No   **Added**

Books on Tape: Yes   **Cost:** $2,000

Calculator allowed in exam: Y/N   **Taping of books not on tape:** Yes

Tape recording in class: Yes   **Dictionary/computer/spellcheck during exam:** No

How are professors notified of LD: By the student and the Program Director

GENERAL ADMISSIONS INFORMATION

Director of Admissions: Jim Mulligan   **Telephone:** 617-969-7000

Entrance Requirements:

4 yrs. English; 2 yrs. Math; 3 yrs. Social Studies; 2 yrs. Science.

Test Scores: **SAT:** Not required   **ACT:** Not required

G.P.A.: 2.0   **Class Rank:**

Application Deadline: **Achievement Tests:**

COLLEGE GRADUATION REQUIREMENTS

Foreign Language: No   **Waivers:**

Math: No   **Waivers:**

Minimum Course Load per Term: Yes

ADDITIONAL INFORMATION

Location: Mount Ida's 85 acre campus is in a suburban neighborhood 8 miles west of Boston.

Enrollment Information: Undergraduate: 1,775   **Women:** 57%   **Men:** 43%

In-State Students: 50%   **Out of State:** 50%

Cost Information: In-State Tuition: $7,985   **Out of State:** same

Room & Board: $5,535   **Additional Costs:**

Housing Information: University Housing: Yes   **Sorority:** No

% Living on Campus: 50%   **Fraternity:** No

Athletics: Intercollegiate sports

Support: CS   **Institution:** 4 yr. Private

LEARNING DISABILITY PROGRAM AND SERVICES

Comments:

The Disability Resource Center offers extensive support services to all University students. For all learning disabled students admitted to Northeastern, a series of individualized meetings are conducted to establish learning strategies and specific goals. Faculty are inserviced to ensure follow-through services. There is an independent highly structured LD program called The Learning Disability Program which is housed on-campus. This privately sponsored program, only for LD students, has an additional cost of $2,400 per/semester.

LEARNING DISABILITY ADMISSIONS INFORMATION

		Telephone
Program Name:	Disability Resource Center	
Program Director:	Dean G. Ruth Kukiela Bork	617-437-2675
Contact Person:	Marge Rabinovitch, Director of The LD Program	617-437-4526

Admissions:

There are two separate application processes involved in admission to Northeastern. Admission requirements to the University are the same for all students and any student may be eligible for help in the Disability Resource Center. There is a separate application and interview needed for The Learning Disability Program, which is the independent program. Students must take a full 6-10 hour battery of tests for this program, and must also submit previous diagnostic tests.

Interview: Yes   **Diagnostic Tests:** Yes

Documentation: Taken within 3 years

College Entrance Exams Required: Yes   **Untimed Accepted:** Yes

Course Entrance Requirements: Yes

Are Waivers Available: Yes

Additional Information:

Depending on the Program, courses and diagnosis of the students learning disability, courses may be substituted for admission.

Individualized high school coursework accepted:

Essay Required: No

Special Application Required: Yes   **Submitted To:**

Number of Applications Submitted Each Year:

Number of Applications Accepted Each Year:

Number of Students Served: 200 LD, 35 in Learning Disability Program

Application Deadline for Special Admission: Rolling Admissions

Acceptance into Program means acceptance

into college: No, must be accepted by the college first

LEARNING DISABILITY SERVICES

Learning Resource Room:

Kurzweil Personal Reader: Yes

LD Specialists: 3

Oral Exams: Yes

Services for LD Only: Y/N

Books on Tape: Yes

Calculator allowed in exam: Y/N

Tape recording in class: Yes

How are professors notified of LD: By the student or Program Director

Curriculum Modification Available: Yes

Tutorial Help: Yes   **Peer Tutors:** Yes

Max. Hours/Week for services:

  Varies

**Added
Cost:** $2,400 per/semester for the LD Program

Taping of books not on tape: Yes

Dictionary/computer/spellcheck during exam: Y/N

GENERAL ADMISSIONS INFORMATION

Director of Admissions: Phillip R. McCabe   **Telephone:** 617-731-7104

Entrance Requirements:

4 yrs. English; 4 yrs. Math; 3 yrs. Foreign Language; 3 yrs. Science; 2 yrs. Social Studies; 1 yr. History. Recommendations are helpful. Essay required.

Test Scores: **SAT:** 946   **ACT:**

G.P.A.:   **Class Rank:** Top 40-50%

Application Deadline: Rolling Admissions   **Achievement Tests:** 3

COLLEGE GRADUATION REQUIREMENTS

Foreign Language: **Waivers:** Depends on Program

Math: **Waivers:** Yes

Minimum Course Load per Term: Depends if student is on financial aid or on a sports team.

ADDITIONAL INFORMATION

Location: The school is located on 55 acres in the city of Boston.

Enrollment Information: Undergraduate: 15,249   **Women:** 41%   **Men:** 59%

In-State Students: 58%   **Out of State:** 42%

Cost Information: In-State Tuition: $9,500   **Out of State:** same

Room & Board: $5,970   **Additional Costs:**

Housing Information: University Housing: Yes   **Sorority:** 2%

% Living on Campus: 25%   **Fraternity:** 4%

Athletics: NCAA Div. I

PINE MANOR COLLEGE
Chestnut Hill, Ma. 02167

617-731-7000

Support: CS   **Institution:** 4 yr. Private

LEARNING DISABILITY PROGRAM AND SERVICES

Comments:

The Learning Resource Center is an academic support center used by all students of Pine Manor. There are four professional tutors: a writing tutor, a math tutor, a learning specialist, and the director who provide tutoring that is individually tailored to the learning style and needs of the student. Students work on strategies and receive tutoring assistance from college professors in the different disciplines.

LEARNING DISABILITY ADMISSIONS INFORMATION

Program Name: Learning Resource Center (LRC)   *Telephone*

Program Director: Mary Walsh   1-800-PMC-1357

Contact Person: same

Admissions:

There is no special application required for students with learning disabilities. There is a special Optional Response Form that is used by the Learning Resource Center after the student is accepted. Although not required, an interview is highly recommended. Admissions is done by the Office of Admissions. However, the Director of the LRC assists in interpreting testing.

Interview: **Diagnostic Tests:** Yes

Documentation:

College Entrance Exams Required: No   **Untimed Accepted:** Yes

Course Entrance Requirements: Yes

Are Waivers Available:

Additional Information:

They are looking for an SAT range of 800-950 and an ACT range of 17-20.

Individualized high school coursework accepted: Yes

Essay Required: Yes

Special Application Required: No   **Submitted To:**

Number of Applications Submitted Each Year:

Number of Applications Accepted Each Year:

Number of Students Served:

Application Deadline for Special Admission: No

Acceptance into Program means acceptance into college: Yes

149

LEARNING DISABILITY SERVICES

Learning Resource Room: Yes	**Curriculum Modification Available:** Yes	
Kurzweil Personal Reader:	**Tutorial Help:** Yes	**Peer Tutors:** Yes
LD Specialists: 3	**Max. Hours/Week for services:**	
Oral Exams: Yes	As many as needed	
Services for LD Only: No	**Added Cost:**	
Books on Tape: Yes		
Calculator allowed in exam:	**Taping of books not on tape:** Yes	
Tape recording in class: Yes	**Dictionary/computer/spellcheck during exam:**	

How are professors notified of LD:

GENERAL ADMISSIONS INFORMATION

Director of Admissions: Gillian Lloyd   **Telephone:** 617-731-7104

Entrance Requirements:

16 academic units including: 4 yrs. English; 2 yrs. Math; 2 yrs. Foreign Language; 2 yrs. Social Science; 2 yrs. Natural Science.

Test Scores: **SAT:** 810   **ACT:** 17-20

G.P.A.: 2.0+   **Class Rank:**

Application Deadline: Rolling   **Achievement Tests:**

COLLEGE GRADUATION REQUIREMENTS

Foreign Language: **Waivers:**

Math: Yes   **Waivers:** Student has to pass math exam to be exempt

Minimum Course Load per Term:

ADDITIONAL INFORMATION

Location: Pine Manor is located on a 79 acre campus in Chestnut Hill, 5 miles west of Boston.

Enrollment Information:	**Undergraduate:** 600	**Women:** 100%	**Men:**	
	In-State Students: 19%		**Out of State:** 81%	
Cost Information:	**In-State Tuition:** $12,000		**Out of State:** same	
	Room & Board: $5,700		**Additional Costs:** $600	
Housing Information:	**University Housing:** Yes		**Sorority:** No	
	% Living on Campus: 95%		**Fraternity:**	

Athletics: NCAA Div. III

Support: S   **Institution:** 4 yr. Private

LEARNING DISABILITY PROGRAM AND SERVICES

Comments:

Although Smith College does not have a formal learning disability program it does offer services aimed to eliminate barriers through modification of the program where necessary. The student is encouraged to tell the professor about her accommodation needs. The Center for Academic Development provides writing counseling, tutoring, study skills workshops and quantitative skills counseling. There is a Special Needs Advisory Committee that evaluates and makes recommendations regarding supportive services.

LEARNING DISABILITY ADMISSIONS INFORMATION

Program Name: Special Needs Services   **Telephone**

Program Director: Mary Jane Maccardini   413-585-2071

Contact Person: same

Admissions:

There is no special admissions procedure for students with learning disabilities. Tests that evaluate cognitive ability, achievement and information processing should be included with the regular application. It is also helpful to have a letter from a diagnostician documenting services which will be needed in college.

Interview: Yes   **Diagnostic Tests:** Yes

Documentation:

College Entrance Exams Required: Yes   **Untimed Accepted:** Yes

Course Entrance Requirements: No

Are Waivers Available:

Additional Information:

Three achievement tests are required in addition to the SAT or ACT.

Individualized high school coursework accepted: Yes

Essay Required: Yes

Special Application Required: No   **Submitted To:**

Number of Applications Submitted Each Year: N/A

Number of Applications Accepted Each Year: N/A

Number of Students Served: N/A

Application Deadline for Special Admission:

Acceptance into Program means acceptance into college:

LEARNING DISABILITY SERVICES

Learning Resource Room: Yes   **Curriculum Modification Available:** No

Kurzweil Personal Reader: No   **Tutorial Help:** Yes   **Peer Tutors:** Yes

LD Specialists: No   **Max. Hours/Week for services:**

Oral Exams: Yes   No maximum

Services for LD Only: No   **Added**

Books on Tape: Yes   **Cost:** None

Calculator allowed in exam: Yes   **Taping of books not on tape:** Yes

Tape recording in class: Yes   **Dictionary/computer/spellcheck during exam:** Yes

How are professors notified of LD: By the student

GENERAL ADMISSIONS INFORMATION

Director of Admissions: Lorna R. Blake   **Telephone:** 413-584-0515

Entrance Requirements:

4 yrs. English; 3 yrs. Math; 2 yrs. Foreign Language; 2 yrs. Science; 2 yrs. History. Students who submit the SAT must also take 3 achievements.

Test Scores: **SAT:** 1200   **ACT:** 27

G.P.A.:   **Class Rank:**

Application Deadline: 1/15   **Achievement Tests:** 3 (with SAT)

COLLEGE GRADUATION REQUIREMENTS

Foreign Language: No   **Waivers:**

Math: No   **Waivers:**

Minimum Course Load per Term: No, normal course program

ADDITIONAL INFORMATION

Location: The 204 acre campus is located in a small city 85 miles west of Boston, and 15 minutes from Amherst.

Enrollment Information: **Undergraduate:** 2,660   **Women:** 100%   **Men:**

     In-State Students: 22%   **Out of State:** 78%

Cost Information: **In-State Tuition:** $14,400   **Out of State:** same

     Room & Board: $5,600   **Additional Costs:** $110

Housing Information: **University Housing:** Yes   **Sorority:** No

     % Living on Campus: 87%   **Fraternity:**

Athletics: NCAA Div. III

Support: CS   **Institution:** 4 yr. Private

LEARNING DISABILITY PROGRAM AND SERVICES

Comments:

There is extensive academic support services for all handicapped students. The more the students are mainstreamed in the high school, the greater their chances of success at Adrian in their mainstream program. There is no special or separate curriculum for learning disabled students. Project EXCEL is the umbrella program for all services at Adrian.

LEARNING DISABILITY ADMISSIONS INFORMATION

Program Name: EXCELL   **Telephone**

Program Director: Mary Ann Stibbe   517-265-5161

Contact Person: same

Admissions:

No special admissions. All students should demonstrate the ability to do college level work through an acceptable Grade Point Average in college preparatory classes, ACT or SAT and/or psychological report. Furthermore, by their senior year students should, for the most part, be mainstreamed.

Interview: Suggested   **Diagnostic Tests:** Yes

Documentation: Complete and current psychological

College Entrance Exams Required: Yes   **Untimed Accepted:** Yes

Course Entrance Requirements: Yes

Are Waivers Available: Yes

Additional Information:

High School GPA and SAT/ACT; ACT preferred; waivers are available under special conditions and with application to academic status review. In most cases, adaptations made by the professors within the college courses helps to make the content of the courses more understandable so that waivers would not be necessary once enrolled in Adrian.

Individualized high school coursework accepted: Yes

Essay Required: No

Special Application Required: No   **Submitted To:**

Number of Applications Submitted Each Year:

Number of Applications Accepted Each Year:

Number of Students Served: 25

Application Deadline for Special Admission: No

**Acceptance into Program means acceptance
into college:**

LEARNING DISABILITY SERVICES

Learning Resource Room:	Yes	**Curriculum Modification Available:** Yes	
Kurzweil Personal Reader:		**Tutorial Help:** Yes	**Peer Tutors:** Yes
LD Specialists:	1	**Max. Hours/Week for services:**	
Oral Exams:	Yes	No limit	
Services for LD Only:	No	**Added**	
Books on Tape:	Yes	**Cost:** None	
Calculator allowed in exam:	Yes	**Taping of books not on tape:** Yes	
Tape recording in class:	Yes	**Dictionary/computer/spellcheck during exam:** Yes	

How are professors notified of LD: By student and Director of the Program

GENERAL ADMISSIONS INFORMATION

Director of Admissions: Barbara Cunningham   **Telephone:** 517-265-5161

Entrance Requirements:

15 academic units required:4 yrs. English; 2-3 yrs. Math; 2 yrs. Social Science; 1 yr. History; 1 yr. Foreign Language; 3 electives.

Test Scores: **SAT:** 971   **ACT:** 19-23

G.P.A.: 2.6-3.4   **Class Rank:** upper 50%

Application Deadline: 8/15   **Achievement Tests:**

COLLEGE GRADUATION REQUIREMENTS

Foreign Language: Yes   **Waivers:** Try to adapt the courses and accommodations

Math: Yes   **Waivers:** Consider psychological effect as a determining factor

Minimum Course Load per Term: 12 hours

ADDITIONAL INFORMATION

Location: The school is located on 100 acres in a residential section of Michigan 35 miles northeast of Ann Arbor.

Enrollment Information:	**Undergraduate:** 1,207	**Women:** 60%	**Men:** 40%
	In-State Students: 70%		**Out of State:** 30%
Cost Information:	**In-State Tuition:** $8,096		**Out of State:** same
	Room & Board: $2,645		**Additional Costs:**
Housing Information:	**University Housing:** Yes		**Sorority:** 23%
	% Living on Campus: 76%		**Fraternity:** 31%

Athletics: NCAA Div. III

Support: CS   *Institution:* 2 yr. Public

LEARNING DISABILITY PROGRAM AND SERVICES

Comments:

Individuals who have been specifically identified by evaluation as Learning Disabled are given individualized, appropriate assistance through the Learning Disabilities Office. The mission of the faculty and staff of the College is to help the student achieve as much as possible. Support services include tutoring, notetakers, testing options, readers, and counseling. A special remedial course for credit will be offered in 1991-92.

LEARNING DISABILITY ADMISSIONS INFORMATION

Program Name:	Learning Disabilities Services	*Telephone*
Program Director:	Lowell Plaugher	517-686-9556
Contact Person:	same	

Admissions:

There is no special application procedure for admissions of learning disabled student. There is an open-door admission policy. All students who apply are admitted. It is recommended that students be able to read at least at the 7th grade level.

Interview: Yes   *Diagnostic Tests:* Yes

Documentation: W-J-R administered at Delta

College Entrance Exams Required: No   *Untimed Accepted:*

Course Entrance Requirements: No

Are Waivers Available:

Additional Information:

Learning disabled students who have not had assessment tests given to them within the last three years can be given the Woodcock-Johnson on campus. Results of this assessment are written up and given to each of the student's professors to help with accommodations necessary for success in College.

Individualized high school coursework accepted: Yes

Essay Required: No

Special Application Required: No   *Submitted To:*

Number of Applications Submitted Each Year:

Number of Applications Accepted Each Year: Unlimited

Number of Students Served: 60

Application Deadline for Special Admission: No

Acceptance into Program means acceptance

into college: Yes

LEARNING DISABILITY SERVICES

Learning Resource Room: Yes   **Curriculum Modification Available:** Yes

Kurzweil Personal Reader: No   **Tutorial Help:** Yes   **Peer Tutors:** Yes

LD Specialists: 1   **Max. Hours/Week for services:**

Oral Exams: Yes   Unlimited

Services for LD Only: Yes   **Added**

Books on Tape: Yes   **Cost:** None

Calculator allowed in exam: Y/N   **Taping of books not on tape:** Yes

Tape recording in class: Y/N   **Dictionary/computer/spellcheck during exam:** Y/N

How are professors notified of LD: By the student and the Program Director

GENERAL ADMISSIONS INFORMATION

Director of Admissions: Margaret Mosqueda   **Telephone:** 517-686-9092

Entrance Requirements:

High school transcript. Open admissions (At least a 7th grade reading level is recommended for success in the College courses).

Test Scores: **SAT:**   **ACT:**

G.P.A.:   **Class Rank:**

Application Deadline: Rolling   **Achievement Tests:**

COLLEGE GRADUATION REQUIREMENTS

Foreign Language: No   **Waivers:**

Math: Yes   **Waivers:** Yes, case-by-case

Minimum Course Load per Term: 6 credits part-time/ 12 credits full-time

ADDITIONAL INFORMATION

Location: The College is located on 640 acres in northern Michigan.

Enrollment Information: **Undergraduate:** 10,923   **Women:** 62%   **Men:** 38%

               In-State Students: 99%   **Out of State:** 1%

Cost Information: **In-State Tuition:** $1,200   **Out of State:** $2,640

               Room & Board: $2,822   **Additional Costs:**

Housing Information: **University Housing:** Yes   **Sorority:**

             % Living on Campus: 2%   **Fraternity:**

Athletics: NJCAA

Support: CS   **Institution:** 4 yr. Public

LEARNING DISABILITY PROGRAM AND SERVICES

Comments:

Michigan State University is serious in their commitment to helping students no-matter what the handicap. The Office of Programs for Handicapper Students provides many services for alternative learners, from personal consultation with a staff specialist to alternative test taking and peer group support. Eligibility for services requires documentation of a certifiable learning characteristic from a professional source, not more than three years prior to enrollment.

LEARNING DISABILITY ADMISSIONS INFORMATION

Program Name: Office of Programs for Handicapper Students   **Telephone**

Program Director: Valerie Nilson   517-353-9642

Contact Person:

Admissions:

Admission for a learning disabled student to the University is based on the same criteria as other students must meet. Learning disabled students are enrolled in the same programs and courses. MSU does not use a cut off for test scores or GPA's for admission; rather they look at the prospective student's entire transcript, including the academic strength of the high school, the type of courses students have enrolled in, the trend of the grades, and the GPA of the academic, college preparatory courses. A letter of recommendation for a student who may have borderline credentials could be included with the application.

Interview: **Diagnostic Tests:** Yes

Documentation: Any tests that can document the disability

College Entrance Exams Required: Yes   **Untimed Accepted:** Yes

Course Entrance Requirements: Yes

Are Waivers Available:

Additional Information:

Individualized high school coursework accepted:

Essay Required: No

Special Application Required: N/A   **Submitted To:**

Number of Applications Submitted Each Year: N/A

Number of Applications Accepted Each Year: N/A

Number of Students Served:

Application Deadline for Special Admission:

Acceptance into Program means acceptance into college:

LEARNING DISABILITY SERVICES

Learning Resource Room: Yes   **Curriculum Modification Available:**

Kurzweil Personal Reader: **Tutorial Help:** Yes   **Peer Tutors:** Yes

LD Specialists: 2   **Max. Hours/Week for services:**

Oral Exams: Yes   Individualized

Services for LD Only: No   **Added Cost:**

Books on Tape: Yes

Calculator allowed in exam: Yes   **Taping of books not on tape:** Yes

Tape recording in class: Yes   **Dictionary/computer/spellcheck during exam:** Yes

How are professors notified of LD:

GENERAL ADMISSIONS INFORMATION

Director of Admissions: William Turner   **Telephone:** 517-355-8332

Entrance Requirements:

4 yrs. English; 3 yrs. Math; 3 yrs. Social Science; 3 yrs. Science; 2 yrs. Foreign Language.

Test Scores: **SAT:** 900 (Minimum)   **ACT:** 20 (Minimum)

G.P.A.: 2.5+   **Class Rank:** Top 35%

Application Deadline: Rolling   **Achievement Tests:**

COLLEGE GRADUATION REQUIREMENTS

Foreign Language: Y/N   **Waivers:** Individual case-by-case

Math: Y/N   **Waivers:** Individual case-by-case

Minimum Course Load per Term:

ADDITIONAL INFORMATION

Location: Michigan State is located 1 hour from Ann Arbor and 1 1/2 hours from Detroit.

Enrollment Information: **Undergraduate:** 34,829   **Women:** 52%   **Men:** 48%

In-State Students: 88%   **Out of State:** 12%

Cost Information: **In-State Tuition:** $2,734   **Out of State:** $7,200

Room & Board: $2,960   **Additional Costs:** $318

Housing Information: **University Housing:** Yes   **Sorority:** 10%

% Living on Campus: 51%   **Fraternity:** 10%

Athletics: NCAA Div. I

Support: SP   **Institution:** 2 yr.   Private

LEARNING DISABILITY PROGRAM AND SERVICES

Comments:

The title of the Learning Disability Program is Talent Development. This is a curriculum designed for students needing personalized attention and additional education before entering a liberal arts or career program. An individualized program is designed for each student drawing on courses available in one of the three distinctive programs offered: Talent Development; Liberal Arts or Career Development.

LEARNING DISABILITY ADMISSIONS INFORMATION

Program Name: Talent Development   **Telephone**

Program Director: Edith G. Wiard   906-487-7326

Contact Person: same

Admissions:

General requirements for all students must be met including an evaluation within the last three years documenting the learning disability; an IEP; and a handwritten essay by the student describing the learning disability.

Interview: Yes   **Diagnostic Tests:** Yes

Documentation: to be selected

College Entrance Exams Required: **Untimed Accepted:**

Course Entrance Requirements: Yes

Are Waivers Available: Yes

Additional Information:

An applicant must have the academic ability and background for work on a college level. A "Pro-College Program" is available for students who do not have a 2.0 GPA or did not take college preparatory courses or who have reading, math or writing deficiencies.

Individualized high school coursework accepted: Yes

Essay Required: Yes

Special Application Required: No   **Submitted To:**

Number of Applications Submitted Each Year: NA

Number of Applications Accepted Each Year: 15

Number of Students Served: 30

Application Deadline for Special Admission: Late Junior year/ Early Senior year

Acceptance into Program means acceptance into college: No

159

LEARNING DISABILITY SERVICES

Learning Resource Room: Yes	**Curriculum Modification Available:** Yes	
Kurzweil Personal Reader: Yes	**Tutorial Help:** Yes	**Peer Tutors:** Yes
LD Specialists: 2	**Max. Hours/Week for services:**	
Oral Exams: Yes	Varies	
Services for LD Only: Yes	**Added Cost:**	
Books on Tape: Yes		
Calculator allowed in exam: Yes	**Taping of books not on tape:** Yes	
Tape recording in class: Yes	**Dictionary/computer/spellcheck during exam:** Yes	

How are professors notified of LD: By student and Program Director

GENERAL ADMISSIONS INFORMATION

Director of Admissions: Keith Reynolds   **Telephone:** 906-482-5300

Entrance Requirements:

An applicant must have the academic ability and background for work on a college level. Students should have a 'C' average or better with acceptable references and standardized grade equivalent scores for reading and math. Students are urged to take the ACT or SAT.

Test Scores: **SAT:**   **ACT:**

G.P.A.:   **Class Rank:**

Application Deadline: Rolling Admissions   **Achievement Tests:**

COLLEGE GRADUATION REQUIREMENTS

Foreign Language: No   **Waivers:**

Math: Yes   **Waivers:** No

Minimum Course Load per Term: 12 credits

ADDITIONAL INFORMATION

Location: The school founded by Finnish immigrants is located in a beautiful and rugged area of the Upper Peninsula of Michigan.

Enrollment Information: Undergraduate: 562   **Women:** 67%   **Men:** 33%

In-State Students: 96%   **Out of State:** 4%

Cost Information: In-State Tuition: $6,900   **Out of State:** same

Room & Board: $2,655   **Additional Costs:**

Housing Information: University Housing: Yes   **Sorority:** No

% Living on Campus: 70%   **Fraternity:** No

Athletics: Intramural sports

WESTERN MICHIGAN UNIVERSITY
Kalamazoo, Mi. 49008
616-387-2000

Support: CS   **Institution:** 4 yr. Public

LEARNING DISABILITY PROGRAM AND SERVICES

Comments:

The University's Special Services Program provides academic support for the learning disabled student in a number of different ways. There are content tutors who work individually with a student on a regular weekly basis. LD tutors meet individually with students on a regular basis to assist in planning time, arranging study materials for the student's best learning modality, gathering research material for papers. There are also writing tutors who help students improve their writing skills. This is a very thorough service.

LEARNING DISABILITY ADMISSIONS INFORMATION

Program Name: Special Services Program   **Telephone**

Program Director: Trudy Stauffer   616-387-4400

Contact Person: same

Admissions:

There is no special admission process. Learning disabled students must meet general admissions requirements and may request services once admitted.

Interview: No   **Diagnostic Tests:** No

Documentation:

College Entrance Exams Required: Yes   **Untimed Accepted:** Yes

Course Entrance Requirements: Yes

Are Waivers Available:

Additional Information:

College Prep core classes

Individualized high school coursework accepted: Yes

Essay Required: No

Special Application Required: No   **Submitted To:**

Number of Applications Submitted Each Year: N/A

Number of Applications Accepted Each Year: N/A

Number of Students Served: 90+

Application Deadline for Special Admission: No

Acceptance into Program means acceptance

into college: Yes

161

LEARNING DISABILITY SERVICES

Learning Resource Room:	Yes	Curriculum Modification Available:	No
Kurzweil Personal Reader:	Yes	Tutorial Help: Yes	Peer Tutors: Yes
LD Specialists:	1	Max. Hours/Week for services:	
Oral Exams:	Yes	N/A	
Services for LD Only:	No	Added	
Books on Tape:	Yes	Cost:	
Calculator allowed in exam:	Yes	Taping of books not on tape: Yes	
Tape recording in class:	Yes	Dictionary/computer/spellcheck during exam: Yes	

How are professors notified of LD: By the student and/or the Program Director

GENERAL ADMISSIONS INFORMATION

Director of Admissions: Stanley E. Henderson   **Telephone:** 616-387-2000

Entrance Requirements:

ACT; 83% of the students are in the top 50% of their class.

Test Scores:	SAT:	ACT:	21
G.P.A.:		Class Rank:	
Application Deadline: Rolling		Achievement Tests:	

COLLEGE GRADUATION REQUIREMENTS

Foreign Language: **Waivers:** Depends on major

Math: **Waivers:** Depends on major

Minimum Course Load per Term: Varies

ADDITIONAL INFORMATION

Location: The school is located on 451 acres in an urban area 140 miles west of Detroit.

Enrollment Information:	Undergraduate:	19,928	Women: 52%	Men:	48%
	In-State Students:	91%		Out of State:	9%
Cost Information:	In-State Tuition:	$2,130		Out of State:	$5,033
	Room & Board:	$3,160		Additional Costs:	$180
Housing Information:	University Housing:	Yes		Sorority:	7%
	% Living on Campus:	31%		Fraternity:	9%

Athletics: NCAA Div. I

Support: SP   **Institution:** 4 yr. Private

LEARNING DISABILITY PROGRAM AND SERVICES

Comments:

The C.L.A.S.S. program at Augsburg College is a result of the College's commitment to provide a high-quality liberal arts education for students with diverse backgrounds, experiences, and preparation. Augsburg has a commitment to recruit, retain and graduate learning disabled students who demonstrate the willingness and ability to participate in college-level learning.

LEARNING DISABILITY ADMISSIONS INFORMATION

Program Name: Center for Learning and Adaptive Student Services   **Telephone**

Program Director: John P. Weir   612-330-1053

Contact Person: same

Admissions:

Admission to the C.L.A.S.S. program is separate from admission to the College. The student must complete both an application to the College and one to the Program. Included with the application to the special program should be diagnostic tests. This data must include an intelligence test and one or more achievement tests which demonstrate reading, writing, spelling, and math skills. These tests must be less than 3 years old. An interview is also important.

Interview: Yes   **Diagnostic Tests:** Yes

Documentation: WAIS-R; W-J(I.Q. and achievement)

College Entrance Exams Required: Yes   **Untimed Accepted:** Yes

Course Entrance Requirements: Yes

Are Waivers Available: Yes

Additional Information:

College prep coursework is important. Foreign language can be waived. They are looking for ACT of 18.

Individualized high school coursework accepted: Yes

Essay Required: Yes

Special Application Required: Yes   **Submitted To:**

Number of Applications Submitted Each Year: 75

Number of Applications Accepted Each Year: 10-20

Number of Students Served: 95

Application Deadline for Special Admission: Early senior year

Acceptance into Program means acceptance

into college: Yes

LEARNING DISABILITY SERVICES

Learning Resource Room: Yes

Curriculum Modification Available: Yes

Kurzweil Personal Reader: No

Tutorial Help: Yes

Peer Tutors: Yes

LD Specialists: 3

Max. Hours/Week for services:

Oral Exams: Yes

As needed

Services for LD Only: Yes

Added Cost: None

Books on Tape: Yes

Calculator allowed in exam: Yes

Taping of books not on tape: Yes

Tape recording in class: Yes

Dictionary/computer/spellcheck during exam: Yes

How are professors notified of LD: By the student and the Program Director

GENERAL ADMISSIONS INFORMATION

Director of Admissions: Carol A. Stack

Telephone: 612-330-1001

Entrance Requirements:

High school academic courses with 4 years of English; 3 yrs. Math; 3 yrs. Science: 2 yrs. Foreign Language; 3 yrs. Social Studies; 3 yrs. History.

Test Scores: **SAT:** 930

ACT: 20

G.P.A.: 2.5

Class Rank: Upper 50%

Application Deadline: 9/1

Achievement Tests:

COLLEGE GRADUATION REQUIREMENTS

Foreign Language: Yes **Waivers:** Yes

Math: Yes **Waivers:** No

Minimum Course Load per Term: 3 courses to be considered full-time

ADDITIONAL INFORMATION

Location: The College is located on 25 acres near downtown Minneapolis.

Enrollment Information:	**Undergraduate:**	2,638	**Women:** 57%	**Men:**	43%
	In-State Students:	78%		**Out of State:**	22%
Cost Information:	**In-State Tuition:**	$8,835		**Out of State:**	same
	Room & Board:	$3,328		**Additional Costs:**	$95
Housing Information:	**University Housing:**	Yes		**Sorority:**	No
	% Living on Campus:	86%		**Fraternity:**	No

Athletics: NCAA Div. III

Support: CS   **Institution:** 4 yr. Private

LEARNING DISABILITY PROGRAM AND SERVICES

Comments:

The O'Neill Learning Center houses the special learning programs for students with learning disabilities. The Learning Center and Counseling Center staff offer inservices to faculty to help them accommodate LD students in their classroom. Students are strongly encouraged to take a reduced course load their first semester and are able to have course substitutions when necessary. The only special credit course offered is called "Strategies for Academic Success" which covers the writing, reading and study skills necessary for college.

LEARNING DISABILITY ADMISSIONS INFORMATION

Program Name: O'Neill Learning Centers / Learning Programs   **Telephone**

Program Director: Elaine McDonough   612-690-6563

Contact Person:

Admissions:

There is no special admission procedure for LD students, although they tend to give special consideration if a student discloses this information.

Interview: **Diagnostic Tests:**

Documentation:

College Entrance Exams Required: **Untimed Accepted:**

Course Entrance Requirements: Yes

Are Waivers Available:

Additional Information:

During orientation students take a math placement test, a quantitative skills test, and a writing sample. The math placement test is used for placement into the appropriate math course; the other tests are used to determine whether the student needs special help. Sometimes a reading test is given to be used for diagnostic purposes.

Individualized high school coursework accepted:

Essay Required:

Special Application Required: **Submitted To:**

Number of Applications Submitted Each Year:

Number of Applications Accepted Each Year:

Number of Students Served:

Application Deadline for Special Admission:

Acceptance into Program means acceptance into college:

LEARNING DISABILITY SERVICES

Learning Resource Room: Yes **Curriculum Modification Available:** Yes

Kurzweil Personal Reader: **Tutorial Help:** Yes **Peer Tutors:**

LD Specialists: Yes **Max. Hours/Week for services:**

Oral Exams: Yes No limit

Services for LD Only: Yes **Added Cost:**

Books on Tape: Yes

Calculator allowed in exam: Yes **Taping of books not on tape:** Yes

Tape recording in class: Yes **Dictionary/computer/spellcheck during exam:** Yes

How are professors notified of LD: By the Program Director

GENERAL ADMISSIONS INFORMATION

Director of Admissions: Jennifer Hantho **Telephone:** 612-690-6505

Entrance Requirements:

4 yrs. English; 3 yrs. Math; 2 yrs. Foreign Language; 2 yrs. Science; 2 yrs. Social Studies.

Test Scores: **SAT:** 980 **ACT:** 23

G.P.A.: 2.0 **Class Rank:**

Application Deadline: 8/15 **Achievement Tests:**

COLLEGE GRADUATION REQUIREMENTS

Foreign Language: **Waivers:**

Math: **Waivers:**

Minimum Course Load per Term:

ADDITIONAL INFORMATION

Location: The College is located on 110 acres in an urban area in central St. Paul.

Enrollment Information: **Undergraduate:** 2,419 **Women:** 100% **Men:**

In-State Students: 88% **Out of State:** 12%

Cost Information: **In-State Tuition:** $8,544 **Out of State:** same

Room & Board: $3,140 **Additional Costs:** $156

Housing Information: **University Housing:** Yes **Sorority:** No

% Living on Campus: 27% **Fraternity:**

Athletics: NCAA Div. III

Support: CS   **Institution:** 4 yr. Private

LEARNING DISABILITY PROGRAM AND SERVICES

Comments:

The college provides as many individualized services as needed by the student. Through assistance in the learning resource center students may get help with reading, writing, life sciences, math and natural sciences. Students may drop-in for tutoring.

LEARNING DISABILITY ADMISSIONS INFORMATION

Program Name:	Learning Center	**Telephone**
Program Director:	Charles Norman	612-696-6121

Contact Person:

Admissions:

There is no special application nor admission requirements. Although the College accepts untimed SAT or ACT scores, those scores must be comparable to timed ranges of students who are in the top 50% of their class.

Interview: Yes   **Diagnostic Tests:** No

Documentation:

College Entrance Exams Required: Yes   **Untimed Accepted:** Yes

Course Entrance Requirements: No

Are Waivers Available:

Additional Information:

Individualized high school coursework accepted: Depends

Essay Required: Yes

Special Application Required: No   **Submitted To:**

Number of Applications Submitted Each Year:

Number of Applications Accepted Each Year:

Number of Students Served: 1/3 of campus uses services

Application Deadline for Special Admission: No

Acceptance into Program means acceptance into college: N/A

LEARNING DISABILITY SERVICES

Learning Resource Room: Yes   **Curriculum Modification Available:** No

Kurzweil Personal Reader: Yes   **Tutorial Help:** Yes   **Peer Tutors:** Yes

LD Specialists: 3   **Max. Hours/Week for services:**

Oral Exams: Yes   N/A

Services for LD Only: No   **Added Cost:** None

Books on Tape: Yes

Calculator allowed in exam: Y/N   **Taping of books not on tape:** Yes

Tape recording in class: Yes   **Dictionary/computer/spellcheck during exam:** No

How are professors notified of LD: Usually by the student or Deans Office

GENERAL ADMISSIONS INFORMATION

Director of Admissions: William M. Shain   **Telephone:** 612-696-6357

Entrance Requirements:

16 credits including: 4 yrs. English; 3 yrs. Math; 3 yrs. Science; 3 yrs. Foreign Language; 3 yrs. Social Studies/History.

Test Scores: **SAT:** 1225 (mid 50%)   **ACT:** 27-30

G.P.A.:   **Class Rank:**

Application Deadline: 2/1   **Achievement Tests:** 3 recommended

COLLEGE GRADUATION REQUIREMENTS

Foreign Language: No   **Waivers:**

Math: **Waivers:**

Minimum Course Load per Term: 3 hrs. to be full-time

ADDITIONAL INFORMATION

Location: The 55 acre campus is located 4 miles from downtown St. Paul.

Enrollment Information: **Undergraduate:** 1,855   **Women:** 53%   **Men:** 47%

     In-State Students: 31%   **Out of State:** 69%

Cost Information: **In-State Tuition:** $12,300   **Out of State:** same

     Room & Board: $3,700   **Additional Costs:** $86

Housing Information: **University Housing:** Yes   **Sorority:** No

     % Living on Campus: 70%   **Fraternity:** No

Athletics: NCAA Div. III

WINONA STATE UNIVERSITY
Winona, Mn. 55987
507-457-5100

Support: S   **Institution:** 4 yr. Public

LEARNING DISABILITY PROGRAM AND SERVICES

Comments:

SSP is available to all students and offers intensive study skills and time management tutoring as well as personal academic advising. There is a program called GOALS for incoming Freshman. Freshman are eligible for GOALS based on admission status and scores on English and Math Placement tests. Students involved in GOALS are closely monitored. The Program includes academic advising, individualized tutoring, planning study time, counseling and monitored classes which are regular college classes with special attention given to individualized learning styles.

LEARNING DISABILITY ADMISSIONS INFORMATION

Program Name: Student Support Services /Special Service (SSP/SS)   **Telephone**

Program Director: Karen Owen   507-457-5344

Contact Person:

Admissions:

Admissions is the same for all students.

Interview: **Diagnostic Tests:** Yes

Documentation: To receive accommodations send psycho-educational information

College Entrance Exams Required: Yes   **Untimed Accepted:** Yes

Course Entrance Requirements: Yes

Are Waivers Available: No

Additional Information:

Regular admission: top 50% or ACT of 21 or SAT of 900 University Studies admission: top 40-49% and an ACT of 19-21 or SAT of 700-899 Deferred admission: top 40-49% or an ACT of 19-20 or SAT of 700-899 (if accepted, students are limited to taking 12 hours the first semester).

Individualized high school coursework accepted:

Essay Required: Yes, in certain departments/colleges

Special Application Required: **Submitted To:**

Number of Applications Submitted Each Year: N/A

Number of Applications Accepted Each Year: N/A

Number of Students Served: 50

Application Deadline for Special Admission: No

Acceptance into Program means acceptance

into college: No, there is an appeal procedure available.

LEARNING DISABILITY SERVICES

Learning Resource Room: Yes	**Curriculum Modification Available:** No		
Kurzweil Personal Reader: No	**Tutorial Help:** Yes	**Peer Tutors:** Yes	
LD Specialists: No	**Max. Hours/Week for services:**		
Oral Exams: No	1 hr. per/subject per/week		
Services for LD Only: No	**Added**		
Books on Tape: No	**Cost:** None		
Calculator allowed in exam: No	**Taping of books not on tape:** No		
Tape recording in class:	**Dictionary/computer/spellcheck during exam:** No		

How are professors notified of LD:

GENERAL ADMISSIONS INFORMATION

Director of Admissions: Dr. J.A. Mootz   **Telephone:** 507-457-5100

Entrance Requirements:

4 yrs. English (1 may be speech); 3 yrs. Math; 3 yrs. Social Studies; 3 yrs. Science; 2 yrs. Art; 2 yrs. Foreign Language; 1/2 yr. Computer Science. Automatic admission for top 50% of high school graduating class or an ACT of 21 or SAT of 900. University Studies for in-state requires top 2/3 and out-of-state, top 3/5, both need ACT of 19 or SAT of 700. Provisonal admissions 700 SAT, 19 ACT.

Test Scores: **SAT:** 900   **ACT:** 21

G.P.A.:   **Class Rank:** 50%

Application Deadline: Rolling   **Achievement Tests:**

COLLEGE GRADUATION REQUIREMENTS

Foreign Language: **Waivers:**

Math: **Waivers:**

Minimum Course Load per Term:

ADDITIONAL INFORMATION

Location: The University is located on 40 acres in a small city 110 miles southeast of Minneapolis and St. Paul and 2 1/2 hours west of Madison, Wisconsin.

Enrollment Information: **Undergraduate:** 7,000	**Women:** 60%	**Men:** 40%	
In-State Students: 65%		**Out of State:** 35%	
Cost Information: **In-State Tuition:** $1,750		**Out of State:** $3,000	
Room & Board: $2,450		**Additional Costs:** $250	
Housing Information: **University Housing:** Yes		**Sorority:** 4%	
% Living on Campus: 35%		**Fraternity:** 4%	

Athletics: NCAA Div. II

UNIVERSITY OF SOUTHERN MISSISSIPPI
Hattiesburg, Ms. 39406
601-266-5555

Support: S   *Institution:* 4 yr. Public

LEARNING DISABILITY PROGRAM AND SERVICES

Comments:

The Office of Disabled Student Services helps the student locate tutors, notetakers and other ancillary aids for their classwork. The Office works with Vocational Rehabilitation in order to pay for these services. The Office staff works with students on a one-to-one basis in order to determine how they learn best. There are remedial programs in math, writing and reading.

LEARNING DISABILITY ADMISSIONS INFORMATION

Program Name: Disabled Student Services   *Telephone*

Program Director: Warren Dunn   601-266-5007

Contact Person:

Admissions:

There is no special admissions procedure for students with learning disabilities. An interview is not required, but preferred. The University offers a pre-admission summer program.

Interview: No   *Diagnostic Tests:* No

Documentation:

College Entrance Exams Required: Yes   *Untimed Accepted:*

Course Entrance Requirements: Yes

Are Waivers Available:

Additional Information:

Individualized high school coursework accepted:

Essay Required: No

Special Application Required: *Submitted To:*

Number of Applications Submitted Each Year:

Number of Applications Accepted Each Year:

Number of Students Served:

Application Deadline for Special Admission: No

Acceptance into Program means acceptance into college:

LEARNING DISABILITY SERVICES

Learning Resource Room: Yes   **Curriculum Modification Available:**

Kurzweil Personal Reader: **Tutorial Help:** Yes   **Peer Tutors:** Yes

LD Specialists: **Max. Hours/Week for services:**

Oral Exams: Varies

Services for LD Only: No   **Added**

Books on Tape: Yes   **Cost:** Varies

Calculator allowed in exam: **Taping of books not on tape:** Yes

Tape recording in class: Yes   **Dictionary/computer/spellcheck during exam:**

How are professors notified of LD: By the student

GENERAL ADMISSIONS INFORMATION

Director of Admissions: Wayne Pyle   **Telephone:** 601-266-5555

Entrance Requirements:

High school transcript; 14 credits including: 4 yrs. English; 3 yrs. Math; 3 yrs. Science; 2 1/2 yrs. Social Studies; 1 elective. Up to 5%may be admitted with up to 3 deficiencies. ACT is required for in-state student. Others may use the SAT.

Test Scores: **SAT:** 720 (minimum)   **ACT:** 18 (minimum)

G.P.A.: 2.0   **Class Rank:**

Application Deadline: Rolling   **Achievement Tests:**

COLLEGE GRADUATION REQUIREMENTS

Foreign Language: **Waivers:**

Math: **Waivers:**

Minimum Course Load per Term:

ADDITIONAL INFORMATION

Location: The University is located on 840 acres in a small city 90 miles southeast of Jackson.

Enrollment Information: **Undergraduate:** 9,777   **Women:** 57%   **Men:** 43%

                     In-State Students: 87%   **Out of State:** 13%

Cost Information: **In-State Tuition:** $1,830   **Out of State:** $3,000

                     Room & Board: $2,111   **Additional Costs:** $10

Housing Information: University Housing: Yes   **Sorority:** 13%

             % Living on Campus: 40%   **Fraternity:** 16%

Athletics: NCAA Div. I

SOUTHWEST MISSOURI STATE UNIVERSITY
Springfield, Mo. 65804
417-836-5000

Support: S　　　*Institution:* 4 yr. Public

LEARNING DISABILITY PROGRAM AND SERVICES

Comments:

There are numerous support services and programs offered to all students. A battery of tests are required in order to be able to evaluate the student's potential at SMSU. These tests include: WAIS-R or Stanford-Binet; K-TEA or Woodcock-Johnson; PPVT-R; EOWPVT; TLC; Detroit Tests of Learning Aptitude; BVMG; Malcomesius; PSLT; PIAT. Services include individual tutoring, individual skills remediation in spelling, math, written language, reading, study and learning strategies, and test accommodations.

LEARNING DISABILITY ADMISSIONS INFORMATION

Program Name:　Learning Diagnostic Clinic　　　　　　　　　　*Telephone*

Program Director:　Sylvia T. Buse, Ph.D　　　　　　　　　　417-836-4787

Contact Person:　same

Admissions:

A student must be admitted to the University to be eligible for the program. There is a special application to be completed as well as a required evaluation fee of $250 for in-state students and $350 for out-of-state students. Eligibility for admissions is based on a sliding scale determined by ACT composite scores and class rank.

Interview: Yes　　　　　　　　　　　　　*Diagnostic Tests:* Yes

Documentation: Intelligence and Achievement tests

College Entrance Exams Required: Yes　　　　*Untimed Accepted:* Yes

Course Entrance Requirements:　Yes

Are Waivers Available:　　　No

Additional Information:

SMSU administers Math and English placement tests to all incoming students in order to determine enrollment in appropriate courses.

Individualized high school coursework accepted: No

Essay Required: No

Special Application Required: Yes　　*Submitted To:*

Number of Applications Submitted Each Year:

Number of Applications Accepted Each Year:

Number of Students Served:　　　　　60

Application Deadline for Special Admission:　Early Senior year

Acceptance into Program means acceptance into college: No

LEARNING DISABILITY SERVICES

Learning Resource Room: Yes

Curriculum Modification Available: No

Kurzweil Personal Reader: Yes

Tutorial Help: Yes   **Peer Tutors:** Yes

LD Specialists:

Max. Hours/Week for services:

Oral Exams: Yes

3 hours weekly

Services for LD Only: No

Added

Books on Tape: Yes

Cost: $100 tutoring fee

Calculator allowed in exam: No

Taping of books not on tape: Yes

Tape recording in class: Yes

Dictionary/computer/spellcheck during exam: Yes

How are professors notified of LD: By student and Program Director

GENERAL ADMISSIONS INFORMATION

Director of Admissions: Mr. Donald Simpson   **Telephone:** 417-836-5517

Entrance Requirements:

4 yrs. English; 3 yrs. Math; 2 yrs. Foreign Language; 2 yrs. Science; 2 yrs. Social Studies. A sliding scale of GPA and test scores is used as an evaluation tool for admission.

Test Scores: **SAT:**

ACT: 17 in-state / 20 out-of-state

G.P.A.:

Class Rank: 50%

Application Deadline: 8/1

Achievement Tests:

COLLEGE GRADUATION REQUIREMENTS

Foreign Language: No   **Waivers:** No

Math: Yes   **Waivers:** No

Minimum Course Load per Term: 12 semester hours

ADDITIONAL INFORMATION

Location: 200 acre rural campus located 170 miles from Kansas City and 120 miles from St. Louis.

Enrollment Information: **Undergraduate:** 16,612   **Women:** 55%   **Men:** 45%

In-State Students: 95%   **Out of State:** 5%

Cost Information: **In-State Tuition:** $1,622   **Out of State:** $3,218

Room & Board: $2,280   **Additional Costs:**

Housing Information: University Housing: Yes   **Sorority:** 8%

% Living on Campus: 20%   **Fraternity:** 10%

Athletics: NCAA Div. I

Support: S   **Institution:** 4 yr. Private

LEARNING DISABILITY PROGRAM AND SERVICES

Comments:

Although the University does not have a specific learning disability program, a wide range of services and accommodations are provided to help remove barriers posed by the students' disability. Students are encouraged to be their own advocates and have the major responsibility for securing services and accommodations. The most common accommodation is extended test time and relocation of testing site.

LEARNING DISABILITY ADMISSIONS INFORMATION

Program Name: Disabled Student Services   **Telephone**

Program Director: Donald A. Strano, Ed.D   314-889-5040

Contact Person: same

Admissions:

Although there is no special admissions process for students with learning disabilities, the student can choose to voluntarily identify themselves as learning disabled in the admissions process. That information can be considered as part of the applications process for example, to explain lower grades in some subjects.

Interview: Recommended   **Diagnostic Tests:** Yes

Documentation: psycho-educational evaluation

College Entrance Exams Required: Yes   **Untimed Accepted:** Yes

Course Entrance Requirements: Yes

Are Waivers Available:

Additional Information:

Individualized high school coursework accepted:

Essay Required: Yes

Special Application Required: **Submitted To:**

Number of Applications Submitted Each Year:

Number of Applications Accepted Each Year:

Number of Students Served:

Application Deadline for Special Admission:

Acceptance into Program means acceptance into college:

175

LEARNING DISABILITY SERVICES

Learning Resource Room: Yes   **Curriculum Modification Available:** Yes

Kurzweil Personal Reader: Yes   **Tutorial Help:** Yes   **Peer Tutors:** Yes

LD Specialists: No   **Max. Hours/Week for services:**

Oral Exams: Yes   Varies

Services for LD Only: No   **Added**

Books on Tape: Yes   **Cost:**

Calculator allowed in exam: Yes   **Taping of books not on tape:** Yes

Tape recording in class: Yes   **Dictionary/computer/spellcheck during exam:** Yes

How are professors notified of LD: By the student and the Program Director

GENERAL ADMISSIONS INFORMATION

Director of Admissions: Dr. Charles S. Nolan   **Telephone:** 314-889-6000

Entrance Requirements:

4 yrs. English; 4 yrs. Math; 3 yrs. Science (including 2 yrs. Lab.); 2 yrs. Foreign Language; 2 yrs. History; 1 yr. Social Studies.

Test Scores: **SAT:** 1250   **ACT:** 29

G.P.A.:   **Class Rank:**

Application Deadline: 2/1   **Achievement Tests:** Recommended

COLLEGE GRADUATION REQUIREMENTS

Foreign Language: No   **Waivers:**

Math: Yes   **Waivers:** Depends on major

Minimum Course Load per Term: Varies by students needs

ADDITIONAL INFORMATION

Location: The Washington University campus is located 7 miles west of St. Louis on 169 acres.

Enrollment Information: Undergraduate: 5,024   **Women:** 49%   **Men:** 51%

     In-State Students: 13%   **Out of State:** 87%

Cost Information: **In-State Tuition:** $13,600   **Out of State:** same

     Room & Board: $4,610   **Additional Costs:** $135

Housing Information: University Housing: Yes   **Sorority:** 29%

     % Living on Campus: 90%   **Fraternity:** 31%

Athletics: NCAA Div. III

Support: SP   **Institution:** 4 yr. Private

LEARNING DISABILITY PROGRAM AND SERVICES

Comments:

Westminster offers a student with a learning disability a supportive environment, small classes and professors who are readily accessible. The learning resources available to students in the Learning Disabilities Program include audio tapes of textbooks for those with reading difficulties, self-instructional materials, and special classes in study skills. Close supervision of the curriculum is essential in the freshman year. This enables the College to monitor the student's progress and to respond quickly to any difficulties that may arise.

LEARNING DISABILITY ADMISSIONS INFORMATION

Program Name: Learning Disabilities Program   **Telephone**

Program Director: Henry F. Ottinger   314-642-3361

Contact Person:

Admissions:

There is a special application and special admissions procedure. LD students submit a completed regular College application form and a separate application form for the LD Program. All students who plan to enroll in the program must visit the campus for interviews and testing prior to admission. Students must also submit the results of the following: eye exam; hearing exam; WAIS-R or WISC-R; achievement tests; SAT or ACT administered on an untimed basis; and 2 copies of the high school transcript.

Interview: Yes   **Diagnostic Tests:** Yes

Documentation: WRAT; WAIS-R or WISC-R

College Entrance Exams Required: Yes   **Untimed Accepted:** Yes

Course Entrance Requirements: Yes

Are Waivers Available:

Additional Information:

The learning disabilities staff offers intensive instruction in reading, writing, and study skills. Much of this instruction is conducted on a one-to-one basis and is directed to the individual student's specific language related problems.

Individualized high school coursework accepted: Depends

Essay Required: Yes

Special Application Required: Yes   **Submitted To:**

Number of Applications Submitted Each Year: 60

Number of Applications Accepted Each Year: 15

Number of Students Served: 35+

Application Deadline for Special Admission: Early Fall of Senior year

Acceptance into Program means acceptance into college: Yes

LEARNING DISABILITY SERVICES

Learning Resource Room: Yes   **Curriculum Modification Available:** No

Kurzweil Personal Reader: **Tutorial Help:** Yes   **Peer Tutors:** Yes

LD Specialists: 2   **Max. Hours/Week for services:**

Oral Exams: Yes   Varies

Services for LD Only: Yes

Books on Tape: Yes   **Added Cost:** $2,200 Fresh. year.,$1,100 upper classes

Calculator allowed in exam: Yes   **Taping of books not on tape:** Yes

Tape recording in class: Yes   **Dictionary/computer/spellcheck during exam:** Y/N

How are professors notified of LD: By the Program Director

GENERAL ADMISSIONS INFORMATION

Director of Admissions: Gary Forney   **Telephone:** 314-642-3361

Entrance Requirements:

4 yrs. English; 3 yrs. Math; 2 yrs. Social Studies; 2 yrs. Science. An essay is required.

Test Scores: **SAT:** 1020 (mid 50%)   **ACT:** 24 (average)

G.P.A.: 3.30 (average)   **Class Rank:** Top 30%

Application Deadline: Rolling   **Achievement Tests:**

COLLEGE GRADUATION REQUIREMENTS

Foreign Language: No   **Waivers:**

Math: Yes   **Waivers:** No

Minimum Course Load per Term: No

ADDITIONAL INFORMATION

Location: The 250 acre College campus is located in a small town, 20 miles east of Columbia, Missouri.

Enrollment Information: **Undergraduate:** 725   **Women:** 34%   **Men:** 66%

In-State Students: 51%   **Out of State:** 49%

Cost Information: **In-State Tuition:** $7,520   **Out of State:** same

Room & Board: $3,280   **Additional Costs:**

Housing Information: **University Housing:** Yes   **Sorority:** 65%

% Living on Campus: 97%   **Fraternity:** 85%

Athletics: NAIA

NOTRE DAME COLLEGE
Manchester, N.H. 03104
603-669-4298

Support: CS   **Institution:** 4 yr. Private

LEARNING DISABILITY PROGRAM AND SERVICES

Comments:

The SNAP program at Notre Dame College is an accommodation, not a remediation program. All SNAP students are enrolled in regular classes. Specific accommodations and assistance are available, such as reduced course loads, note-takers, oral exams, advance lecture notes, extended exam times, faculty support and meetings. The SNAP Program is designed for the high school student who has the potential to earn a college degree but needs support to compensate for a learning disability.

LEARNING DISABILITY ADMISSIONS INFORMATION

Program Name:	Special Needs Assistance Program (SNAP)	**Telephone**
Program Director:	Dr. Felicia Wilczenjki	603-669-4298
Contact Person:	Joseph P. Wagner	same

Admissions:

The student must submit a regular application for admission and be accepted under regular admissions criteria. Applicants desiring admission to the SNAP Program must submit to the admissions office documentation of a diagnosis of the learning disability by a certified professional within a school system, or state certified agency or office. Upon receipt of a completed application, the applicant will meet with the SNAP Director who will make a recommendation to the admissions committee.

Interview: Yes   **Diagnostic Tests:** Yes

Documentation:

College Entrance Exams Required: Yes   **Untimed Accepted:** Yes

Course Entrance Requirements: Yes

Are Waivers Available: Yes

Additional Information:

The admissions office is flexible in the SAT range required for entrance. LD documentation must include: identification and description of the specific type of learning disability; description of the effects of the learning disability including strengths, weaknesses; learning style, and recent Individualized Educational Plan showing placement, goals, objectives and types of assistance received.

Individualized high school coursework accepted: Yes

Essay Required: No

Special Application Required: No   **Submitted To:**

Number of Applications Submitted Each Year: 20-25

Number of Applications Accepted Each Year: 15-18

Number of Students Served: 18

Application Deadline for Special Admission: No

Acceptance into Program means acceptance into college:

179

LEARNING DISABILITY SERVICES

Learning Resource Room: Yes

Kurzweil Personal Reader:

LD Specialists: 1

Oral Exams: Yes

Services for LD Only: No

Books on Tape: Yes

Calculator allowed in exam: Yes

Tape recording in class: Yes

How are professors notified of LD: By the student

Curriculum Modification Available: Yes

Tutorial Help: Yes   **Peer Tutors:** Yes

Max. Hours/Week for services:

   N/A

Added Cost:

Taping of books not on tape: Yes

Dictionary/computer/spellcheck during exam: Yes

GENERAL ADMISSIONS INFORMATION

Director of Admissions: Joseph P. Wagner   **Telephone:** 603-669-4298

Entrance Requirements:

16 academic units including: 4 yrs. English; 2 yrs. Foreign Language; 2 yrs. History; 2 yrs. Math; 2 yrs. Science; 2 yrs. Social Studies.

Test Scores: **SAT:** 880   **ACT:**

G.P.A.: 2.0 (minimum)   **Class Rank:**

Application Deadline: Rolling   **Achievement Tests:**

COLLEGE GRADUATION REQUIREMENTS

Foreign Language: Yes   **Waivers:** Yes

Math: Yes   **Waivers:** Yes

Minimum Course Load per Term:

ADDITIONAL INFORMATION

Location: Notre Dame College is located on 7 acres in a suburban area north of Manchester.

Enrollment Information: **Undergraduate:** 638   **Women:** 82%   **Men:** 18%

In-State Students: 50%   **Out of State:** 50%

Cost Information: **In-State Tuition:** $7,400   **Out of State:** same

Room & Board: $4,290   **Additional Costs:** $160

Housing Information: **University Housing:** Yes   **Sorority:** No

% Living on Campus: 40%   **Fraternity:** No

Athletics: Intercollegiate sports

Support: S   **Institution:** 4 yr. Private

LEARNING DISABILITY PROGRAM AND SERVICES

Comments:

There is no formal program or services. However, the University does provide tutoring for all students. There is no tutoring center and all arrangements for peer-tutoring help are made by the student on an as-need basis. The Associate Dean of Students will facilitate at a first semester meeting with the student and the professor.

LEARNING DISABILITY ADMISSIONS INFORMATION

Program Name: Program for Students with Learning Disabilities   **Telephone**

Program Director: Johanna Glazwski   201-408-3323

Contact Person: same

Admissions:

There is no special application nor special admissions procedure. All students must meet the same criteria. Most students are in the top one-fifth of their class, but there is flexibility and no test cut-off.

Interview: Recommended   **Diagnostic Tests:** Yes

Documentation: Any official testing

College Entrance Exams Required: Yes   **Untimed Accepted:** Yes

Course Entrance Requirements: Yes

Are Waivers Available: Yes

Additional Information:

Handled on an individual basis. Generally they look for an SAT of 800+ or an ACT of 18+, achievement tests are recommended but not required.

Individualized high school coursework accepted: Yes, if appropriate

Essay Required: Yes

Special Application Required: No   **Submitted To:**

Number of Applications Submitted Each Year: 5-10

Number of Applications Accepted Each Year: Varies

Number of Students Served: 36

Application Deadline for Special Admission:

Acceptance into Program means acceptance into college: Yes

LEARNING DISABILITY SERVICES

Learning Resource Room: No   **Curriculum Modification Available:** No

Kurzweil Personal Reader: No   **Tutorial Help:** Yes   **Peer Tutors:** Yes

LD Specialists: No   **Max. Hours/Week for services:**

Oral Exams: Yes   Unlimited-individual basis

Services for LD Only: No   **Added**

Books on Tape: No   **Cost:** None

Calculator allowed in exam: Yes   **Taping of books not on tape:** No

Tape recording in class: Yes   **Dictionary/computer/spellcheck during exam:** Yes

How are professors notified of LD: Each situation is handled on an individual basis

GENERAL ADMISSIONS INFORMATION

Director of Admissions: William T. Conley   **Telephone:** 201-408-3252

Entrance Requirements:

4 yrs. English; 2 yrs. Science; 2 yrs. Foreign Language; 3 yrs. Math; 2 yrs. Social Studies; Electives; 3 Achievement tests required.

Test Scores: **SAT:** 1140   **ACT:** 27

G.P.A.:   **Class Rank:**

Application Deadline: 2/15   **Achievement Tests:** 3

COLLEGE GRADUATION REQUIREMENTS

Foreign Language: Yes   **Waivers:** Yes, based on diagnostic testing recommendations

Math: Yes   **Waivers:** Yes, same

Minimum Course Load per Term: 12 credits minimal

ADDITIONAL INFORMATION

Location: The University is located on 186 acres in a suburban area 30 miles west of New York City.

Enrollment Information: **Undergraduate:** 1,475   **Women:** 57%   **Men:** 43%

       In-State Students: 51%   **Out of State:** 49%

Cost Information: **In-State Tuition:** $14,600   **Out of State:** same

       Room & Board: $4,376   **Additional Costs:** $264

Housing Information: **University Housing:** Yes   **Sorority:** No

       % Living on Campus: 95%   **Fraternity:** No

Athletics: NCAA Div. III

FAIRLEIGH DICKINSON UNIVERSITY
Teaneck, N.J. 07666
201-692-2559

Support: CS   *Institution:* 4 yr. Private

LEARNING DISABILITY PROGRAM AND SERVICES

Comments:

Fairleigh Dickinson University's program is a comprehensive support program staffed by professionals. The LD program has services at both the Teaneck and the Madison campus. The LD program and the special services are free of charge. Assistance to students is intensive and the program is fully integrated into the coursework. Freshman receive tutorial support for every subject. Students are in touch with faculty on a regular basis. The program encourages involvement in the community, particularly service-type activities relevant to the LD students.

LEARNING DISABILITY ADMISSIONS INFORMATION

Program Name:	Learning Disabled College Student Program	*Telephone*
Program Director:	Dr. Mary Farrell	201-692-2089

Contact Person:

Admissions:

Decisions on admissions for LD students are made jointly by the University and the LD Program Director. Criteria include: Mainstreamed classes in high school, "C" average, 2 teacher recommendations (one from a 11th or 12th grade English teacher). Recommendations should describe motivation level. Students who have taken all special education classes to accommodate LD are usually not admissable to the University. Lower level mainstream classes are acceptable from high schools which offer different levels in the same subjects. ACT/SAT are required but usually not a factor in the admission decision.

Interview: Recommended   *Diagnostic Tests:* Yes

Documentation:

College Entrance Exams Required: Yes   *Untimed Accepted:* Yes

Course Entrance Requirements: Yes

Are Waivers Available:

Additional Information:

The SAT/ACT tests do not carry much weight in the admissions process. High school grades are viewed as the best predictors for success. Students with a 2.0 GPA and an 800 SAT can be accepted. If below a 2.0 GPA and 800 SAT the student may be referred to Edward Williams College, a 2 year college located on the Teaneck campus. Edward Williams also offers full services for the learning disabled student.

Individualized high school coursework accepted: Yes

Essay Required:

Special Application Required: Yes   *Submitted To:* Dr. Mary Farrell

Number of Applications Submitted Each Year: 200+

Number of Applications Accepted Each Year: 25-40 Teaneck/15-20 Madison

Number of Students Served:

Application Deadline for Special Admission: Apply early with the special application form

Acceptance into Program means acceptance

into college:

LEARNING DISABILITY SERVICES

Learning Resource Room: Yes   **Curriculum Modification Available:**

Kurzweil Personal Reader: **Tutorial Help:** Yes   **Peer Tutors:** Yes

LD Specialists: Yes   **Max. Hours/Week for services:**

Oral Exams: Yes   5-6 hours

Services for LD Only: Yes   **Added**
Books on Tape: Yes   **Cost:** None

Calculator allowed in exam: Yes   **Taping of books not on tape:** Yes

Tape recording in class: Yes   **Dictionary/computer/spellcheck during exam:** Yes

How are professors notified of LD: By student and Program Director

GENERAL ADMISSIONS INFORMATION

Director of Admissions: Rita Bennett   **Telephone:** 201-593-8900

Entrance Requirements:

4 yrs. English; 2 yrs. Math; 2 yrs. Social Studies; 1 yr. Science; 4 electives. Additional Math and Science courses are required for Science, Engineering and Health Science majors.

Test Scores: **SAT:** 948   **ACT:**

G.P.A.: 2.0 (minimum)   **Class Rank:** Top 50%

Application Deadline: **Achievement Tests:** No

COLLEGE GRADUATION REQUIREMENTS

Foreign Language: **Waivers:**

Math: **Waivers:**

Minimum Course Load per Term:

ADDITIONAL INFORMATION

Location: The Teaneck campus is located on the banks of the Hackensack River. It is within walking distance of Edward Williams Junior College.

Enrollment Information: **Undergraduate:** 2,550   **Women:** 54%   **Men:** 46%

                      In-State Students: 81%   **Out of State:** 19%

Cost Information: **In-State Tuition:** $8,482   **Out of State:** same

                      Room & Board: $5,091   **Additional Costs:** $380

Housing Information: **University Housing:** Yes   **Sorority:** Yes

                      % Living on Campus: 60%   **Fraternity:** Yes

Athletics: NCAA Div. III

GEORGIAN COURT COLLEGE
Lakewood, N.J. 08701

201-367-4440

Support: CS   **Institution:** 4 yr. Private

LEARNING DISABILITY PROGRAM AND SERVICES

Comments:

The Learning Center (TLC) program is an assistance program designed to provide an environment for students with mild to moderate learning disabilities who desire a college education. The program is not one of remediation, but an individualized support program to assist candidates in becoming successful college students. Emphasis is placed on developing self-help strategies and study techniques. Services include study techniques, strategies for planning and writing research papers, and techniques in memorization and concentration.

LEARNING DISABILITY ADMISSIONS INFORMATION

Program Name:	The Leaning Center (TLC)	**Telephone**
Program Director:	Dr. Marilyn Gonyo	201-364-2200
Contact Person:	same	

Admissions:

Applicants must meet the following: 16 academics units that include 4 years of English; 2 years of Foreign Language; 2 years of Math; 1 year of Lab Science; 1 year History; electives. The class rank and transcript giving evidence of the ability to succeed in college and the SAT must be sent to the College as well.

Interview: Yes   **Diagnostic Tests:** No

Documentation:

College Entrance Exams Required: Yes   **Untimed Accepted:** Yes

Course Entrance Requirements: No

Are Waivers Available:

Additional Information:

College graduation requirements are not waived for TLC students. Therefore, program completion may take longer than 4 years.

Individualized high school coursework accepted: No

Essay Required: No

Special Application Required: **Submitted To:**

Number of Applications Submitted Each Year: 10

Number of Applications Accepted Each Year: 5

Number of Students Served: 9

Application Deadline for Special Admission: No

Acceptance into Program means acceptance

into college: No, there is no appeal process

LEARNING DISABILITY SERVICES

Learning Resource Room: Yes

Curriculum Modification Available: No

Kurzweil Personal Reader:

Tutorial Help: Yes   **Peer Tutors:** Yes

LD Specialists: 1

Max. Hours/Week for services:

Oral Exams: Yes

    15 hours

Services for LD Only: Yes

Added Cost: $1,750.

Books on Tape: Yes

Calculator allowed in exam: Yes

Taping of books not on tape: Yes

Tape recording in class: Yes

Dictionary/computer/spellcheck during exam: Yes

How are professors notified of LD: By the student and the Program Director

GENERAL ADMISSIONS INFORMATION

Director of Admissions: John P. Burke   **Telephone:** 201-367-4440

Entrance Requirements:

4 yrs. English, 2 yrs. Foreign Language; 2 yrs. Math; 1 yr. History; 1 yr. Lab Science; 6 electives. Students can be admitted with course deficiencies. SAT is required.

Test Scores: **SAT:** 950 (recommended)   **ACT:** 19 (minimum)

G.P.A.: 2.75   **Class Rank:** Upper 50%

Application Deadline: 8/1   **Achievement Tests:**

COLLEGE GRADUATION REQUIREMENTS

Foreign Language: Yes   **Waivers:** No

Math: **Waivers:**

Minimum Course Load per Term: Reduced course load is highly recommended.

ADDITIONAL INFORMATION

Location: Georgian Court College is a small private institution, centrally located in New Jersey.

Enrollment Information: **Undergraduate:** 1,584   **Women:** 90%   **Men:** 10%

    In-State Students: 98%   **Out of State:** 2%

Cost Information: **In-State Tuition:** $6,255   **Out of State:** same

    Room & Board: $3,550   **Additional Costs:** $225

Housing Information: **University Housing:** Yes   **Sorority:** No

    % Living on Campus: 30%   **Fraternity:**

Athletics: NCAA Div. I

Support: SP   **Institution:** 4 yr. Private

LEARNING DISABILITY PROGRAM AND SERVICES

Comments:

Adelphi's Program for Learning Disabled College Students has achieved recognition and success because it provides each student with the support of an inter - disciplinary team of experienced and concerned professionals. Although each student meets individually with an Educator and a Counselor, these professionals work as a team. There is a 5 week Summer Program that is mandatory before freshman year. Tutoring occurs 2 times a week and students must attend these sessions.

LEARNING DISABILITY ADMISSIONS INFORMATION

Program Name: Program for Learning Disabled College Students   **Telephone**

Program Director: Sandra Holzinger   516-663-1006

Contact Person: same

Admissions:

The Admissions Committee first studies all submitted materials for a total picture of the applicant's strengths and disabilities. An interview for applicants who show an ability to succeed academically is then arranged. To be considered, an applicant must send a high school transcript, school records identifying a learning disability, untimed SAT scores, and a handwritten essay answering the question; "What special considerations should be taken into account when evaluating your application?" The Director of the Program is actively involved in the admissions decision. Motivation is the key.

Interview: Yes   **Diagnostic Tests:** Yes

Documentation: WAIS-R within 1 year of application; reading test scores are important

College Entrance Exams Required: Yes   **Untimed Accepted:** Yes

Course Entrance Requirements: Yes

Are Waivers Available:

Additional Information:

They look for college preparatory work with at least average grades. Attitude and motivation is assessed through the comments by teachers, attendance in school, services received, and an interview. 150 students may be admitted through the General Studies Program. This is a 1 year program and students take 13 credits and work with a counselor and a tutor.

Individualized high school coursework accepted: Possibly

Essay Required: Yes

Special Application Required: **Submitted To:**

Number of Applications Submitted Each Year: 250

Number of Applications Accepted Each Year: 40-60

Number of Students Served: 145

Application Deadline for Special Admission: Fall of Senior year

Acceptance into Program means acceptance
into college: Yes

LEARNING DISABILITY SERVICES

Learning Resource Room: Yes   **Curriculum Modification Available:** No

Kurzweil Personal Reader: **Tutorial Help:** Yes   **Peer Tutors:** No

LD Specialists: 17   **Max. Hours/Week for services:**

Oral Exams: Yes   As needed

Services for LD Only: Yes   **Added**

Books on Tape: Yes   **Cost:** $1,500 per/semester

Calculator allowed in exam: Yes   **Taping of books not on tape:** Yes

Tape recording in class: Yes   **Dictionary/computer/spellcheck during exam:** Yes

How are professors notified of LD: By student and Program Director

GENERAL ADMISSIONS INFORMATION

Director of Admissions: Laura Richter   **Telephone:** 516-663-1100

Entrance Requirements:

16 academic credits including: 4 yrs. English; 3 yrs. Math; 3 yrs. Science; 2/3 yrs. Foreign Language; 4 yrs. History/Social Studies.

Test Scores: **SAT:** 950   **ACT:** 24

G.P.A.: 3.0   **Class Rank:** upper 33%

Application Deadline: Rolling   **Achievement Tests:** No

COLLEGE GRADUATION REQUIREMENTS

Foreign Language: No   **Waivers:**

Math: No   **Waivers:**

Minimum Course Load per Term: 12-13 credits for first Fall semester.

ADDITIONAL INFORMATION

Location: The University is located on a 75 acres campus, 20 miles from New York City.

Enrollment Information: **Undergraduate:** 4,824   **Women:** 66%   **Men:** 34%

In-State Students: 87%   **Out of State:** 13%

Cost Information: **In-State Tuition:** $8,600   **Out of State:** same

Room & Board: $4,450   **Additional Costs:** $650

Housing Information: **University Housing:** Yes   **Sorority:** 6%

% Living on Campus: 46%   **Fraternity:** 7%

Athletics: NCAA Div. I and II

Support: CS   *Institution:* 4 yr. Private/Public

LEARNING DISABILITY PROGRAM AND SERVICES

Comments:

Cornell University does not have a program but the services offered are comprehensive. Cornell believes that learning disabled students can and do succeed. These students can meet course requirements and performance standards when allowed to use learning strategies that compensate for their specific deficits. Professors and the LD specialists are in direct communication. The faculty are provided with information about working with the learning disabled student through presenting materials in a clear, repetitive, and flexible teaching style.

LEARNING DISABILITY ADMISSIONS INFORMATION

Program Name:	Disability Services	*Telephone*
Program Director:	Joan Fisher	607-255-3976

Contact Person:

Admissions:

Each college within the University makes their own admission decision as well as sets their own criteria for admission and graduation. Learning disabled students who submit testing documentation will have this information reviewed by Disability Services and there is communication between this office and the various admission committees. Occasionally students with lower test scores or deficiencies in high school curriculum may be admitted. The students must provide sufficient information to explain deficiency and highlight strengths, motivation and ability to succeed.

Interview: No   *Diagnostic Tests:* Yes

Documentation: WAIS-R; complete psychological as well as summary

College Entrance Exams Required: Yes   *Untimed Accepted:* Yes

Course Entrance Requirements: Yes

Are Waivers Available: Yes

Additional Information:

With documentation a student may not have to take a Foreign Language for entrance or a specific higher Math class if not needed for a major. Students are encouraged to use one of the essay questions on the application to describe their learning disability. They can also use the section that encourages descriptions of anything else the admission office should know about the student.

Individualized high school coursework accepted: Not recommended

Essay Required: Yes

Special Application Required: No   *Submitted To:*

Number of Applications Submitted Each Year:

Number of Applications Accepted Each Year:

Number of Students Served: 70

Application Deadline for Special Admission:

Acceptance into Program means acceptance

into college: No

LEARNING DISABILITY SERVICES

Learning Resource Room: Yes   **Curriculum Modification Available:** Yes

Kurzweil Personal Reader: Yes   **Tutorial Help:** Yes   **Peer Tutors:** Yes

LD Specialists: 2   **Max. Hours/Week for services:**

Oral Exams: Yes   Unlimited

Services for LD Only: No   **Added**

Books on Tape: Yes   **Cost:** None

Calculator allowed in exam: Yes   **Taping of books not on tape:** Yes

Tape recording in class: Yes   **Dictionary/computer/spellcheck during exam:** Yes

How are professors notified of LD: By the student and Program Director

GENERAL ADMISSIONS INFORMATION

Director of Admissions: Nancy Meislahn   **Telephone:** 607-255-4099

Entrance Requirements:

Depends on College, but basically: 4 yrs. English; 3-4 yrs. Math; 3-4 yrs. Science; 2-3 yrs. Foreign Language. The Colleges of Agriculture, Human Ecology, and Industrial and Labor Relations are public, state programs. Architecture, Arts & Sciences, Engineering, and Hotel Management are private programs. Each has their own admissions criteria.

Test Scores: SAT: **ACT:** 27-30

G.P.A.: 3.6 average   **Class Rank:** Top 10%

Application Deadline: 1/1   **Achievement Tests:** Varies w/College

COLLEGE GRADUATION REQUIREMENTS

Foreign Language: Y/N   **Waivers:** Yes

Math: Y/N   **Waivers:** Yes

Minimum Course Load per Term: Individual case-by-case

ADDITIONAL INFORMATION

Location: Cornell is located 45 minutes from Syracuse, on the southern end of Lake Cayuga in the Finger Lakes Region.

Enrollment Information: Undergraduate: 12,715   **Women:** 43%   **Men:** 57%

In-State Students: 44%   **Out of State:** 56%

Cost Information: In-State Tuition: $14,000   **Out of State:** same

Room & Board: $4,630   **Additional Costs:** $40

Housing Information: University Housing: Yes   **Sorority:** 32%

% Living on Campus: 43%   **Fraternity:** 36%

Athletics: NCAA Div. I

CULINARY INSTITUTE OF AMERICA
Hyde Park, N.Y. 12538
914-452-9600

Support: CS **Institution:** 2 yr. Private

LEARNING DISABILITY PROGRAM AND SERVICES

Comments:

The curriculum consists of 3 week blocks. Therefore, there are 16 entry dates per year and students may apply all year round. Classes move along very quickly. The Office of Special Services strives to assist students in compensating for weaknesses due to learning disabilities. Students with severe math difficulties may not be successful. Special Service Counselors meet periodically with LD students to discuss strategies for each individual curriculum. No one fails at the Institute because students can repeat courses when necessary.

LEARNING DISABILITY ADMISSIONS INFORMATION

Program Name:	Office of Special Services	**Telephone**
Program Director:	Frederick J. Gaines	914-452-9600
Contact Person:	Rebecca Way	same

Admissions:

There is no special admissions. Students apply through admissions, then provide documentation to Special Services after acceptance. However, Special Service Staff will be available to prospective students for pre-admission counseling. An interview may be required by the Admissions office. Pre-admissions meeting with Special Services Staff is also recommended. A complete diagnostic evaluation is required once a student has been accepted. A special Basic Math test is offered to students who may not meet the admissions requirements.

Interview: Yes **Diagnostic Tests:** Yes

Documentation: WAIS-R

College Entrance Exams Required: No **Untimed Accepted:** Yes

Course Entrance Requirements: No

Are Waivers Available:

Additional Information:

Students whose math background are weak are asked to take a school-designed math test at the Institute. In addition, an essay should be handwritten, though many learning disabled students hand in a typed copy as well.

Individualized high school coursework accepted: Yes

Essay Required: Yes

Special Application Required: **Submitted To:**

Number of Applications Submitted Each Year:

Number of Applications Accepted Each Year:

Number of Students Served: 50

Application Deadline for Special Admission: May apply year round

Acceptance into Program means acceptance into college: N/A

LEARNING DISABILITY SERVICES

Learning Resource Room: Yes   **Curriculum Modification Available:** Yes

Kurzweil Personal Reader: No   **Tutorial Help:** Yes   **Peer Tutors:** Yes

LD Specialists: **Max. Hours/Week for services:**

Oral Exams: Yes   N/A

Services for LD Only: No   **Added**

Books on Tape: Yes   **Cost:** $5 per/hr. for peer tutoring

Calculator allowed in exam: Yes   **Taping of books not on tape:** Yes

Tape recording in class: Yes   **Dictionary/computer/spellcheck during exam:** Yes

How are professors notified of LD: By student

GENERAL ADMISSIONS INFORMATION

Director of Admissions: Dr. Janis Wertz   **Telephone:** 914-452-9600

Entrance Requirements:

3 yrs. Math; Science; Foreign Language.

Test Scores: **SAT:**   **ACT:**

G.P.A.:   **Class Rank:**

Application Deadline: rolling   **Achievement Tests:**

COLLEGE GRADUATION REQUIREMENTS

Foreign Language: Yes   **Waivers:** No

Math: Yes   **Waivers:** No

Minimum Course Load per Term: No one set course of study

ADDITIONAL INFORMATION

Location: Hyde Park is located on the eastern bank of the Hudson River, 75 miles north of New York City.

Enrollment Information: **Undergraduate:** 1,833   **Women:** 21%   **Men:** 79%

In-State Students: 25%   **Out of State:** 75%

Cost Information: **In-State Tuition:** $8,490   **Out of State:** same

Room & Board: $2,450   **Additional Costs:**

Housing Information: **University Housing:** Yes   **Sorority:** No

% Living on Campus: 80%   **Fraternity:** No

Athletics: Intercollegiate

HOFSTRA UNIVERSITY
Hempstead, N.Y. 11550
516-463-6700

Support: CS   *Institution:* 4 yr. Private

LEARNING DISABILITY PROGRAM AND SERVICES

Comments:

The PALS program seeks candidates who have been diagnosed as learning disabled and show above-average intellectual ability and emotional stability. The program concentrates on identifying qualified applicants for entrance to the University, and on enhancing the skills that will help students achieve academic success. This program is part of the Division of Special Studies. Normally, candidates will be accepted into PALS for a period of one academic year. In the first semester students enroll in courses offered through DSS, and in the second semester in regular classes.

LEARNING DISABILITY ADMISSIONS INFORMATION

Program Name: Program for Academic Learning Skills (PALS)   *Telephone*

Program Director: I.H. Gotz, Ph.D   516-463-5841

Contact Person: same

Admissions:

The Division of Special Studies, which administers PALS, has always conducted a highly individualized admissions process. A student with learning disabilities who may be in the bottom 30% of their high school class and have an 800-850 SAT may be eligible for the PALS program. The interview is very important and the student may be asked to write an essay at this time. Only 18 applicants are accepted each year to the program which is a part of the Division of Special Studies. The Director has total authority for selecting students for admission to this program.

Interview: Yes   *Diagnostic Tests:* Yes

Documentation: WAIS-R; IEP

College Entrance Exams Required: No   *Untimed Accepted:* Yes

Course Entrance Requirements: No

Are Waivers Available: Yes

Additional Information:

There are waivers available, however the University prefers to substitute courses where possible. Once admitted the students meet with a specialist 2 times a week and information regarding progress is sent home.

Individualized high school coursework accepted: Yes

Essay Required: No, but preferred

Special Application Required: Submitted To:

Number of Applications Submitted Each Year: 350

Number of Applications Accepted Each Year: 18

Number of Students Served: 70-100

Application Deadline for Special Admission: When satisfied with SAT score

Acceptance into Program means acceptance

into college: Yes, there is also an appeal process available

LEARNING DISABILITY SERVICES

Learning Resource Room:	Yes	**Curriculum Modification Available:** No	
Kurzweil Personal Reader:	Yes	**Tutorial Help:** Yes	**Peer Tutors:** Yes
LD Specialists:	6	**Max. Hours/Week for services:**	
Oral Exams:	Yes	No limit	
Services for LD Only:	Yes	**Added**	
Books on Tape:	Yes	**Cost:** $3,200 for Fresh. year only	
Calculator allowed in exam:	Yes	**Taping of books not on tape:** Yes	
Tape recording in class:	Yes	**Dictionary/computer/spellcheck during exam:** Yes	

How are professors notified of LD: By student and Program Director

GENERAL ADMISSIONS INFORMATION

Director of Admissions: Joan Isaac   **Telephone:** 516-463-6700

Entrance Requirements:

4 yrs. English; 3 yrs. History and Social Studies; 2 yrs. Math; 2 yrs. Foreign Language; 1 yr. Science.

Test Scores: **SAT:** 1026   **ACT:** 23

G.P.A.:   **Class Rank:** Top 20-35%

Application Deadline: 2/15   **Achievement Tests:**

COLLEGE GRADUATION REQUIREMENTS

Foreign Language: Yes   **Waivers:** Depends on program of study

Math: Yes   **Waivers:** Substitute classes

Minimum Course Load per Term: Yes

ADDITIONAL INFORMATION

Location: Hempstead is a residential community in Long Island, just outside New York City.

Enrollment Information:	**Undergraduate:**	8,449	**Women:** 51%	**Men:** 49%
	In-State Students:	71%	**Out of State:** 29%	
Cost Information:	**In-State Tuition:**	$8,430	**Out of State:** same	
	Room & Board:	$4,586	**Additional Costs:**	
Housing Information:	**University Housing:**	Yes	**Sorority:** 12%	
	% Living on Campus:	57%	**Fraternity:** 14%	

Athletics: NCAA Div. I

Support: SP   **Institution:** 4 yr. Private

LEARNING DISABILITY PROGRAM AND SERVICES

Comments:

Iona welcomes learning disabled students into the College Assistance Program(CAP) offered on the Yonkers campus through the Elizabeth Seton School of Associate Degree Studies. CAP is designed to provide instruction on an individual basis and will provide any compensatory service or strategy deemed necessary for success. At every step of the way, from improving basic skills to deciding which courses to take, extensive support and guidance is available from professional staff in the CAP office and from highly qualified counselors.

LEARNING DISABILITY ADMISSIONS INFORMATION

Program Name: College Assistance Program (CAP)   **Telephone**

Program Director: Elsa Brady DeVits   914-969-4000

Contact Person: same

Admissions:

The Program is designed for students with a learning disability who have been mainstreamed in their high school academic courses. They should be average or above-average in intellectual ability, socially mature, emotionally stable and motivated. Each applicant must submit an official high school transcript, complete psychological evaluation, IEP, two letters of recommendation (including one from the student's high school resource teacher or special educator) and a completed admissions application.

Interview: Yes   **Diagnostic Tests:** Yes

Documentation: WAIS-R

College Entrance Exams Required: No   **Untimed Accepted:**

Course Entrance Requirements: Yes

Are Waivers Available: Yes

Additional Information:

Complete sequence in English, History, Science, Math (unless waiver exists), Foreign Language (unless waiver exists).

Individualized high school coursework accepted:

Essay Required: Yes

Special Application Required: **Submitted To:**

Number of Applications Submitted Each Year: 60

Number of Applications Accepted Each Year: 20

Number of Students Served: 40

Application Deadline for Special Admission: As early as November (no later than March)

Acceptance into Program means acceptance into college: No

LEARNING DISABILITY SERVICES

Learning Resource Room: Yes

Kurzweil Personal Reader:

LD Specialists: 6

Oral Exams: Yes

Services for LD Only: Yes

Books on Tape: Yes

Calculator allowed in exam: Yes

Tape recording in class: Yes

How are professors notified of LD: By student and Program Director

Curriculum Modification Available: No

Tutorial Help: Yes   **Peer Tutors:** Yes

Max. Hours/Week for services:

    2 hours are required, more as needed

**Added
Cost:** $1,800 per/yr. $660 summer session

Taping of books not on tape: Yes

Dictionary/computer/spellcheck during exam: Yes

GENERAL ADMISSIONS INFORMATION

Director of Admissions: Barbara C. Sweeney   **Telephone:** 814-633-2502

Entrance Requirements:

16 credits including: 4 yrs. English; 3 yrs. Math; 2 yrs. Foreign Language; 1 yr. History; 1 yr. Science; 1 yr. Social Studies.

Test Scores: **SAT:** 880 (mid 50%)   **ACT:**

G.P.A.: 2.5   **Class Rank:** Upper 50%

Application Deadline: **Achievement Tests:** 3

COLLEGE GRADUATION REQUIREMENTS

Foreign Language: No   **Waivers:**

Math: Yes   **Waivers:** Yes

Minimum Course Load per Term: 12 credits

ADDITIONAL INFORMATION

Location: The College is on 58 acres in Westchester County, a suburb of New York City.

Enrollment Information: **Undergraduate:** 3,419   **Women:** 50%   **Men:** 50%

    In-State Students: 92%   **Out of State:** 8%

Cost Information: **In-State Tuition:** $7,300   **Out of State:** same

    Room & Board: $5,050   **Additional Costs:**

Housing Information: **University Housing:** Yes   **Sorority:** 25%

    % Living on Campus: 3%   **Fraternity:** 20%

Athletics: NCAA Div. I and III

LONG ISLAND UNIVERSITY-C.W. POST COLLEGE
Brookville, N.Y. 11548
516-299-2999

Support: SP   **Institution:** 4 yr. Private

LEARNING DISABILITY PROGRAM AND SERVICES

Comments:

Motivation is the key to acceptance and success at Long Island University-C.W. Post where 90% of the admitted students are successful and are active participants in the Program. Students receive excellent assistance and advise. Peers are a big part of this Program. Students learn time management, reading, study and test-taking strategies, organizational skills and note-taking techniques.

LEARNING DISABILITY ADMISSIONS INFORMATION

Program Name: Academic Resource Center   **Telephone**

Program Director: Dr. Marian T. Power   516-299-2937

Contact Person: Carol Rundlett

Admissions:

The student must be admitted to the University first and then apply to the Resource Center. If the GPA is low or tests are low the student may be admitted through the Directed Studies Program. During the interview students must convince the Admissions Counselor that they have changed and are now willing to work hard at College. Motivation is very important. Students who apply for this special admissions usually have a B-/C+ average. Students with an SAT below 700 or a Verbal below 350 are required to have either a B- average, or 400 verbal or 400 math SAT, or rank in the top 60% of the class.

Interview: Yes,important   **Diagnostic Tests:** Yes

Documentation: WAIS-R

College Entrance Exams Required: Yes   **Untimed Accepted:** Yes

Course Entrance Requirements: Yes

Are Waivers Available: Yes

Additional Information:

If the student has a deficiency, the person responsible for testing must write a letter stating what specifically in the test data indicates the student should be granted a waiver. There is also a 12 credit program with limited matriculation for the student with a 2.0 GPA and less than 900 SAT or 19 ACT.

Individualized high school coursework accepted: Yes

Essay Required: Yes, also the student will write a short essay during interview

Special Application Required: No   **Submitted To:**

Number of Applications Submitted Each Year: 150

Number of Applications Accepted Each Year: 20-30

Number of Students Served: 80

Application Deadline for Special Admission: As soon as possible Senior year

Acceptance into Program means acceptance into college: No, there is an appeal process

197

LEARNING DISABILITY SERVICES

Learning Resource Room: Yes   **Curriculum Modification Available:** No

Kurzweil Personal Reader: No   **Tutorial Help:** Yes   **Peer Tutors:** Yes

LD Specialists: 13   **Max. Hours/Week for services:**

Oral Exams: Yes   As needed

Services for LD Only: Yes   **Added**

Books on Tape: Yes   **Cost:** $3,000 per/year

Calculator allowed in exam: Y/N   **Taping of books not on tape:** Yes

Tape recording in class: Yes   **Dictionary/computer/spellcheck during exam:** Y/N

How are professors notified of LD: By student and Program Director

GENERAL ADMISSIONS INFORMATION

Director of Admissions: Christine Natali   **Telephone:** 516-299-2999

Entrance Requirements:

4 yrs. English; 2 yrs. Math; 3 yrs. History; 2 yrs. Foreign Language; 1 yr. Science.

Test Scores: **SAT:** 900 (minimum)   **ACT:** 19 average

G.P.A.: 2.0   **Class Rank:** upper 60%

Application Deadline: Rolling   **Achievement Tests:**

COLLEGE GRADUATION REQUIREMENTS

Foreign Language: Yes   **Waivers:** Yes, but cannot get waivers for both Language and Math

Math: Yes   **Waivers:** Yes, but cannot get waivers for both

Minimum Course Load per Term: 12 credits

ADDITIONAL INFORMATION

Location: The College is located in Long Island about 30 minutes from New York City.

Enrollment Information: **Undergraduate:** 5,322   **Women:** 56%   **Men:** 44%

In-State Students: 93%   **Out of State:** 7%

Cost Information: **In-State Tuition:** $8,520   **Out of State:** same

Room & Board: $3,920   **Additional Costs:** $470

Housing Information: **University Housing:** Yes   **Sorority:** Yes

% Living on Campus: 50%   **Fraternity:** Yes

Athletics: NCAA Div. II

MARIST COLLEGE
Poughkeppsie,N.Y. 12601-1387
914-471-3240

Support: CS   **Institution:** 4 yr. Private

LEARNING DISABILITY PROGRAM AND SERVICES

Comments:

Believing that bright, motivated students with specific learning disabilities can achieve a higher education, Marist has a Special Services program. An Interdisciplinary team of professionals helps students identify and use their strengths through an individualized program. An extensive internship provides many students with off-campus training to complement their major field studies while experiencing the world of work. Campus life provides students an opportunity to participate in a range of activities.

LEARNING DISABILITY ADMISSIONS INFORMATION

Program Name: Special Services

Program Director: Dr. Diane Perreira

Contact Person: Linda Scorza

Telephone

914-471-3274

Admissions:

Students applying to Marist should submit an Application for Admission and all required materials to the Office of Admissions. Students wishing to participate in the support program must also complete a Supplementary Application for Admission which should be forwarded directly to the Office of Special Services. The student must also submit an unedited essay describing the impact of the learning disability on academic achievement. Once enrolled the students are assigned bi-weekly meetings with a learning disabilities specialist.

Interview: Yes   **Diagnostic Tests:** Yes

Documentation: WAIS-R (plus all other available information)

College Entrance Exams Required: No   **Untimed Accepted:** Yes

Course Entrance Requirements: Yes

Are Waivers Available:

Additional Information:

College preparatory courses should be taken in high school. With some evidence of high school math. There should also be: 4 yrs. English; 3 yrs. Science; 3 yrs. Social Science.

Individualized high school coursework accepted:

Essay Required: Yes

Special Application Required: Yes   **Submitted To:**

Number of Applications Submitted Each Year: 200

Number of Applications Accepted Each Year: 25

Number of Students Served: 40

Application Deadline for Special Admission: Early Fall of Senior year

Acceptance into Program means acceptance into college: Yes, there is an appeal process

LEARNING DISABILITY SERVICES

Learning Resource Room: Yes   **Curriculum Modification Available:** No

Kurzweil Personal Reader: Yes   **Tutorial Help:** Yes   **Peer Tutors:** Yes

LD Specialists: 3   **Max. Hours/Week for services:**

Oral Exams: Y/N   4-6 hours per/week for as long as necessary

Services for LD Only: No   **Added**

Books on Tape: Yes   **Cost:** $1,500/varies in upper classes

Calculator allowed in exam: Yes   **Taping of books not on tape:** Yes

Tape recording in class: Yes   **Dictionary/computer/spellcheck during exam:** Yes

How are professors notified of LD: By the student

GENERAL ADMISSIONS INFORMATION

Director of Admissions: Harry W. Wood   **Telephone:** 914-471-3240

Entrance Requirements:

4 yrs. English; 3 yrs. Math; 4 yrs. Science; 4 yrs. Social Studies; 1 year Art; 1 yr. Music.

Test Scores: **SAT:** 900 (minimum)   **ACT:** 22

G.P.A.:   **Class Rank:** Upper 40%

Application Deadline: 3/1   **Achievement Tests:**

COLLEGE GRADUATION REQUIREMENTS

Foreign Language: No   **Waivers:** Yes

Math: Yes   **Waivers:** Documentation is necessary/difficult to get waiver

Minimum Course Load per Term: 12 credits required for resident student

ADDITIONAL INFORMATION

Location: The College is located on 120 acres in upstate New York, 75 miles from New York City.

Enrollment Information: **Undergraduate:** 3,963   **Women:** 52%   **Men:** 48%

   In-State Students: 75%   **Out of State:** 25%

Cost Information: **In-State Tuition:** $8,344   **Out of State:** same

   Room & Board: $4,582   **Additional Costs:** $144

Housing Information: **University Housing:** Yes   **Sorority:** No

   % Living on Campus: 70%   **Fraternity:** 10%

Athletics: NCAA Div. I

PAUL SMITHS COLLEGE
Paul Smiths, N.Y. 12970
518-327-6227

Support: CS   **Institution:** 2 yr. Private

LEARNING DISABILITY PROGRAM AND SERVICES

Comments:

The College offers students accommodations on a need-by-need basis. Non-credit courses are offered in Reading and Study Skills, Science and Math. The programs that are offered by the College are career specific and offer a hands-on approach experience. Associate degrees are offered in Forest Technology, Forest Recreation,Survey, Urban Tree Management, Ecology, Environment and Chef training. Students individual needs are met and all necessary accommodations are provided.

LEARNING DISABILITY ADMISSIONS INFORMATION

Program Name: Academic Support Services   **Telephone**

Program Director: Carol McKillip   518-327-6425

Contact Person:

Admissions:

Upon request of the learning disabled student,parent or high school personnel a learning specialist will interview perspective students and review their admissions file.

Interview: Yes   **Diagnostic Tests:** Yes

Documentation:

College Entrance Exams Required: Yes   **Untimed Accepted:**

Course Entrance Requirements: No

Are Waivers Available:

Additional Information:

Placement exams are given. If the student contacts the learning specialist a collective decision is made regarding which courses are required.

Individualized high school coursework accepted: Yes

Essay Required: Recommended

Special Application Required: No   **Submitted To:**

Number of Applications Submitted Each Year: 97

Number of Applications Accepted Each Year: 84

Number of Students Served: 71

Application Deadline for Special Admission: By Fall of senior year

Acceptance into Program means acceptance into college:

LEARNING DISABILITY SERVICES

Learning Resource Room: Yes   **Curriculum Modification Available:** Yes

Kurzweil Personal Reader: Yes   **Tutorial Help:** Yes   **Peer Tutors:** Yes

LD Specialists: 2   **Max. Hours/Week for services:**

Oral Exams: Yes   Unlimited

Services for LD Only: No   **Added**

Books on Tape: Yes   **Cost:** None

Calculator allowed in exam: Yes   **Taping of books not on tape:** Yes

Tape recording in class: Yes   **Dictionary/computer/spellcheck during exam:** Yes

How are professors notified of LD: By the student and the Program Director

GENERAL ADMISSIONS INFORMATION

Director of Admissions: Joel R. Wincowski   **Telephone:** 518-327-6227

Entrance Requirements:

High school transcript including: 3 yrs. Math; 3 yrs. Science. An essay and recommendation are helpful.

Test Scores: **SAT:** 950 (mid 50%)   **ACT:** 21-28

G.P.A.:   **Class Rank:**

Application Deadline: Rolling   **Achievement Tests:**

COLLEGE GRADUATION REQUIREMENTS

Foreign Language: **Waivers:**

Math: Yes   **Waivers:** Depends on major

Minimum Course Load per Term: 12 hours for financial aid purposes

ADDITIONAL INFORMATION

Location: Paul Smiths College is located in a rural setting on 15,000 acres in Paul Smiths.

Enrollment Information: **Undergraduate:** 784   **Women:** 35%   **Men:** 65%

In-State Students: 70%   **Out of State:** 30%

Cost Information: **In-State Tuition:** $6,470   **Out of State:** same

Room & Board: $3,794   **Additional Costs:** $200

Housing Information: **University Housing:** Yes   **Sorority:**

% Living on Campus: 90%   **Fraternity:**

Athletics: NJCAA

ROCHESTER INSTITUTE OF TECHNOLOGY
Rochester, N.Y. 14623-0887

716-475-6631

Support: CS   **Institution:** 4 yr. Private

LEARNING DISABILITY PROGRAM AND SERVICES

Comments:

The Special Services program at R.I.T. is available to all students. A full complement of programs and services is provided to assist the student in strengthening areas of academic concern and/or weakness, to assist in understanding and refining the learning process and to assist in using academic resources more effectively. It is mandatory for learning disabled students to participate in a six week series of workshops designed to enhance performance at R.I.T.

LEARNING DISABILITY ADMISSIONS INFORMATION

Program Name: Special Services   **Telephone**

Program Director: Marie Giardino   716-475-2832

Contact Person: Jacqueline Lynch Czamanshe

Admissions:

There is no special admissions process for students with learning disabilities. However, learning disabled students should include diagnostic information with their application. Although an interview is not required, it is recommended. The required scores on the SAT or ACT will depend on the College the student is applying to within R.I.T. It is also helpful to identify compensatory strategies used in high school and what will be needed for success in college.

Interview: No   **Diagnostic Tests:** Yes

Documentation: WAIS; Achievement tests

College Entrance Exams Required: Yes   **Untimed Accepted:** Yes

Course Entrance Requirements: Yes

Are Waivers Available:

Additional Information:

Sometimes waivers are accepted.

Individualized high school coursework accepted:

Essay Required: For some programs

Special Application Required: No   **Submitted To:**

Number of Applications Submitted Each Year: 75-200

Number of Applications Accepted Each Year:

Number of Students Served: 120 (not all LD)

Application Deadline for Special Admission: No

Acceptance into Program means acceptance into college:

LEARNING DISABILITY SERVICES

Learning Resource Room: Yes   **Curriculum Modification Available:**

Kurzweil Personal Reader: Yes   **Tutorial Help:** Yes   **Peer Tutors:** Yes

LD Specialists: 1   **Max. Hours/Week for services:**

Oral Exams: Yes   On an individual basis

Services for LD Only: No   **Added**

Books on Tape: Yes   **Cost:** None

Calculator allowed in exam: Yes   **Taping of books not on tape:** Yes

Tape recording in class: Yes   **Dictionary/computer/spellcheck during exam:** Yes

How are professors notified of LD: By the student

GENERAL ADMISSIONS INFORMATION

Director of Admissions: Robert C. French   **Telephone:** 716-475-6631

Entrance Requirements:

4 yrs. English; 1-4 yrs. Math; 1-4 yrs. Science; 3 yrs. Social Studies. Recommended distribution depends on specific College the student is applying to for admission.

Test Scores: **SAT:** 1041   **ACT:** 24

G.P.A.:   **Class Rank:**

Application Deadline: 7/1   **Achievement Tests:**

COLLEGE GRADUATION REQUIREMENTS

Foreign Language: No   **Waivers:**

Math: **Waivers:** Depends on major

Minimum Course Load per Term: Yes

ADDITIONAL INFORMATION

Location: R.I.T. is located on a 1,300 acre campus 5 miles south of the city of Rochester, the third largest city in New York State.

Enrollment Information: **Undergraduate:** 11,092   **Women:** 34%   **Men:** 66%

     In-State Students: 66%   **Out of State:** 34%

Cost Information: **In-State Tuition:** $9,972   **Out of State:** same

     Room & Board: $4,470   **Additional Costs:** $180

Housing Information: **University Housing:** Yes   **Sorority:** 3%

     % Living on Campus: 85%   **Fraternity:** 5%

Athletics: NCAA Div. III

Support: S   **Institution:** 2 yr. Public

LEARNING DISABILITY PROGRAM AND SERVICES

Comments:

The Learning Center offers support services to students who have been admited and who have documented learning disablities. Students may meet individually with a learning disability specialist for 1 hour per week, or in group meetings. Services include academic remediation with emphasis on compensatory strategies, study skills strartegies training, test accommodations, time management instruction, tutoring and self understanding of disability.

LEARNING DISABILITY ADMISSIONS INFORMATION

Program Name:	Learning Center	**Telephone**
Program Director:	Malka Edelman	516-420-2411
Contact Person:	same	

Admissions:

There is no special admissions procedure. Learning disabled students should self-identify on the application.

Interview: On request   **Diagnostic Tests:**

Documentation: WAIS-R to receive services: IEP

College Entrance Exams Required: No   **Untimed Accepted:**

Course Entrance Requirements: Yes

Are Waivers Available:

Additional Information:

The College would like the IEP and the WAIS-R to help identify the services necessary to help the student to be successful. Pre-College Pathways Program has more flexible entrance requirements. Elementary algebra is minimum requirement in math.

Individualized high school coursework accepted:

Essay Required:

Special Application Required: No   **Submitted To:**

Number of Applications Submitted Each Year: 20

Number of Applications Accepted Each Year: All students accepted

Number of Students Served:

Application Deadline for Special Admission: No

Acceptance into Program means acceptance into college: Appeal process available

LEARNING DISABILITY SERVICES

Learning Resource Room: **Curriculum Modification Available:**

Kurzweil Personal Reader: No   **Tutorial Help:** Yes   **Peer Tutors:** Yes

LD Specialists: 1   **Max. Hours/Week for services:**

Oral Exams: Yes   No maximum

Services for LD Only: No   **Added**

Books on Tape: Yes   **Cost:** None

Calculator allowed in exam: Yes   **Taping of books not on tape:** Yes

Tape recording in class: **Dictionary/computer/spellcheck during exam:** Yes

How are professors notified of LD:

GENERAL ADMISSIONS INFORMATION

Director of Admissions: Janet Synder   **Telephone:** 516-420-2200

Entrance Requirements:

High school transcript. Course requirements vary by curriculum. 3 years Math required for some. Tests are used for counseling and placement. 70% of those admitted were in the top half of their class.

Test Scores: **SAT:**   **ACT:** recommended

G.P.A.:   **Class Rank:** Top 50%

Application Deadline: Rolling   **Achievement Tests:** Yes for placement

COLLEGE GRADUATION REQUIREMENTS

Foreign Language: Yes   **Waivers:** No, required in Liberal Arts

Math: Yes   **Waivers:** No

Minimum Course Load per Term: 12 credits if living on campus

ADDITIONAL INFORMATION

Location: Farmingdale is a small town located within easy access to New York City.

Enrollment Information: **Undergraduate:** 10,880   **Women:** 48%   **Men:** 52%

                  In-State Students: 99%   **Out of State:** 1%

Cost Information: **In-State Tuition:** $1,350   **Out of State:** $4,700

                  Room & Board: $1,910   **Additional Costs:** $150

Housing Information: **University Housing:** Yes   **Sorority:** 1%

               % Living on Campus: 10%   **Fraternity:** 1%

Athletics: NJCAA

Support: S   *Institution:* 4 yr. Private

LEARNING DISABILITY PROGRAM AND SERVICES

Comments:

St. Lawrence University has an accommodation policy which services primarily LD students. There is a special emphasis on orienting freshman in early weeks of the first semester to good time/task management. Services include academic skills and writing tutorials. The Director of the Service will advocate for students when needed.

LEARNING DISABILITY ADMISSIONS INFORMATION

Program Name: Office of Services for Students with Special Needs   *Telephone*

Program Director: Jim Cohn   315-379-5106

Contact Person: same

Admissions:

Admissions is standard for all students

Interview: Yes   *Diagnostic Tests:* No

Documentation:

College Entrance Exams Required: Yes   *Untimed Accepted:* Yes

Course Entrance Requirements: Yes

Are Waivers Available: Yes

Additional Information:

Individualized high school coursework accepted: Yes

Essay Required: Yes

Special Application Required: No   *Submitted To:*

Number of Applications Submitted Each Year:

Number of Applications Accepted Each Year:

Number of Students Served: 100

Application Deadline for Special Admission:

Acceptance into Program means acceptance

into college: No

LEARNING DISABILITY SERVICES

Learning Resource Room: No   **Curriculum Modification Available:** Yes

Kurzweil Personal Reader: **Tutorial Help:** Yes   **Peer Tutors:** Yes

LD Specialists: 1   **Max. Hours/Week for services:**

Oral Exams: Yes   Unlimited

Services for LD Only: No   **Added Cost:**

Books on Tape: Yes

Calculator allowed in exam: Yes   **Taping of books not on tape:** Yes

Tape recording in class: Yes   **Dictionary/computer/spellcheck during exam:** Yes

How are professors notified of LD: By student and Program Director

GENERAL ADMISSIONS INFORMATION

Director of Admissions: Peter Richardson   **Telephone:** 315-379-5261

Entrance Requirements:

4 yrs. English: 3 yrs. Math; 3 yrs. Science; 3 yrs. Foreign Language; 2 yrs. Social Science; 2 recommendations; 1 achievement test; English Composition Test.

Test Scores: **SAT:** 1105   **ACT:** 24

G.P.A.: 3.0 (recommended)   **Class Rank:** Top 20%

Application Deadline: 2/1   **Achievement Tests:** 3

COLLEGE GRADUATION REQUIREMENTS

Foreign Language: No   **Waivers:**

Math: No   **Waivers:**

Minimum Course Load per Term: 3 courses

ADDITIONAL INFORMATION

Location: Rural setting on 1,000 acres 20 miles from the Canadian border.

Enrollment Information: **Undergraduate:** 2,278   **Women:** 48%   **Men:** 52%

In-State Students: 50%   **Out of State:** 50%

Cost Information: **In-State Tuition:** $14,710   **Out of State:** same

Room & Board: $4,730   **Additional Costs:**

Housing Information: **University Housing:** Yes   **Sorority:** 20%

% Living on Campus: 80%   **Fraternity:** 20%

Athletics: NCAA Div. III

ST. THOMAS AQUINAS COLLEGE

Sparkill, N.Y. 10976

914-359-9500

Support: CS   **Institution:** 4 yr. Private

LEARNING DISABILITY PROGRAM AND SERVICES

Comments:

The services provided in "The STAC Exchange" program are extremely comprehensive and based on research and actual experiences with undergraduates who have learning process dysfunctions. As the students progress each year, the program is designed to gradually reduce the need for some services, thus lessening dependency and increasing independence and confidence. At the heart of the program are the Seminars conducted by Program Mentors. These instructional units are small group sessions, each covering a specific area.

LEARNING DISABILITY ADMISSIONS INFORMATION

Program Name: THE "STAC" EXCHANGE   *Telephone*

Program Director: Dr. M. Doonan   914-359-9500

Contact Person: same

Admissions:

The school requires proof of graduation, documentation of a diagnosis of learning disability by certified professionals within a school system, current high school transcript, scores of the untimed SAT, 3 letters of recommendation, handwritten statement from the students stating reasons for wanting to attend college and what effects the learning disability has had on the student's life.

Interview: Yes   **Diagnostic Tests:** Yes

Documentation: WAIS-R; IEP

College Entrance Exams Required: Yes   **Untimed Accepted:** Yes

Course Entrance Requirements: Yes

Are Waivers Available:

Additional Information:

Individualized high school coursework accepted: No

Essay Required: Yes

Special Application Required: **Submitted To:**

Number of Applications Submitted Each Year: 16

Number of Applications Accepted Each Year: 25

Number of Students Served: 75

Application Deadline for Special Admission: No

Acceptance into Program means acceptance into college:

LEARNING DISABILITY SERVICES

Learning Resource Room: Yes

Kurzweil Personal Reader:

LD Specialists: Yes

Oral Exams:

Services for LD Only: Yes

Books on Tape: Yes

Calculator allowed in exam: Yes

Tape recording in class: Yes

How are professors notified of LD: By Student and LD Director

Curriculum Modification Available: No

Tutorial Help: Yes   **Peer Tutors:** No

Max. Hours/Week for services:

As needed

**Added
Cost:** $1,000 per/semester

Taping of books not on tape: Yes

Dictionary/computer/spellcheck during exam: Yes

GENERAL ADMISSIONS INFORMATION

Director of Admissions: Andrea Kraeft   **Telephone:** 914-359-9500

Entrance Requirements:

16 credits including: 4 yrs. English; 2 yrs. Math; 2 yrs. Science; 1 yr. Foreign Language; 1 yr. History. Applicants whose secondary school record varies from the requirements may be considered if motivation is high.

Test Scores: **SAT:** 830   **ACT:** May be substituted

G.P.A.:   **Class Rank:**

Application Deadline: Rolling   **Achievement Tests:** No

COLLEGE GRADUATION REQUIREMENTS

Foreign Language: Yes   **Waivers:** Decided on case-by-case basis

Math: Yes   **Waivers:** Decided on case-by-case basis

Minimum Course Load per Term: 12 credit hours

ADDITIONAL INFORMATION

Location: The school is located on 42 acres in a suburban area, 13 miles from New York City.

Enrollment Information: **Undergraduate:** 1,989   **Women:** 50%   **Men:** 50%

      In-State Students: 75%   **Out of State:** 25%

Cost Information: **In-State Tuition:** $6,100   **Out of State:** same

      Room & Board: $3,400   **Additional Costs:** $100

Housing Information: **University Housing:** Yes   **Sorority:** No

      % Living on Campus: 5%   **Fraternity:** No

Athletics: NAIA

STATE UNIVERSITY OF NEW YORK - ALBANY
Albany, N.Y. 12222
518-442-5435

Support: S   *Institution:* 4 yr. Public

LEARNING DISABILITY PROGRAM AND SERVICES

Comments:

The Disabled Student Services Program offers a full complement of support services to ensure students with disabilities equal access to the University at Albany. The services attempt to be flexible enough to meet a broad range of needs as well as individual priorities relative to a particular student. The Program provides a Writing Center staffed by faculty, advocacy, assistance with recommended courses, tutoring assistance, and a willingness to explore innovative ways of providing the most efficient assistance possible.

LEARNING DISABILITY ADMISSIONS INFORMATION

Program Name:	Disabled Student Services	*Telephone*
Program Director:	Nancy Belowich-Negron	518-442-5491
Contact Person:	Same	

Admissions:

There is no special application. The student should self-identify on the application. Letters of recommendation, auxiliary testing, and a personal interview are helpful.

Interview: No

Diagnostic Tests: Yes

Documentation: IEP; WAIS; etc.

College Entrance Exams Required: Yes

Untimed Accepted: Yes

Course Entrance Requirements: Yes

Are Waivers Available: No

Additional Information:

Individualized high school coursework accepted:

Essay Required: Preferred

Special Application Required: *Submitted To:*

Number of Applications Submitted Each Year:

Number of Applications Accepted Each Year:

Number of Students Served: 52 LD students

Application Deadline for Special Admission:

Acceptance into Program means acceptance into college: Yes

211

LEARNING DISABILITY SERVICES

Learning Resource Room: Yes   **Curriculum Modification Available:** Yes

Kurzweil Personal Reader: **Tutorial Help:** Yes   **Peer Tutors:** Yes

LD Specialists: 1   **Max. Hours/Week for services:**

Oral Exams: Y/N   Open

Services for LD Only: No   **Added**

Books on Tape: Yes   **Cost:** None

Calculator allowed in exam: Yes   **Taping of books not on tape:** Yes

Tape recording in class: Yes   **Dictionary/computer/spellcheck during exam:** Yes

How are professors notified of LD: By student and by the Program Director

GENERAL ADMISSIONS INFORMATION

Director of Admissions: Micheleen Tredwell   **Telephone:** 518-442-5435

Entrance Requirements:

4 yrs. English; 2 yrs. Math; 2 yrs. Science; 2-3 yrs. Foreign Language.

Test Scores: **SAT:** 1154   **ACT:**

G.P.A.:   **Class Rank:**

Application Deadline: 2/15   **Achievement Tests:**

COLLEGE GRADUATION REQUIREMENTS

Foreign Language: No   **Waivers:** Possible

Math: Yes   **Waivers:** Possible

Minimum Course Load per Term: 12 credits

ADDITIONAL INFORMATION

Location: Urban campus on 515 acres located on the fringe of the state capital.

Enrollment Information: **Undergraduate:** 11,870   **Women:** 49%   **Men:** 51%

In-State Students: 97%   **Out of State:** 3%

Cost Information: **In-State Tuition:** $1,478   **Out of State:** $4,828

Room & Board: $3,301   **Additional Costs:**

Housing Information: **University Housing:** Yes   **Sorority:** 7%

% Living on Campus: 60%   **Fraternity:** 15%

Athletics: NCAA Div. III

STATE UNIVERSITY OF NEW YORK - CANTON

Canton, N.Y. 13617-1098

315-386-7123

Support: S   **Institution:** 2 yr. Public

LEARNING DISABILITY PROGRAM AND SERVICES

Comments:

At the State University of New York-College of Technology the Accommodative Services Program has a number of services. Its Academic Development Program on campus is for under-prepared students. Help is given in the Reading/Writing Lab, Math Lab and by peer tutors. Acceptance into the University assures the student will receive services.

LEARNING DISABILITY ADMISSIONS INFORMATION

Program Name:	Accommodative Services Program	**Telephone**
Program Director:	Debora L. Camp	315-386-7121
Contact Person:	same	same

Admissions:

There is a special admissions procedure which includes an interview with the Coordinator of the Services Program. Students should also submit auxiliary testing, letters of recommendation, and a personal statement. An interview is very important.

Interview: Yes   **Diagnostic Tests:** Yes

Documentation: WAIS

College Entrance Exams Required: No   **Untimed Accepted:**

Course Entrance Requirements: Yes

Are Waivers Available:

Additional Information:

Individualized high school coursework accepted: Yes

Essay Required: No

Special Application Required: No   **Submitted To:**

Number of Applications Submitted Each Year: 85

Number of Applications Accepted Each Year: All

Number of Students Served: 61

Application Deadline for Special Admission: No

Acceptance into Program means acceptance into college: No

213

LEARNING DISABILITY SERVICES

Learning Resource Room: **Curriculum Modification Available:** Yes

Kurzweil Personal Reader: **Tutorial Help:** Yes   **Peer Tutors:** Yes

LD Specialists: No   **Max. Hours/Week for services:**

Oral Exams: Yes   2-3 hours per week

Services for LD Only: No   **Added**

Books on Tape: Yes   **Cost:** None

Calculator allowed in exam: Yes   **Taping of books not on tape:** Yes

Tape recording in class: Yes   **Dictionary/computer/spellcheck during exam:** Yes

How are professors notified of LD: By student and Program Director

GENERAL ADMISSIONS INFORMATION

Director of Admissions: Enrico A. Miller   **Telephone:** 315-386-7123

Entrance Requirements:

3 yrs. Math; 3 yrs. Science.

Test Scores: **SAT:**   **ACT:**

G.P.A.:   **Class Rank:**

Application Deadline: Rolling   **Achievement Tests:**

COLLEGE GRADUATION REQUIREMENTS

Foreign Language: No   **Waivers:**

Math: Yes   **Waivers:** No

Minimum Course Load per Term: 12 credits

ADDITIONAL INFORMATION

Location: Small-town setting on 550 acre campus 135 miles northeast of Syracuse.

Enrollment Information: **Undergraduate:** 2,437   **Women:** 475   **Men:** 53%

                           In-State Students: 98%   **Out of State:** 2%

Cost Information: **In-State Tuition:** $1,350   **Out of State:** $4,700

                          Room & Board: $3,520   **Additional Costs:** $165

Housing Information: **University Housing:** Yes   **Sorority:** 25%

                        % Living on Campus: 45%   **Fraternity:** 23%

Athletics: NJCAA

STATE UNIVERSITY OF NEW YORK - DELHI
Delhi, N.Y. 13753
607-746-4246

Support: S   *Institution:* 2 yr. Public

LEARNING DISABILITY PROGRAM AND SERVICES

Comments:

There are extensive academic support services and equipment for students with learning disabilities. They include professional tutors; exams in a distraction-free environment; submission of exams on tape or dictating exams to an attendant; remedial courses in reading, math, English, study skills, personal development; a computer with DecTalk Synthesizer and enlarged video display computer terminals.

LEARNING DISABILITY ADMISSIONS INFORMATION

Program Name:	Services for Learning Disabled Students	*Telephone*
Program Director:	Suzanne Aragoni	607-746-4129
Contact Person:	same	

Admissions:

To be eligible for services the student must disclose information about their learning disability with the regular application documentation. ACT scores are used for placement within courses.

Interview: Yes   *Diagnostic Tests:* Yes

Documentation: WAIS; Achievement tests

College Entrance Exams Required: No   *Untimed Accepted:* Yes

Course Entrance Requirements: No

Are Waivers Available:

Additional Information:

Other requirements vary according to programs.

Individualized high school coursework accepted: Yes

Essay Required: Yes

Special Application Required: No   *Submitted To:*

Number of Applications Submitted Each Year: 130

Number of Applications Accepted Each Year:

Number of Students Served: 100

Application Deadline for Special Admission: No

Acceptance into Program means acceptance into college: Yes

215

LEARNING DISABILITY SERVICES

Learning Resource Room: Yes   **Curriculum Modification Available:**

Kurzweil Personal Reader: Yes   **Tutorial Help:** Yes   **Peer Tutors:** Yes

LD Specialists: No   **Max. Hours/Week for services:**

Oral Exams: Yes   No maximum

Services for LD Only: No   **Added**

Books on Tape: Yes   **Cost:** None

Calculator allowed in exam: Yes   **Taping of books not on tape:** Yes

Tape recording in class: Yes   **Dictionary/computer/spellcheck during exam:** Yes

How are professors notified of LD: By student

GENERAL ADMISSIONS INFORMATION

Director of Admissions: Richard A. Cardoza   **Telephone:** 607-746-4246

Entrance Requirements:

3 yrs. Math; Recommendations and campus interview are helpful.

Test Scores: **SAT:**   **ACT:**

G.P.A.:   **Class Rank:**

Application Deadline: Rolling   **Achievement Tests:**

COLLEGE GRADUATION REQUIREMENTS

Foreign Language: **Waivers:**

Math: **Waivers:**

Minimum Course Load per Term: Decision made according to student needs.

ADDITIONAL INFORMATION

Location: Small town setting on 1,100 acres in upstate New York.

Enrollment Information: **Undergraduate:** 2,415   **Women:** 42%   **Men:** 58%

In-State Students: 95%   **Out of State:** 5%

Cost Information: **In-State Tuition:** $1,460   **Out of State:** $4,700

Room & Board: $3,310   **Additional Costs:** $110

Housing Information: **University Housing:** Yes   **Sorority:**

% Living on Campus: 50%   **Fraternity:** Yes

Athletics: NJCAA

SYRACUSE UNIVERSITY
Syracuse, NY 13244-2330

315-423-3611

Support: CS   **Institution:** 4 yr. Private

LEARNING DISABILITY PROGRAM AND SERVICES

Comments:

The Center for Academic Achievement provides an integrated network of diagnostic, academic support, and counseling services. Every learning disabled student who is accepted to the University is eligible for services as long as the necessary documentation is provided. The staff is very supportive and sensitive to the needs of the LD student. The Assistant Director and staff work closely with the LD students to provide necessary accommodations.

LEARNING DISABILITY ADMISSIONS INFORMATION

Program Name:	Learning Disability Services (LDS)	**Telephone**
Program Director:	James Duah-Agyeman	315-443-4498
Contact Person:	Joanne Heinz, Ass't Director & Coordinator	same

Admissions:

Students use general application but may indicate they are learning disabled by checking a question on the application which refers to any disability. Students should include current testing and documentation and request that it be sent to the Center for Academic Achievement. The Director of LDS reviews application and documentation and makes a recommendation to admissions. The LD student should write an accompanying letter describing the disability and goals and services needed. Less weight is put on ACT and SAT. Student's grades should show an up-ward trend.

Interview: recommended   **Diagnostic Tests:** Yes

Documentation: WAIS-R; W-J; Achievements

College Entrance Exams Required: Yes   **Untimed Accepted:** Yes

Course Entrance Requirements: Yes

Are Waivers Available: No

Additional Information:

LD students may request substitutions for high school Math or Foreign Language if documentation can substantiate a disability in any one of these areas.

Individualized high school coursework accepted: No

Essay Required: Yes

Special Application Required: No   **Submitted To:**

Number of Applications Submitted Each Year: 200+

Number of Applications Accepted Each Year: 90-100

Number of Students Served: 260

Application Deadline for Special Admission: Apply 10 months prior

Acceptance into Program means acceptance into college: No

217

LEARNING DISABILITY SERVICES

Learning Resource Room: No	*Curriculum Modification Available:* Yes	
Kurzweil Personal Reader: Yes	*Tutorial Help:* Yes	*Peer Tutors:* Yes
LD Specialists: 2	*Max. Hours/Week for services:*	
Oral Exams: Yes	2 hours per/week	
Services for LD Only: No	*Added*	
Books on Tape: Yes	*Cost:* None	
Calculator allowed in exam: Yes	*Taping of books not on tape:* Yes	
Tape recording in class: Yes	*Dictionary/computer/spellcheck during exam:* Yes	

How are professors notified of LD: By the student

GENERAL ADMISSIONS INFORMATION

Director of Admissions: Susan Donovan   *Telephone:* 315-423-3611

Entrance Requirements:

4 yrs. English; 3 yrs. Math; Social Studies; 1 yr. Science; 2 yrs. Foreign Language; 5 electives.

Test Scores: *SAT:* 1100 (mid 50%)   *ACT:*

G.P.A.:   *Class Rank:* Top 25%

Application Deadline: 2/1   *Achievement Tests:* No

COLLEGE GRADUATION REQUIREMENTS

Foreign Language: Yes   *Waivers:* Yes

Math: Yes   *Waivers:* Yes

Minimum Course Load per Term: 12 credits

ADDITIONAL INFORMATION

Location: The school is located on 200 acres set on a hill overlooking the city of Syracuse.

Enrollment Information:	*Undergraduate:* 12,585	*Women:* 51%	*Men:* 49%
	In-State Students: 37%		*Out of State:* 63%
Cost Information:	*In-State Tuition:* $12,120		*Out of State:* same
	Room & Board: $5,535		*Additional Costs:* $290
Housing Information:	*University Housing:* Yes		*Sorority:* 30%
	% Living on Campus: 80%		*Fraternity:* 17%

Athletics: NCAA Div. I

APPALACHIAN STATE UNIVERSITY
Boone, N.C. 28608

704-262-2120

Support: S   **Institution:** 4 yr. Public

LEARNING DISABILITY PROGRAM AND SERVICES

Comments:

The University LD Program is part of a larger academic support service called the Learning Assistance Program. The LD program is designed to provide academic services for students who identified themselves n a voluntary basis as being learning disabled. LD students are mainstreamed throughout the University community.

LEARNING DISABILITY ADMISSIONS INFORMATION

Program Name: Learning Disability Program   **Telephone**

Program Director: Arlene J. Lunquist   704-262-9122

Contact Person: same

Admissions:

LD students are admitted to the University through the regular admission procedure. Scores from untimed tests are accepted. Once the student has been accepted by the University, a form is provided in which the LD student can identify their disability. This identification process is necessary for the student to have access to the services of the LD Program.

Interview: No   **Diagnostic Tests:** Yes

Documentation:

College Entrance Exams Required: Yes   **Untimed Accepted:** Yes

Course Entrance Requirements: Yes

Are Waivers Available: No

Additional Information:

Individualized high school coursework accepted: No

Essay Required:

Special Application Required: No   **Submitted To:**

Number of Applications Submitted Each Year: N/A

Number of Applications Accepted Each Year: N/A

Number of Students Served: 96

Application Deadline for Special Admission: No

Acceptance into Program means acceptance into college: No

LEARNING DISABILITY SERVICES

Learning Resource Room: Yes   **Curriculum Modification Available:** No

Kurzweil Personal Reader: Yes   **Tutorial Help:** Yes   **Peer Tutors:** Yes

LD Specialists: No   **Max. Hours/Week for services:**

Oral Exams: Yes   Need-by-need basis

Services for LD Only: No   **Added**

Books on Tape: Yes   **Cost:** None

Calculator allowed in exam: Y/N   **Taping of books not on tape:** Yes

Tape recording in class: Yes   **Dictionary/computer/spellcheck during exam:** Y/N

How are professors notified of LD: By student and Program Director

GENERAL ADMISSIONS INFORMATION

Director of Admissions: Joe Watts   **Telephone:** 704-262-2120

Entrance Requirements:

4 yrs. English; 3 yrs. Math; 3 yrs. Science; 2 yrs. Social Studies, including 1 in history; Music Special admission for high risk students or disadvantaged.

Test Scores: SAT: 910   **ACT:** 21

G.P.A.: 3.1 average   **Class Rank:**

Application Deadline: 2/15   **Achievement Tests:** No

COLLEGE GRADUATION REQUIREMENTS

Foreign Language: No   **Waivers:**

Math: Yes   **Waivers:** No

Minimum Course Load per Term: 12 credits

ADDITIONAL INFORMATION

Location: 255 acre campus in small town 90 miles northwest of Winston-Salem. The University also maintains 2 external campuses for experimental studies in Washington, D.C. and in

Enrollment Information: Undergraduate: 10,658   **Women:** 51%   **Men:** 49%

In-State Students: 90%   **Out of State:** 10%

Cost Information: In-State Tuition: $1,075   **Out of State:** $7,447

Room & Board: $2,110   **Additional Costs:**

Housing Information: University Housing: Yes   **Sorority:** 5%

% Living on Campus: 40%   **Fraternity:** 5%

Athletics: NCAA Div. I

Support: S   **Institution:** 4 Yr. Public

LEARNING DISABILITY PROGRAM AND SERVICES

Comments:

The overall purpose of the University's program for learning disabled students is to provide auxiliary support services to students with various disabilities so they may derive equal benefits from all that East Carolina University has to offer. Routine services which are available to the general student body are also available to the disabled student population. However, additional services if required are available to minimize the long range effects the disability may impose on the attainment of the basic goals of a postsecondary institution.

LEARNING DISABILITY ADMISSIONS INFORMATION

Program Name: Office of Handicapped Student Services   **Telephone**

Program Director: C.C. Rowe   919-757-6799

Contact Person: same

Admissions:

A student with a disability applies for admission and is considered for admission in the same manner as any other applicant. A student's admission is based solely on academic qualifications. Out-of-state students must present slightly higher GPA's and test scores.

Interview: Yes   **Diagnostic Tests:** Yes

Documentation: WAIS-R; W-JPEB

College Entrance Exams Required: Yes   **Untimed Accepted:** Yes

Course Entrance Requirements: Yes

Are Waivers Available: No

Additional Information:

Once a student is admitted, recent evaluations identifying the nature of the learning disability must be provided.

Individualized high school coursework accepted: Yes

Essay Required: No

Special Application Required: No   **Submitted To:**

Number of Applications Submitted Each Year: N/A

Number of Applications Accepted Each Year:

Number of Students Served: 70

Application Deadline for Special Admission: No

Acceptance into Program means acceptance into college:

LEARNING DISABILITY SERVICES

Learning Resource Room: Yes   **Curriculum Modification Available:** No

Kurzweil Personal Reader: Yes   **Tutorial Help:** Yes   **Peer Tutors:** Yes

LD Specialists: No   **Max. Hours/Week for services:**

Oral Exams: Yes   Depends on need of student

Services for LD Only: Yes   **Added**

Books on Tape: Yes   **Cost:** None

Calculator allowed in exam: Yes   **Taping of books not on tape:** Yes

Tape recording in class: Yes   **Dictionary/computer/spellcheck during exam:** Yes

How are professors notified of LD: By the student and the Program Director

GENERAL ADMISSIONS INFORMATION

Director of Admissions: Dr. Thomas E. Powell, Jr.   **Telephone:** 919-757-6640

Entrance Requirements:

20 units of academic credit including: 4 yrs. English; 3 yrs. Math; 3 yrs. Science; 2 yrs. Social Studies; 2 yrs. Foreign Language.

Test Scores: **SAT:** 880   **ACT:** Accepted

G.P.A.:   **Class Rank:**

Application Deadline: 2/15   **Achievement Tests:**

COLLEGE GRADUATION REQUIREMENTS

Foreign Language: **Waivers:** Depends on major

Math: Yes   **Waivers:** Yes

Minimum Course Load per Term: Students pay according to the number of hours they take.

ADDITIONAL INFORMATION

Location: The school is located on over 370 acres within the city of Greenville 85 miles from Raleigh.

Enrollment Information: **Undergraduate:** 13,292   **Women:** 56%   **Men:** 44%

        In-State Students: 85%   **Out of State:** 15%

Cost Information: **In-State Tuition:** $978   **Out of State:** $4,892

        Room & Board: $2425   **Additional Costs:** $458

Housing Information: **University Housing:** Yes   **Sorority:** 1%

        % Living on Campus: 42%   **Fraternity:** 1%

Athletics: NCAA Div. I

NORTH CAROLINA STATE UNIVERSITY
Raleigh, N.C. 27695-7103
919-737-2434

NC

Support: CS   **Institution:** 4 yr. Public

LEARNING DISABILITY PROGRAM AND SERVICES

Comments:

At North Carolina State University services for students with learning disabilities are handled by the LD Coordinator through Handicapped Student Services. The functions of the coordinator include identifying LD students, helping to accommodate and interpret the needs of these students to the faculty, and providing services to students according to their individual needs. N.C. State provides services only for independent high achieving students. Services include priority scheduling, reader or taping service, notetaker, testing accommodations and support groups.

LEARNING DISABILITY ADMISSIONS INFORMATION

		Telephone
Program Name:	Handicapped Student Services	
Program Director:	Patricia Smith	919-737-7653
Contact Person:	Lelia Brettmann	same

Admissions:

Admission to the University is determined on the basis of academic qualifications. Students with disabilities are considered for admission in the same manner as any other applicant. However, it is helpful for the student to write a cover letter stating that a learning disability exists. This alerts the admission staff to take this into consideration. It is highly recommended that the SAT be taken on an untimed basis as this gives a better estimate of the student's ability. Out-of-state test score may need to be higher than those from in-state.

Interview: No   **Diagnostic Tests:** Yes

Documentation: WAIS-R: W-J

College Entrance Exams Required: Yes   **Untimed Accepted:** Yes

Course Entrance Requirements: Yes

Are Waivers Available: No

Additional Information:

Individualized high school coursework accepted: No

Essay Required: Yes, not heavily weighted

Special Application Required: No   **Submitted To:**

Number of Applications Submitted Each Year: Varies

Number of Applications Accepted Each Year: All

Number of Students Served: 130

Application Deadline for Special Admission: After acceptance into the University

Acceptance into Program means acceptance into college: No

LEARNING DISABILITY SERVICES

Learning Resource Room:	No	**Curriculum Modification Available:**	No
Kurzweil Personal Reader:		**Tutorial Help:** Yes	**Peer Tutors:** Yes
LD Specialists:	1	**Max. Hours/Week for services:**	

Oral Exams: 3+ hours per/course

Services for LD Only: Yes **Added**

Books on Tape: Yes **Cost:** None

Calculator allowed in exam: Y/N **Taping of books not on tape:** Yes

Tape recording in class: Yes **Dictionary/computer/spellcheck during exam:** Yes

How are professors notified of LD: By the student and the Program Director

GENERAL ADMISSIONS INFORMATION

Director of Admissions: George R. Dixon **Telephone:** 919- 737-2434

Entrance Requirements:

4 yrs. English; 3 yrs. Math (Alg. I, Alg. II, Geometry, or courses higher than Alg. II); 2 yrs. Social Studies (including 1 unit American History); 3 yrs. Science; 2 yrs. Foreign Language recommended. SAT required.

Test Scores: **SAT:** 1055 **ACT:**

G.P.A.: 2.5 in-state/3.0 (out) **Class Rank:** Top 30%

Application Deadline: 2/1 **Achievement Tests:** Math recommended

COLLEGE GRADUATION REQUIREMENTS

Foreign Language: Yes **Waivers:** No

Math: Yes **Waivers:** No

Minimum Course Load per Term: Any student can take as few courses as desired

ADDITIONAL INFORMATION

Location: The University sits on 623 acres in the central part of the state, and has an adjacent 900 acre research campus.

Enrollment Information:	**Undergraduate:** 17,736	**Women:** 37%	**Men:** 63%
	In-State Students: 85%		**Out of State:** 15%
Cost Information:	**In-State Tuition:** $1,000		**Out of State:** $5,500
	Room & Board: $2,900		**Additional Costs:** $440
Housing Information:	**University Housing:** Yes		**Sorority:** 5%
	% Living on Campus: 35%		**Fraternity:** 5%

Athletics: NCAA Div. I

UNIVERSITY OF NORTH CAROLINA
Wilmington, N.C. 28403-3297
919-395-3243

Support: S   **Institution:** 4 yr. Public

LEARNING DISABILITY PROGRAM AND SERVICES

Comments:

The University of North Carolina, Wilmington has a number of services available to accommodate learning disabled students. These services are coordinated through (DSS) Disabled Student Services. It is up to the student to contact the Coordinator of the program. All services are based on individual need as assessed through recent diagnostic information and personal interview. As new needs are identified, additional services may be developed or modified. Services include priority scheduling, advocacy, counseling, study skills, notetakers, and test accommodations.

LEARNING DISABILITY ADMISSIONS INFORMATION

Program Name: Disabled Student Services   **Telephone**

Program Director: Margaret T. Sheridan, M. Ed   919-395-3746

Contact Person: same   same

Admissions:

Learning disabled students applying to UNCW must meet the same entrance requirements as all other applicants. Newly accepted students interested in services should complete and sign the disclosure form which is included with the letter of acceptance.

Interview: **Diagnostic Tests:** Yes

Documentation: WAIS-R; Woodcock-Johnson Within 3 years prior to admission.

College Entrance Exams Required: Yes   **Untimed Accepted:** Yes

Course Entrance Requirements: Yes

Are Waivers Available: Yes

Additional Information:

Accepted with deficiency in foreign language. A U.S. History deficiency must be made-up by sophomore year.

Individualized high school coursework accepted: Yes

Essay Required:

Special Application Required: **Submitted To:**

Number of Applications Submitted Each Year:

Number of Applications Accepted Each Year: Unlimited

Number of Students Served: Unlimited

Application Deadline for Special Admission:

Acceptance into Program means acceptance

into college: No, there is an appeal procedure

LEARNING DISABILITY SERVICES

Learning Resource Room:

Kurzweil Personal Reader:

LD Specialists: No

Oral Exams: Yes

Services for LD Only: No

Books on Tape: Yes

Calculator allowed in exam: Y/N

Tape recording in class: Y/N

How are professors notified of LD: By student and Program Director

Curriculum Modification Available: No

Tutorial Help: Yes   **Peer Tutors:** Yes

Max. Hours/Week for services:

  Individually determined

Added Cost: None

Taping of books not on tape: Yes

Dictionary/computer/spellcheck during exam: Y/N

GENERAL ADMISSIONS INFORMATION

Director of Admissions: Diane M. Zeeman   **Telephone:** 919-385-3243

Entrance Requirements:

4 yrs. English; 2 yrs. Math; 2 yrs. Social Studies; 2 yrs. Foreign Language; 1 yr. Biology; 1 yr. Physical Science. SAT preferred.

Test Scores: SAT: 900   **ACT:** 18

G.P.A.: 2.0   **Class Rank:**

Application Deadline: 12/1   **Achievement Tests:** No

COLLEGE GRADUATION REQUIREMENTS

Foreign Language: Yes   **Waivers:** No

Math: Yes   **Waivers:** No

Minimum Course Load per Term: Yes one course

ADDITIONAL INFORMATION

Location: The University is located on 650 acres in a suburban neighborhood, 125 miles southeast of Raleigh.

Enrollment Information: Undergraduate: 6,651   **Women:** 57%   **Men:** 43%

In-State Students: 90%   **Out of State:** 10%

Cost Information: In-State Tuition: $1,068   **Out of State:** $5,430

Room & Board: $2,756   **Additional Costs:**

Housing Information: University Housing: Yes   **Sorority:** 13%

% Living on Campus: 27%   **Fraternity:** 14%

Athletics: NCAA Div. I

WAKE FOREST UNIVERSITY
Winston-Salem, N.C. 27109
919-759-5201

Support: S   *Institution:* 4 yr. Public

LEARNING DISABILITY PROGRAM AND SERVICES

Comments:

All students are eligible for group tutoring sessions in basic academic subjects. Those students enrolled in the LAP Academic Skills program are eligible for individual tutoring services. LAP tutors are specially trained to focus on academic skill building within course content areas. Tutor services are free and subject to availability of tutors and space. The LD student has a series of conferences with staff members who specialize in academic skills and who help design an overall study plan to improve scholastic performance in those areas needing assistance.

LEARNING DISABILITY ADMISSIONS INFORMATION

Program Name:	Learning Assistance Program (LAP)	*Telephone*
Program Director:	Sandra C. Chadwick	919-759-5929
Contact Person:	W.G. Starling	919-759-5201

Admissions:

No special admissions.

Interview: Yes   *Diagnostic Tests:* Yes

Documentation: Any available

College Entrance Exams Required: Yes   *Untimed Accepted:* Yes

Course Entrance Requirements: Yes

Are Waivers Available: No

Additional Information:

Applications are accepted for course substitutions.

Individualized high school coursework accepted: Yes

Essay Required: Yes

Special Application Required: No   *Submitted To:*

Number of Applications Submitted Each Year: 4-7

Number of Applications Accepted Each Year: All

Number of Students Served: 4

Application Deadline for Special Admission:

Acceptance into Program means acceptance into college: No

LEARNING DISABILITY SERVICES

Learning Resource Room: Yes

Curriculum Modification Available: Yes

Kurzweil Personal Reader:

Tutorial Help: Yes   **Peer Tutors:** Yes

LD Specialists: 1

Max. Hours/Week for services:

Oral Exams: Yes

3 hours per course

Services for LD Only: No

Added Cost: None

Books on Tape: Yes

Calculator allowed in exam: Yes

Taping of books not on tape: Yes

Tape recording in class: Yes

Dictionary/computer/spellcheck during exam: Y/N

How are professors notified of LD: By the student and the Program Director

GENERAL ADMISSIONS INFORMATION

Director of Admissions: William G. Starling   **Telephone:** 919-759-5201

Entrance Requirements:

4 yrs. English; 3 yrs. Math; 2 yrs. Foreign Language, History, Social Studies; 1 yr. Science. The SAT is required.

Test Scores: **SAT:** 1180 (mid 50%)   **ACT:**

G.P.A.:   **Class Rank:** top 5-10%

Application Deadline: 1/15   **Achievement Tests:** Recommended

COLLEGE GRADUATION REQUIREMENTS

Foreign Language: Yes   **Waivers:** No

Math: Yes   **Waivers:** No

Minimum Course Load per Term: 12 credits

ADDITIONAL INFORMATION

Location: The 550 acre campus, located in the Piedmont region of North Carolina, is recognized as among the most beautiful in the South.

Enrollment Information: **Undergraduate:** 3,531   **Women:** 46%   **Men:** 54%

In-State Students: 36%   **Out of State:** 64%

Cost Information: **In-State Tuition:** $9,700   **Out of State:** same

Room & Board: $2,470   **Additional Costs:**

Housing Information: **University Housing:** Yes   **Sorority:** 43%

% Living on Campus: 84%   **Fraternity:** 38%

Athletics: NCAA Div. I

WESTERN CAROLINA UNIVERSITY
Cullowhee, N.C. 28723

704-227-7317

Support: CS   **Institution:** 4 yr. Public

LEARNING DISABILITY PROGRAM AND SERVICES

Comments:

The Disabled Student Services program attempts to respond to the needs of learning disabled students by making services and equipment available as needed, and by making judicious use of reading and tutoring services. Each student in the program is assigned a counselor/advisor. The student must meet this counselor at least twice a month to discuss topics such as academic progress, study skills, adjustment to college life, career decision-making, or personal concerns. In addition, students may take specially designed classes in English and Reading.

LEARNING DISABILITY ADMISSIONS INFORMATION

		Telephone
Program Name:	Disabled Student Services	
Program Director:	Dr. Bonita Jacobs, Dean	704-227-7234
Contact Person:	Ginny Hawkin	704-227-7127

Admissions:

Students with learning disabilities are admitted under the same admission standards as a student who has no learning disability. Non-standardized ACT/SAT are acceptable.

Interview: No   **Diagnostic Tests:** Yes

Documentation: W-J; IQ tests

College Entrance Exams Required: Yes   **Untimed Accepted:** Yes

Course Entrance Requirements: Yes

Are Waivers Available:

Additional Information:

To qualify for services the student must be enrolled at the University, evaluated within the last 3 years, be willing to participate in additional evaluation to confirm the disability, and be willing to participate in planning support services. Admitted LD students are also expected to maintain good class attendance, strive for good grades, cooperate with counselors and advisors, set realistic career goals, and meet and confer with the learning disabilities team as scheduled.

Individualized high school coursework accepted:

Essay Required: No

Special Application Required: No   **Submitted To:**

Number of Applications Submitted Each Year:

Number of Applications Accepted Each Year: All accepted into the University

Number of Students Served:

Application Deadline for Special Admission: No

Acceptance into Program means acceptance into college: No

LEARNING DISABILITY SERVICES

Learning Resource Room: Yes   **Curriculum Modification Available:** No

Kurzweil Personal Reader: No   **Tutorial Help:** Yes   **Peer Tutors:** Yes

LD Specialists: 1   **Max. Hours/Week for services:**

Oral Exams: Yes   Not set at this time

Services for LD Only: Yes   **Added**

Books on Tape: Yes   **Cost:** None

Calculator allowed in exam: Y/N   **Taping of books not on tape:** Yes

Tape recording in class: Yes   **Dictionary/computer/spellcheck during exam:** Y/N

How are professors notified of LD: By the student and the Program Director

GENERAL ADMISSIONS INFORMATION

Director of Admissions: Drumont I. Bowman, Jr.   **Telephone:** 704-227-7317

Entrance Requirements:

4 yrs. English; 3 yrs. Math; 3 yrs. Science; 2 yrs. Social Studies; 1 yr. History; 2 yrs. Foreign Language. SAT required.

Test Scores: **SAT:** 845   **ACT:**

G.P.A.: 2.0   **Class Rank:**

Application Deadline: Rolling   **Achievement Tests:**

COLLEGE GRADUATION REQUIREMENTS

Foreign Language: **Waivers:**

Math: Yes   **Waivers:** No

Minimum Course Load per Term: 12 hours

ADDITIONAL INFORMATION

Location: The University is located on 400 acres in a rural area 50 miles southwest of Asheville.

Enrollment Information: **Undergraduate:** 5,106   **Women:** 51%   **Men:** 49%

In-State Students: 88%   **Out of State:** 12%

Cost Information: **In-State Tuition:** $1,028   **Out of State:** $5,400

Room & Board: $2,180   **Additional Costs:**

Housing Information: **University Housing:** Yes   **Sorority:** 12%

% Living on Campus: 56%   **Fraternity:** 25%

Athletics: NCAA Div. I

Support: CS   **Institution:** 4 yr. Private

LEARNING DISABILITY PROGRAM AND SERVICES

Comments:

Wingate College provides a program designed to assist students with diagnosed specific learning disabilities/dyslexia. The Program Director works closely with each student in an effort to maximize the opportunity for a successful college experience. While each student will have specific needs, there are some modes of assistance available to assist each student with the maximum support necessary. Services include developing study plans, tutoring, liaison with faculty, and regular evaluation sessions.

LEARNING DISABILITY ADMISSIONS INFORMATION

		Telephone
Program Name:	Specific Learning Disabilities / Dyslexia	
Program Director:	Dr. Lucia R. Karnes	919-945-5803
Contact Person:	Patricia LeDonne	1-800-755-5550

Admissions:

In order to ensure that the individual needs of each student are met, enrollment in the program is limited. Applications are reviewed thoroughly by the admissions committee and the Program Director. The student should: complete high school with a "C" average; have been diagnosed by a qualified professionall; supply supportive testing information with the application; provide satisfactory SAT or ACT scores; have an interview; provide assurance of motivation to attend Wingate College; and submit application for admission with all required documentation.

Interview: Yes   **Diagnostic Tests:** Yes

Documentation: IQ performance, verbal, full-range

College Entrance Exams Required: Yes   **Untimed Accepted:** Yes

Course Entrance Requirements: Yes

Are Waivers Available: Yes

Additional Information:

Math is required through Algebra II (sometimes this is waived).

Individualized high school coursework accepted: No

Essay Required: Yes

Special Application Required: No   **Submitted To:**

Number of Applications Submitted Each Year: 40

Number of Applications Accepted Each Year: 20

Number of Students Served: 27

Application Deadline for Special Admission: No

Acceptance into Program means acceptance into college: Yes

231

LEARNING DISABILITY SERVICES

Learning Resource Room: No   **Curriculum Modification Available:** Yes

Kurzweil Personal Reader: No   **Tutorial Help:** Yes   **Peer Tutors:** Yes

LD Specialists: 1   **Max. Hours/Week for services:**

Oral Exams: Yes   As needed

Services for LD Only: No   **Added**

Books on Tape: No   **Cost:** $1,000 for 1st year./$500 thereafter

Calculator allowed in exam: **Taping of books not on tape:** No

Tape recording in class: Yes   **Dictionary/computer/spellcheck during exam:** Yes

How are professors notified of LD: By the student and the Program Director

GENERAL ADMISSIONS INFORMATION

Director of Admissions: Steve Poston   **Telephone:** 704-233-8201

Entrance Requirements:

4 yrs. English; 3 yrs. Math; 2 yrs. History; 2 yrs. Science; 1 yr. Social Studies. 2 yrs. Foreign Language is recommended.

Test Scores: **SAT:** 845   **ACT:** Accepted

G.P.A.: 2.0   **Class Rank:**

Application Deadline: **Achievement Tests:**

COLLEGE GRADUATION REQUIREMENTS

Foreign Language: Yes   **Waivers:** Depends on major

Math: Yes   **Waivers:**

Minimum Course Load per Term: 8/15

ADDITIONAL INFORMATION

Location: The College is located on 330 acres in a small town 25 miles east of Charlotte.

Enrollment Information: **Undergraduate:** 1,666   **Women:** 51%   **Men:** 49%

    In-State Students: 75%   **Out of State:** 25%

Cost Information: **In-State Tuition:** $4,850   **Out of State:** same

    Room & Board: $2,550   **Additional Costs:** $220

Housing Information: **University Housing:** Yes   **Sorority:**

    % Living on Campus: 77%   **Fraternity:**

Athletics: NAIA

NORTH DAKOTA STATE UNIVERSITY
Fargo, N.D. 58105
701-237-8643

Support: CS   *Institution:* 4 yr. Public

LEARNING DISABILITY PROGRAM AND SERVICES

Comments:

All students with disabilities which may affect their academic functioning are eligible for services through Disabled Student Services. Specialized assistance and resources are offered. Students may receive one-on-one sessions in study strategies as well as courses in reading, assertiveness, and career planning. The Counseling Center is available to all students.

LEARNING DISABILITY ADMISSIONS INFORMATION

		Telephone
Program Name:	Disabled Student Services	
Program Director:	Pete Bower	701-237-7198
Contact Person:	Liz Sepe	701-237-7671

Admissions:

There is a voluntary information sheet included with all admissions materials allowing learning disabled students to self-identify. Admissions to the University is basically open-door, except to selective majors in Nursing, Architecture, Engineering and Pharmacy.

Interview: Yes   *Diagnostic Tests:* Yes

Documentation: Woodcock-Johnson; WISC or WAIS-R given within 2 years

College Entrance Exams Required: Yes   *Untimed Accepted:* Yes

Course Entrance Requirements: Yes

Are Waivers Available:

Additional Information:

Learning disabled students should submit an IEP from their high school as well as a statement from their LD teacher or case manager.

Individualized high school coursework accepted: Yes

Essay Required: No

Special Application Required: *Submitted To:*

Number of Applications Submitted Each Year: 20

Number of Applications Accepted Each Year: 15

Number of Students Served: 40

Application Deadline for Special Admission: No

Acceptance into Program means acceptance

into college: No, there is an appeal procedure

233

LEARNING DISABILITY SERVICES

Learning Resource Room: No

Kurzweil Personal Reader:

LD Specialists: 1

Oral Exams: Yes

Services for LD Only: Yes

Books on Tape: Yes

Calculator allowed in exam: No

Tape recording in class: Yes

Curriculum Modification Available: Yes

Tutorial Help: Yes   **Peer Tutors:** Yes

Max. Hours/Week for services:

Individually arranged

Added Cost: None

Taping of books not on tape: Yes

Dictionary/computer/spellcheck during exam: Yes

How are professors notified of LD: By both the student and the Program Director

GENERAL ADMISSIONS INFORMATION

Director of Admissions: George Wallman   **Telephone:** 701-237-8643

Entrance Requirements:

Graduation from an accredited secondary school, with 17 academic credits including high school Algebra and English. May consider PSAT.

Test Scores: **SAT:** 958   **ACT:** 21(Preferred)

G.P.A.:   **Class Rank:**

Application Deadline: Rolling   **Achievement Tests:**

COLLEGE GRADUATION REQUIREMENTS

Foreign Language: Y/N   **Waivers:** Yes

Math: Yes   **Waivers:** Yes with documentation and a strong case

Minimum Course Load per Term: Financial aid is at risk if less than 12 credits

ADDITIONAL INFORMATION

Location: The University is located in a small city 250 miles from Minneapolis, Sioux Falls, and Winnipeg, Canada.

Enrollment Information: **Undergraduate:** 8,518   **Women:** 39%   **Men:** 61%

In-State Students: 61%   **Out of State:** 39%

Cost Information: **In-State Tuition:** $1,506   **Out of State:** $3,768

Room & Board: $2,854   **Additional Costs:** $150

Housing Information: **University Housing:** Yes   **Sorority:** 1%

% Living on Campus: 45%   **Fraternity:** 1%

Athletics: NCAA Div. II

BOWLING GREEN STATE UNIVERSITY
Bowling Green, Oh. 43403-0013
419-372-2086

Support: S   **Institution:** 4 yr. Public

LEARNING DISABILITY PROGRAM AND SERVICES

Comments:

The Office of Handicapped Services provides services on an as-need basis. Services include an informational letter sent to professors describing the student's disability; referral for tutorial assistance; proctors for tests; pre-registration assistance; and assistance to faculty members in helping them to provide reasonable accommodations for learning disabled students. Students who have a documented disability which precludes learning a foreign language may petition for an exemption from the language requirement.

LEARNING DISABILITY ADMISSIONS INFORMATION

Program Name:	Office of Handicapped Services	**Telephone**
Program Director:	Rob Cunningham	419-372-8495
Contact Person:	same	

Admissions:

There is no special application or special admissions process. Students fill out a regular application and request special services. There is a Summer Freshman Program for freshman applicants who do not meet the academic standards for fall admission.

Interview: No   **Diagnostic Tests:** Yes

Documentation: Flexible

College Entrance Exams Required: Yes   **Untimed Accepted:** Yes

Course Entrance Requirements: Yes

Are Waivers Available: No

Additional Information:

Individualized high school coursework accepted:

Essay Required: No

Special Application Required: **Submitted To:**

Number of Applications Submitted Each Year:

Number of Applications Accepted Each Year:

Number of Students Served: 150

Application Deadline for Special Admission: No

Acceptance into Program means acceptance into college:

235

LEARNING DISABILITY SERVICES

Learning Resource Room: No   **Curriculum Modification Available:** No

Kurzweil Personal Reader: No   **Tutorial Help:** Yes   **Peer Tutors:** Yes

LD Specialists: **Max. Hours/Week for services:**

Oral Exams: Yes   Flexible

Services for LD Only: No   **Added**

Books on Tape: Yes   **Cost:** None

Calculator allowed in exam: Yes   **Taping of books not on tape:** Yes

Tape recording in class: Yes   **Dictionary/computer/spellcheck during exam:** Yes

How are professors notified of LD: By student and Program Director

GENERAL ADMISSIONS INFORMATION

Director of Admissions: John Martin   **Telephone:** 419-372-2086

Entrance Requirements:

4 yrs. English; 3 yrs. Math; 3 yrs. Science; 3 yrs. Social Studies/History; 2 yrs. Foreign Language;
1 yr. Art or Music.

Test Scores: **SAT:** 963   **ACT:** 22

G.P.A.: 2.5 minimum   **Class Rank:** top 1/4-1/2

Application Deadline: Rolling   **Achievement Tests:** No

COLLEGE GRADUATION REQUIREMENTS

Foreign Language: Yes   **Waivers:** Depends on Major

Math: **Waivers:**

Minimum Course Load per Term: 12 hours. per semester

ADDITIONAL INFORMATION

Location: The 1,250 acre campus is in a small town, 25 miles south of Toledo. There is a Gulf
Coast Research Lab in Marine Biology.

Enrollment Information: Undergraduate: 15,847   **Women:** 59%   **Men:** 41%

In-State Students: 92%   **Out of State:** 8%

Cost Information: In-State Tuition: $2,644   **Out of State:** $5,804

Room & Board: $2,344   **Additional Costs:** $482

Housing Information: University Housing: Yes   **Sorority:** 17%

% Living on Campus: 51%   **Fraternity:** 22%

Athletics: NCAA Div. I

COLLEGE OF MOUNT ST. JOSEPH
Mount St. Joseph, Ohio 45051
513-244-4531

Support: SP   **Institution:** 4 yr. Private

LEARNING DISABILITY PROGRAM AND SERVICES

Comments:

Project Excel is an academic support program for LD students enrolled in the College. The program fosters the development of learning strategies and compensatory skills which enable students to succeed in a regular academic program. The structure of the program and supportive environment at the Mount give Project Excel its singular quality.

LEARNING DISABILITY ADMISSIONS INFORMATION

Program Name: Project Excel   **Telephone**

Program Director: Dollie Kelly   513-244-4859

Contact Person: same

Admissions:

Students interested in Project Excel are encouraged to apply as early as possible. Call or write to schedule an interview and testing; fill out admission form; send ACT or SAT scores and high school transcript; complete a psycho-educational evaluation to be conducted at the Mount.

Interview: Yes   **Diagnostic Tests:** Yes

Documentation:

College Entrance Exams Required: Yes   **Untimed Accepted:** Yes

Course Entrance Requirements: Yes

Are Waivers Available:

Additional Information:

Students not meeting all admission requirements may be admitted on a part-time conditional basis.

Individualized high school coursework accepted:

Essay Required:

Special Application Required: **Submitted To:**

Number of Applications Submitted Each Year:

Number of Applications Accepted Each Year:

Number of Students Served: 40-45

Application Deadline for Special Admission: Junior year

**Acceptance into Program means acceptance
into college:** Yes

LEARNING DISABILITY SERVICES

Learning Resource Room: Yes   **Curriculum Modification Available:** No

Kurzweil Personal Reader: **Tutorial Help:** Yes   **Peer Tutors:** Yes

LD Specialists: 7   **Max. Hours/Week for services:**

Oral Exams: Yes   No Limit

Services for LD Only: Yes   **Added**

Books on Tape: Yes   **Cost:** $1,650

Calculator allowed in exam: **Taping of books not on tape:** Yes

Tape recording in class: Yes   **Dictionary/computer/spellcheck during exam:** Yes

How are professors notified of LD: By student and Director of Program

GENERAL ADMISSIONS INFORMATION

Director of Admissions: Edward Eckel   **Telephone:** 513-244-4531

Entrance Requirements:

16 credits including: 3 yrs. English; 2 yrs. Math; Social Studies; 1 yr. Lab Science; 8 electives.

Test Scores: **SAT:** 873   **ACT:** 19

G.P.A.: 2.5   **Class Rank:**

Application Deadline: Rolling   **Achievement Tests:**

COLLEGE GRADUATION REQUIREMENTS

Foreign Language: No   **Waivers:** Yes

Math: **Waivers:**

Minimum Course Load per Term:

ADDITIONAL INFORMATION

Location: The Mount is a Catholic coeducational liberal arts college located approximately 15 miles from downtown Cincinnati.

Enrollment Information: **Undergraduate:** 2,398   **Women:** 80%   **Men:** 20%

In-State Students: 96%   **Out of State:** 4%

Cost Information: **In-State Tuition:** $7,600   **Out of State:** same

Room & Board: $3,700   **Additional Costs:**

Housing Information: **University Housing:** Yes   **Sorority:** No

% Living on Campus: 18%   **Fraternity:** No

Athletics: NAIA

KENT STATE UNIVERSITY
Kent, Ohio 44242
216-672-2444

Support: CS   **Institution:** 4 yr. Public

LEARNING DISABILITY PROGRAM AND SERVICES

Comments:

The University believes that the ability to do college work is highly correlated with grades in high school. If a learning disability support system has been available and the student has been diligent and still has a low grade point average in high school, lack of skills or disabilities may be too severe for that student to be successful at Kent State. If the student has received accommodations in high school and has been successful, the student can receive assistance at Kent State. Students should meet with a DSS staff member 6 months before enrollment.

LEARNING DISABILITY ADMISSIONS INFORMATION

Program Name: Disabled Student Services (DSS)   **Telephone**

Program Director:

Contact Person: Janet L. Filer   216-672-3391

Admissions:

Students must meet the same admission criteria as all other applicants. There is no special admissions procedure for students with learning disabilities. However, the high school may adjust grade-point average if the student was not diagnosed until late in high school. Documentation of disability is required. Admitted students can receive subject tutoring through the Learning Development Program.

Interview: Yes   **Diagnostic Tests:** Yes

Documentation: Educational assessment should show areas of specific learning disability

College Entrance Exams Required: Yes   **Untimed Accepted:** Yes

Course Entrance Requirements: Yes

Are Waivers Available: No

Additional Information:

Individualized high school coursework accepted: Yes

Essay Required: No

Special Application Required: No   **Submitted To:**

Number of Applications Submitted Each Year: Varies

Number of Applications Accepted Each Year: Varies

Number of Students Served: 105 LD students

Application Deadline for Special Admission: No

Acceptance into Program means acceptance into college: No, there is an appeal procedure

239

LEARNING DISABILITY SERVICES

Learning Resource Room:	No	**Curriculum Modification Available:** No	
Kurzweil Personal Reader:		**Tutorial Help:** Yes	**Peer Tutors:** Yes
LD Specialists:	2	**Max. Hours/Week for services:**	
Oral Exams:	Yes	No limit	
Services for LD Only:	No	**Added**	
Books on Tape:	Yes	**Cost:**	
Calculator allowed in exam:	Yes	**Taping of books not on tape:** Yes	
Tape recording in class:	Yes	**Dictionary/computer/spellcheck during exam:** Yes	

How are professors notified of LD: Recommended Accommodations memo is sent

GENERAL ADMISSIONS INFORMATION

Director of Admissions: Bruce L. Riddle   **Telephone:** 216-672-2444

Entrance Requirements:

4 yrs. English; 2 yrs. Foreign Language; 3 yrs. Math; 3 yrs. Science; 3 yrs. Social Studies; 1 yr. Art. A 2.5 GPA is required for out-of-state students. Some programs have additional requirements.

Test Scores: **SAT:** 890   **ACT:** 21

G.P.A.: 2.5   **Class Rank:** Upper 50%

Application Deadline: 3/15   **Achievement Tests:**

COLLEGE GRADUATION REQUIREMENTS

Foreign Language: Yes   **Waivers:** Depends on major

Math: Yes   **Waivers:** Depends on major

Minimum Course Load per Term: Yes

ADDITIONAL INFORMATION

Location: The University is a residential campus located on 1,200 acres 45 miles south east of Cleveland.

Enrollment Information: **Undergraduate:**	18,993	**Women:** 58%	**Men:** 42%
In-State Students:	92%	**Out of State:** 8%	
Cost Information: **In-State Tuition:**	$2,826	**Out of State:** $5,426	
Room & Board:	$2,872	**Additional Costs:**	
Housing Information: **University Housing:**	Yes	**Sorority:** 3%	
% Living on Campus:	30%	**Fraternity:** 5%	

Athletics: NCAA Div. I

Support: SP   **Institution:** 4 yr. Private

LEARNING DISABILITY PROGRAM AND SERVICES

Comments:

Muskingum College's philosophy holds that each student is unique, with a potential to succeed in the academic world. This philosophy is best reflected in their PLUS program. Professional content area tutors offer academic support services. Tutors maintain a liaison with faculty to assure that the services provided are consistent with the individual faculty member's objectives. The student is provided with every opportunity to achieve according to their academic potential and to take responsibility for their own learning.

LEARNING DISABILITY ADMISSIONS INFORMATION

Program Name: PLUS Program   **Telephone**

Program Director: Dr. Paul Naour   614-826-8246

Contact Person: Susan Dannemann   614-826-8137

Admissions:

Admission for LD students is based on a careful evaluation of all the material that are submitted with the application. The student is evaluated for potential for academic success as a participant in the PLUS program. Admission policies are flexible for LD students. Applicants are reviewed and selected candidates are invited to interview. Space in the program is limited, early application is encouraged.

Interview: Yes   **Diagnostic Tests:** Yes

Documentation: WISC-R; WAIS-R; or any other documentation

College Entrance Exams Required: Yes   **Untimed Accepted:** Yes

Course Entrance Requirements: Yes

Are Waivers Available: Yes

Additional Information:

Some high school courses may be waived if test information substantiates an area of difficulty. Required are: 4 yrs. English; 3 yrs. Math; 2 yrs. Science; 2 yrs. Foreign Language and other college prep courses.

Individualized high school coursework accepted: Considered

Essay Required: Optional

Special Application Required: No   **Submitted To:**

Number of Applications Submitted Each Year: 150

Number of Applications Accepted Each Year: 40

Number of Students Served: 110

Application Deadline for Special Admission: Fall of senior year

Acceptance into Program means acceptance into college: Yes

LEARNING DISABILITY SERVICES

Learning Resource Room: Yes   **Curriculum Modification Available:** No

Kurzweil Personal Reader: No   **Tutorial Help:** Yes   **Peer Tutors:** No

LD Specialists: 23   **Max. Hours/Week for services:**

Oral Exams: Yes   No maximum

Services for LD Only: Yes   **Added**

Books on Tape: Yes   **Cost:** $3,000 p/year

Calculator allowed in exam: Yes   **Taping of books not on tape:** Yes

Tape recording in class: Yes   **Dictionary/computer/spellcheck during exam:** No

How are professors notified of LD: By the tutor liaison

GENERAL ADMISSIONS INFORMATION

Director of Admissions: Stan Howell   **Telephone:** 614-826-8137

Entrance Requirements:

4 yrs. English; 3 yrs. Math; 3 yrs. Science; 2 yrs. Social Studies; 2 yrs. Foreign Language.

Test Scores: **SAT:** 922   **ACT:** 19

G.P.A.: 2.5   **Class Rank:** Upper 50%

Application Deadline: Rolling   **Achievement Tests:**

COLLEGE GRADUATION REQUIREMENTS

Foreign Language: No   **Waivers:**

Math: Yes   **Waivers:** No

Minimum Course Load per Term: 12 hrs./ PLUS students carry about 13-14 rather than 15-16

ADDITIONAL INFORMATION

Location: The College is located on 215 ares in a rural area 9 miles west of Cambridge.

Enrollment Information: Undergraduate: 1,122   **Women:** 47%   **Men:** 53%

    In-State Students: 82%   **Out of State:** 18%

Cost Information: **In-State Tuition:** $10,325   **Out of State:** same

    Room & Board: $3,080   **Additional Costs:** $205

Housing Information: University Housing: Yes   **Sorority:** 55%

    % Living on Campus: 95%   **Fraternity:** 55%

Athletics: NCAA Div. III

UNIVERSITY OF CINCINNATI
Cincinnati, Ohio 45221-0091
513-556-1100

Support: S   **Institution:** 4 yr. Public

LEARNING DISABILITY PROGRAM AND SERVICES

Comments:

The University of Cincinnati does not have a specific structured Learning Disability Program. However, students who utilize the available services and resources of the University find they can be successful in achieving their academic objectives. Remedial developmental courses are available along with campus-wide tutoring. There is special consideration for testing, and a specialized mini computer lab.

LEARNING DISABILITY ADMISSIONS INFORMATION

Program Name:	Disability Services	**Telephone**
Program Director:	Lawrence M. Goodall	513-556-6816
Contact Person:	same	same

Admissions:

There is no special admissions. However, there is open-door admissions to University College. This is a 2 year Associate degree program. University College offers developmental courses in Effective Reading, Psychology, English for Effective Communication, Mathematics, Math Lab, and a college study course.

Interview: Yes   **Diagnostic Tests:** Yes

Documentation:

College Entrance Exams Required: Yes   **Untimed Accepted:** Yes

Course Entrance Requirements: Yes

Are Waivers Available: Yes

Additional Information:

Course requirements and waivers vary depending on which College within the University the student applies to. University College is an open door admissions with no minimum GPA, tests scores or course requirements. Transferring to other majors may be difficult.

Individualized high school coursework accepted: According to the College

Essay Required: No

Special Application Required: No   **Submitted To:**

Number of Applications Submitted Each Year: 20-30

Number of Applications Accepted Each Year: 20-30

Number of Students Served: 90

Application Deadline for Special Admission: No

Acceptance into Program means acceptance into college: No

LEARNING DISABILITY SERVICES

Learning Resource Room: No   **Curriculum Modification Available:** No

Kurzweil Personal Reader: Yes   **Tutorial Help:** Yes   **Peer Tutors:** Yes

LD Specialists: No   **Max. Hours/Week for services:**

Oral Exams: Yes   Varies

Services for LD Only: No   **Added
                                        Cost:**
Books on Tape: Yes

Calculator allowed in exam: Yes   **Taping of books not on tape:** Yes

Tape recording in class: Yes   **Dictionary/computer/spellcheck during exam:** Yes

How are professors notified of LD: By student

GENERAL ADMISSIONS INFORMATION

Director of Admissions: Robert W. Neel   **Telephone:** 513-556-1100

Entrance Requirements:

4 yrs. English; 3 yrs. Math; 2 yrs. each Science, Social Science, Foreign Language; electives; 1 yr. Fine Art. Open admissions to University College, a 2 year Associates degree program.

Test Scores: **SAT:** 980   **ACT:** 23

G.P.A.:   **Class Rank:**

Application Deadline: Rolling   **Achievement Tests:**

COLLEGE GRADUATION REQUIREMENTS

Foreign Language: Yes   **Waivers:** Yes

Math: Yes   **Waivers:**

Minimum Course Load per Term: Up to the student

ADDITIONAL INFORMATION

Location: The University is located on 392 acres in downtown Cincinnati.

Enrollment Information: **Undergraduate:** 24,263   **Women:** 47%   **Men:** 53%

In-State Students: 95%   **Out of State:** 5%

Cost Information: **In-State Tuition:** $2,679   **Out of State:** $6,393

Room & Board: $3,950   **Additional Costs:** $432

Housing Information: **University Housing:** Yes   **Sorority:** 11%

% Living on Campus: 16%   **Fraternity:** 10%

Athletics: NCAA Div. I

OKLAHOMA STATE UNIVERSITY
Stillwater, Ok. 74078-0660
405-744-6858

Support: S   **Institution:** 4 yr. Public

LEARNING DISABILITY PROGRAM AND SERVICES

Comments:

Oklahoma State University does not have a formal learning disabilities program but uses a service based model to assist the students in obtaining the necessary accommodations for specific learning disabilities. Specific services include assistance from Discover Career and Study Skills Center; writing lab; reading clinic; and Disabled Student Counseling. Other services developed in coordination with the Special Education area work to minimize the students difficulties in relation to coursework. These services could include test accommodations, course substitutions and independent study.

LEARNING DISABILITY ADMISSIONS INFORMATION

Program Name:	Disabled Student Services	**Telephone**
Program Director:	Maureen A. McCarthy	405-744-7116
Contact Person:	same	

Admissions:

Although there is no special admissions policy for students with learning disabilities a strong counselor recommendation could help a student who does not meet general admission requirements.

Interview: No   **Diagnostic Tests:** Yes

Documentation:

College Entrance Exams Required: Yes   **Untimed Accepted:** Yes

Course Entrance Requirements: Yes

Are Waivers Available:

Additional Information:

The purpose of alternative admissions is to provide a mechanism for students desiring to attend the University who may not qualify under the published criteria. These students must present their case as an exception and establish evidence of potential success. The University also operates the Oklahoma City Technical Institute which offers 2-year, career-oriented programs. Five percent of those applying may be admitted to the University on probation.

Individualized high school coursework accepted: No

Essay Required: No

Special Application Required: No   **Submitted To:**

Number of Applications Submitted Each Year:

Number of Applications Accepted Each Year:

Number of Students Served:

Application Deadline for Special Admission: No

Acceptance into Program means acceptance into college:

LEARNING DISABILITY SERVICES

Learning Resource Room: No   **Curriculum Modification Available:** Yes

Kurzweil Personal Reader: Yes   **Tutorial Help:** Yes   **Peer Tutors:** Yes

LD Specialists: **Max. Hours/Week for services:**

Oral Exams: Yes

Services for LD Only: **Added Cost:**

Books on Tape: Yes

Calculator allowed in exam: **Taping of books not on tape:** Yes

Tape recording in class: Yes   **Dictionary/computer/spellcheck during exam:**

How are professors notified of LD: By the student and the Program Director

GENERAL ADMISSIONS INFORMATION

Director of Admissions: Dr. Robin H. Lacy   **Telephone:** 405- 744-6876

Entrance Requirements:

11 academic units including: 4 yrs. English; 3 yrs. Math(algebra and above): 2 yrs. History; 2 yrs. Laboratory Science. Applicants should rank in the top 1/3 or have an ACT of 22 and a 3.0 GPA. Five percent are admitted on probation. GPA will be set annually based on the rank and the analysis of the relation between rank and GPA.

Test Scores: **SAT:**   **ACT:** 19

G.P.A.: 3.0 average   **Class Rank:** Top 50%

Application Deadline: **Achievement Tests:**

COLLEGE GRADUATION REQUIREMENTS

Foreign Language: Yes   **Waivers:**

Math: Yes   **Waivers:**

Minimum Course Load per Term: No

ADDITIONAL INFORMATION

Location: This 415 acre campus is located in a small city 65 miles north of Oklahoma City.

Enrollment Information: **Undergraduate:** 15,954   **Women:** 45%   **Men:** 55%

In-State Students: 90%   **Out of State:** 10%

Cost Information: **In-State Tuition:** $1,520   **Out of State:** $4,480

Room & Board: $2,700   **Additional Costs:** $244

Housing Information: **University Housing:** Yes   **Sorority:** 22%

% Living on Campus: 22%   **Fraternity:** 20%

Athletics: NCAA Div. I

Support: S   *Institution:* 4 yr. Public

LEARNING DISABILITY PROGRAM AND SERVICES

Comments:

The University offers a variety of support services to enhance academic success. These services are offered to all the students at the University. There are no special LD or remedial classes. As some classes are very large, students with attention deficits must consider this situation and determine if they can be successful in courses with a large student population. Accommodations include recorded texts, recorded lectures, special testing situations, counseling and advisement. LD students are encouraged to contact the Program Director to discuss individual needs and concerns.

LEARNING DISABILITY ADMISSIONS INFORMATION

Program Name: Handicapped Student Services   *Telephone*

Program Director: Linda Zinner   405-325-4006

Contact Person: Leslie Baumert

Admissions:

Admission requirements for learning disabled students are the same as for all other students. The University does accept ACT scores given under special conditions.

Interview: No   *Diagnostic Tests:* Yes

Documentation: WAIS-R; W-J

College Entrance Exams Required: Yes   *Untimed Accepted:* Yes

Course Entrance Requirements: Yes

Are Waivers Available: No

Additional Information:

Individualized high school coursework accepted:

Essay Required: No

Special Application Required: No   *Submitted To:*

Number of Applications Submitted Each Year:

Number of Applications Accepted Each Year:

Number of Students Served: 30

Application Deadline for Special Admission:

Acceptance into Program means acceptance

into college: N/A, there is an appeal procedure

LEARNING DISABILITY SERVICES

Learning Resource Room: No	**Curriculum Modification Available:**	
Kurzweil Personal Reader:	**Tutorial Help:** Yes	**Peer Tutors:** Yes
LD Specialists: No	**Max. Hours/Week for services:**	
Oral Exams:	First semester of senior year	
Services for LD Only: No	**Added**	
Books on Tape: Yes	**Cost:** None	
Calculator allowed in exam: Yes	**Taping of books not on tape:** Yes	
Tape recording in class: Yes	**Dictionary/computer/spellcheck during exam:** Yes	

How are professors notified of LD: By either the student or Program Director

GENERAL ADMISSIONS INFORMATION

Director of Admissions: Marc Borish   **Telephone:** 405-325-2251

Entrance Requirements:

11 academic credits including: 4 yrs. English; 3 yrs. Math; 2 yrs. Science; 2 yrs. History; 2 yrs. Foreign Language.

Test Scores: **SAT:** 880 (minimum)   **ACT:** 22 (minimum)

G.P.A.: 3.0   **Class Rank:** Upper 50%

Application Deadline: Rolling   **Achievement Tests:**

COLLEGE GRADUATION REQUIREMENTS

Foreign Language: **Waivers:** Depends on major

Math: **Waivers:** Depends on major

Minimum Course Load per Term: 1 credit hour

ADDITIONAL INFORMATION

Location: The 1,219 acre campus is located in a suburb 17 miles south of Oklahoma City.

Enrollment Information:	**Undergraduate:** 14,925	**Women:** 46%	**Men:** 54%
	In-State Students: 82%		**Out of State:** 18%
Cost Information:	**In-State Tuition:** $1,070		**Out of State:** $3,271
	Room & Board: $3,172		**Additional Costs:** $130
Housing Information:	**University Housing:** Yes		**Sorority:** 5%
	% Living on Campus: 13%		**Fraternity:** 5%

Athletics: NCAA Div. I

OREGON STATE UNIVERSITY
Corvallis, Or. 97331
503-737-0123

Support: S   **Institution:** 4 yrs. Public

LEARNING DISABILITY PROGRAM AND SERVICES

Comments:

SSD is available for all students who need extra services. EOP offers students who are learning disabled, economically disadvantaged, or first generation college-bound a variety of remedial courses for credit. They try to provide tutoring for any undergraduate class if tutors are available. Other services include developmental classes in writing, math, study skills, and test accommodations. There is also a course for learning disabled students to get assistance with learning strategies for notetaking. The Director acts as a liaison between student and faculty.

LEARNING DISABILITY ADMISSIONS INFORMATION

Program Name:	Services for Students with Disabilities (SSD)	**Telephone**
Program Director:	Tracy Bentley	503-737-3661
Contact Person:	Shiela Tacy	503-737-3628

Admissions:

LD students are eligible for a special admission process. They need to mark on the application that they are LD. Students must submit documentation of their learning disability including educational history and diagnostic testing administered by professionals. It is helpful if the information includes a description of cognitive strengths and weaknesses, recommendations for accommodations or services, and any other additional information in the form of a family history. Students must also submit a handwritten 1-2 page statement outlining educational goals and explaining motivation to succeed at OSU.

Interview: Yes   **Diagnostic Tests:** Yes

Documentation: IQ: Achievement tests: Processing tests

College Entrance Exams Required: Yes   **Untimed Accepted:** Yes

Course Entrance Requirements: Yes

Are Waivers Available:

Additional Information:

The Director of SSD, who helps to make admission decisions, may recommend EOP for the learning disabled student. EOP will review documentation and will provide extra help in selecting programs including placement in study skills classes, and English and Math classes with fewer students enrolled.

Individualized high school coursework accepted: No

Essay Required: Yes

Special Application Required: Yes   **Submitted To:**

Number of Applications Submitted Each Year: 350-400

Number of Applications Accepted Each Year: 250

Number of Students Served: 650

Application Deadline for Special Admission: 3/1 of Senior year

Acceptance into Program means acceptance

into college: No, can appeal

249

LEARNING DISABILITY SERVICES

Learning Resource Room: Yes   **Curriculum Modification Available:** Y/N

Kurzweil Personal Reader: Yes   **Tutorial Help:** Yes   **Peer Tutors:** Yes

LD Specialists: No   **Max. Hours/Week for services:**

Oral Exams: Yes   2 hours per week/per class / EOP, varies

Services for LD Only: No   **Added**

Books on Tape: Yes   **Cost:** None

Calculator allowed in exam: Y/N   **Taping of books not on tape:** Yes

Tape recording in class: Yes   **Dictionary/computer/spellcheck during exam:** Y/N

How are professors notified of LD: By student and Program Director

GENERAL ADMISSIONS INFORMATION

Director of Admissions: Wallace E. Gibbs   **Telephone:** 503-737-4411

Entrance Requirements:

4 yrs. English; 3 yrs. Math; 3 yrs. Social Studies; 2 yrs. Science; Foreign Language; plus 2 yrs. of additional college prep courses. They require a 30 on the test of Standard Written English or a 12 on the English section of the ACT.

Test Scores: SAT: 950   **ACT:** 21

G.P.A.: 2.75 (in-state)   **Class Rank:**

Application Deadline: Rolling   **Achievement Tests:** No

COLLEGE GRADUATION REQUIREMENTS

Foreign Language: Y/N   **Waivers:** Depends on Department

Math: Y/N   **Waivers:** Basic core requirements

Minimum Course Load per Term: 9 hrs. (but might affect financial aid)

ADDITIONAL INFORMATION

Location: The University is located on 530 acres in a small town 85 miles south of Portland.

Enrollment Information: Undergraduate: 13,249   **Women:** 40%   **Men:** 60%

In-State Students: 77%   **Out of State:** 23%

Cost Information: In-State Tuition: $1,707   **Out of State:** $4,968

Room & Board: $2,558   **Additional Costs:**

Housing Information: University Housing: Yes   **Sorority:** 7%

% Living on Campus: 25%   **Fraternity:** 12%

Athletics: NCAA Div. I

CLARION UNIVERSITY OF PENNSYLVANIA
Clarion, Pa. 16214
814-226-2306

Support: S   *Institution:* 4 Yr. Public

LEARNING DISABILITY PROGRAM AND SERVICES

Comments:

Clarion does not have a "special admissions" program for students with learning disabilities, nor does it offer a structured "LD Program." The Special Services Program is the University's primary vehicle for providing a Tutoring Center and Academic Support Center which is available to all students but is especially beneficial for students with learning disabilities. These services are free of charge and include extensive peer tutoring, study skills workshops and individual "learning to learn" activities.

LEARNING DISABILITY ADMISSIONS INFORMATION

Program Name: Special Services Program   *Telephone*

Program Director: Gregory K. Clay   814-226-2347

Contact Person: same

Admissions:

Students who wish to be admitted to the University must meet regular admissions requirements. As part of the application process, LD students are encouraged to provide documentation of their learning disability in order to establish a clear need for individualized support services. Students should also include a copy of their IEP.

Interview: Yes   *Diagnostic Tests:* Yes

Documentation: WAIS-R

College Entrance Exams Required: Yes   *Untimed Accepted:* Yes

Course Entrance Requirements: Yes

Are Waivers Available:

Additional Information:

Individualized high school coursework accepted: Yes

Essay Required: Yes

Special Application Required: *Submitted To:*

Number of Applications Submitted Each Year: 15

Number of Applications Accepted Each Year: 8

Number of Students Served: 36 LD

Application Deadline for Special Admission: No

Acceptance into Program means acceptance into college: No

251

LEARNING DISABILITY SERVICES

Learning Resource Room: Yes

Kurzweil Personal Reader:

LD Specialists: No

Oral Exams: Yes

Services for LD Only: No

Books on Tape: Yes

Calculator allowed in exam: Y/N

Tape recording in class: Yes

How are professors notified of LD: By student and Program Director

Curriculum Modification Available: Yes

Tutorial Help: Yes   **Peer Tutors:** Yes

Max. Hours/Week for services:

    1 hour per/course

Added Cost: None

Taping of books not on tape: Yes

Dictionary/computer/spellcheck during exam: No

GENERAL ADMISSIONS INFORMATION

Director of Admissions: John S. Shropshire   **Telephone:** 814-226-2306

Entrance Requirements:

4 yrs. English; 3 yrs. Social Studies; 3 yrs. Math; 3 yrs. Science; 2 yrs. Foreign Language. Summer Pre-college Experience for students not usually admitted. No SAT verbal or math below 400.

Test Scores: **SAT:** 850 (minimum)   **ACT:** 19 (minimum)

G.P.A.: 2.5   **Class Rank:** Upper 60%

Application Deadline: Rolling   **Achievement Tests:** For Foreign Lang.

COLLEGE GRADUATION REQUIREMENTS

Foreign Language: Yes   **Waivers:** Depends on major

Math: Yes   **Waivers:** Depends on major, substitution possible

Minimum Course Load per Term: 12 hours, however many have fewer

ADDITIONAL INFORMATION

Location: The University is located in a small town on 100 acres 85 miles northeast of Pittsburgh.

Enrollment Information: **Undergraduate:** 5,789   **Women:** 59%   **Men:** 41%

    In-State Students: 92%   **Out of State:** 8%

Cost Information: **In-State Tuition:** $2,458   **Out of State:** $4,314

    Room & Board: $2,360   **Additional Costs:** $385

Housing Information: University Housing: Yes   **Sorority:** 13%

    % Living on Campus: 50%   **Fraternity:** 18%

Athletics: NCAA Div. II

COLLEGE MISERICORDIA
Dallas, Pa. 18612
717-675-2507

Support: CS   **Institution:** 4 yr. Private

LEARNING DISABILITY PROGRAM AND SERVICES

Comments:

All students who participate in the Alternate Learners Project are enrolled in regular college classes. In most cases they take a carefully selected, reduced credit load each semester. Students who participate in ALP are supported by an assortment of services delivered by a specially trained full-time staff. Services include "Learning Strategies," which are designed to make students more efficient, and accommodations designed to work around students' disabilities whenever possible.

LEARNING DISABILITY ADMISSIONS INFORMATION

Program Name: Alternative Learners Project (ALP)   **Telephone**

Program Director: Dr. Joseph Rogan   717-674-6347

Contact Person: same

Admissions:

College Misericordia's experience with learning disabled students has stated that students who who are highly motivated and socially mature have an excellent chance to be successful. Each applicant has to secure a standard admissions form, enclose written cover letter summarizing their learning disability; additionally, they should submit a copy of their psychological report, high school transcript, and 3 letters of recommendation (one must be written by a special education professional).

Interview: Yes   **Diagnostic Tests:** Yes

Documentation: Recent psychological including WAIS-R

College Entrance Exams Required: Yes   **Untimed Accepted:** Yes

Course Entrance Requirements: Yes

Are Waivers Available:

Additional Information:

SAT is required but not used for admissions.

Individualized high school coursework accepted: Maybe

Essay Required: Yes

Special Application Required: **Submitted To:**

Number of Applications Submitted Each Year: 100

Number of Applications Accepted Each Year: 25

Number of Students Served: 55

Application Deadline for Special Admission: November of Senior year

Acceptance into Program means acceptance

into college: Joint acceptance

LEARNING DISABILITY SERVICES

Learning Resource Room: Yes   **Curriculum Modification Available:** No

Kurzweil Personal Reader: Yes   **Tutorial Help:** Yes   **Peer Tutors:** Yes

LD Specialists: 5   **Max. Hours/Week for services:**

Oral Exams: Yes   Unlimited

Services for LD Only: No   **Added**

Books on Tape: Yes   **Cost:** None

Calculator allowed in exam: Yes   **Taping of books not on tape:** Yes

Tape recording in class: Yes   **Dictionary/computer/spellcheck during exam:** Yes

How are professors notified of LD: By staff

GENERAL ADMISSIONS INFORMATION

Director of Admissions: David M. Payne   **Telephone:** 717-675-4449

Entrance Requirements:

16 units including: 4 yrs. English; 4 yrs. Math; 4 yrs. History; 4 yrs. Science (including 2 yrs. of Lab); 4 yrs. Social Studies; 4 yrs. electives which may include 2 non-academic units. The school requires at least a 400 verbal and a 400 math on the SAT.

Test Scores: **SAT:** 800 (minimum)   **ACT:**

G.P.A.: 2.0 (minimum)   **Class Rank:**

Application Deadline: Rolling   **Achievement Tests:**

COLLEGE GRADUATION REQUIREMENTS

Foreign Language: No   **Waivers:**

Math: Yes   **Waivers:**

Minimum Course Load per Term: 12 credits

ADDITIONAL INFORMATION

Location: The College is located in a suburban small town. on a 100 acre campus 9 miles south of Wilks-Barre.

Enrollment Information: **Undergraduate:** 1,035   **Women:** 70%   **Men:** 30%

In-State Students: 80%   **Out of State:** 20%

Cost Information: **In-State Tuition:** $7,280   **Out of State:** same

Room & Board: $3,700   **Additional Costs:** $400

Housing Information: **University Housing:** Yes   **Sorority:** 3%

% Living on Campus: 50%   **Fraternity:** 3%

Athletics: NAIA

Support: S   **Institution:** 4 yr. Private

LEARNING DISABILITY PROGRAM AND SERVICES

Comments:

Drexel does not have a learning disability program, but services are provided through the Office of Student Support Services. SSS helps students achieve their personal and educational goals through assistance from the staff. Programs are designed to develop academic and life skills, increase cultural awareness, contribute to career planning and development, and lend the support necessary to complete a college degree. The program offers two, four-week, residential summer programs, which are designed to prepare incoming freshman to adjust to academic life.

LEARNING DISABILITY ADMISSIONS INFORMATION

Program Name: Office of Student Support Services (SSS)   **Telephone**

Program Director: Ina Ellen   215-895-2525

Contact Person:

Admissions:

The regular admission requirements are the same for all students.

Interview: Yes   **Diagnostic Tests:** No

Documentation: Documentation is needed to provide services.

College Entrance Exams Required: Yes   **Untimed Accepted:** Yes

Course Entrance Requirements: Yes

Are Waivers Available: No

Additional Information:

Individualized high school coursework accepted: Yes

Essay Required: Yes

Special Application Required: No   **Submitted To:**

Number of Applications Submitted Each Year:

Number of Applications Accepted Each Year:

Number of Students Served: 35

Application Deadline for Special Admission: No

Acceptance into Program means acceptance

into college: N/A, there is an appeal process

LEARNING DISABILITY SERVICES

Learning Resource Room: Yes

Kurzweil Personal Reader:

LD Specialists: No

Oral Exams: Yes

Services for LD Only: No

Books on Tape: Yes

Calculator allowed in exam: Y/N

Tape recording in class: Yes

Curriculum Modification Available: No

Tutorial Help: Yes   **Peer Tutors:** Yes

Max. Hours/Week for services:

According to the needs of the student

Added Cost: None

Taping of books not on tape: Yes

Dictionary/computer/spellcheck during exam: Y/N

How are professors notified of LD: By the student and the Program Director

GENERAL ADMISSIONS INFORMATION

Director of Admissions: David Hawsey   **Telephone:** 215-895-2400

Entrance Requirements:

4 yrs. English; 3 yrs. Math; 1 yr. Science (Chemistry, Biology or Physics); 1 yr. Social Studies; 7 electives which may include 3 nonacademic courses. Requirements for those entering with majors in engineering and science are: Algebra 1 & 2, Geometry, Trigonometry; and 2 Lab Sciences. All other majors require: Algebra 1 & 2; Geometry; and Lab Science. Achievements required for Engineering and Science.

Test Scores: **SAT:** 1057   **ACT:**

G.P.A.:   **Class Rank:**

Application Deadline: 8/15   **Achievement Tests:** For Eng./Sci.

COLLEGE GRADUATION REQUIREMENTS

Foreign Language: No   **Waivers:**

Math: Yes   **Waivers:** No

Minimum Course Load per Term: 12 credits for full-time status

ADDITIONAL INFORMATION

Location: The campus is located on 38 acres near the center of Philadelphia.

Enrollment Information: **Undergraduate:** 8,976   **Women:** 31%   **Men:** 69%

In-State Students: 60%   **Out of State:** 40%

Cost Information: **In-State Tuition:** $9,551   **Out of State:** same

Room & Board: $4,004   **Additional Costs:** $546

Housing Information: University Housing: Yes   **Sorority:** 9%

% Living on Campus: 45%   **Fraternity:** 11%

Athletics: NCAA Div. I

EAST STROUDSBURG UNIVERSITY
East Stroudsburg, Pa. 18301
717-424-3542

Support: CS **Institution:** 4 yr. Public

LEARNING DISABILITY PROGRAM AND SERVICES

Comments:

There is no special program at East Stroudsburg University. There is a learning center directed by Germaine Francois, 717-424-3504. The University is committed to supporting otherwise qualified learning disabled students in their pursuit of an education. There are many services to assist LD students. They are encouraged to meet with the Director once accepted. Services include early registration, testing accommodations, advocacy, tutoring and drop-in labs in Math and Writing, remedial instruction and reduced course load.

LEARNING DISABILITY ADMISSIONS INFORMATION

Program Name: Programs for Academic Support

Program Director: Bo Keppel

Telephone

717-424-3470

Contact Person:

Admissions:

Learning disabled students file a general application, and are encouraged to complete the section titled "disabilities Information." Notification of a learning disability is used as a part of the admissions process only if the student is denied admission. At this time the admissions office waits for a recommendation from the learning disability specialist. The Office of Academic Support may request a reconsideration of the denial of admissions.

Interview: No

Documentation: Psychological; IEP

College Entrance Exams Required: Yes

Course Entrance Requirements: Yes

Are Waivers Available: No

Diagnostic Tests: Yes

Untimed Accepted: Yes

Additional Information:

Pre-admission summer program for Pennsylvania residents only. This program is called the Summer Intensive Study Program.

Individualized high school coursework accepted: Yes

Essay Required: Yes for entrance into Frsh. English

Special Application Required: Yes **Submitted To:** Program Director

Number of Applications Submitted Each Year: 60-90

Number of Applications Accepted Each Year:

Number of Students Served: 35

Application Deadline for Special Admission:

Acceptance into Program means acceptance into college:

LEARNING DISABILITY SERVICES

Learning Resource Room: Yes

Curriculum Modification Available: No

Kurzweil Personal Reader: No

Tutorial Help: Yes

Peer Tutors: Yes

LD Specialists: Yes

Max. Hours/Week for services:

Oral Exams: Yes

2 hours per/course

Services for LD Only: No

Added

Books on Tape: Yes

Cost: None

Calculator allowed in exam: Yes

Taping of books not on tape: Yes

Tape recording in class: Yes

Dictionary/computer/spellcheck during exam: No

How are professors notified of LD: By student and Program Director

GENERAL ADMISSIONS INFORMATION

Director of Admissions: Alan T. Chesterton

Telephone: 717-424-3542

Entrance Requirements:

4 yrs. English; 2 yrs. Math; 3 yrs. Social Studies; 2 yrs. Lab Science. Non-academic factors also considered are: special talent and alumni status. Essays are recommended. Achievement tests are necessary for Language majors.

Test Scores: **SAT:** 850

ACT:

G.P.A.:

Class Rank: top 33%

Application Deadline: 3/1

Achievement Tests: Yes

COLLEGE GRADUATION REQUIREMENTS

Foreign Language: No   **Waivers:**

Math: No   **Waivers:**

Minimum Course Load per Term:

ADDITIONAL INFORMATION

Location: The 813 acre campus is set in the foothills of the Pocono Mountains.

Enrollment Information: **Undergraduate:** 4,695   **Women:** 58%   **Men:** 42%

In-State Students: 61%   **Out of State:** 39%

Cost Information: **In-State Tuition:** $2,275   **Out of State:** $4,400

Room & Board: $2,765   **Additional Costs:** $250

Housing Information: **University Housing:** Yes   **Sorority:** Yes

% Living on Campus: 48%   **Fraternity:** Yes

Athletics: NCAA Div. II

EDINBORO UNIVERSITY OF PENNSYLVANIA
Edinboro, Pa. 16444

814-732-2761

Support: S *Institution:* 4 yr. Public

LEARNING DISABILITY PROGRAM AND SERVICES

Comments:

Edinboro University seeks students who have the ability and motivation to succeed academically. The staff of the Office of Disabled Student Services holds high expectations of students with disabilities. Although ODSS acts as an advocate for its disabled students, the students are expected to fulfill all degree requirements. The student is not permitted course waivers as the supportive services are in place to assist the student in handling the rigors of college level work.

LEARNING DISABILITY ADMISSIONS INFORMATION

Program Name: Office of Disabled Student Services (ODSS) *Telephone*

Program Director: James Foulk   814-732-2462

Contact Person: Kathleen Strosser   same

Admissions:

Students apply for admission to Edinboro University of Pennsylvania, and when accepted, apply for ODSS services. Students need to provide a multifactored educational assessment not more than 3 years old; age level scores in reading vocabulary and comprehension, math, and spelling; individual intelligence test administered by a psychologist, including a list of the tests given.

Interview: Recommended   **Diagnostic Tests:** Yes

Documentation:

College Entrance Exams Required: Yes   **Untimed Accepted:** Yes

Course Entrance Requirements: Yes

Are Waivers Available:

Additional Information:

Completion of Confidential Background Information form with an attached writing sample. A minimum of 2 paragraphs of unedited, non-assisted writing, used to establish appropriate writing support services.

Individualized high school coursework accepted: Yes

Essay Required: Yes

Special Application Required: **Submitted To:**

Number of Applications Submitted Each Year: N/A

Number of Applications Accepted Each Year: N/A

Number of Students Served: 84

Application Deadline for Special Admission: No

Acceptance into Program means acceptance into college: No

LEARNING DISABILITY SERVICES

Learning Resource Room: Yes   **Curriculum Modification Available:** No

Kurzweil Personal Reader: Yes   **Tutorial Help:** Yes   **Peer Tutors:** Yes

LD Specialists: No   **Max. Hours/Week for services:**

Oral Exams: Yes   15 hours per/week

Services for LD Only: No   **Added**

Books on Tape: Yes   **Cost:** $1,600 p/y/ Summer Program $2,500

Calculator allowed in exam: Yes   **Taping of books not on tape:** Yes

Tape recording in class: Yes   **Dictionary/computer/spellcheck during exam:** Yes

How are professors notified of LD: By student

GENERAL ADMISSIONS INFORMATION

Director of Admissions: Mr. Terry Carlin   **Telephone:** 814-732-2761

Entrance Requirements:

There is no specific high school courses required. There is a precolloege Summer Program for students not usually admitted. The successful completion of this program allows for unconditional admission to the Fall semester.

Test Scores: **SAT:**   **ACT:** Required

G.P.A.:   **Class Rank:**

Application Deadline: Rolling   **Achievement Tests:**

COLLEGE GRADUATION REQUIREMENTS

Foreign Language: No   **Waivers:**

Math: Yes   **Waivers:** No/ Computer class also considered

Minimum Course Load per Term: 12 hours, waivers available for 9 credits

ADDITIONAL INFORMATION

Location: Small town setting, 600 acres of campus 20 miles south of Erie. Edinboro is a public University with facilities that include a planetarium and an art gallery.

Enrollment Information: **Undergraduate:** 6,750   **Women:** 57%   **Men:** 43%

   In-State Students: 85%   **Out of State:** 15%

Cost Information: **In-State Tuition:** $2,178   **Out of State:** $4,034

   Room & Board: $2,320   **Additional Costs:**

Housing Information: **University Housing:** Yes   **Sorority:** 15%

   % Living on Campus: 40%   **Fraternity:** 10%

Athletics: NCAA Div. II

Support: SP   **Institution:** 2 yr. Private

LEARNING DISABILITY PROGRAM AND SERVICES

Comments:

The Talent Development program at Harcum Junior College is a new service which offers an individualized approach in helping students with learning disabilities. The staff is full-time. Part of the philosophy of the program is not only to offer academic learning disability services but also to help develop a career track that will help the student become independent once they leave the College.

LEARNING DISABILITY ADMISSIONS INFORMATION

Program Name: Talent Development   **Telephone**

Program Director: Tania Bailey   215-526-6034

Contact Person: same

Admissions:

There is a special application and admissions procedure to follow. This includes an interview with the Talent Development staff, interview with Admissions counselor, completed applications form including a written essay, and all referrals describing the specific learning differences and the results of the WAIS-R. The SAT and ACT are not required for the Talent Development program, but is required for specific majors. There is a summer program offered for 6 weeks during the summer prior to the start of school.

Interview: Yes   **Diagnostic Tests:** Yes

Documentation: Detroit Test of Learning Aptitude-not required but helpful

College Entrance Exams Required: No   **Untimed Accepted:** Yes

Course Entrance Requirements: Yes

Are Waivers Available:

Additional Information:

Students must submit their high school diploma and/or transfer documentation from another college. Harcum Junior College Placement Testing in Reading Vocabulary and Comprehension (English grammar and writing samples), and Mathematics are administered to all students. Those who do not meet the cut-offs are placed in developmental courses.

Individualized high school coursework accepted: Yes

Essay Required: Yes

Special Application Required: Yes   **Submitted To:**

Number of Applications Submitted Each Year: N/A

Number of Applications Accepted Each Year: new program

Number of Students Served: 22

Application Deadline for Special Admission: No

Acceptance into Program means acceptance

into college: Spring of Junior year in high school

LEARNING DISABILITY SERVICES

Learning Resource Room: Yes   **Curriculum Modification Available:** No

Kurzweil Personal Reader: No   **Tutorial Help:** Yes   **Peer Tutors:** Yes

LD Specialists: 2   **Max. Hours/Week for services:**

Oral Exams: Yes   6 hours per/week;3 hours per/course

Services for LD Only: Yes   **Added**

Books on Tape: Yes   **Cost:** $2,400

Calculator allowed in exam: **Taping of books not on tape:** Yes

Tape recording in class: Yes   **Dictionary/computer/spellcheck during exam:**

How are professors notified of LD: By the student and the Program Director

GENERAL ADMISSIONS INFORMATION

Director of Admissions: Mary Pontius   **Telephone:** 215-526-6050

Entrance Requirements:

High school transcript. For some majors the requirement is 3 years of math and the SAT. Recommendations are helpful.

Test Scores: SAT: **ACT:**

G.P.A.:   **Class Rank:**

Application Deadline: Rolling   **Achievement Tests:**

COLLEGE GRADUATION REQUIREMENTS

Foreign Language: No   **Waivers:**

Math: Yes   **Waivers:** Yes, Individually determined

Minimum Course Load per Term: 12 credits

ADDITIONAL INFORMATION

Location: The school is located on a 12 acre campus with easy access to Philadelphia.

Enrollment Information: Undergraduate: 677   **Women:** 99%   **Men:** 1%

In-State Students: 65%   **Out of State:** 35%

Cost Information: In-State Tuition: $5,590   **Out of State:** same

Room & Board: $3,630   **Additional Costs:** $410

Housing Information: University Housing: Yes   **Sorority:**

% Living on Campus: 80%   **Fraternity:**

Athletics: Intercollegiate sports

Support: SP   **Institution:** 4 yr. Private

LEARNING DISABILITY PROGRAM AND SERVICES

Comments:

The specialized program at Mercyhurst College is designed to assist students, who have been identified as learning disabled, to achieve in college and to earn a degree. The emphasis is on the students individual strengths, abilities and interests, as well as learning deficits. Each freshman is required to take a 6 week summer session prior to entrance. Services include counseling, tutoring, 3 credit courses to identify learning styles and study skills. There are basic courses available in writing, reading and math.

LEARNING DISABILITY ADMISSIONS INFORMATION

		Telephone
Program Name:	Program for Learning Disabled	
Program Director:	Dr. Barbara Weiqert	814-825-0447
Contact Person:	Andrew Roth	814-825-0239

Admissions:

There is a special application and admission process. Any person who has completed high school and who has been identified as learning disabled may be qualified for admission to this program. A "C" average is required. Recommendations from case managers and/or counselors are required.

Interview: Yes   **Diagnostic Tests:** Yes

Documentation: WISC or WAIS-R

College Entrance Exams Required: Yes   **Untimed Accepted:** Yes

Course Entrance Requirements: Yes

Are Waivers Available:

Additional Information:

Summer Foundations Program for conditional admission.

Individualized high school coursework accepted: Yes

Essay Required: Yes

Special Application Required: Yes   **Submitted To:**

Number of Applications Submitted Each Year: 75

Number of Applications Accepted Each Year: 15

Number of Students Served: 47

Application Deadline for Special Admission: Summer before or February 15 of senior year

Acceptance into Program means acceptance into college: Yes, there is a waiting list

LEARNING DISABILITY SERVICES

Learning Resource Room: Yes   **Curriculum Modification Available:** No

Kurzweil Personal Reader: Yes   **Tutorial Help:** Yes   **Peer Tutors:** Yes

LD Specialists: 1   **Max. Hours/Week for services:**

Oral Exams: Yes   No limit

Services for LD Only: Yes   **Added**

Books on Tape: Yes   **Cost:** $750 plus summer school for Fresh.

Calculator allowed in exam: Y/N   **Taping of books not on tape:** Yes

Tape recording in class: Yes   **Dictionary/computer/spellcheck during exam:** Y/N

How are professors notified of LD: By the student and Program Director

GENERAL ADMISSIONS INFORMATION

Director of Admissions: Andrew Roth   **Telephone:** 814-825-0240

Entrance Requirements:

16 credits which include: 4 yrs. English; 3 yrs. Math; 3 yrs. Social Studies; 2 yrs. History; 2 yrs. Science; Nursing applicants need a "B" average and an SAT of 850. The school recommends a 400 verbal and a 400 math on the SAT.

Test Scores: **SAT:** 800 (minimum)   **ACT:** 16 (minimum)

G.P.A.: 2.2   **Class Rank:** Upper 65%

Application Deadline: Rolling   **Achievement Tests:**

COLLEGE GRADUATION REQUIREMENTS

Foreign Language: No   **Waivers:**

Math: Yes   **Waivers:** No

Minimum Course Load per Term: Student may take reduced load if not on financial aid

ADDITIONAL INFORMATION

Location: The 80 acre campus of the College overlooks Lake Erie.

Enrollment Information: **Undergraduate:** 2,091   **Women:** 52%   **Men:** 48%

                        In-State Students: 63%   **Out of State:** 37%

Cost Information: **In-State Tuition:** $7,450   **Out of State:** same

                          Room & Board: $3,000   **Additional Costs:** $380

Housing Information: **University Housing:** Yes   **Sorority:** No

                  % Living on Campus: 61%   **Fraternity:** No

Athletics: NCAA Div. III

PENNSYLVANIA STATE UNIVERSITY
University Park, Pa. 16802
814-865-5471

Support: S   **Institution:** 4 yr. Public

LEARNING DISABILITY PROGRAM AND SERVICES

Comments:

Penn State is interested in all academically qualified students. In terms of a learning disability, they seek to enroll students who can complete college level courses with the help of support services and classroom accommodations. The Learning Assistance Center is available to help all students with math, writing, reading and study skills. There is individual and group tutoring available. The support program providing one-to-one assistance is, at this time, in a transition stage while the University hires someone to develop and implement services.

LEARNING DISABILITY ADMISSIONS INFORMATION

Program Name: Office for Disability Services   **Telephone**

Program Director: Brenda G. Hameister   814-863-1807

Contact Person:

Admissions:

There is no special application process, however, the student may choose to self-identify a learning disability on the application. If the high school grades and the SAT score are low, students many choose to send a letter explaining why their ability to succeed in college is higher than indicated by their academic records, The Admissions Office will consider this information as it is voluntarily provided. The acceptable ACT or SAT score will depend upon the high school grades and class rank of the student.

Interview: No   **Diagnostic Tests:** No

Documentation:

College Entrance Exams Required: Yes   **Untimed Accepted:** Yes

Course Entrance Requirements: Yes

Are Waivers Available:

Additional Information:

Individualized high school coursework accepted:

Essay Required: No

Special Application Required: No   **Submitted To:**

Number of Applications Submitted Each Year:

Number of Applications Accepted Each Year:

Number of Students Served: 150

Application Deadline for Special Admission: No

Acceptance into Program means acceptance into college: No, there is an appeal procedure

265

LEARNING DISABILITY SERVICES

Learning Resource Room: Yes   **Curriculum Modification Available:** Yes

Kurzweil Personal Reader: Yes   **Tutorial Help:** Yes   **Peer Tutors:**

LD Specialists: **Max. Hours/Week for services:**

Oral Exams: Yes

Services for LD Only: No   **Added Cost:** None

Books on Tape: Yes

Calculator allowed in exam: Yes   **Taping of books not on tape:** Yes

Tape recording in class: Yes   **Dictionary/computer/spellcheck during exam:** Yes

How are professors notified of LD: By the student

GENERAL ADMISSIONS INFORMATION

Director of Admissions: Scott Healy   **Telephone:** 814-865-5471

Entrance Requirements:

4 yrs. English; 3 yrs. Science; 3 yrs. Math; a total of 5 units in Arts, Humanities, and Social Sciences. Possibly 2 yrs. Foreign Language.

Test Scores: **SAT:** 1060   **ACT:**

G.P.A.: 3.04   **Class Rank:**

Application Deadline: Rolling   **Achievement Tests:**

COLLEGE GRADUATION REQUIREMENTS

Foreign Language: Yes   **Waivers:** Depends on major

Math: Yes   **Waivers:** Depends on major

Minimum Course Load per Term: Yes

ADDITIONAL INFORMATION

Location: The school is located on over 5,000 acres in a small city 90 miles west of Harrisburg.

Enrollment Information: **Undergraduate:** 31,621   **Women:** 44%   **Men:** 56%

In-State Students: 82%   **Out of State:** 18%

Cost Information: **In-State Tuition:** $3,754   **Out of State:** $7,900

Room & Board: $3,330   **Additional Costs:**

Housing Information: **University Housing:** Yes   **Sorority:** 15%

% Living on Campus: 40%   **Fraternity:** 14%

Athletics: NCAA Div. I

JOHNSON & WALES UNIVERSITY
Providence, R.I. 02903

401-456-1000

Support: C S   *Institution:* 4 yr. Private

LEARNING DISABILITY PROGRAM AND SERVICES

Comments:

Johnson and Wales University is dedicated to providing reasonable accommodation to allow learning disabled students to succeed in their academic pursuits. While maintaining the highest academic integrity, the University strives to balance scholarship with support services which will assist special needs students to function in the postsecondary learning process. Accommodations could include reduced class load, preferential scheduling, oral exams, untimed exams, notetakers, LD support group, and individualized tutoring.

LEARNING DISABILITY ADMISSIONS INFORMATION

		Telephone
Program Name:	Special Needs Services	
Program Director:	Dr. Angela Renoud	401-456-4660
Contact Person:	Student Success Counselors	401-456-4660

Admissions:

There is no special application process. After regular admissions has been completed and the student is accepted, the student must self- identify and verify their disability with the following: neurological or medical report by a psychiatrist or neurologist, or a psycho-educational evaluation by a licensed clinician. This would include tests administered by the student's high school or private testing service within the past three years. Once admitted the coordinator of the program will meet with the student to develop an individualized educational plan listing appropriate learning strategies and suggestions.

Interview: Sometimes   *Diagnostic Tests:* Yes

Documentation: Battery includes psycho-educational evaluation

College Entrance Exams Required: No   *Untimed Accepted:*

Course Entrance Requirements: No

Are Waivers Available:

Additional Information:

Student must meet the high school course requirements.

Individualized high school coursework accepted: Yes

Essay Required: No

Special Application Required: No   *Submitted To:*

Number of Applications Submitted Each Year: N/A

Number of Applications Accepted Each Year: N/A

Number of Students Served: 140

Application Deadline for Special Admission: No

Acceptance into Program means acceptance into college: N/A

267

LEARNING DISABILITY SERVICES

Learning Resource Room: Yes   **Curriculum Modification Available:** Yes

Kurzweil Personal Reader: **Tutorial Help:** Yes   **Peer Tutors:** Yes

LD Specialists: 2   **Max. Hours/Week for services:**

Oral Exams: Yes   N/A

Services for LD Only: No   **Added**

Books on Tape: Yes   **Cost:** To be announced

Calculator allowed in exam: Yes   **Taping of books not on tape:** Yes

Tape recording in class: Yes   **Dictionary/computer/spellcheck during exam:** Yes

How are professors notified of LD: By the student and Program Director

GENERAL ADMISSIONS INFORMATION

Director of Admissions: Manuel Pimentel, Jr.   **Telephone:** 401-456-1055

Entrance Requirements:

Whatever the high school requires to graduate. Recommended: 3 yrs. English; 2 yrs. Math; 1 yr. Science; 2 yrs. Social Studies.

Test Scores: **SAT:**   **ACT:** Recommended

G.P.A.:   **Class Rank:**

Application Deadline: Rolling   **Achievement Tests:**

COLLEGE GRADUATION REQUIREMENTS

Foreign Language: Yes   **Waivers:** Yes

Math: Yes   **Waivers:** No

Minimum Course Load per Term: Decision made on an individual basis

ADDITIONAL INFORMATION

Location: The University is located on 100 acres with easy access to Boston.

Enrollment Information: **Undergraduate:** 6,846   **Women:** 50%   **Men:** 50%

In-State Students: 12%   **Out of State:** 88%

Cost Information: **In-State Tuition:** $7,860   **Out of State:** same

Room & Board: $3,390   **Additional Costs:** $234

Housing Information: **University Housing:** Yes   **Sorority:** 1%

% Living on Campus: 50%   **Fraternity:** 1%

Athletics: Intramural sports

Support: S   *Institution:* 4 yr. Private

LEARNING DISABILITY PROGRAM AND SERVICES

Comments:

There is no formal program for students with learning disablilites. However, the Director of the Learning Assistance Center and the faculty of the College are very supportive and are diligent about providing comprehensive services. The goal of the College is to be available to assist students whenever help is requested. After admission, the Director meets with the LD student during the summer prior to entry to help them select the appropriate courses for Freshman year. Students are monitored for 4 years. The Director also conducts workshops for the faculty.

LEARNING DISABILITY ADMISSIONS INFORMATION

Program Name:	Learning Assistance Center	*Telephone*
Program Director:	Frances Musco Shipps	401-865-2494
Contact Person:	Same	same

Admissions:

There is no special admissions process for students with learning disabilities. However, an interview is highly recommended. They will look at individualized high school coursework. Learning disabled students who have lower test scores but a fairly good academic record may be accepted. The admission committee has the flexibility to overlook poor test scores for LD students. Those who have higher test scores and reasonable grades in college prep courses (C+/B) may also gain admission. Students should identify as learning disabled on their application.

Interview: Yes   *Diagnostic Tests:* Yes

Documentation: All tests that are available

College Entrance Exams Required: Yes   *Untimed Accepted:* Yes

Course Entrance Requirements: Yes

Are Waivers Available: No

Additional Information:

All learning disability documentation should be sent to the Director of the Learning Assistance Center. This information will help in determining the types of services the students will need.

Individualized high school coursework accepted: Yes

Essay Required: Yes

Special Application Required: No   *Submitted To:*

Number of Applications Submitted Each Year:

Number of Applications Accepted Each Year: 15-20

Number of Students Served: 3,000

Application Deadline for Special Admission: No

Acceptance into Program means acceptance into college: No, there is an appeal process

LEARNING DISABILITY SERVICES

Learning Resource Room: Yes

Curriculum Modification Available: No

Kurzweil Personal Reader: No

Tutorial Help: Yes   **Peer Tutors:** Yes

LD Specialists: No

Max. Hours/Week for services:

Oral Exams: Y/N

No maximum for LD students

Services for LD Only: No

Added Cost: None

Books on Tape: Yes

Calculator allowed in exam: Y/N

Taping of books not on tape: Yes

Tape recording in class: Y/N

Dictionary/computer/spellcheck during exam: Y/N

How are professors notified of LD: By the Program Director

GENERAL ADMISSIONS INFORMATION

Director of Admissions: Michael G. Backes   **Telephone:** 401-865-2535

Entrance Requirements:

4 yrs. English; 3 yrs. Foreign Language; 3 yrs. Math; 2 yrs. History; 2 yrs. Science; 2 yrs. Social Studies. Essay required. Activities and recommendations are also important.

Test Scores: SAT: 1070   **ACT:** 25

G.P.A.: 2.5+   **Class Rank:** Top 50%

Application Deadline: 2/1   **Achievement Tests:** No

COLLEGE GRADUATION REQUIREMENTS

Foreign Language: No   **Waivers:**

Math: Yes   **Waivers:** No, Students may get tutoring services

Minimum Course Load per Term: Individualized

ADDITIONAL INFORMATION

Location: Providence College is on a 105 acre campus is located in a small city 50 miles south of Boston.

Enrollment Information: Undergraduate: 3,805   **Women:** 51%   **Men:** 49%

In-State Students: 15%   **Out of State:** 85%

Cost Information: In-State Tuition: $10,935   **Out of State:** same

Room & Board: $5,000   **Additional Costs:** $95

Housing Information: University Housing: Yes   **Sorority:** No

% Living on Campus: 62%   **Fraternity:** No

Athletics: NCAA Div. I

UNIVERSITY OF SOUTH CAROLINA
Columbia, S.C. 29208
803-777-7700

Support: S   **Institution:** 4 yr. Public

LEARNING DISABILITY PROGRAM AND SERVICES

Comments:

The Learning Disability Program was established at USC because of their belief that students with learning disabilities are able to succeed and contribute to the University and to society. Students with learning disabilities are part of every segment of the University. The program is designed to provide educational support and assistance including: analysis of learning needs to determine appropriate interventions, consulting with the faculty about special academic needs, monitoring of progress by a staff member, study skills training and tutorial referrals.

LEARNING DISABILITY ADMISSIONS INFORMATION

Program Name:	Learning Disability Program	**Telephone**
Program Director:	Deborah C. Haynes	803-777-6142
Contact Person:	same	

Admissions:

There is no special application or admission process for students with learning disabilities. Required scores on the SAT and ACT vary with high school grades and class rank. The freshman class average is an SAT of 960. After learning disabled students are admitted, they contact the Educational Support Services Center to arrange an interview to determine services necessary to accommodate needs.

Interview: Yes   **Diagnostic Tests:** Yes

Documentation:

College Entrance Exams Required: Yes   **Untimed Accepted:** Yes

Course Entrance Requirements: Yes

Are Waivers Available: No

Additional Information:

Students may petition the Admissions Committee for an exception to the regular admissions requirements if they are denied admission or feel they do not meet the required standards.

Individualized high school coursework accepted: Yes

Essay Required: No

Special Application Required: No   **Submitted To:**

Number of Applications Submitted Each Year: N/A

Number of Applications Accepted Each Year: N/A

Number of Students Served: 44

Application Deadline for Special Admission: No

Acceptance into Program means acceptance

into college: No, but there is an appeal procedure

LEARNING DISABILITY SERVICES

Learning Resource Room:	Yes	**Curriculum Modification Available:** Yes	
Kurzweil Personal Reader:		**Tutorial Help:**	**Peer Tutors:** No
LD Specialists:	No	**Max. Hours/Week for services:**	
Oral Exams:	Yes		
Services for LD Only:	No	**Added**	
Books on Tape:	Yes	**Cost:** None	
Calculator allowed in exam:	Y/N	**Taping of books not on tape:** Yes	
Tape recording in class:	Yes	**Dictionary/computer/spellcheck during exam:** Y/N	

How are professors notified of LD: By the student and the Program Director

GENERAL ADMISSIONS INFORMATION

Director of Admissions: Deborah C. Haynes   **Telephone:** 803-777-7700

Entrance Requirements:

16 units including: 4 yrs. English; 3 yrs. Math (Algebra I and II, Geometry); 2 yrs. Lab Science (Biology and Chemistry or Physics); 2 yrs. Foreign Language; 3 yrs. Social Studies; 2 yrs. electives.

Test Scores: **SAT:** 940 (mid 50%)   **ACT:** Can be substituted for SAT

G.P.A.: 2.0 minimum   **Class Rank:** top 25%

Application Deadline: Rolling   **Achievement Tests:**

COLLEGE GRADUATION REQUIREMENTS

Foreign Language: Yes   **Waivers:** Student can petition for waivers

Math: Yes   **Waivers:** Student can petition for waivers

Minimum Course Load per Term: Yes, based on disability, student may enroll in 9 hours per/semester

ADDITIONAL INFORMATION

Location: The University is located on 242 acres in downtown Columbia.

Enrollment Information:	**Undergraduate:** 16,000	**Women:** 53%	**Men:** 47%	
	In-State Students: 81%		**Out of State:** 19%	
Cost Information:	**In-State Tuition:** $2,448		**Out of State:** $5,548	
	Room & Board: $2,790		**Additional Costs:** $384	
Housing Information:	**University Housing:** Yes		**Sorority:** 8%	
	% Living on Campus: 42%		**Fraternity:** 9%	

Athletics: NCAA Div. I

SOUTH DAKOTA STATE UNIVERSITY
Brookings, SD.57007
605-688-4121

SD

Support: S   *Institution:* 4 yr. Public

LEARNING DISABILITY PROGRAM AND SERVICES

Comments:

South Dakota State University is committed to providing equal opportunities for higher education to academically qualified learning disabled students who have a reasonable expectation of college success. There is no specialized curriculum, but the University does share the responsibility with students for modifying the programs to meet individual needs. This is a relatively new program that is slowly developing.

LEARNING DISABILITY ADMISSIONS INFORMATION

Program Name:	Disabled Student Services	*Telephone*
Program Director:	James W. Carlson	605-688-4496
Contact Person:	same	same

Admissions:

There is no special admission.

Interview: No

Diagnostic Tests: No

Documentation:

College Entrance Exams Required: Yes

Untimed Accepted: Yes

Course Entrance Requirements: Yes

Are Waivers Available: Yes

Additional Information:

Same as for regular admissions.

Individualized high school coursework accepted: No

Essay Required: No

Special Application Required: No   *Submitted To:*

Number of Applications Submitted Each Year: 10

Number of Applications Accepted Each Year: All

Number of Students Served: 50

Application Deadline for Special Admission: No

Acceptance into Program means acceptance into college:

LEARNING DISABILITY SERVICES

Learning Resource Room: Yes   **Curriculum Modification Available:** No

Kurzweil Personal Reader: **Tutorial Help:** Yes   **Peer Tutors:** Yes

LD Specialists: No   **Max. Hours/Week for services:**

Oral Exams: Yes   2 hours per/week per/course

Services for LD Only: No   **Added**

Books on Tape: Yes   **Cost:** None

Calculator allowed in exam: Yes   **Taping of books not on tape:** Yes

Tape recording in class: Yes   **Dictionary/computer/spellcheck during exam:** Yes

How are professors notified of LD: By student

GENERAL ADMISSIONS INFORMATION

Director of Admissions: Mark Binkley   **Telephone:** 605-688-4121

Entrance Requirements:

4 yrs. English; 3 yrs. Math; 3 yrs. Social Studies; 2-3 yrs. Science; 1/2 yr. Art or Music; 1/2 yr. Computer Science; electives. Students deficient in course requirements need an ACT of 21 (from South Dakota or Minnesota) or an ACT of 22 from out-of-state.

Test Scores: **SAT:**   **ACT:** 17-25 (mid 50%)

G.P.A.:   **Class Rank:** Top 50%

Application Deadline: 8/1   **Achievement Tests:**

COLLEGE GRADUATION REQUIREMENTS

Foreign Language: No   **Waivers:**

Math: Yes   **Waivers:** No

Minimum Course Load per Term: Yes

ADDITIONAL INFORMATION

Location: The school is located on 220 acres in a rural area 50 miles north of Sioux Falls.

Enrollment Information: **Undergraduate:** 6,283   **Women:** 46%   **Men:** 54%

                     In-State Students: 78%   **Out of State:** 22%

Cost Information: **In-State Tuition:** $1,200   **Out of State:** $2,725

                   Room & Board: $1,730   **Additional Costs:** $640

Housing Information: **University Housing:** Yes   **Sorority:** 3%

            % Living on Campus: 60%   **Fraternity:** 5%

Athletics: NCAA Div. II

LEE COLLEGE

Cleveland, TN. 37311

615-472-2111

TN

Support: S   *Institution:* 4 yr. Private

LEARNING DISABILITY PROGRAM AND SERVICES

Comments:

The college assists the individual needs of each student. Assistance is available for test-taking skills, listening skills, note-taking skills, reading, and time management skills. Tutoring is available in History, English, Science, Biology, Math, Psychology, Religion, Sociology, at no fee. There are also remedial courses for credit in basic math, algebra and college reading. The Center is staffed by friendly people in comfortable surroundings.

LEARNING DISABILITY ADMISSIONS INFORMATION

Program Name: Student Support Services   *Telephone*

Program Director: Bill Winters   615-478-7475

Contact Person: Dauonna Keir   same

Admissions:

There is a special application to be filled out by the learning disabled student.

Interview: No   *Diagnostic Tests:* Yes

Documentation: Nelson Denny Reading

College Entrance Exams Required: Yes   *Untimed Accepted:* Yes

Course Entrance Requirements: Yes

Are Waivers Available: Yes

Additional Information:

Waivers may be possible after a review by Admission-Retention Committee. Students with an ACT of 17 or below, or a GPA lower than 2.0 may be accepted on probation.

Individualized high school coursework accepted: Yes

Essay Required: No

Special Application Required: Yes   *Submitted To:*

Number of Applications Submitted Each Year: 300

Number of Applications Accepted Each Year: 175

Number of Students Served: 175

Application Deadline for Special Admission: Early Summer-Prior to Attendance

Acceptance into Program means acceptance into college: Yes

LEARNING DISABILITY SERVICES

Learning Resource Room: Yes   **Curriculum Modification Available:** Yes

Kurzweil Personal Reader: **Tutorial Help:** Yes   **Peer Tutors:** Yes

LD Specialists: **Max. Hours/Week for services:**

Oral Exams: Yes   5-8 hours

Services for LD Only: No   **Added Cost:** None

Books on Tape:

Calculator allowed in exam: Yes   **Taping of books not on tape:**

Tape recording in class: Yes   **Dictionary/computer/spellcheck during exam:** Yes

How are professors notified of LD: By student and Program Director

GENERAL ADMISSIONS INFORMATION

Director of Admissions: Dr. Stanley Butler   **Telephone:** 615-472-2111

Entrance Requirements:

High School transcript; Secondary school graduation or GED required. No specific courses are required. Probationary admission is available for students who have an ACT lower than 17 or a GPA below a 2.0.

Test Scores: **SAT:** 750 (minimum)   **ACT:** 17 (minimum)

G.P.A.: 2.0   **Class Rank:**

Application Deadline: Rolling   **Achievement Tests:**

COLLEGE GRADUATION REQUIREMENTS

Foreign Language: Yes   **Waivers:**

Math: Yes   **Waivers:**

Minimum Course Load per Term: 9-12 hrs.

ADDITIONAL INFORMATION

Location: The College is located in a small town on 37 acres 30 miles from Chattanooga.

Enrollment Information: **Undergraduate:** 1,535   **Women:** 54%   **Men:** 46%

In-State Students: 96%   **Out of State:** 4%

Cost Information: **In-State Tuition:** $4,013   **Out of State:** same

Room & Board: $2,700   **Additional Costs:** $313

Housing Information: **University Housing:** Yes   **Sorority:** 6%

% Living on Campus: 50%   **Fraternity:** 6%

Athletics: NAIA

UNIVERSITY OF TENNESSEE
Chattanooga, Tn. 37403-2598
615-755-4662

Support: CS   **Institution:** 4 yr. Public

LEARNING DISABILITY PROGRAM AND SERVICES

Comments:

The College Access Program (CAP) at the University provides academic, social and emotional support for the learning disabled student. CAP provides academic advisement, tutoring in all coursework, career planning, counseling, social skills development, survival skills, career advisement, word processing skills, untimed tests, freshman orientation and psychological testing.

LEARNING DISABILITY ADMISSIONS INFORMATION

Program Name:	College Access Program (CAP)	**Telephone**
Program Director:	Dr. Pat Snowden	615-755-4006
Contact Person:	Melissa Taylor	same

Admissions:

There are two separate applications, one to the regular admissions office and one to the CAP program. Students can be considered for conditional admission if they fall below 2.75 GPA and 16 ACT or 640 SAT. However, they need a minimum of a 2.0 GPA and a minimum 16 ACT or 640 SAT and the minimum unit requirements for regular admission. Students admitted on condition must earn at least a 1.0 GPA during their first semester or suspension will result. The Dean of Admissions and Records, or the admission committee may recommend conditions for acceptance.

Interview: Yes   **Diagnostic Tests:** Yes

Documentation: W-J: WAIS-R

College Entrance Exams Required: Yes   **Untimed Accepted:** Yes

Course Entrance Requirements: Yes

Are Waivers Available: Yes

Additional Information:

The University will look at lower test scores for CAP applicants. Students admitted conditionally may be required to carry a reduced course-load, take specific courses, have a specific advisor, and take specific programs of developmental study.

Individualized high school coursework accepted: Yes

Essay Required: Yes

Special Application Required: Yes   **Submitted To:**

Number of Applications Submitted Each Year: 60

Number of Applications Accepted Each Year: 30

Number of Students Served: 105-110

Application Deadline for Special Admission: As early in Senior year as possible

Acceptance into Program means acceptance into college: No, there is an appeal procedure

277

LEARNING DISABILITY SERVICES

Learning Resource Room: Yes   **Curriculum Modification Available:** No

Kurzweil Personal Reader: **Tutorial Help:** Yes   **Peer Tutors:** Yes

LD Specialists: 3   **Max. Hours/Week for services:**

Oral Exams: Yes   3 hours per week/per course

Services for LD Only: Yes   **Added**
Cost: Parents donate tax-deductable $700

Books on Tape: Yes

Calculator allowed in exam: Yes   **Taping of books not on tape:**   Yes

Tape recording in class: Yes   **Dictionary/computer/spellcheck during exam:**   Yes

How are professors notified of LD: By the student and the Program Director

GENERAL ADMISSIONS INFORMATION

Director of Admissions: Patsy Reynolds   **Telephone:**   615-755-4662

Entrance Requirements:

4 yrs. English; 3 yrs. Math; 2 yrs. Foreign Language; 2 yrs. Science; 2 yrs. Social Studies. Conditional admissions for students with a GPA between 2.0 and 2.74, and an SAT between 640-899 or ACT beiween 12 and 19.

Test Scores: **SAT:** 900 (minimum)   **ACT:** 20 (minimum)

G.P.A.: 2.75   **Class Rank:**

Application Deadline: Rolling   **Achievement Tests:** No

COLLEGE GRADUATION REQUIREMENTS

Foreign Language: Yes   **Waivers:** Depends on major

Math: Yes   **Waivers:** Depends on major

Minimum Course Load per Term: 12 hrs. for full-time, others must request special consideration

ADDITIONAL INFORMATION

Location: The University of located on 60 acres in an urban area in Chattanooga.

Enrollment Information: **Undergraduate:**   6,595   **Women:** 54%   **Men:** 46%

In-State Students: 90%   **Out of State:** 10%

Cost Information: **In-State Tuition:** $1,376   **Out of State:** $4,328

Room & Board: $3,514   **Additional Costs:**

Housing Information: **University Housing:** Yes   **Sorority:** 30%

% Living on Campus: 14%   **Fraternity:** 25%

Athletics: NCAA Div. I

SCHREINER COLLEGE

Kerrville, Tx. 78025

512-896-5411

Support: SP   **Institution:** 4 yr. Private

LEARNING DISABILITY PROGRAM AND SERVICES

Comments:

Extensive learning support is given to each student and the ultimate goal is for students to be able to succeed without special help. The Learning Support Services Program is staffed by LD specialists and many tutors. Students are enrolled in regular college courses and receive individual tutorial assistance in each subject.

LEARNING DISABILITY ADMISSIONS INFORMATION

Program Name: Learning Support Services Program   **Telephone**

Program Director: Harry Heiser, M.A. / Karen Dooley, Ph.D   512-896-5411

Contact Person: same

Admissions:

High school diploma and all significant materials relevant to the specific learning disability must be submitted. They prefer the Woodcock-Johnson Achievement Battery but will accept other tests. An interview is required and is an important part of the admissions decision. Applicants are considered individually and selected on the basis of their intellectual ability, motivation, academic preparation and potential for success.

Interview: Yes   **Diagnostic Tests:** Yes

Documentation: WAIS-R; Achievement Tests; Woodcock-Johnson

College Entrance Exams Required: Yes   **Untimed Accepted:** Yes

Course Entrance Requirements: Yes

Are Waivers Available:

Additional Information:

Schreiner College offers both an Associates Degree and a Bachelors Degree.

Individualized high school coursework accepted: Yes

Essay Required: No

Special Application Required: No   **Submitted To:**

Number of Applications Submitted Each Year:

Number of Applications Accepted Each Year: 25

Number of Students Served: 80

Application Deadline for Special Admission: No

Acceptance into Program means acceptance

into college: Yes

LEARNING DISABILITY SERVICES

Learning Resource Room: Yes   **Curriculum Modification Available:** No

Kurzweil Personal Reader: **Tutorial Help:** Yes   **Peer Tutors:** Yes

LD Specialists: 2   **Max. Hours/Week for services:**

Oral Exams: Yes   Unlimited

Services for LD Only: Yes   **Added**

Books on Tape: Yes   **Cost:** $2,210

Calculator allowed in exam: Yes   **Taping of books not on tape:** Yes

Tape recording in class: Yes   **Dictionary/computer/spellcheck during exam:** Yes

How are professors notified of LD: By student and Director

GENERAL ADMISSIONS INFORMATION

Director of Admissions: Dewayne Bannister   **Telephone:** 512-896-5411

Entrance Requirements:

3 yrs. Math; 3 yrs. Science; some Foreign Language

Test Scores: **SAT:** 800 (minimum)   **ACT:** 18 (minimum)

G.P.A.: 2.0   **Class Rank:** top 50%

Application Deadline: Rolling   **Achievement Tests:**

COLLEGE GRADUATION REQUIREMENTS

Foreign Language: Yes   **Waivers:** Yes

Math: Yes   **Waivers:** One theoretical math course

Minimum Course Load per Term: 12-13 hours

ADDITIONAL INFORMATION

Location: The College is located on 175 acres in a rural wooded area, 60 miles northwest of San Antonio.

Enrollment Information: **Undergraduate:** 700   **Women:** 50%   **Men:** 50%

In-State Students: 94%   **Out of State:** 6%

Cost Information: **In-State Tuition:** $6,835   **Out of State:** same

Room & Board: $4,700   **Additional Costs:**

Housing Information: **University Housing:** Yes   **Sorority:** No

% Living on Campus: 50%   **Fraternity:** No

Athletics: NAIA

SOUTHWEST TEXAS STATE UNIVERSITY
San Marcos, Tx. 78666
516-245-2803

Support: S   *Institution:* 4 yr. Public

LEARNING DISABILITY PROGRAM AND SERVICES

Comments:

The University tries to accommodate the student as much as possible. LD students are encouraged to self-identify and once admitted should submit documentation of their disabilities. Tutoring services are offered to all students and are available during standard business hours, at night and on weekends. The professors are required to maintain office hours in order for students having problems, to meet with them. The following campus agencies provide LD students with special academic support services: DSS; Learning Resource Center and Student Learning Assistance Center.

LEARNING DISABILITY ADMISSIONS INFORMATION

Program Name:	Disabled Student Services (DSS)	*Telephone*
Program Director:	Tom Hutson	512-245-3451
Contact Person:	same	

Admissions:

The admission procedure is the same for all students regardless of their disability. Students who are not accepted are free to write letters of appeal to Admissions. However, the office of Disabled Students Services has no authority over the office of Admissions. Non-standardized ACT or SAT tests are acceptable. Admitted students may take reduced loads and live in University housing.

Interview: No   *Diagnostic Tests:* Yes

Documentation: WISC-R; achievement measures; others as necessary

College Entrance Exams Required: Yes   *Untimed Accepted:* Yes

Course Entrance Requirements: Yes

Are Waivers Available: No

Additional Information:

There are courses which are prerequisites to other courses. They are currently working on a substitution list for certain courses. They are flexible with test score requirements. Predicted Index Option is available for admission for students not meeting eligibility index. For the Predicted Index Option ACT scores are averaged in with secondary school grades to predict success in college.

Individualized high school coursework accepted: Y/N

Essay Required: No

Special Application Required: No   *Submitted To:*

Number of Applications Submitted Each Year: 800

Number of Applications Accepted Each Year: All who apply

Number of Students Served:

Application Deadline for Special Admission:

Acceptance into Program means acceptance

into college: No, student can appeal

LEARNING DISABILITY SERVICES

Learning Resource Room: Yes   **Curriculum Modification Available:** Y/N

Kurzweil Personal Reader: Yes   **Tutorial Help:** Yes   **Peer Tutors:** Yes

LD Specialists: No   **Max. Hours/Week for services:**

Oral Exams: Yes   Days, evenings, weekends

Services for LD Only: No   **Added**

Books on Tape: Yes   **Cost:** None

Calculator allowed in exam: Yes   **Taping of books not on tape:** Yes

Tape recording in class: Yes   **Dictionary/computer/spellcheck during exam:** Yes

How are professors notified of LD: By the student and Program Director

GENERAL ADMISSIONS INFORMATION

Director of Admissions: Lissa Norgan   **Telephone:** 512-245-2364

Entrance Requirements:

14 academic credits including: 4 yrs. English; 3 yrs. Math; 2 yrs. Science; 2.5 yrs. Social Science; 1/2 yr. Economics. The minimum score required on the SAT or ACT is determined by the student's high school class rank. Use eligibility indexes: Bottom 25% requires 1100 SAT or 26 ACT; 75% require 900 SAT or 22 ACT; 50% to top 25% require 800 SAT or 20 ACT; top 25% has no minimum test scores.

Test Scores: **SAT:** 850 (mid 50%)   **ACT:** 20

G.P.A.:   **Class Rank:**

Application Deadline: 8/1   **Achievement Tests:** N/A

COLLEGE GRADUATION REQUIREMENTS

Foreign Language: **Waivers:** Depends on major

Math: Yes   **Waivers:** No waivers, there are substitutions

Minimum Course Load per Term: Depends on if the student is receiving financial aid

ADDITIONAL INFORMATION

Location: The 1,091 acre campus is located 30 miles south of Austin and within easy access of San Antonio.

Enrollment Information: **Undergraduate:** 18,168   **Women:** 52%   **Men:** 48%

     In-State Students: 97%   **Out of State:** 3%

Cost Information: **In-State Tuition:** $1,042   **Out of State:** $4,162

     Room & Board: $2,707   **Additional Costs:** $502

Housing Information: **University Housing:** Yes   **Sorority:** 5%

     % Living on Campus: 35%   **Fraternity:** 5%

Athletics: NCAA Div. II

Support: CS   **Institution:** 4 yr. Public

LEARNING DISABILITY PROGRAM AND SERVICES

Comments:

Individual programs are developed for each student's needs. Services include tutoring from peer tutors or qualified tutors from the community, test accommodations, and curriculum modification.

LEARNING DISABILITY ADMISSIONS INFORMATION

Program Name:	Handicapped Student Services	**Telephone**
Program Director:	Dr. Lynn Martin	409-845-1247
Contact Person:	same	

Admissions:

Learning disabled students denied admission may request that the Director of the Handicapped Student Services ask for an over-ride of the decision.

Interview: Yes   **Diagnostic Tests:** Yes

Documentation: Any

College Entrance Exams Required: Yes   **Untimed Accepted:** Yes

Course Entrance Requirements: Yes

Are Waivers Available: Yes

Additional Information:

Some students not meeting priority admissions criteria may have their application reviewed. Admissions will be affected by the students choice of major, activities,and leadership skills. Students not meeting academic criteria for automatic admission may be offered admission to a Summer Provisional Program. These students must take 9 credits and receive a "C."

Individualized high school coursework accepted: Yes

Essay Required: No

Special Application Required: No   **Submitted To:**

Number of Applications Submitted Each Year: 150

Number of Applications Accepted Each Year: 150

Number of Students Served: 150

Application Deadline for Special Admission:

Acceptance into Program means acceptance into college: No

LEARNING DISABILITY SERVICES

Learning Resource Room:	Yes	**Curriculum Modification Available:** Yes	
Kurzweil Personal Reader:	Yes	**Tutorial Help:** Yes	**Peer Tutors:** Yes
LD Specialists:		**Max. Hours/Week for services:**	
Oral Exams:	Yes	Unlimited	
Services for LD Only:	No	**Added Cost:**	
Books on Tape:	Yes		
Calculator allowed in exam:	Yes	**Taping of books not on tape:** Yes	
Tape recording in class:	Yes	**Dictionary/computer/spellcheck during exam:** Yes	

How are professors notified of LD: The student and Program Director

GENERAL ADMISSIONS INFORMATION

Director of Admissions: Gary Engelgal   **Telephone:** 409-845-1031

Entrance Requirements:

4 yrs. English; 3.5 yrs Math and Computer Science; 2 yrs. Science; 2.5 yrs. Social Studies; 4 yrs. Electives. Foreign Language is not required for admission but is required as part of the core curriculum to graduate from the University. Two years of high school Foreign Language will satisfy this requirement. Computer Science is not required for admission but is required for graduation. Substitutions are possible.

Test Scores: **SAT:** 1100 out of state   **ACT:** 28 out of state

G.P.A.:   **Class Rank:** Top 25% out of state

Application Deadline: 3/1   **Achievement Tests:**

COLLEGE GRADUATION REQUIREMENTS

Foreign Language: Yes   **Waivers:** Possible

Math: Yes   **Waivers:** Possible

Minimum Course Load per Term:

ADDITIONAL INFORMATION

Location: The school is located on over 5,000 acres in a college town of 100,000, about 90 miles from Houston.

Enrollment Information:	Undergraduate:	32,951	**Women:** 44%	**Men:** 56%	
	In-State Students:	93%		Out of State: 7%	
Cost Information:	In-State Tuition:	$540		Out of State: $3,660	
	Room & Board:	$3,700		Additional Costs: $486	
Housing Information:	University Housing:	Yes		Sorority: 1%	
	% Living on Campus:	28%		Fraternity: 7%	

Athletics: NCAA Div. I

UNIVERSITY OF NORTH TEXAS
Denton, Tx. 76203-3797
817-565-2000

Support: CS   **Institution:** 4 yr. Public

LEARNING DISABILITY PROGRAM AND SERVICES

Comments:

The University has no specialized program specifically geared to the learning disabled. The Disabled Student Services program serves as a liaison for students needing special assistance or accommodation to access UNT's educational program and facilities. Each faculty member is given a booklet discussing learning disabilities and how the professor can help the student with learning limitations. Assistance is provided by locating readers and interpreters, offering study skills workshops, counseling and testing, tutorial services/learning assistance and career development classes.

LEARNING DISABILITY ADMISSIONS INFORMATION

		Telephone
Program Name:	Disabled Student Services (DSS)	
Program Director:	Barbara Jungjahan	817-565-2199
Contact Person:	Steve Pickert	817-565-4303

Admissions:

The student must apply through Admissions and meet regular admission criteria. LD students ultimately apply for special services to DSS by furnishing proof of their disability. Applicants who do not meet all entrance requirements may be considered for admission by individual approval. A member of the professional admission staff must feel that an individual case has enough merit to refer it to the Admissions Review Committee for consideration and final decision. Referral may be granted only after the applicant has submitted recommendation letters from teachers or counselors and completed an interview prior to the admission deadline.

Interview: Yes   **Diagnostic Tests:** Yes

Documentation: Nationally recognized tests used for identifying the learning disability.

College Entrance Exams Required: Yes   **Untimed Accepted:** Yes

Course Entrance Requirements: Yes

Are Waivers Available: Yes

Additional Information:

Individualized high school coursework accepted: No

Essay Required: No

Special Application Required: No   **Submitted To:**

Number of Applications Submitted Each Year: 250

Number of Applications Accepted Each Year: 40-50

Number of Students Served: 110

Application Deadline for Special Admission: No

Acceptance into Program means acceptance

into college: No, there is an appeal procedure

LEARNING DISABILITY SERVICES

Learning Resource Room: Yes   **Curriculum Modification Available:** Yes

Kurzweil Personal Reader: Yes   **Tutorial Help:** Yes   **Peer Tutors:** Yes

LD Specialists: 2   **Max. Hours/Week for services:**

Oral Exams: Yes   No maximum

Services for LD Only: No   **Added**

Books on Tape: Yes   **Cost:** None

Calculator allowed in exam: Yes   **Taping of books not on tape:** Yes

Tape recording in class: Yes   **Dictionary/computer/spellcheck during exam:** Yes

How are professors notified of LD: By the student and the Program Director

GENERAL ADMISSIONS INFORMATION

Director of Admissions: Don Palermo   **Telephone:** 817-565-2681

Entrance Requirements:

Graduation from secondary school is required with 16 units of credit. No minimum test scores are required for students in the top 10% of their high school. Students in the top 25% need an 800 SAT or a 19 ACT; 50% needs a 900 SAT or 21 ACT; 75% needs a 1000 SAT or a 24 ACT; a student in the bottom 25% needs a 1100 SAT or 27 ACT.

Test Scores: **SAT:** 800-1100   **ACT:** 19-27

G.P.A.:   **Class Rank:**

Application Deadline: 6/15   **Achievement Tests:**

COLLEGE GRADUATION REQUIREMENTS

Foreign Language: No   **Waivers:**

Math: Yes   **Waivers:** With the approval of the Dean of Arts and Sciences

Minimum Course Load per Term: No

ADDITIONAL INFORMATION

Location: The University campus is located on 425 acres north of Dallas/Fort Worth.

Enrollment Information: **Undergraduate:** 19,970   **Women:** 51%   **Men:** 49%

                            In-State Students: 94%   **Out of State:** 6%

Cost Information: **In-State Tuition:** $540   **Out of State:** $3,660

                            Room & Board: $3,304   **Additional Costs:** $496

Housing Information: **University Housing:** Yes   **Sorority:** 2%

                        % Living on Campus: 15%   **Fraternity:** 3%

Athletics: NCAA Div. I

Support: S   **Institution:** 2 yr. Private

LEARNING DISABILITY PROGRAM AND SERVICES

Comments:

Champlain College does not offer a special program for students with learning disabilities. It does have many support services for the general student population. In addition, accommodations in certain areas such as test taking are provided. The Student Resource Center offers peer tutoring, writing assistance, accounting lab, math lab, study skill workshop series in notetaking, mastering a college text, writing, revising and editing papers and personal counseling. Special Services for LD Students includes weekly meetings with the Coordinator, readers, and scribes.

LEARNING DISABILITY ADMISSIONS INFORMATION

Program Name: Student Resource Center   **Telephone**

Program Director: Shelli Goldsweig   802-658-0800

Contact Person:

Admissions:

There is no special admissions procedure for students with learning disabilities. Admissions are fairly flexible, although some requirements for certain majors are more difficult. Upward grade trend is very helpful and a good senior year is looked upon favorably. Recommendations are critical. The College is very sensitive to learning disabled students and is most interested in determining if the student can succeed. Students not admitted may take a reduced load and attend part-time.

Interview: Y/N   **Diagnostic Tests:** No

Documentation:

College Entrance Exams Required: No   **Untimed Accepted:** Yes

Course Entrance Requirements: Yes

Are Waivers Available:

Additional Information:

The College has a developemental course in Math and English for those students who may have a deficit in those areas. (These credits do not count towards graduation.)

Individualized high school coursework accepted: Y/N

Essay Required: Yes

Special Application Required: No   **Submitted To:**

Number of Applications Submitted Each Year: N/A

Number of Applications Accepted Each Year:

Number of Students Served: 55

Application Deadline for Special Admission: No

Acceptance into Program means acceptance
into college: N/A

LEARNING DISABILITY SERVICES

Learning Resource Room: Yes	**Curriculum Modification Available:** No	
Kurzweil Personal Reader:	**Tutorial Help:** Yes	**Peer Tutors:** Yes
LD Specialists: No	**Max. Hours/Week for services:**	
Oral Exams: Yes	2 hrs./per course/per week	
Services for LD Only: No	**Added**	
Books on Tape: No	**Cost:** None	
Calculator allowed in exam: Yes	**Taping of books not on tape:** No	
Tape recording in class: Yes	**Dictionary/computer/spellcheck during exam:** Y/N	

How are professors notified of LD: By the student and Program Director

GENERAL ADMISSIONS INFORMATION

Director of Admissions: Josephine Churchill   **Telephone:** 802-860-2727

Entrance Requirements:

High school transcript; SAT or ACT.

Test Scores: **SAT:**   **ACT:**

G.P.A.:   **Class Rank:**

Application Deadline: Rolling   **Achievement Tests:** No

COLLEGE GRADUATION REQUIREMENTS

Foreign Language: No   **Waivers:**

Math: Yes   **Waivers:** No

Minimum Course Load per Term: Yes, 12 credits for full-time status

ADDITIONAL INFORMATION

Location: The College is located on 16 acres in a small city surrounded by rural area mountains and Lake Champlain.

Enrollment Information:	Undergraduate:	1,590	**Women:** 68%	**Men:** 32%	
	In-State Students:	72%		**Out of State:** 28%	
Cost Information:	In-State Tuition:	$6,410		**Out of State:** same	
	Room & Board:	$4,630		**Additional Costs:** $100	
Housing Information:	University Housing:	Yes		**Sorority:**	
	% Living on Campus:	40%		**Fraternity:**	

Athletics: NJCAA

Support: CS   **Institution:** 4 yr. Private

LEARNING DISABILITY PROGRAM AND SERVICES

Comments:

The Learning Support Center offers comprehensive support services in all areas of academic life. Services begin when students enter the University. Freshman are given Placement Tests, designed to assess each individual's readiness for college reading, writing and math. Students are instructed by the center staff in Freshman Academic Survival Training (F.A.S.T.) which covers a wide range of study and college survival skills. The center also works closely with advisors and faculty members. The staff is a strong advocate for the learning disabled student.

LEARNING DISABILITY ADMISSIONS INFORMATION

Program Name: Learning Support Center   **Telephone**

Program Director: Paula A. Gills   802-485-2130

Contact Person: same

Admissions:

Students go through the regular application process. The Director of Support Services reviews all applications from learning disabled students and makes the admission decision. Students should provide detailed information about any existing handicap. A complete psycho-diagnostic evaluation is required. The required SAT score of 700 can be lower with written explanation. While Norwich does not have a formal program for learning disabled students, the University does offer support services on a voluntary basis.

Interview: No   **Diagnostic Tests:** Yes

Documentation: Complete psycho-diagnostic evaluation with full report and recommendation recom

College Entrance Exams Required: Yes   **Untimed Accepted:** Yes

Course Entrance Requirements: Yes

Are Waivers Available:

Additional Information:

No waivers, but course substitutions are allowed. The University is flexible on test scores.

Individualized high school coursework accepted: Y/N

Essay Required: Yes

Special Application Required: No   **Submitted To:**

Number of Applications Submitted Each Year:

Number of Applications Accepted Each Year:

Number of Students Served: 141

Application Deadline for Special Admission: No

Acceptance into Program means acceptance into college: N/A

LEARNING DISABILITY SERVICES

Learning Resource Room: Yes   **Curriculum Modification Available:** Yes

Kurzweil Personal Reader: **Tutorial Help:** Yes   **Peer Tutors:** 14

LD Specialists: 2   **Max. Hours/Week for services:**

Oral Exams: Yes   No limit

Services for LD Only: No   **Added**

Books on Tape: Yes   **Cost:** None

Calculator allowed in exam: Yes   **Taping of books not on tape:** Yes

Tape recording in class: Yes   **Dictionary/computer/spellcheck during exam:** Yes

How are professors notified of LD: By the student and the Program Director

GENERAL ADMISSIONS INFORMATION

Director of Admissions: Bruce E. Stewart, Jr.   **Telephone:** 802-485-2001

Entrance Requirements:

18 academic credits: 4 yrs. English; 3 yrs. Math; 2 yrs. Science; 2 yrs. Social Studies.

Test Scores: **SAT:**   **ACT:** 20 (explain if lower)

G.P.A.: 2.0 (usually)   **Class Rank:**

Application Deadline: Rolling   **Achievement Tests:**

COLLEGE GRADUATION REQUIREMENTS

Foreign Language: Yes   **Waivers:** Depends on major

Math: Yes   **Waivers:** Depends on major

Minimum Course Load per Term: The student can enroll on a continuing education basis.

ADDITIONAL INFORMATION

Location: Norwich University is comprised of the Military College of Vermont and Vermont College. The 1,000 acre Military College is located 11 miles south of the state capital Montpelier.

Enrollment Information: **Undergraduate:** 1,729   **Women:** 25%   **Men:** 75%

In-State Students: 20%   **Out of State:** 80%

Cost Information: **In-State Tuition:** $11,200   **Out of State:** same

Room & Board: $4,300   **Additional Costs:**

Housing Information: **University Housing:** Yes   **Sorority:** No

% Living on Campus: 90%   **Fraternity:** No

Athletics: NCAA Div. III

SOUTHERN VERMONT COLLEGE
Bennington, Vt. 05201
802-442-5427

Support: SP   **Institution:** 4 yr. Private

LEARNING DISABILITY PROGRAM AND SERVICES

Comments:

The Learning Disability Program is highly structured and provides the flexibility to meet individual needs. The Program is part of Special Services which offers many resources and a very supportive staff. Internships help to balance students formal classroom studies. Many of these internships range from government-related experiences to the media, and private industry, developing into job offers upon graduation. Southern Vermont College provides a holistic approach to education with special emphasis on the individual student.

LEARNING DISABILITY ADMISSIONS INFORMATION

Program Name: Learning Disability Program

Program Director: Virginia Sturdtevant

Contact Person: same

Telephone

802-442-5427

Admissions:

If a student does not meet regular entrance requirements the application goes to a review committee made up of the Director of Admissions, Director of Special Services, Director of the LD Program and a faculty member. This committee must reach consensus in order for a student to be given special admission. Each case is decided on an individual basis. The WAIS-R is required and should have been administered within the last 2 years. Special attention is given to subscores.

Interview: Yes   **Diagnostic Tests:** Yes

Documentation: Psychological testing with subscores and full report.

College Entrance Exams Required: Optional   **Untimed Accepted:**

Course Entrance Requirements: Yes

Are Waivers Available:

Additional Information:

General Admissions requirements. However, students not meeting the regular requirement courses are reviewed by committee.

Individualized high school coursework accepted:

Essay Required: Writing sample

Special Application Required: **Submitted To:**

Number of Applications Submitted Each Year: 100

Number of Applications Accepted Each Year: 20

Number of Students Served: 54

Application Deadline for Special Admission: No

Acceptance into Program means acceptance
into college:

LEARNING DISABILITY SERVICES

Learning Resource Room: Yes   **Curriculum Modification Available:** Yes

Kurzweil Personal Reader: **Tutorial Help:** Yes   **Peer Tutors:** Yes

LD Specialists: 2   **Max. Hours/Week for services:**

Oral Exams: Yes   unlimited

Services for LD Only: Yes   **Added**

Books on Tape: Yes   **Cost:**

Calculator allowed in exam: Yes **Taping of books not on tape:** Yes

Tape recording in class: Yes **Dictionary/computer/spellcheck during exam:** Yes

How are professors notified of LD: By student

GENERAL ADMISSIONS INFORMATION

Director of Admissions: Ms. Ann M. Kirvin   **Telephone:** 802-442-5427

Entrance Requirements:

3 yrs. Math; 3 yrs. Science; Foreign Language, SAT or ACT. Average Math and English grades of at least C/C-.

Test Scores: **SAT:**   **ACT:**

G.P.A.: 2.0   **Class Rank:** top 3/4

Application Deadline: Rolling Admissions   **Achievement Tests:**

COLLEGE GRADUATION REQUIREMENTS

Foreign Language: No   **Waivers:**

Math: Yes   **Waivers:** Basic Math course, self-paced is available

Minimum Course Load per Term: 4 courses

ADDITIONAL INFORMATION

Location: The college is located in a town of 17,000, forty miles northeast of Albany, New York.

Enrollment Information: **Undergraduate:** 633   **Women:** 54%   **Men:** 46%

In-State Students: 41%   **Out of State:** 59%

Cost Information: **In-State Tuition:** $6,330   **Out of State:** same

Room & Board: $3,360   **Additional Costs:** $200

Housing Information: **University Housing:** Yes   **Sorority:** No

% Living on Campus: 33%   **Fraternity:** No

Athletics: NAIA

UNIVERSITY OF VERMONT
Burlington, Vt. 05405
802-656-3370

Support: CS   *Institution:* 4 yr. Public

LEARNING DISABILITY PROGRAM AND SERVICES

Comments:

The staff of the OSSS work closely with students having learning problems to ensure that campus-wide resources are used effectively. Initially, a comprehensive assessment is undertaken to identify a student's strengths and weaknesses in learning. This information is used to carefully design classroom and study accommodations to compensate for learning problems. Through this process students and program staff have identified a number of techniques and strategies to enable success at class and study tasks. There are no developmental courses, only tutoring.

LEARNING DISABILITY ADMISSIONS INFORMATION

Program Name:	Office of Specialized Student Services (OSSS)	*Telephone*
Program Director:	Nancy Oliker	802-656-3340
Contact Person:	Susan Krasnow	

Admissions:

Students need to self-identify on the regular application. OSSS Director and staff read approximately 150 files of learning disabled students and meet with the Office of Admissions to jointly make final decisions. They look at WAIS-R, letters of support from counselors and case-managers, the support needed by the student in high school, recent psychological testing and pre-admissions interview. The more documentation included the better the admissions counselors can review the application beyond traditional measures. Interested students may request a pre-admission evaluation.

Interview: No   *Diagnostic Tests:* Yes

Documentation: WAIS-R; W-J 1 or 2; or other similar tests

College Entrance Exams Required: Yes   *Untimed Accepted:* Yes

Course Entrance Requirements: Yes

Are Waivers Available: Yes

Additional Information:

The 2 years of foreign language which is required can be waived with appropriate documentation. The same is true for math.

Individualized high school coursework accepted:

Essay Required: Yes

Special Application Required: No   *Submitted To:*

Number of Applications Submitted Each Year: 100+

Number of Applications Accepted Each Year: Varies

Number of Students Served: 95+

Application Deadline for Special Admission: No

Acceptance into Program means acceptance into college: No, there is an appeal procedure

293

LEARNING DISABILITY SERVICES

Learning Resource Room: Yes   **Curriculum Modification Available:** Yes

Kurzweil Personal Reader: **Tutorial Help:** Yes   **Peer Tutors:** Yes

LD Specialists: 2   **Max. Hours/Week for services:**

Oral Exams: Yes   2-3 hours per course

Services for LD Only: Yes   **Added**

Books on Tape: Yes   **Cost:** None

Calculator allowed in exam: Y/N   **Taping of books not on tape:** Yes

Tape recording in class: Y/N   **Dictionary/computer/spellcheck during exam:** Y/N

How are professors notified of LD: By both the student and the Program Director

GENERAL ADMISSIONS INFORMATION

Director of Admissions: Linda Kreamer   **Telephone:** 802-656-3370

Entrance Requirements:

16 units including: 4 yrs. English; 3 yrs. of an Algebra 1 or 11/ Geometry grouping; 2 yrs. Foreign Language; 2 yrs. Science; 2 yrs. Social Studies.

Test Scores: **SAT:** 1070 (mid 50%)   **ACT:** Accepted

G.P.A.: 2.6-3.0   **Class Rank:** Top 3/5

Application Deadline: 2/1   **Achievement Tests:** No

COLLEGE GRADUATION REQUIREMENTS

Foreign Language: Yes   **Waivers:** Depends on major, in Arts and Sciences

Math: Yes   **Waivers:** In Arts and Sciences, and Education Programs

Minimum Course Load per Term: Defined by the student

ADDITIONAL INFORMATION

Location: The University sits on 425 acres on Lake Champlain 90 miles south of Montreal.

Enrollment Information: **Undergraduate:** 8,029   **Women:** 54%   **Men:** 46%

   In-State Students: 51%   **Out of State:** 49%

Cost Information: **In-State Tuition:** $3,986   **Out of State:** $11,986

   Room & Board: $3,858   **Additional Costs:** $336

Housing Information: **University Housing:** Yes   **Sorority:** 7%

   % Living on Campus: 50%   **Fraternity:** 15%

Athletics: NCAA Div. I

JAMES MADISON UNIVERSITY
Harrisonburg, Va. 22807
703-568-6147

Support: CS   **Institution:** 4 yr. Public

LEARNING DISABILITY PROGRAM AND SERVICES

Comments:

James Madison has a variety of services available for its learning disabled students. Many such students receive individualized assistance with their work in the Reading, Writing, and Math Lab with an appropriate instructor. Students must register with the Office of Disability Services to receive help.

LEARNING DISABILITY ADMISSIONS INFORMATION

Program Name:	Office of Disability Services	**Telephone**
Program Director:	Carole C. Grove	703-568-6705
Contact Person:	Carole C. Grove, Kathy Crews	703-568-6147

Admissions:

LD students must meet the same requirements for admissions as any other student. The University does accept SAT scores from alternative testing arrangements. Specific questions concerning admissions can be answered through the Admissions Office. If a student with a learning disability is denied admission, the Disability Services office will, when requested, ask admissions to re-evaluate the application.

Interview: No   **Diagnostic Tests:** Yes

Documentation: Full battery- I.Q. and Achievement

College Entrance Exams Required: Yes   **Untimed Accepted:** Yes

Course Entrance Requirements: Yes

Are Waivers Available:

Additional Information:

Math placement exam, Foreign Language Placement and Student Development Assessment (survey).

Individualized high school coursework accepted: Yes

Essay Required: No

Special Application Required: No   **Submitted To:**

Number of Applications Submitted Each Year: 97

Number of Applications Accepted Each Year: 80

Number of Students Served: 50 LD students

Application Deadline for Special Admission: No

Acceptance into Program means acceptance

into college: No, there is a re-evaluation process

LEARNING DISABILITY SERVICES

Learning Resource Room: Yes

Curriculum Modification Available: No

Kurzweil Personal Reader:

Tutorial Help: Yes   **Peer Tutors:** Yes

LD Specialists: 2

Max. Hours/Week for services:

Oral Exams: Yes

Services for LD Only: No

Added Cost: None

Books on Tape: Yes

Calculator allowed in exam: Y/N

Taping of books not on tape: Yes

Tape recording in class: Yes

Dictionary/computer/spellcheck during exam: Yes

How are professors notified of LD: By student and Program Director

GENERAL ADMISSIONS INFORMATION

Director of Admissions: Alan L. Cerveny   **Telephone:** 703-568-6147

Entrance Requirements:

Student must show solid achievement in 5 or more academic courses each year. Recommended: 4 yrs. English; 2-3 yrs. Foreign Language; 3 yrs. Social Studies; 4 yrs. History

Test Scores: **SAT:** 1100   **ACT:**

G.P.A.: 3.0   **Class Rank:** Upper 50%

Application Deadline: 2/1   **Achievement Tests:**

COLLEGE GRADUATION REQUIREMENTS

Foreign Language: No   **Waivers:** Only for BA

Math: Yes   **Waivers:** No

Minimum Course Load per Term: 12 hours in order to remain on campus as a full-time student

ADDITIONAL INFORMATION

Location: The University is located in the Shenandoah Valley surrounded by the Blue Ridge Mountains and the Alleghenies, 120 miles from Washington, D.C.

Enrollment Information: **Undergraduate:** 9,557   **Women:** 55%   **Men:** 45%

In-State Students: 77%   **Out of State:** 23%

Cost Information: **In-State Tuition:** $2,834   **Out of State:** $5,426

Room & Board: $3,496   **Additional Costs:**

Housing Information: **University Housing:** Yes   **Sorority:** 19%

% Living on Campus: 54%   **Fraternity:** 17%

Athletics: NCAA Div. I

OLD DOMINION UNIVERSITY
Norfolk, Va. 23508
804-683-3637

Support: S   **Institution:** 4 yr. Public

LEARNING DISABILITY PROGRAM AND SERVICES

Comments:

Student Support Services is a TRIO program funded by the U.S. Department of Education providing academic support. The program assists students in achieving and maintaining the academic performance level required for satisfactory academic standing at the University, thereby increasing their chances of graduating. Special help is offered through; on-site orientation programs; taped materials; tutorial services by peers; oral testing; untimed testing; and individual counseling.

LEARNING DISABILITY ADMISSIONS INFORMATION

Program Name: Disabled Student Services   **Telephone**

Program Director: Mary Welch   804-683-4655

Contact Person: same

Admissions:

There is no special admissions process for students with learning disabilities. Application to the University is made through standard procedures by submitting SAT scores and high school transcripts with the University application. Upon admission to the University documentation of the disability is required to receive services. Testing must not be older than 3 years.

Interview: No   **Diagnostic Tests:** Yes

Documentation: WAIS-R

College Entrance Exams Required: Yes   **Untimed Accepted:** Yes

Course Entrance Requirements: No

Are Waivers Available:

Additional Information:

Individualized high school coursework accepted:

Essay Required:

Special Application Required: **Submitted To:**

Number of Applications Submitted Each Year: Varies

Number of Applications Accepted Each Year: All

Number of Students Served: 70

Application Deadline for Special Admission: No

Acceptance into Program means acceptance
into college: No, there is an appeal process

297

LEARNING DISABILITY SERVICES

Learning Resource Room: No   **Curriculum Modification Available:** Yes

Kurzweil Personal Reader: **Tutorial Help:** Yes   **Peer Tutors:** Yes

LD Specialists: No   **Max. Hours/Week for services:**

Oral Exams: Yes   Varies

Services for LD Only: Yes   **Added**

Books on Tape: Yes   **Cost:** None

Calculator allowed in exam: Yes   **Taping of books not on tape:** Yes

Tape recording in class: Yes   **Dictionary/computer/spellcheck during exam:** Yes

How are professors notified of LD: The student is given a letter to present to the professor

GENERAL ADMISSIONS INFORMATION

Director of Admissions: Dr. Richard Parent   **Telephone:** 804-683-3637

Entrance Requirements:

3 yrs. English; 4 yrs. Math; 3 yrs. Foreign Language; 3 yrs. Science; 3 yrs. Social Science.

Test Scores: **SAT:** 800 (minimum)   **ACT:** 19 (minimum)

G.P.A.: 2.5   **Class Rank:** Upper 50%

Application Deadline: 5/1   **Achievement Tests:**

COLLEGE GRADUATION REQUIREMENTS

Foreign Language: Yes   **Waivers:** Yes, substitutions

Math: Yes   **Waivers:** Yes, substitutions

Minimum Course Load per Term: No

ADDITIONAL INFORMATION

Location: The University is located on 46 acres in a suburban area of Norfolk.

Enrollment Information: **Undergraduate:** 11,526   **Women:** 50%   **Men:** 50%

                          In-State Students: 80%   **Out of State:** 20%

Cost Information: **In-State Tuition:** $2,462   **Out of State:** $4,982

                          Room & Board: $4,052   **Additional Costs:**

Housing Information: **University Housing:** Yes   **Sorority:** Yes

                          % Living on Campus: 20%   **Fraternity:** Yes

Athletics: NCAA Div. I

UNIVERSITY OF VIRGINIA
Charlottesville, Va. 22904
804-924-7751

Support: C S   **Institution:** 4 yr. Public

LEARNING DISABILITY PROGRAM AND SERVICES

Comments:

The University of Virginia believes in making academic progress accessible to learning disabled students. The University is continuing their quest to address academic and student service areas. Information is available to describe the various disabilities and professors are encouraged to ask students, who may wish accommodations, to see them after the first class meeting.

LEARNING DISABILITY ADMISSIONS INFORMATION

Program Name: Learning Needs and Evaluation Center   **Telephone**

Program Director: Eleanor C. Westhead, Ph.D   804-924-3139

Contact Person: any staff

Admissions:

The learning disabled student goes through the same admissions procedure as all incoming applicants. After admission to the school, learning disabled students contact the Center in order to receive services. Learning disabled students admitted to the University have qualified for admission because of their ability. No criteria for admission is waived because of a disability. However no learning disabled student, who is qualified, is denied because of their disability.

Interview: No   **Diagnostic Tests:** Yes

Documentation: Any valid documentation

College Entrance Exams Required: Yes   **Untimed Accepted:** Yes

Course Entrance Requirements: Yes

Are Waivers Available: Yes

Additional Information:

Should a candidate self-declare a learning disability, any data which is missing, because of the disability, may be allowed or differentially weighted.

Individualized high school coursework accepted: Yes

Essay Required: Yes

Special Application Required: No   **Submitted To:**

Number of Applications Submitted Each Year:

Number of Applications Accepted Each Year: All

Number of Students Served: 450+

Application Deadline for Special Admission: No

Acceptance into Program means acceptance into college: No

LEARNING DISABILITY SERVICES

Learning Resource Room: Yes   **Curriculum Modification Available:** Yes

Kurzweil Personal Reader: Yes   **Tutorial Help:** Yes   **Peer Tutors:** Yes

LD Specialists: 2   **Max. Hours/Week for services:**

Oral Exams: Yes   Individualized

Services for LD Only: No   **Added**

Books on Tape: Yes   **Cost:** None

Calculator allowed in exam: Yes   **Taping of books not on tape:** Yes

Tape recording in class: Yes   **Dictionary/computer/spellcheck during exam:** Yes

How are professors notified of LD: By student with a letter from the Center

GENERAL ADMISSIONS INFORMATION

Director of Admissions: Jack Blackburn   **Telephone:** 804-924-7551

Entrance Requirements:

16 academic courses including: 4 yrs. English; 4 yrs. Math (beginning with Algebra I); 2 yrs. total of either Physics, Biology or Chemistry; 2 years Foreign Language. More competitive for out-of-state applicants.

Test Scores: **SAT:** 1230   **ACT:**

G.P.A.:   **Class Rank:**

Application Deadline: 1/2   **Achievement Tests:** 3

COLLEGE GRADUATION REQUIREMENTS

Foreign Language: Yes   **Waivers:** Yes

Math: Yes   **Waivers:** Yes

Minimum Course Load per Term: As few as 6 hours with permission

ADDITIONAL INFORMATION

Location: The 2,440 acre campus is located in a small city 70 miles northwest of Richmond.

Enrollment Information: **Undergraduate:** 11,199   **Women:** 50%   **Men:** 50%

In-State Students: 65%   **Out of State:** 35%

Cost Information: **In-State Tuition:** $2,708   **Out of State:** $8,200

Room & Board: $2,911   **Additional Costs:** $568

Housing Information: **University Housing:** Yes   **Sorority:** 28%

% Living on Campus: 51%   **Fraternity:** 30%

Athletics: NCAA Div. I

VIRGINIA INTERMONT COLLEGE

Bristol, Va. 24201

703-669-6101

Support: CS   **Institution:** 4 yr. Private

LEARNING DISABILITY PROGRAM AND SERVICES

Comments:

Student Support Services is a federally funded program providing free supportive services to students who participate in the program. There are extensive services offered to those with learning disabilities. The objective of the services is to help students stay in school and graduate. Therefore, services span a wide range based on student's needs and requests. A few accommodations require appointments, though generally there is an open door policy. The Program is available to the student throughout the 4 years of college.

LEARNING DISABILITY ADMISSIONS INFORMATION

		Telephone
Program Name:	Student Support Services	
Program Director:	Talmage Dobbins	703-669-6101
Contact Person:	Marta Bush	same,ext. 216

Admissions:

There is no special admissions procedure for the student with learning disabities. However, an application form should include documentation related to the learning disability. The ACT or SAT score requirements are flexible depending upon the LD documentation.

Interview: Helpful   **Diagnostic Tests:** Yes

Documentation: WISC-R or WAIS-R; W-J or Peabody Individual Achievement Test

College Entrance Exams Required: Yes   **Untimed Accepted:** Yes

Course Entrance Requirements: Yes

Are Waivers Available: No

Additional Information:

Placement tests for Reading, English, and Math are given to all in-coming Freshman to determine if placement in a developmental course will be necessary. LD students, based on documentation showing need, are given options of extended time, calculators, and other accommodations.

Individualized high school coursework accepted: Yes

Essay Required: Yes

Special Application Required: **Submitted To:**

Number of Applications Submitted Each Year: 400

Number of Applications Accepted Each Year: 210

Number of Students Served: Varies

Application Deadline for Special Admission: No

Acceptance into Program means acceptance

into college: No, there is no appeal procedure

301

LEARNING DISABILITY SERVICES

Learning Resource Room: No   **Curriculum Modification Available:** Y/N

Kurzweil Personal Reader: Yes   **Tutorial Help:** Yes   **Peer Tutors:** Yes

LD Specialists: 1   **Max. Hours/Week for services:**

Oral Exams: Yes   Try not to put a limit

Services for LD Only: No   **Added Cost:** None

Books on Tape: Yes

Calculator allowed in exam: Yes   **Taping of books not on tape:** Yes

Tape recording in class: Yes   **Dictionary/computer/spellcheck during exam:** Yes

How are professors notified of LD: By student and the Program Director

GENERAL ADMISSIONS INFORMATION

Director of Admissions: R. Lawton Blandford, Jr.   **Telephone:** 703-669-6101

Entrance Requirements:

15 academic credits including: 4 yrs. English; 3 yrs. Math; 3 yrs, Science; 6 electives.

Test Scores: **SAT:** 650 (minimum)   **ACT:** 15 (minimum)

G.P.A.: 2.0   **Class Rank:**

Application Deadline: Rolling   **Achievement Tests:**

COLLEGE GRADUATION REQUIREMENTS

Foreign Language: No   **Waivers:**

Math: Yes   **Waivers:** No

Minimum Course Load per Term: 12 hours

ADDITIONAL INFORMATION

Location: The College is located on a 16 acre campus in the Blue Ridge Mountains.

Enrollment Information: **Undergraduate:** 521   **Women:** 71%   **Men:** 29%

   In-State Students: 52%   **Out of State:** 48%

Cost Information: **In-State Tuition:** $5,880   **Out of State:** same

   Room & Board: $3,620   **Additional Costs:** $100

Housing Information: **University Housing:** Yes   **Sorority:** No

   % Living on Campus: 65%   **Fraternity:** No

Athletics: Intercollegiate sports

Support: S   **Institution:** 4 yr. Public

LEARNING DISABILITY PROGRAM AND SERVICES

Comments:

The Disabled Student Services/Student and Advising Learning Center (SALC) coordinates services for students with learning disabilities. DSS works with other offices within the University to increase accessibility and sensitivity to the nature of the students disability. The Academic Development Program is available to all students who need help in developing learning strategies to become more successful college students. This program offers academic support through advising, testing, and individualized and group instruction in many different areas.

LEARNING DISABILITY ADMISSIONS INFORMATION

Program Name:	Disabled Student Services / SALC	**Telephone**
Program Director:	Marshall Mitchell	509-335-4357
Contact Person:	same	

Admissions:

Students who do not qualify for regular admission may appeal at which time DSS is invited to make a recommendation. The University looks at the combination of the score on the ACT/SAT and the high school GPA. Documentation of the learning disability and diagnostic tests given less than 3 years before application, should be included with the application.

Interview: Yes   **Diagnostic Tests:** Yes

Documentation:

College Entrance Exams Required: Yes   **Untimed Accepted:** Yes

Course Entrance Requirements: Yes

Are Waivers Available:

Additional Information:

Waivers are available for students who do not have the ability to learn a foreign language. Documentation must be provided.

Individualized high school coursework accepted:

Essay Required: Yes

Special Application Required: **Submitted To:**

Number of Applications Submitted Each Year:

Number of Applications Accepted Each Year:

Number of Students Served: 65-70

Application Deadline for Special Admission: No

Acceptance into Program means acceptance

into college: No, there is an appeal process

LEARNING DISABILITY SERVICES

Learning Resource Room:

Kurzweil Personal Reader: No

LD Specialists:

Oral Exams: Yes

Services for LD Only: No

Books on Tape: Yes

Calculator allowed in exam: Yes

Tape recording in class: Yes

Curriculum Modification Available:

Tutorial Help: Yes **Peer Tutors:**

Max. Hours/Week for services:
No maximum

Added Cost: None

Taping of books not on tape: Yes

Dictionary/computer/spellcheck during exam: Yes

How are professors notified of LD: By the student and the Program Director

GENERAL ADMISSIONS INFORMATION

Director of Admissions: Ms. Terry Flynn **Telephone:** 509-335-5586

Entrance Requirements:

4 yrs. English; 3 yrs. Math; 2 yrs. Foreign Language; 3 yrs. Social Science; 2 yrs. Science (including 1 yr. of Lab)

Test Scores: **SAT:** **ACT:** required

G.P.A.: 2.0 **Class Rank:**

Application Deadline: 5/1 **Achievement Tests:**

COLLEGE GRADUATION REQUIREMENTS

Foreign Language: Yes **Waivers:** Yes, Depends on major

Math: Yes **Waivers:** Yes, Depends on major

Minimum Course Load per Term: Depends on financial aid requirements

ADDITIONAL INFORMATION

Location: The University is located on 600 acres in a small town 80 miles south of Spokane.

Enrollment Information: **Undergraduate:** 14,802 **Women:** 45% **Men:** 55%

In-State Students: 85% **Out of State:** 15%

Cost Information: **In-State Tuition:** $1,945 **Out of State:** $5,414

Room & Board: $3,300 **Additional Costs:** $150

Housing Information: University Housing: Yes **Sorority:** 9%

% Living on Campus: 60% **Fraternity:** 15%

Athletics: NCAA Div. I

WESTERN WASHINGTON UNIVERSITY
Bellingham, Wa. 98225
206-676-3440

WA

Support: CS   *Institution:* 4 Yr. Public

LEARNING DISABILITY PROGRAM AND SERVICES

Comments:

The Disabled Student Service program offers services to students admitted into the University through regular admissions. The learning disabled student must submit documentation to receive accommodations. The Director of the program is a certified LD Instructor.

LEARNING DISABILITY ADMISSIONS INFORMATION

Program Name:	Disabled Student Services	*Telephone*
Program Director:	Dorothy Crow	206-676-3083
Contact Person:	same	

Admissions:

There is no special admissions program for students with learning disabilities. However, if the documentation that is submitted with the regular application describes the learning disability, some entrance requirements may be waived. The required SAT score varies and is weighed with the students GPA.

Interview: No   *Diagnostic Tests:* Yes

Documentation: WAIS-R; Achievement tests; Tests of auditory and visual perception

College Entrance Exams Required: Yes   *Untimed Accepted:* Yes

Course Entrance Requirements: Yes

Are Waivers Available: Some

Additional Information:

Entrance requirement for all students is the state of Washington's exam, the WPCT.

Individualized high school coursework accepted: Yes

Essay Required: No

Special Application Required: No   *Submitted To:*

Number of Applications Submitted Each Year: Varies

Number of Applications Accepted Each Year: Varies

Number of Students Served: 180

Application Deadline for Special Admission: No

Acceptance into Program means acceptance into college:

305

LEARNING DISABILITY SERVICES

Learning Resource Room: Yes   **Curriculum Modification Available:** Yes

Kurzweil Personal Reader: Yes   **Tutorial Help:** Yes   **Peer Tutors:** Yes

LD Specialists: 2   **Max. Hours/Week for services:**

Oral Exams: Yes   3 to 4

Services for LD Only: No   **Added**
Cost: None, $60 for diagnostic exam
Books on Tape: Yes

Calculator allowed in exam: Yes   **Taping of books not on tape:** Yes

Tape recording in class: Yes   **Dictionary/computer/spellcheck during exam:** Yes

How are professors notified of LD: The student takes a letter from the DSS office.

GENERAL ADMISSIONS INFORMATION

Director of Admissions: Cal Mathews   **Telephone:** 206-676-3440

Entrance Requirements:

14 academic credits including: 4 yrs. English Composition and Literature; 3 yrs. Math including 2 of Algebra; 2 yrs. of Science including 1 of Chemistry or Physics; 2 yrs. Foreign Language; 3 yrs. Social Studies/History.

Test Scores: **SAT:** 1000   **ACT:** 21

G.P.A.: 2.5   **Class Rank:** Upper 50%

Application Deadline: 3/1   **Achievement Tests:** WPCT

COLLEGE GRADUATION REQUIREMENTS

Foreign Language: No   **Waivers:**

Math: Yes   **Waivers:** No

Minimum Course Load per Term: Yes, depends on needs of student

ADDITIONAL INFORMATION

Location: Western Washington University is located on 190 acres in a small city 60 miles south of Vancouver, British Columbia.

Enrollment Information: **Undergraduate:** 8,569   **Women:** 55%   **Men:** 45%

In-State Students: 94%   **Out of State:** 6%

Cost Information: **In-State Tuition:** $1,161   **Out of State:** $5,649

Room & Board: $3,400   **Additional Costs:**

Housing Information: **University Housing:** Yes   **Sorority:** No

% Living on Campus: 35%   **Fraternity:** No

Athletics: NAIA

Support: SP   **Institution:** 4 yr. Private

LEARNING DISABILITY PROGRAM AND SERVICES

Comments:

The Program at Davis & Elkins College is based on the needs of the individual student. Personnel are trained by the Special Services Director to meet specialized needs of the learning disabled college population. The content of the sessions with the students is based on an Individual Program Plan. The strategies provided are based on current research in the field of learning disabilities. With the increasing number of learning disabled students being encouraged to consider college and the obvious lure of a small college environment, the College wants to meet the need.

LEARNING DISABILITY ADMISSIONS INFORMATION

Program Name: Special Services   **Telephone**

Program Director: Dr. Margaret N. Turner   304-636-1900

Contact Person: same

Admissions:

All applications are screened by the Special Services Director and the Director of Admissions. Students must be admitted to Davis & Elkin College prior to being considered for Special Services. The admissions counselors have been trained to recognize potentially successful LD students. Students requesting services must send: a high school transcript; psychological tests taken within the last 3 years; recommendation of an LD teacher, counselor or psychologist; copy of recent IEP; handwritten essay requesting services and indicating why services are being requested.

Interview: Yes   **Diagnostic Tests:** Yes

Documentation:

College Entrance Exams Required: No   **Untimed Accepted:** Yes

Course Entrance Requirements: Yes

Are Waivers Available: No

Additional Information:

Learning disabled students must participate in the Special Services Program. The ACT/SAT are used for placement purposes only.

Individualized high school coursework accepted: Yes

Essay Required: Yes

Special Application Required: Yes   **Submitted To:**

Number of Applications Submitted Each Year:

Number of Applications Accepted Each Year:

Number of Students Served: 70

Application Deadline for Special Admission: Fall of senior year

Acceptance into Program means acceptance into college: No

LEARNING DISABILITY SERVICES

Learning Resource Room: Yes   **Curriculum Modification Available:** No

Kurzweil Personal Reader: **Tutorial Help:** Yes   **Peer Tutors:** Yes

LD Specialists: 6   **Max. Hours/Week for services:**

Oral Exams: Yes   No maximum

Services for LD Only: No   **Added**

Books on Tape: Yes   **Cost:** $2,000 p/year

Calculator allowed in exam: Yes   **Taping of books not on tape:** Yes

Tape recording in class: Yes   **Dictionary/computer/spellcheck during exam:** Yes

How are professors notified of LD: By student and Special Services Director

GENERAL ADMISSIONS INFORMATION

Director of Admissions: David H. Wilkey   **Telephone:** 304-636-5850

Entrance Requirements:

16 credits including: 4 yrs. English; 2 yrs. Math; 3 yrs. Social Studies; 2 yrs. Science.

Test Scores: **SAT:** 766   **ACT:** 18 average

G.P.A.: 2.0 (minimum)   **Class Rank:**

Application Deadline: 6/1   **Achievement Tests:**

COLLEGE GRADUATION REQUIREMENTS

Foreign Language: **Waivers:** Depends on major

Math: **Waivers:** Depends on major

Minimum Course Load per Term: Yes

ADDITIONAL INFORMATION

Location: The College is located in a community of 10,000 in the foothills of the Allegheny Mountains.

Enrollment Information: **Undergraduate:** 856   **Women:** 52%   **Men:** 48%

    In-State Students: 45%   **Out of State:** 55%

Cost Information: **In-State Tuition:** $6,853   **Out of State:** same

    Room & Board: $3,512   **Additional Costs:** $95

Housing Information: **University Housing:** Yes   **Sorority:** 15%

    % Living on Campus: 50%   **Fraternity:** 15%

Athletics: NCAA Div. II

Support: CS *Institution:* 4 yr. Public

LEARNING DISABILITY PROGRAM AND SERVICES

Comments:

Higher Education for Learning Problems (H.E.L.P.) encourages a feeling of camaraderie between the students enrolled in the Program. They often provide the support that is needed when depression or frustration become a problem. There are now about 120 students being served, most are dyslexic. There is a large professional staff who offer a wide variety of services on a individual basis to the student. Services include assistance with skills for notetaking, studying, and organization.

LEARNING DISABILITY ADMISSIONS INFORMATION

Program Name:	Higher Education for Learning Problems (H.E.L.P.)	*Telephone*
Program Director:	Barbara P. Guyer	304-696-6252
Contact Person:	Barbara P. Guyer or Lynne M. Weston	same

Admissions:

There is a special application required as well as a special admissions procedure to follow. The student must enclose with their application an updated Psychological and Educational Evaluation and a one page handwritten statement by the student on their college goals. The student is required to have an interview, and have letters of recommendations sent to the College as well.

Interview: Yes   *Diagnostic Tests:* Yes

Documentation: Intelligence and Achievement tests

College Entrance Exams Required: Yes   *Untimed Accepted:* Yes

Course Entrance Requirements: Yes

Are Waivers Available: No

Additional Information:

If the ACT score in English is less than 17 the student must pass an English Proficiency Exam.

Individualized high school coursework accepted:

Essay Required: Yes, for HELP applicants only

Special Application Required: Yes   *Submitted To:*

Number of Applications Submitted Each Year: 200+

Number of Applications Accepted Each Year: 30+

Number of Students Served: 120+

Application Deadline for Special Admission: 1 year in advance

Acceptance into Program means acceptance

into college: No

LEARNING DISABILITY SERVICES

Learning Resource Room: Yes

Kurzweil Personal Reader:

LD Specialists: 13

Oral Exams: Yes

Services for LD Only: Yes

Books on Tape: Yes

Calculator allowed in exam: Y/N

Tape recording in class: Yes

Curriculum Modification Available:

Tutorial Help: Yes   **Peer Tutors:** Yes

Max. Hours/Week for services:
No Maximum

**Added
Cost:** Included on application form

Taping of books not on tape: Yes

Dictionary/computer/spellcheck during exam: Y/N

How are professors notified of LD: By the Student who submits a form letter to the professor

GENERAL ADMISSIONS INFORMATION

Director of Admissions: James W. Haless   **Telephone:** 304-696-3160

Entrance Requirements:

4 yrs. English; 2 yrs. higher Math; 3 yrs. Social Studies; 2 yrs. Lab Science; 2 yrs. Foreign Language. Minimum 2.0 or 17 ACT ,19 ACT for the Nursing programs

Test Scores: **SAT:**   **ACT:** 17

G.P.A.: 2.0   **Class Rank:**

Application Deadline: Rolling   **Achievement Tests:** No

COLLEGE GRADUATION REQUIREMENTS

Foreign Language: Yes   **Waivers:** Depends on major/Foreign culture may be substituted

Math: Yes   **Waivers:** Depends on major

Minimum Course Load per Term: 12 hours qualifies student as full-time

ADDITIONAL INFORMATION

Location: Marshall University is located on 55 acres, 135 miles from Columbus,West Virginia.

Enrollment Information: **Undergraduate:** 10,581   **Women:** 56%   **Men:** 44%

In-State Students: 86%   **Out of State:** 14%

Cost Information: **In-State Tuition:** $1,487   **Out of State:** $3,557

Room & Board: $4,582   **Additional Costs:** $144

Housing Information: **University Housing:** Yes   **Sorority:** 7%

% Living on Campus: 30%   **Fraternity:** 12%

Athletics: NCAA Div. 1

WEST VIRGINIA WESLEYAN COLLEGE
Buckhannon, W.V. 26201
304-473-8510

Support: SP   **Institution:** 4 yr. Private

LEARNING DISABILITY PROGRAM AND SERVICES

Comments:

The Special Support Services program is designed to help students prepare for academic success and a productive career. Students are mainstreamed into regular classes and assisted by a variety of people and services coordinated by Wesleyan's Learning Center. During the first year, learning disabled students take 3 courses: a Reading and Study Development course and 2 Laboratory Practicums which focus on improving writing and personal development. Support groups, individual conferences, personal counseling and academic development are available.

LEARNING DISABILITY ADMISSIONS INFORMATION

Program Name:	Special Support Services Program (SSSP)	**Telephone**
Program Director:	Phyllis Coston	304-473-8380
Contact Person:	Tammy Frederick or Phyllis Coston	same

Admissions:

The following requirements must be completed before an applicant will be considered for admission: completion of Application of Admission, high school transcript, SAT or ACT, letters of recommendation from a guidance counselor, a teacher and another professional, and an interview on campus. Applicants for the SSSP for learning disabled students must complete all admission requirements by December 15. The interview is the most important component of the process, and student motivation is the key.

Interview: Yes   **Diagnostic Tests:** Yes

Documentation: WAIS-R or WISC-R (90+ range) test should be given within 2 years

College Entrance Exams Required: Yes   **Untimed Accepted:** Yes

Course Entrance Requirements: Yes

Are Waivers Available:

Additional Information:

Three letters of recommendation are required. The interview is with the learning center and admission counselor.

Individualized high school coursework accepted: Yes, should be mainstreamed by junior year

Essay Required: Writing sample required for accepted students.

Special Application Required: No   **Submitted To:**

Number of Applications Submitted Each Year: 300+

Number of Applications Accepted Each Year: 60 (usually) sometimes higher

Number of Students Served: 232

Application Deadline for Special Admission: December of Senior year

Acceptance into Program means acceptance into college: Yes

LEARNING DISABILITY SERVICES

Learning Resource Room: Yes   **Curriculum Modification Available:** No

Kurzweil Personal Reader: No   **Tutorial Help:** Yes   **Peer Tutors:** Yes

LD Specialists: 4   **Max. Hours/Week for services:**

Oral Exams: Yes   No limit

Services for LD Only: No   **Added**

Books on Tape: Yes   **Cost:** $3,700 yr 1, $2,000 yr 2, $1,000 yr 3, $500 yr 4

Calculator allowed in exam: Y/N   **Taping of books not on tape:** Yes

Tape recording in class: Yes   **Dictionary/computer/spellcheck during exam:** Y/N

How are professors notified of LD: By the student and Program Director

GENERAL ADMISSIONS INFORMATION

Director of Admissions: John Fluke   **Telephone:** 304- 473-8510

Entrance Requirements:

Application for admission, High School Record Request Form, SAT or ACT scores, 3 letters of recommendation, recent photo (optional). There are no minimum test scores. Admissions favors the best qualified candidates.

Test Scores: **SAT:** No minimum   **ACT:** No minimum

G.P.A.: 2.2 (but may accept lower)   **Class Rank:**

Application Deadline: Rolling   **Achievement Tests:**

COLLEGE GRADUATION REQUIREMENTS

Foreign Language: No   **Waivers:**

Math: No   **Waivers:**

Minimum Course Load per Term: 12 credits is full time. Most SSSP students carry 12-15 hours

ADDITIONAL INFORMATION

Location: The College is located on 80 acres 135 miles from Pittsburgh, in the Appalachian foothills.

Enrollment Information: **Undergraduate:** 1,511   **Women:** 50%   **Men:** 50%

         In-State Students: 43%   **Out of State:** 57%

Cost Information: **In-State Tuition:** $11,830   **Out of State:** same

         Room & Board: $3,150.   **Additional Costs:**

Housing Information: **University Housing:** Yes   **Sorority:** 21%

         % Living on Campus: 77%   **Fraternity:** 28%

Athletics: NAIA

Support: CS   **Institution:** 4 yrs. Private

LEARNING DISABILITY PROGRAM AND SERVICES

Comments:

The Assistance to Students with Learning Differences is available for incoming freshman who have demonstrated learning disabilities. This program is designed to support these students in their regular coursework. Five to seven students, of at least average intelligence who are highly motivated to succeed in college, will be accepted yearly into this program. Each student accepted into the program will participate in the ASLD Summer Program and will be eligible to receive support services.

LEARNING DISABILITY ADMISSIONS INFORMATION

Program Name:	Assistance to Students with Learning Differences (ASLD)	**Telephone**
Program Director:	Kathie Moran	608-257-4861
Contact Person:	same	

Admissions:

In addition to the regular admission application and requirements, the following will be necessary: ASLD program applicational letters of recommendation from 2 high school teachers/counselors; on-campus interview with Admissions Counselor, Learning Skills Coordinator, and Associate Academic Dean. If a student with a learning disability is denied admission, that student may request reconsideration and send additional documentation.

Interview: Yes   **Diagnostic Tests:** Yes

Documentation: Woodcock-Johnson; WAIS-R or WISC-R

College Entrance Exams Required: Yes   **Untimed Accepted:** Yes

Course Entrance Requirements: Yes

Are Waivers Available: No

Additional Information:

Currently, placement tests are given after acceptance to Edgewood to determine Math and English placement. It is likely the College will begin using expanded ACT scores to determine placement.

Individualized high school coursework accepted: No

Essay Required: Yes

Special Application Required: Yes   **Submitted To:**

Number of Applications Submitted Each Year: 15

Number of Applications Accepted Each Year: 5-6

Number of Students Served: 4

Application Deadline for Special Admission: Fall of Senior year

Acceptance into Program means acceptance into college: Yes

313

LEARNING DISABILITY SERVICES

Learning Resource Room: Yes   **Curriculum Modification Available:** No

Kurzweil Personal Reader: **Tutorial Help:** Yes   **Peer Tutors:** Yes

LD Specialists: 1   **Max. Hours/Week for services:**

Oral Exams: Yes   Need-by-need basis

Services for LD Only: No   **Added**

Books on Tape: Yes   **Cost:** None

Calculator allowed in exam: Y/N   **Taping of books not on tape:** Yes

Tape recording in class: Yes   **Dictionary/computer/spellcheck during exam:** Y/N

How are professors notified of LD: As directed by student

GENERAL ADMISSIONS INFORMATION

Director of Admissions: Robert Blust   **Telephone:** 608-257-4861

Entrance Requirements:

4 yrs. English; 3 yrs. Math; 2 yrs. Foreign Language; 2 yrs. Science; 2 yrs. Social Studies; 1 yr. History; 4 electives(may be non-academic). There is conditional admission for students not usually admitted. Those students must maintain a 2.0 GPA for 12 credits.

Test Scores: **SAT:**   **ACT:** 17-18 (minimum)

G.P.A.: 2.0 (minimum)   **Class Rank:**

Application Deadline: 8/1   **Achievement Tests:**

COLLEGE GRADUATION REQUIREMENTS

Foreign Language: Yes   **Waivers:** If 2 years have been taken in high school

Math: Yes   **Waivers:** Being discussed

Minimum Course Load per Term: 12 credits, first semester

ADDITIONAL INFORMATION

Location: The College is located in Madison, a University-oriented city.

Enrollment Information: **Undergraduate:** 967   **Women:** 68%   **Men:** 32%

    In-State Students: 88%   **Out of State:** 12%

Cost Information: **In-State Tuition:** $6,400   **Out of State:** same

    Room & Board: $3,000   **Additional Costs:**

Housing Information: **University Housing:** Yes   **Sorority:** No

    % Living on Campus: 15%   **Fraternity:** No

Athletics: NAIA, NLCAA

Support: S   **Institution:** 4 yr. Private

LEARNING DISABILITY PROGRAM AND SERVICES

Comments:

Marian College offers support services for students with learning disabilities. The ultimate goal of this program is to offer the services necessary to allow learning disabled students to succeed in their college classes. This program offers the following services: information on community, state and national resources available to learning disabled people; untimed exams; test readers; assistance in writing and proofreading papers and assignments; help in organizational and study skills; notetakers; recorded textbooks; tutors(individual and group; and liaison service.

LEARNING DISABILITY ADMISSIONS INFORMATION

Program Name: Academic Support Services   **Telephone**

Program Director: Gretchen Gall   414-923-8097

Contact Person: same

Admissions:

There is no special application nor admissions procedure for the student with learning disabilities.

Interview: Yes   **Diagnostic Tests:** Yes

Documentation: Psychological and achievement tests

College Entrance Exams Required: Yes   **Untimed Accepted:** Yes

Course Entrance Requirements: Yes

Are Waivers Available: No

Additional Information:

High school transcripts and ACT scores are used for Math placement. High school Chemistry (with a C or better) is needed prior to taking College Chemistry. Mastery (C or above) of high school Algebra is extremely helpful before taking college level Chemistry and Physical Science courses.

Individualized high school coursework accepted: Yes

Essay Required: Yes, a writing sample

Special Application Required: No   **Submitted To:**

Number of Applications Submitted Each Year: 6-12

Number of Applications Accepted Each Year:

Number of Students Served: 23

Application Deadline for Special Admission: No

Acceptance into Program means acceptance

into college: There is an appeal procedure

315

LEARNING DISABILITY SERVICES

Learning Resource Room: No   **Curriculum Modification Available:** No

Kurzweil Personal Reader: No   **Tutorial Help:**   **Peer Tutors:** Yes

LD Specialists: **Max. Hours/Week for services:**

Oral Exams: Yes   Varies

Services for LD Only: No   **Added**

Books on Tape: Yes   **Cost:** None

Calculator allowed in exam: Y/N   **Taping of books not on tape:** Yes

Tape recording in class: Yes   **Dictionary/computer/spellcheck during exam:** Yes

How are professors notified of LD: By the student and the Program Director

GENERAL ADMISSIONS INFORMATION

Director of Admissions: Carol Reichenberger   **Telephone:** 414-923-7650

Entrance Requirements:

4 yrs. English; 3 yrs. Math; 3 yrs. Science; Foreign Language.

Test Scores: **SAT:**   **ACT:** 18

G.P.A.: 2.0   **Class Rank:** top 50%

Application Deadline: Rolling   **Achievement Tests:**

COLLEGE GRADUATION REQUIREMENTS

Foreign Language: No   **Waivers:**

Math: Yes   **Waivers:** Study option available

Minimum Course Load per Term: 12 credits to be considered full-time

ADDITIONAL INFORMATION

Location: Marian College is located on 50 acres in a suburb of Fond-du-Lac.

Enrollment Information: **Undergraduate:** 1,228   **Women:** 74%   **Men:** 26%

In-State Students: 90%   **Out of State:** 10%

Cost Information: **In-State Tuition:** $6,448   **Out of State:** same

Room & Board: $2,600   **Additional Costs:** $110

Housing Information: **University Housing:** Yes   **Sorority:** No

% Living on Campus: 40%   **Fraternity:** No

Athletics: NAIA

UNIVERSITY OF WISCONSIN - EAU CLAIRE
Eau Claire, Wi. 54701
715-836-5415

Support: CS   **Institution:** 4 yr. Public

LEARNING DISABILITY PROGRAM AND SERVICES

Comments:

When the student is admitted to UW they should make their special needs known to the SSD coordinator at least 8 weeks before classes begin so that necessary adaptations can be arranged. The student is required to submit diagnostic documentation of disability to receive requested accommodations. The Coordinator facilitates communication with department advisors when special scheduling, course selection or auxiliary aids are needed. The University also has an Academic Skills Center staffed with specialists in Math and Science, composition, Foreign Language, and more.

LEARNING DISABILITY ADMISSIONS INFORMATION

Program Name: Services for Students with Disabilities (SSD)   **Telephone**

Program Director: Joseph C. Hisrich   715-836-4542

Contact Person: same

Admissions:

Individuals with learning disabilities complete the standard University application form and must meet the regular University admission criteria. Once admitted, students may access services. Students not admitted in the Fall, may find a January admission somewhat less competitive.

Interview: No   **Diagnostic Tests:** Yes

Documentation: LD assessment

College Entrance Exams Required: Yes   **Untimed Accepted:** Yes

Course Entrance Requirements: Yes

Are Waivers Available: No

Additional Information:

The University offers a Collegiate Bridge Program which is a 5 week summer program. This program is mainly for minority students, first generation and disadvantaged students. Learning disabled students are eligible candidates. This program requires a separate application which is sent to students who are conditionally admitted.

Individualized high school coursework accepted: Yes

Essay Required: No

Special Application Required: No   **Submitted To:**

Number of Applications Submitted Each Year: 35-45

Number of Applications Accepted Each Year: 35-45

Number of Students Served: 35-50

Application Deadline for Special Admission: No

Acceptance into Program means acceptance into college: No

317

LEARNING DISABILITY SERVICES

Learning Resource Room: Yes   **Curriculum Modification Available:** Yes

Kurzweil Personal Reader: No   **Tutorial Help:** Yes   **Peer Tutors:** Yes

LD Specialists: 1   **Max. Hours/Week for services:**

Oral Exams: Yes   2-3 hours per course/per week

Services for LD Only: Yes   **Added**

Books on Tape: Yes   **Cost:** None

Calculator allowed in exam: Y/N   **Taping of books not on tape:** Yes

Tape recording in class: Yes   **Dictionary/computer/spellcheck during exam:** Yes

How are professors notified of LD: By the student or the Program Director

GENERAL ADMISSIONS INFORMATION

Director of Admissions: Roger W. Groenwold   **Telephone:** 715-836-5415

Entrance Requirements:

4 yrs. English; 2 yrs. Math; 3 yrs. Social Studies; 2 yrs. Science. Probationary admissions is sometimes offered.

Test Scores: SAT: **ACT:** 21

G.P.A.:   **Class Rank:** Upper 50%

Application Deadline: Rolling   **Achievement Tests:**

COLLEGE GRADUATION REQUIREMENTS

Foreign Language: Yes   **Waivers:** Yes

Math: Yes   **Waivers:** Yes

Minimum Course Load per Term: 12 credits for full-time status

ADDITIONAL INFORMATION

Location: The 333 acre Eau Claire campus is 95 miles east of Minneapolis.

Enrollment Information: Undergraduate: 10,251   **Women:** 60%   **Men:** 40%

In-State Students: 84%   **Out of State:** 16%

Cost Information: In-State Tuition: $1,735   **Out of State:** $5,096

Room & Board: $2,290   **Additional Costs:**

Housing Information: University Housing: Yes   **Sorority:** 1%

% Living on Campus: 33%   **Fraternity:** 1%

Athletics: NAIA

UNIVERSITY OF WISCONSIN - LACROSSE

LaCrosse, Wi. 54601

608-785-8067

Support: CS   **Institution:** 4 yr. Public

LEARNING DISABILITY PROGRAM AND SERVICES

Comments:

A number of academic and personal support services are available through the Services for Students with Special Needs. The Program Director writes a letter to all the student's professors explaining the students learning disability and describing necessary modifications. The Program Director meets with freshman once a week. There is also a support group which meets twice a month. Services include taped texts, testing accommodations, notetakers and remedial courses. Students are encouraged to get tutoring through the academic departments.

LEARNING DISABILITY ADMISSIONS INFORMATION

Program Name:	Services for Students with Special Needs	**Telephone**
Program Director:	June Reinert	608-785-8535
Contact Person:	Tim Lewis	same

Admissions:

There is a special application and admission procedure for students with learning disabilities. Students should check the line on the regular application indicating the presence of a learning disability. These applications are automatically referred to the Program Director who will then request a recent psychological report, 3 letters of recommendation and a personal interview. The admissions office is sensitive to the Director's opinions and will admit students recommended and who can succeed even if these students do not meet standard admissions requirements.

Interview: No   **Diagnostic Tests:** Yes

Documentation: WAIS; W-J

College Entrance Exams Required: Yes   **Untimed Accepted:** Yes

Course Entrance Requirements: Yes

Are Waivers Available: Yes

Additional Information:

Students generally are admitted who are in the top 50% or have an ACT of 22. Students below top 50% or below a 21 ACT may be wait-listed. LD students not meeting entrance criteria may ask for special consideration. Students also may be considered for admission if they meet other quantifiable criteria such as standardized or institutional achievement test scores, alternate high school courses, or grade point average, or demonstrate special talents.

Individualized high school coursework accepted: No

Essay Required: No

Special Application Required: **Submitted To:**

Number of Applications Submitted Each Year: 100

Number of Applications Accepted Each Year: 40

Number of Students Served: 150-200

Application Deadline for Special Admission: No

Acceptance into Program means acceptance

into college: No, appeals are made through admissions office

319

LEARNING DISABILITY SERVICES

Learning Resource Room: Yes   **Curriculum Modification Available:**

Kurzweil Personal Reader: No   **Tutorial Help:** Yes   **Peer Tutors:** Yes

LD Specialists: Yes   **Max. Hours/Week for services:**

Oral Exams: Yes   As Needed

Services for LD Only: No   **Added Cost:**

Books on Tape: Yes

Calculator allowed in exam: Y/N   **Taping of books not on tape:** Yes

Tape recording in class: Yes   **Dictionary/computer/spellcheck during exam:** Y/N

How are professors notified of LD: By student or Program Director

GENERAL ADMISSIONS INFORMATION

Director of Admissions: Timothy R. Lewis   **Telephone:** 608-785-8067

Entrance Requirements:

4 yrs. English; 2 yrs. Science; 2 yrs. Math (Algebra and Geometry); 3 yrs. Social Studies; 3 electives in College Preparatory courses; 2 electives from College Preparatory courses or Fine Arts,Computer Scinece, and other academic areas. Students who rank in the top 60% and have a 21 ACT may be placed on a waiting list.

Test Scores: **SAT:**   **ACT:** 22

G.P.A.:   **Class Rank:** Top 50%

Application Deadline: Rolling   **Achievement Tests:**

COLLEGE GRADUATION REQUIREMENTS

Foreign Language: **Waivers:** Depends on major/ Can be waived on an individual basis

Math: Yes   **Waivers:** Depends on major/ Can be waived on an individual basis

Minimum Course Load per Term: 12 credits per/semester

ADDITIONAL INFORMATION

Location: The University is located on 119 acres in a small city 140 miles west of Madison.

Enrollment Information: **Undergraduate:** 8,411   **Women:** 57%   **Men:** 43%

                  In-State Students: 86%   **Out of State:** 14%

Cost Information: **In-State Tuition:** $1,769   **Out of State:** $5,130

                  Room & Board: $1,950   **Additional Costs:**

Housing Information: **University Housing:** Yes   **Sorority:** 1%

            % Living on Campus: 22%   **Fraternity:** 1%

Athletics: NCAA Div. II

UNIVERSITY OF WISCONSIN - MILWAUKEE
Milwaukee, Wi. 53201
414-229-3800

Support: CS   **Institution:** 4 yr. Public

LEARNING DISABILITY PROGRAM AND SERVICES

Comments:

The Learning Disability Program offers a wide range of support services. The goal of the program is to provide an environment which encourages the development of the unique talents of every student. There is an emphasis on mainstreaming, and participation to the fullest extent in the total life of the university community. Services provided include tape recording, tutorial services, special arrangements for test taking, notetakers, and communication with professors.

LEARNING DISABILITY ADMISSIONS INFORMATION

Program Name: Learning Disability Program   **Telephone**

Program Director: Laurie Gramatzki   414-229-6239

Contact Person: same

Admissions:

There is a special admissions procedure for students with learning disabilities. Students must submit current and complete documentation of their learning disability to the LD Program. An interview is required. If the students are not regularly admissible to the University, they may apply through the Department of Learning Skills and Educational Opportunity. They will need to take placement tests. The LD Program does not make admission decisions.

Interview: Yes   **Diagnostic Tests:** Yes

Documentation: W-J-revised (preferred)

College Entrance Exams Required: Yes   **Untimed Accepted:** Yes

Course Entrance Requirements: Yes

Are Waivers Available: Yes

Additional Information:

Individualized high school coursework accepted: Y/N

Essay Required: No

Special Application Required: No   **Submitted To:**

Number of Applications Submitted Each Year:

Number of Applications Accepted Each Year:

Number of Students Served: 10

Application Deadline for Special Admission: Eleven months prior to admissions

Acceptance into Program means acceptance

into college: There is an appeal procedure

LEARNING DISABILITY SERVICES

Learning Resource Room: Yes **Curriculum Modification Available:** No

Kurzweil Personal Reader: No **Tutorial Help:** Yes **Peer Tutors:** Yes

LD Specialists: 1 **Max. Hours/Week for services:**

Oral Exams: Yes Varies

Services for LD Only: Yes **Added**

Books on Tape: Yes **Cost:** None

Calculator allowed in exam: Y/N **Taping of books not on tape:** Yes

Tape recording in class: Yes **Dictionary/computer/spellcheck during exam:** Yes

How are professors notified of LD: At the student's request, by the Program Director

GENERAL ADMISSIONS INFORMATION

Director of Admissions: Beth Weckmueller **Telephone:** 414-229-6164

Entrance Requirements:

16 units: 4 yrs. English; 1 yr. Algebra; 1 yr. Geometry; 1 yr. Biology or Chemistry Lab; 3 yrs. History

Test Scores: **SAT:** **ACT:** 21

G.P.A.: **Class Rank:** Top 50%

Application Deadline: Rolling **Achievement Tests:**

COLLEGE GRADUATION REQUIREMENTS

Foreign Language: No **Waivers:**

Math: Yes **Waivers:** Student has to pass Math proficiency exam

Minimum Course Load per Term: No limit

ADDITIONAL INFORMATION

Location: The University is located on 93 acres in an urban area 90 miles north of Chicago.

Enrollment Information: Undergraduate: 20,316 **Women:** 53% **Men:** 47%

In-State Students: 93% **Out of State:** 7%

Cost Information: In-State Tuition: $2,054 **Out of State:** $6,187

Room & Board: $3,476 **Additional Costs:**

Housing Information: University Housing: Yes **Sorority:** Yes

% Living on Campus: 10% **Fraternity:** Yes

Athletics: NCAA Div. II

Support: SP   **Institution:** 4 yr. Public

LEARNING DISABILITY PROGRAM AND SERVICES

Comments:

Project Success is an academic and social remediation program for specific language handicapped dyslexic students. These students are academically able and have a determination to succeed in spite of a pronounced problem in a number of areas. Help is offered in the following ways: by direct remediation of deficiencies through the Orton-Gillingham Technique; one-to-one tutoring assistance; math and writing labs; Guidance and Counseling with scheduling course work and interpersonal relations; untimed exams; and by providing an atmosphere that is supportive.

LEARNING DISABILITY ADMISSIONS INFORMATION

		Telephone
Program Name:	Project Success	
Program Director:	Dr. Robert Nash	414-424-1032
Contact Person:	Dr. Robert Nash/ Dr. William Katz	414-424-1032

Admissions:

Students apply to Project Success in their sophomore year of high school. The applicant applies by writing a letter in their own handwriting indicating interest in the Program and why. In junior year the student and parents are required to have an interview with the Director. The interview is used to assess family dynamics in terms of support for the student and reasons for wanting to attend college. The Director is looking for motivation, stability and the ability of the student to describe the disability. Learning disabled students who are admitted must take an 8 week summer program prior to fall semester.

Interview: Yes   **Diagnostic Tests:** Yes

Documentation: testing done by Program Director

College Entrance Exams Required: Yes   **Untimed Accepted:** Yes

Course Entrance Requirements: Yes

Are Waivers Available: Yes

Additional Information:

Acceptance into Project Success does not grant acceptance into the University. Admission to the University and acceptance into Project Success is a joint decision but a separate process is required for each. Current admissions procedures must be followed before acceptance into the special program can be offered.

Individualized high school coursework accepted: Yes

Essay Required: No

Special Application Required: Yes   **Submitted To:**

Number of Applications Submitted Each Year: 100-150

Number of Applications Accepted Each Year: 50-55

Number of Students Served: 150

Application Deadline for Special Admission: 2-3 years prior to admissions

Acceptance into Program means acceptance

into college: Yes

LEARNING DISABILITY SERVICES

Learning Resource Room:	Yes	**Curriculum Modification Available:** No	
Kurzweil Personal Reader:		**Tutorial Help:** Yes	**Peer Tutors:** Yes
LD Specialists:	2	**Max. Hours/Week for services:**	
Oral Exams:	No	No Limit	
Services for LD Only:	Yes	**Added**	
Books on Tape:	No	**Cost:** None	
Calculator allowed in exam:	Yes	**Taping of books not on tape:** No	
Tape recording in class:	Yes	**Dictionary/computer/spellcheck during exam:** No	

How are professors notified of LD: By student

GENERAL ADMISSIONS INFORMATION

Director of Admissions: August Helgerson   **Telephone:** 414-424-0202

Entrance Requirements:

4 yrs. English; 2 yrs. Math; 3 yrs. Social Studies; 2 yrs. Science; 3 college prep electives; 2 yrs. other electives. SAT scores are acceptable from non-residents. Students may be wait-listed if they meet course requirements and test scores, but are not in the top 51% to 75% of their class.

Test Scores: **SAT:**   **ACT:** 22

G.P.A.:   **Class Rank:** 50%

Application Deadline: Rolling admissions   **Achievement Tests:** NA

COLLEGE GRADUATION REQUIREMENTS

Foreign Language: Yes   **Waivers:**

Math: Yes   **Waivers:**

Minimum Course Load per Term: 14 credits

ADDITIONAL INFORMATION

Location: The campus is located 3 hours north of Chicago and 2 hours northeast of Madison.

Enrollment Information:	**Undergraduate:** 9,469	**Women:** 57%	**Men:** 43%
	In-State Students: 97%		**Out of State:** 3%
Cost Information:	**In-State Tuition:** $1,790		**Out of State:** $5,352
	Room & Board: $1,990		**Additional Costs:**
Housing Information:	**University Housing:** Yes		**Sorority:** Yes
	% Living on Campus: 38%		**Fraternity:** Yes

Athletics: NCAA Div.III

UNIVERSITY OF WISCONSIN - STEVENS POINT

Stevens Point, Wi. 54481

715-346-2441

Support: S   **Institution:** 4 yr. Public

LEARNING DISABILITY PROGRAM AND SERVICES

Comments:

The University does not have a formal program for learning disabled students. However, the Director of Services is a strong advocate for LD students and encourages them to identify their learning limitation in their application for admission. Students are encouraged to meet with the Director prior to admissions for information about the services. A full range of accommodations are provided.

LEARNING DISABILITY ADMISSIONS INFORMATION

Program Name: New Students Program & Services for the Disabled   **Telephone**

Program Director: John Timcak   715-346-3361

Contact Person:

Admissions:

There is no separate admission procedure for learning disabled students. However, LD students are encouraged to make a pre-admission inquiry and talk to the Director of Services. The Director of Admission does have the flexibility to admit LD students who are borderline. If the student meets with special services and the Director feels the case is reasonable, the Director will ask admissions to consider the case in light of the learning differences. These students usually have a class rank plus ACT composite index of 60 instead of the required 64.

Interview: Yes   **Diagnostic Tests:** Yes

Documentation: Yes

College Entrance Exams Required: Yes   **Untimed Accepted:** Yes

Course Entrance Requirements: Yes

Are Waivers Available:

Additional Information:

Learning disabled students who do not meet the combined class rank and ACT test score index of 64 should send a letter of recommendation from the high school LD specialist or counselor. Students should also meet with the Director of the services program at Stevens Point.

Individualized high school coursework accepted:

Essay Required: No

Special Application Required: No   **Submitted To:**

Number of Applications Submitted Each Year:

Number of Applications Accepted Each Year:

Number of Students Served: 48

Application Deadline for Special Admission: No

Acceptance into Program means acceptance into college:

LEARNING DISABILITY SERVICES

Learning Resource Room: Yes	**Curriculum Modification Available:** Yes	
Kurzweil Personal Reader: Yes	**Tutorial Help:** Yes	**Peer Tutors:** Yes
LD Specialists: No	**Max. Hours/Week for services:**	
Oral Exams: Yes	3 hours	
Services for LD Only: No	**Added**	
Books on Tape: Yes	**Cost:** None	
Calculator allowed in exam: Yes	**Taping of books not on tape:** Yes	
Tape recording in class: Yes	**Dictionary/computer/spellcheck during exam:** Yes	

How are professors notified of LD: By the student or the Director of the Program

GENERAL ADMISSIONS INFORMATION

Director of Admissions: John Larsen   **Telephone:** 715-346-2441

Entrance Requirements:

4 yrs. English; 2 yrs. Math; 3 yrs. Social Studies; 2 yrs. Science; 5 Electives (preferably college prep.) Use combination of class rank and test scores. ACT plus class rank must equal 64. Students not meeting the specific class rank and test score index should contact the Director of Admissions.

Test Scores: **SAT:**   —   **ACT:** 22

G.P.A.:   **Class Rank:** Top 50%

Application Deadline: Rolling   **Achievement Tests:**

COLLEGE GRADUATION REQUIREMENTS

Foreign Language: Y/N   **Waivers:** Depends on degree; Committee will consider waivers

Math: Yes   **Waivers:** Yes, Offer independent study, substitutions or waivers

Minimum Course Load per Term: Case-by-case determination

ADDITIONAL INFORMATION

Location: The University of Wisconsin at Stevens Point is located on 335 acres, 110 miles north of Madison.

Enrollment Information: **Undergraduate:** 7,680	**Women:** 51%	**Men:** 49%	
In-State Students: 91%	**Out of State:** 9%		
Cost Information: **In-State Tuition:** $1,770	**Out of State:** $5,130		
Room & Board: $2,480	**Additional Costs:**		
Housing Information: **University Housing:** Yes	**Sorority:** Yes		
% Living on Campus: 40%	**Fraternity:** Yes		

Athletics: NCAA Div. III

Quick Contact
Reference List

K&W Quick Reference List

State/School	Location	Contact	Program Name	Telephone
ALABAMA				
U. of Alabama	Birmingham 35294	Jacqueline O. Falls	Handicapped Student Services	208-394-3704
U. of Alabama	Huntsville 35899	Dr. Gary Biller	Student Support Services	205-895-6203
U. of Alabama	Tuscaloosa 35487	Warner Moore	Office of Student Services	205-348-6794
Auburn U.	Montgomery 36193	Letta Gorman	Center for Rehabilitation Resource	205-244-3468
ALASKA				
U. of Alaska	Anchorage 99508	Doran Vaughan	Disabled Student Services	907-786-1570
U. of Alaska	Fairbanks 99775	Diane Presten	Center for Health and Counseling	807-474-7043
ARIZONA				
Arizona State U.	Tempe 85287	Deborah E. Taska	Disabled Student Resources	602-965-1234
U. of Arizona	Tucson 85721	Tedde Scharf	SALT (Strategic Alternate Learning Techniques)	602-621-1242
		Eleanor Harner		
		Rose Wilhite		
ARKANSAS				
Henderson St. U.	Arkadelphia 71923	Mrs. Kathy Muse	Student Support Services	501-246-5511
U. of the Ozarks	Clarksville 72830	Dr. Dale Jordan	Ben D. Caudle Program/ Jones Learning Center	501-754-3839
CALIFORNIA				
Bakersfield C.	Bakersfield 93311	Debbie Shinn	Supportive Service Center	805-395-4464
California State U.	Carson 90747	Ann Wells	Disabled Student Services	213-516-3660
California State U.	Fullerton 92634	John D. Liverpool	Counseling and Learning Disability Program	714-773-2370
California State U.	Hayward 94542	Pennijean Savage	Disabled Student Services	415-881-3868
California State U.	Northridge 91330	Dr. Marshall Rasking	Learning Disability Program	818-885-2684
Calif. Poly. St. U.	San Luis Obispo 93407	Ann Fryer	Disabled Student Services	805-756-1395
		Harriet Clendenen		
Canada C.	Redwood City 94061	Glory Bratton	Learning Disability Program	415-364-1212
Cerritos Comm. C.	Norwalk 90650	Al Spetrino	Instructional Support Center	213-860-2451
Cypress C.	Cypress 90630	Robert Nadell	Educational Services Center	714-826-2220
De Anza C.	Cupertino 95014	Pauline Waathig	Educational Diagnostic Center	408-864-8838
El Camino C.	Torrance 90506	Bill Hoanzl	Special Resource Center	213-715-3276
Evergreen Valley C.	San Jose 95135	Bonnie Clark	Diagnostic Learning Program	408-270-6447
Imperial Valley C.	Imperial 92251	Melvin Wendrick, Dir.	Disabled Student Program and Services	619-352-8320
		Norma Nava-Pinvelas		
Los Medanos C.	Pittsburg 94565	Stan Chin	Disabled Student Program and Services	415-439-2181
Kings River Comm. C.	Reedley 93654	Lynn Mancini	Enabler Services	209-638-3641
Menlo C.	Menlo Park 94025	Jamie Armstrong	Student Support Services	415-323-6141

K&W Quick Reference List

State/School	Location	Contact	Program Name	Telephone
CALIFORNIA (Con't)				
San Diego State U.	San Diego 92182	Joan Kilbourne	Disabled Student Services	619-594-6473
San Francisco State U.	San Francisco 94132	Elizabeth Bacon / Terry Smith / Mollie Brodie	Disabled Student Services	415-338-2472
Santa Clara U.	Santa Clara 95053	Christine McIntyre	Disabled Student Resources	408-554-4111
Santa Monica C.	Santa Monica 90405	Dr. Ann Maddox	Learning Specialist Program	213-450-5150
Santa Rosa Jr. C.	Santa Rosa 95401	Jennifer Mann / Carla Stone	Learning Skills Program	707-527-4278 / 707-527-4580
Sierra C.	Rocklin 95677	Dr. James Hirschinger / Denise Stone/K. Fields	Learning Disabilities Program	916-624-3333
Sonoma State U.	Rohnert Park 94928	Anthony Tusler / Bill Clopton	Disability Resource Center	707-664-2677
Stanford U.	Palo Alto 94305	Molly Sandperl / James Boriquin	Disability Resource Center	415-723-1066 / 415-723-1039
U. of California	Berkeley 94720	Michael Spagna / Susan O'Hara	Disabled Students Program	415-642-0518
U. of California	Davis 95616	Christine O'Dell	Disability Resource Center	916-752-3184
U. of California	Santa Cruz 95064	Lea Van Meter	Disabled Student Services	408-429-2089
U. of the Pacific	Stockton 95211	Ellen Weire	Learning Disability Support Service	209-946-3219
U. of San Francisco	San Francisco 94117	Cally Salzman	Services For The Learning Disabled	415-666-6876
U. of Southern Calif.	Los Angeles 90089	Janet Ewart Eddy	The Learning Center	213-743-6544
West Hills C.	Coalinga 93210	Diane L. Allen	Learning Skills Program	209-935-0801
COLORADO				
Colorado State U.	Fort Collins 80523	Rosemary Kreston	Office of Resources for Disabled	303-491-6385
Fort Lewis C.	Durango 81301	Robert Lindquist	Learning Assistance Center	303-247-7383
Mesa C.	Grand Junction 81502	Sandra Wymore	TLC/PLD	303-248-1304
Regis C.	Denver 80221	Julie Elgin	Commitment Program	303-458-4900
U. of Colorado	Boulder 80309	Terri Bodhaine	Learning Disability Program	303-566-5611
U. of Denver	Denver 80208	Maria Armstrong, Dir. / Sue Hunt	Learning Effectiveness Program	303-871-2280
U. of N. Colorado	Greeley 80639	Gary Gullickson	Disabled Student Services	303-351-2881
CONNECTICUT				
Central Ct. State U.	New Britain 06050	George Tenney	Special Student Services	203-827-7651
Mitchell C.	New London 06320	Dr. Susan Duques	Learning Resource Center	203-443-2811
U. of Connecticut	Storrs 06268	Dr. Joan McGuire	University Program for LD Students	203-486-5035
U. of Hartford	W. Hartford 06117	Patricia Williams	Learning Plus	203-243-4522
U. of New Haven	West Haven 06516	Arlene Faiman	Services for Students with Learning Disabilities	203-932-7409

K&W Quick Reference List

State/School	Location	Contact	Program Name	Telephone
CONNECTICUT (Con't)				
Wesleyan U.	Middletown 06457	Denise Darrigrand	Office of Student Life	203-344-7900
DELAWARE				
Brandywine C. of Widner U.	Willmington 19803	Linda Baun	Program for LD Students	302-477-2290
U. of Delaware	Newark 19716	David Johns	Academic Studies Assistance Program	302-451-8167
DISTRICT OF COLUMBIA				
American U.	20016	Dr. Faith Leonard	Learning Services Program	202-885-3360
George Washington U.	20052	Christy Willis	Disabled Student Services	202-676-8250
Georgetown U.	20057	Dr. Norma Jo Eitington	Learning Services	202-687-6985
FLORIDA				
U. of Florida	Gainesville 32611	Kenneth Osfield	Programs and Services for Students with LD	904-392-1261
Florida A & M	Tallahassee 32307	Dr. Sharon M. Wooten	Learning Develpment and Evaluation Center	904-599-3180
Florida Atlantic	Boca Raton 33431	Dee Davis	Disabled Student Services	407-367-3880
Florida Intern. U.	Miami 33199	Jennifer King	Disabled Student Services	305-554-2434
Florida State U.	Tallahassee 32306	Hallie Wabi	Disabled Student Services	904-644-9569
Jacksonville U.	Jacksonville 32211	Helen Glenn	Launch Program	904-744-3950
Miami-Dade Comm. C.	Miami 33176	Elizabeth Smith	Support Services	305-347-2316
St. Thomas U.	Miami 33054	Ellie Delello	Special Services	305-628-6532
GEORGIA				
Brenau Women's C.	Gainesville 30501	Dr. Vincent Yamilkoski	Learning Center	404-534-6134
Emory U.	Atlanta 30322	Lelia Crawford	Handicapped Student Services	404-727-2300
Georgia Southern C.	Statesboro 30460	Regina Kulzer-Hollen	Disability Services	912-681-5541
U. of Georgia	Athens 30602	Karen Kalivoda	Learning Disabilities Adult Clinic	404-542-4597
IDAHO				
U. of Idaho	Moscow 83843	Meredith Goodwin	Student Support Services	208-885-6746
ILLINOIS				
Barat C.	Lake Forest 60045	Dr. Pamela Adelman	Learning Opportunities Program	708-234-8000
DePaul U.	Chicago 60604	Alisa Brickman	Productive Learning Strategies	312-362-6897
Eastern Illinois U.	Charleston 61920	Bill Phillips	Special Education Department	217-581-5315
Elmhurst C.	Elmhurst 60126	James Cunningham	Learning Center	708-617-3050
Harper C.	Palatine 60067	Tom Thompson	Disabled Student Affairs	708-397-3000
Illinois State U.	Normal 61761	Dr. Judy Smithson	Office of Disability Concerns	309-438-5853

K&W Quick Reference List

State/School	Location	Contact	Program Name	Telephone
ILLINOIS (Con't)				
Joliet Junior C.	Joliet 60436	Jewell Myers	Student Support Services	815-729-9020
Kendall C.	Evanston 60201	Kathy McCarville	Freshman Year Program	708-866-1305
Knox C.	Galesburg 61401	Karyn Halloran	Educational Develpmental Program	309-343-0112
Lincoln C.	Lincoln 62656	Irene Bloch	Supportive Educational Services	217-732-3155
National-Louis U.	Evanston 60201		Center for Academic Development	708-256-5150
Northeastern Ill. U.	Chicago 60625	Victoria Amey-Flippin	Special Services	312-583-4050
Northern Illinois U.	DeKalb 60115	Sue Reinhardt	Services for Students with Disabilities	815-753-1303
		Linda Sorge		
Oakton Community C.	Des Plaines 60016	Paula Griswold	Assist	708-635-1759
Rockford C.	Rockford 61101	Jeannie Grey	Learning Resource Center	815-226-4087
Roosevelt U.	Chicago 60605	Dr. Margaret Policastro	Learning Support Services Program	312-341-3870
Rosary C.	River Forest 60305	Louis Tenzis	Student Support Services	312-366-2490
Southern Illinois U.	Carbondale 62901	Sally DeDecker	Project Achieve	618-453-2595
Triton C.	River Grove 60171	Mary Mahoney	Special Needs Assistance Program	708-456-0300
Waubonsee C. C.	Sugar Grove 60554	Sharon Wyland	LD Support Services Program	708-466-4811
Western Illinois U.	Macomb 61455	Candice McLaughlin	Disabled Student Services	309-298-1846
INDIANA				
Anderson U.	Anderson 46012	Rinda Smith	Special Education Services	317-641-4226
Ball State U.	Muncie 47306	Richard Harris	Office of Disabled Students	317-285-5293
Butler U.	Indianapolis 46208	Richard Tirman	Counseling Services	317-283-9385
Earlham C.	Richmond 47374	Kathy Byrne	Student Support Services	317-983-1341
Indiana State U.	Terre Haute 47809	Dr. Charles Hedrick	Skills Center	812-237-4135
		Rita Worrell	Student Support Services	812-237-3604
Indiana U.	Bloomington 47401	Steve Morris	Disabled Student Services	812-855-7578
Indiana Wesleyan U.	Marion 46953	Dr. Ruth Dixon	Learning Center	317-677-2192
		Neil McFarland	Student Supporty Services	
Purdue U.	W. Lafayette 47907	Sarah Templin	Disabled Student Services	317-494-1726
		Kathy Jones		
St. Joseph's C.	Rensselaer 47978	Diane Jennings	Counseling Services	219-866-6116
U. of Indianapolis	Indianapolis 46227	Dr. Patricia Cook	B.U.I.L.D.	317-788-3285
		Dr. Nancy E. O'Dell		
Vincennes U.	Vincennes 47591	George Varns	COPE Student Support Services	812-885-4515
		Jane Kavanaugh	S.T.E.P.	812-885-4209
IOWA				
Coe C.	Cedar Rapids 52402	Lois Kabela	Educational Support Program	319-399-8500
Cornell C.	Mt. Vernon 52314	Connie Rosene	Counseling & Student Support Services	319-895-4292
Drake U.	Des Moines 50311	Dr. Stephen Schoddee	Special Services	515-271-3866
Grand View C.	Des Moines 50316	Jane Molde	Learning Disability Program	515-263-2884
Indiana Hills C. C.	Ottumwa 52501	Judith K. Brickey	Strauss-Kephart Institute	515-683-5125

K&W Quick Reference List

State/School	Location	Contact	Program Name	Telephone
IOWA (Con't)				
Iowa State U.	Ames 50011	Dr. Jim Copley	Services for Students with Disabilities	515-294-5056
Iowa Wesleyan U.	Mt. Pleasant 52641	Sara Mitchell	Learning Center	319-385-6231
Iowa Western C. C.	Council Bluffs 51502	Ray Olson	Special Support Services	712-325-3252
Loras C.	Dubuque 52001	Dianne Gibson	Learning Disabilities Program	319-588-7134
U. of Dubuque	Dubuque 52001	Lavinia Pattee	Learning Center	319-589-3218
U. of Iowa	Iowa City 52242	Donna Chandler	Services for Persons with Disabilities	319-335-1462
U. of Northern Iowa	Cedar Falls 50614	Paula Gilroy	Services for Handicapped Students	319-273-2281
		Wayne King	Center for Academic Achievement	319-273-2346
KANSAS				
Kansas State U.	Manhattan 66506	Gretchen Holden	Services for Students with Physical Limitations	913-532-6441
U. of Kansas	Lawrence 66045	Lorna Zimmer	Student Assistance Center	913-864-4064
KENTUCKY				
Thomas Moore C.	Crestview Hills 41017	Karen Ford	Student Support Services	606-344-3521
U. of Kentucky	Lexington 40506	Jacob Karnes	Handicapped Student Services	606-257-2754
LOUISIANA				
U. of New Orleans	New Orleans 70148	Jill Zimmerman	Student Support Services	504-286-6222
MAINE				
S. Maine Tech C.	South Portland 04106	Gail Christiansen	Learning Assistance Center	207-799-7303
Unity C.	Unity 04988	James Horan	Student Support Services	207-948-3131
		Ann Dalley		
U. of Maine	Orono 04469	Kathy Schilmueller	Disability Services	207-581-2320
U. of New England	Biddeford 04005	Dr. Robert Manganello	Individual Program	207-283-0171
MARYLAND				
Columbia Union C.	Takoma Park 20912	Dr. Betty Howard	Summer Start	301-891-4106
Frostburg State U.	Frostburg 21532	Carolyn Princes, Dir.	Student Support/Disabled Student	301-689-4481
		Beth Hoffman		
Towson State U.	Towson 21204-7097	Margaret M. Warrington	Handicapped Student Services	301-830-2638
U. of Maryland	College Park 20742	William Scales	Disabled Student Services	301-454-6460
Western Maryland C.	Westminster 21157	Matt Jackson	Office of Special Services	301-848-7000
MASSACHUSETTS				
American Inter. C.	Springfield 01109	Dr. Mary Saltus	Supportive Learning Services	413-737-7000
Aquinas Junior C.	Newton 02158	Sister Eleanor K. Shea	Academic Skills Center	617-969-4400
Bentley C.	Waltham 02154	Dr. Roger Danchise	Counseling and Student Development	617-891-2274
Boston U.	Boston 02215	Mr. Kip Opperman	Learning Disabilities Support Services	617-353-3658

333

K&W Quick Reference List

State/School	Location	Contact	Program Name	Telephone
MASSACHUSETTS (Con't)				
Bradford C.	Bradford 01835	Diane Waldron	College Learning Program	508-372-7161
Clark U.	Worcester 01610	Dr. Marilyn Engelman	Academic Advising Center	508-793-7468
Curry C.	Milton 02186	Dr. Gertrude M. Webb	Program for Advancement for Learning (PAL)	617-335-0500
Dean Jr. C.	Franklin 02038	Phil Tetreault	Special Academic Services	617-528-9100
Emerson C.	Boston 02116	Dr. William Tenbrunsel	Learning Assistance Center	617-578-8653
Endicott C.	Beverly 01915	Donna Qualters	Student Support Program	508-927-0585
Lesley C.	Cambridge 02138	Janet Selzer	Threshold	617-491-3739
Mt. Ida C.	Newton Centre 02159	Dr. Chris Chase / Lisa Douly	Learning Opportunities Program	617-969-7000
Northeastern U.	Boston 02115	Dean Ruth K. Bork / Marge Rabinovitch	Disability Resource Center / The LD Program	617-437-2675 / 617-437-2675
Pine Manor C.	Chestnut Hill 02167	Mary Walsh	Learning Resource Center	800-762-1357
Simmons C.	Boston 02115	Helel Moore	Supportive Instructional Services	617-738-2107
Smith C.	Northampton 01063	Mary Jane Maccardini	Special Needs Services	413-585-2071
Tufts U.	Medford 02155	Dr. Jean Herbert	Academic Resource Center	617-628-5000
U. of Massachusetts	Amherst 01003	Dr. Patricia Gillespie-Silver	Learning Disabled Student Services	413-545-4602
Wellesley C.	Wellesley 02181	Kathleen Kopec	Academic Assistance	617-235-0320
Worcester Poly. Inst.	Worcester 01609	Ann Garvin	Academic Advising	508-831-5381
MICHIGAN				
Adrian C.	Adrian 49221	Mary Ann Stibbe	EXCELL	517-265-5161
Alma C.	Alma 48801	Dr. Robert Perkins	Center for Student Development	517-463-7225
Delta C.	University Center 48710	Lowell Plaugher	Learning Disabilities Services	517-686-9556
Michigan State U.	East Lansing 48824	Valerie Nilson	Program for Handicapped Services	517-353-9642
Northern Michigan U.	Marquette 49855	Dr. Masud Mufti	Student Support Services	906-227-1550
Suomi C.	Hancock 49930	Carol Bates	Talent Development	906-487-7297
U. of Michigan	Ann Arbor 48109	Dr. John Hagen	LD Program	313-763-3000
Western Michigan U.	Kalamazoo 49008	Trudy Stauffer	Special Services Program	616-387-4400
MINNESOTA				
Augsburg C.	Minneapolis 55454	John P. Weir	Center for Learning & Adaptive Student Services	612-330-1053
C. of St. Catherine	St. Paul 55105	Elaine McDonough	O'Neill Learning Centers	612-690-6563
Hamline U.	St. Paul 55104	Barbara Simmons	Study Skills Resource Center	612-641-2207
Macalester C.	St. Paul 55105	Charles Norman	Learning Center	612-696-6121
Southwest State U.	Marshall 56258	Marilyn M. Leach	Learning Resource Center	507-537-6169

K&W Quick Reference List

State/School	Location	Contact	Program Name	Telephone
MINNESOTA (Con't)				
U. of Minnesota	Minneapolis 55455	Carrie Wilson	Learning Disability Program	612-624-4037
Winona State U.	Winona 55987	Karen Owen	Student Support Services	507-457-5344
MISSISSIPPI				
U. of S. Mississippi	Hattiesburg 39406	Warren Dunn	Disabled Student Services	601-266-5007
MISSOURI				
Central Mo. State U.	Warrensburg 64093	Mary Alice Lyon	Project Advance	816-429-4061
Kansas City Art Inst.	Kansas City 64111	Kimberly Tyson	Academic Resource Center	816-561-4852
Northwest Mo. St. U.	Maryville 64468	Lois Hldenbrand	Student Support Services	816-562-1861
Southwest Mo. St. U.	Springfield 65804	Dr. Sylvia Buse	Learning Diagnostic Clinic	417-836-4787
U. of Missouri	Columbia 65211	Carma Messerli	Access Office	314-882-4696
Washington U.	St. Louis 63130	Donald Strano Ed.D.	Disabled Student Services	314-889-5040
Westminster C.	Fulton 65251	Henry F. Ottinger	Learning Disabilities Program	314-642-3361
MONTANA				
Montana State U.	Bozeman 59717	Sandra Mandell	Disabled Student Services	406-994-2452
Western Montana C.	Dillon 59725	Clarence Kostelecky	Learning Center	406-683-7330
NEBRASKA				
Union C.	Lincoln 68506	Dr. Joan C. Stoner	People of Promise	402-486-2506
NEVADA				
U. of Nevada	Las Vegas 89154	Jan Hurtubise	Learning Abilities Program	702-739-3781
NEW HAMPSHIRE				
Dartmouth C.	Hanover 03755	Nancy Pomdian	Student Disabilities	603-646-2014
Keene State C.	Keene 03431	Deborah Merchant	Student Academic Support Services	603-352-1902
New England C.	Henniker 03242	Joanne MacEachran	College Skills Center	603-428-2218
New Hampshire C.	Manchester 03104	Dr. Frances Doucette	The Learning Center	603-645-9611
Notre Dame C.	Manchester 03275	Dr. Felicia Wilczenski	Special Needs Assistance Program	603-669-4298
		Joseph P. Wagner		
U. of New Hampshire	Durham 03824	Donna Sorrentino	Access	603-862-2607
NEW JERSEY				
Drew U.	Madison 07940	Johanna Glazewski	Program for Students with LD	201-408-3323
Fairleigh-Dickinson	Rutherford 07070	Dr. Mary Farrell	Learning Disabled College Student Program	201-692-2089
Georgian Court C.	Lakewood 08701	Dr. Marilyn Gonyo	The Learning Center	201-364-2200

K&W Quick Reference List

State/School	Location	Contact	Program Name	Telephone
NEW YORK				
Adelphi U.	Garden City 11530	Sandra Holzinger	Learning Disabled College Students	516-663-1006
Cornell U.	Ithaca 14853	Joan Fisher	Disability Services	607-255-3976
Culinary Inst. of Amer.	Hyde Park 12538	Rebecca Way	Office of Special Services	914-452-9600
Hofstra U.	Hemstead 11550	Dr. Ignacio Gotz	Program for Academic Learning Skills	516-560-5841
Iona College	New Rochelle 10801	Elsa Brady DeVits	College Assistance Program	914-969-4000
Long Is. C.W. Post	Brookville 11548	Dr. Marian T. Power	Academic Resource Center	516-299-2937
Marist C.	Poughkeepsie 12601	Dr. Diane Perreira	Special Services Program	914-471-3270
		Linda Scorza		
Mercy C.	Dobbs Ferry 10522	Catherine Catania	Support Services	914-693-4500
New York U.	New York City 10011	Georgeann DuChossis	Access to Learning	212-998-4980
Paul Smith's C.	Paul Smith 12970	Carol McKillip	Academic Support Services	518-327-6425
Rochester Inst. of Tech.	Rochester 14623	Jacqueline Czamamshe	Special Services	716-475-2832
St. Lawrence U.	Canton 13617	Jim Cohn	Services for Students with Special Needs	315-379-5106
St. Thomas Aquinas	Sparkill 10976	Dr. Mary Doonan	THE "STAC" EXCHANGE	914-359-9500
SUNY at Albany	Albany 12222	Nancy Belowich-Negron	Disabled Student Services	518-442-5490
SUNY C. of Technology	Canton, NY	Debora Camp	Accommodative Services Program	315-386-7121
SUNY C. of Technology	Delhi, NY	Suzanne Aragoni	Services for Learning Disabled	607-746-4129
SUNY C. of Technology	Farmingdale 11735	Malka Edelman	Support Services	516-420-2411
SUNY at Plattsburgh	Plattsburgh 12901	Elizabeth Pasti	Student Support	518-564-2810
SUNY at Stonybrook	Stonybrook 11794	Carol Dworkin	Support Services	516-632-6748
Syracuse U.	Syracuse 13244	Joanne Heinz	Learning Disability Services	315-443-4498
Utica C.	Utica 13502	Stephen Pattarioli	Student Development	315-792-3009
Vassar C.	Poughkeepsie 12601	Karen Getter	Academic Resource Center	914-437-7000
NORTH CAROLINA				
Appalachian State U.	Boone 28608	Arlene Linquist	Learning Disability Program	704-262-9122
East Carolina U.	Greenville 27858-4353	C.C. Rowe	Office of Handicapped Student Services	919-757-6799
North Carolina St. U.	Raleigh 27695-7103	Lelie Brettmann	Handicapped Student Services	919-737-7653
U. of N. Carolina	Wilmington 28403-3297	Margaret T. Sheridan	Disabled Student Services	919-395-3746
Wake Forest U.	Winston-Salem 27109	W.G. Starling	Learning Assistance Program	919-759-5201
Western Carolina U.	Cullowhee 28723	Ginny Hawken	Disabled Student Services	704-227-7127
		Dr. Bonita Jacobs-Dean		704-227-7234
Wingate C.	Wingate 28174-0157	Dr. Lucia R. Karnes	Specific Learning Disabilities	919-945-5803
		Patricia LeDonne	Dyslexia	800-755-5550
NORTH DAKOTA				
North Dakota St. C.	Wahpeton 58075	Georgia Berg	Resource Program for Handicapped	701-671-2327
North Dakota St. U.	Fargo 58105	Liz Sepe	Learning Disabled Program	701-237-7671

K&W Quick Reference List

State/School	Location	Contact	Program Name	Telephone
OHIO				
Bowling Green State U.	Bowling Green 43403	Rob Cunningham	Office of Handicapped Services	419-372-8495
Case W. Reserve U.	Cleveland 44106	Mayo Bulloch	Educational Support Services	216-368-5230
C. of Wooster	Wooster 44691	Pam Rose	Developmental Learning Center	216-246-2595
C. of Mt. St. Joseph	Mt. St. Joseph 45051	Dollie Kelley	Project Excel	513-244-4859
Denison U.	Granville 43023	Theron P. Shell	Educational Services	614-587-6667
Hocking Technical C.	Nelsonville 45764	Kim Forbes Shanor	Center for Alternative Education	614-753-3591
Kent State U.	Kent 44242	Janet L. Filer	Disabled Student Services	216-672-3391
Miami U.	Oxford 45056	Andrew Ziesler	Support Services	513-529-3600
Muskingum C.	New Concord 43762	Dr. Paul Naor	PLUS Program	614-826-8137
Oberlin C.	Oberlin 44074	Dr. Dean Kelly	Student Support Services	216-775-8466
Ohio State U.	Columbus 43210	Lydia Block	Office for Disabilities Services	614-292-3307
Ohio Wesleyan U.	Delaware 43015	Jean Hooper	Writing Resource Center	614-369-4431
Ohio U.	Athens 45701	Susan Wagner, Assistant Director	Affirmative Action	614-593-2620
U. of Akron	Akron 44325	Beth Olmstead	Services for LD Students	216-375-7928
U. of Cincinnati	Cincinnati 45221	Lawrence Goodall	Disability Services	513-556-6816
U. of Dayton	Dayton 45469	Mr. L.B. Fred	Handicapped Student Services	513-229-2229
U. of Toledo	Toledo 43606	Carl Earwood	Physically or Mentally Challenged Skills Center	419-537-2624
Wilmington C.	Wilmington 45177	Laurie Eckels		513-382-6661
Wright State U.	Dayton 45435	Patricia Schlaerth	Learning Disabilities Support Program	513-873-2140
Xavier U.	Cincinnati 45207	Doris Jackson	Academic Advising Center	513-745-3301
OKLAHOMA				
U. of Oklahoma	Norman 73019	Linda Zinner	Handicapped Student Services	405-325-4006
Oklahoma State U.	Stillwater 74078	Maureen A. McCarthy	Disabled Student Services	405-744-7116
OREGON				
Oregon State U.	Corvallis 97331	Joe Wooten	Special Services Program	503-737-4411
PENNSYLVANIA				
Albright C.	Reading 19612-5234	Dale Vandersall	Office of Student Services	215-921-2381
Carnegie Mellon U.	Pittsburgh 15213	Dr. Maria Wratcher	Learning Services	412-268-6878
Clarion U. of Penn.	Clarion 16214	Gregory Clary	Special Services Program	814-226-2347
College Misericordia	Dallas 18612	Dr. Joseph Rogan	Alternative Learners Project	717-674-6347
Dickinson C.	Carlisle 17013	Kate Brooks	Disabled Student Services	717-245-1740
Drexel U.	Philadelphia 19104	Ina Ellen	Office of Student Supportive Services	215-895-2525
East Stroudsburg U.	East Stroudsburg 18301	Bo Keppel	Program for Academic Success	814-424-3470
Edinboro U.	Edinboro 16444	James B. Foulk	Office of Disabled Student Services	814-732-2461
Elizabethtown C.	Elizabethtown 17022	Carol Isaaks	Developmental Studies	717-367-1151
Gettysburg C.	Gettysburg 17325	Beth Kaplanitz	Student Advisement	800-431-0803

K&W Quick Reference List

State/School	Location	Contact	Program Name	Telephone
PENNSYLVANIA (Con't)				
Harcum Jr. C.	Bryn Mawr 19010	Tania Bailey	Talent Development	215-526-6034
Indiana U. of Penn.	Indiana 15705	Catherine Dugan	Disabled Student Services	412-357-4067
Kutztown U.	Kutztown 19530	Barbara Peters	Affirmative Action	215-683-4108
Lock Haven U. of Penn.	Lock Haven 17745	Bruce Skolnick	Special Services	717-893-2324
Lycoming C.	Williamsport 17701	Margaret P. Piper	Academic Support Services	717-321-4326
Mercyhurst C.	Erie 16546	Andrew Roth	Program for Learning Disabled	814-825-0239
Northampton County C. C.	Bethlehem 18017	Cheryl Ashcroft	Services for Learning Disabled	215-861-5342
Pennsylvania State U.	University Park 16802	Brenda G. Hameister	Disability Services	814-863-1807
U. of Pittsburgh	Pittsburgh 15260	Sabina Bilder	Disability Student Services	412-648-7890
U. of the Arts	Philadelphia 19102	Stephanie Bell	Student Resource Center	215-875-1091
RHODE ISLAND				
Brown U.	Providence 02912	Dean Robert Shaw	Dyslexics at Brown	401-863-2378
Johnson & Whales C.	Providence 02903	Dr. A. Renaud	Special Needs Services	401-456-4660
Providence C.	Providence 02918	Frances Shipps	Learning Assistance Center	401-865-2494
U. of Rhode Island	Kingston 02881	Robert Shaw	Handicapped Services	401-863-2315
SOUTH CAROLINA				
U. of South Carolina	Columbia 29208	Deborah C. Haynes	Learning Disability Program	803-777-6142
SOUTH DAKOTA				
South Dakota State U.	Brookings 57007	James W. Carlson	Disabled Student Services	605-688-4496
TENNESSEE				
Lee C.	Cleveland 37311	Davonna Keir	Student Support Services	615-478-7475
Memphis State U.	Memphis 38152	Dr. John Eubank	Handicapped Student Services	901-678-2101
Tennessee Tech U.	Cookeville 38505	Dr. Flanders	Learning Disabled Support	615-372-3331
U. of Tennessee	Knoxville 37996	Scott Berg	Handicapped Student Services	615-974-6087
U. of Tennessee	Chattanooga 37403	Dr. Patricia B. Snowden	College Access Program	615-775-4006
		Melissa Taylor		
Vanderbilt U.	Nashville 37212	Anita Pulley	Students with Disabilities	615-322-4705
TEXAS				
Amarillo C.	Amarillo 79178	Judy Johnson	Transition Assistance	803-371-5436
			Post-Secondary Studies	
Richland C.	Dallas 75243	Jeanne Brewer	Learning Disabilities Program	214-238-6180
Schreiner C.	Kerrville 78028	Harry Heiser	Learning Support Services Program	512-896-5411
		Karen Dooley		

K&W Quick Reference List

State/School	Location	Contact	Program Name	Telephone
TEXAS (Con't)				
Southwest Texas St. U.	San Marcos 78666	Tom Huston	Disabled Student Services	512-245-3451
Texas A & M U.	Galveston 77553	Lynn Martin	Handicapped Student Services	409-845-1241
U. of North Texas	Denton 76203	Barbara Jungjahan	Disabled Student Services	817-565-2199
		Steve Pickert	Services	817-565-4303
UTAH				
Snow C.	Ephraim 84627	Jean Larsen	Student Support Services	801-283-4021 Ext. 313
U. of Utah	Salt Lake City 84112	Olga Nadeau	Disabled Student Services	801-581-5020
VERMONT				
Champlain C.	Burlington 05402	Shelli Goldsweig	Student Resource Center	802-658-0800
Green Mountain C.	Poultney 05764	Larry E. Turns	Skills Advancement Center	802-287-9313
Johnson State C.	Johnson 05656	Kathleen Richardson	Academic and Support Services	802-635-2356
Landmark C.	Putney 05346	Carolyn Olivier	Landmark College/Pre-College	802-387-4767
Norwich U.	Northfield 05663	Paula Gills	Learning Support Center	802-485-2130
Southern Vermont C.	Bennington 05201	Virginia Sturtevant	Learning Disability Program	802-442-5427
Vermont Technical C.	Randolph Center 05061	Nancye Pierce	Disabled Student Services	802-728-3391
U. of Vermont	Burlington 05405-3596	Nancy Oliker / Susan Krasnow	Office of Specialized Student Services	802-656-3340
VIRGINIA				
James Madison	Harrisonburg 22807	Carol Grove	Office of Disability Services	703-568-6705
George Mason U.	Fairfax 22030	Paul Bousel	Disabled Students	703-323-2523
Lynchburg C.	Lynchburg 24501	Craig Wesley	Disabled Students	804-522-8300
Old Dominican U.	Norfolk 23529	Mary Welch	Disabled Student Services	804-683-4655
Roanoke C.	Salem 24153	Catherine Cook	Student Support Services	703-375-2219
U. of Virginia	Charlottesville 22903	Dr. Eleanor Westhead	Learning Needs & Evaluation Center	804-924-3139
Virginia Intermont C.	Bristol 24201	Talmadge Dobbins / Marta Bush	Student Support Services	703-669-6101
WASHINGTON				
Central Washington U.	Ellensburg 98926	Dave Brown	Disabled Student Services	509-963-2171
U. of Washington	Seattle 98195	Enrique Morales	Disabled Students	206-543-5715
Washington State U.	Pullman 99164	Marshall Mitchell	Disabled Student Services/SALC	509-335-4357
Western Washington U.	Bellingham 98225	Dorothy Crow	Disabled Student Services	206-676-3083
WEST VIRGINIA				
Bethany C.	Bethany 26032	Robin Bolling	Special Advising	304-829-7611
Davis & Elkins C.	Elkins 26241	Dr. Margaret Turner	Special Services	304-636-1900

K&W Quick Reference List

State/School	Location	Contact	Program Name	Telephone
WEST VIRGINIA (Con't)				
Marshall U.	Huntington 25755	Dr. Barbara Guyer	H.E.L.P. Program for Learning Problems	304-696-6252
W. Vir. Wesleyan C.	Buckhannon 26201	Phyllis Coston	Special Support Services Program	304-473-8380
WISCONSIN				
Carroll C.	Waukesha 53186	Ginny Giese	Learning Network	806-547-1233
Carthage C.	Kenosha 53141	Peter Holbrook	Academic Support Program	414-551-8500
Edgewood C.	Madison 53711	Kathie Moran	Assistance to Students with LD	608-257-4861
Marian C.	Fond du Lac 54935	Gretchen Gall	Academic Support Services	414-923-8097
Marquette U.	Milwaukee 53233	Patricia Almon	Handicapped Services	414-224-7302
Milwaukee Sch. of Eng.	Milwaukee 53201	Brenda Benton	Learning Resource Center	414-278-6838
Ripon C.	Ripon 54971	Dan Krhin	Student Services	414-748-8107
U. of Wisconsin	Eau Claire 54701	Joseph Hisrich	Services for Students with Disabilities	715-836-4542
U. of Wisconsin	La Crosse 54601	June Reinert	Students with Special Needs	608-785-8535
U. of Wisconsin	Madison 53706	Cathleen Trueba	Learning Specialist	608-263-5177
		Bill Kitz	Project Success	
U. of Wisconsin	Milwaukee 53201	Laurie Gramatzki	Learning Disability Program	414-229-6239
U. of Wisconsin	Oshkosh 54901	Dr. Robert Nash	Project Success	414-424-1033
		Dr. William Katz		
U. of Wisconsin	Platteville 53818	Bernie Bernhardt	Special Services	608-342-1816
U. of Wisconsin	River Falls 54022	Dr. Hamman	Counseling Center	715-425-3884
U. of Wisconsin	Stevens Point 54481	John Timcak	Services for the Disabled	715-346-3361
U. of Wisconsin	Whitewater 53190	Dr. Connie Dalke	Project Assist	414-472-4788

Definition of Testing Instruments and Assessments

Definitions of Testing Instruments and Assessments

Intelligence Tests

WAIS-R: Wechsler Adult Intelligence Scale – Revised
This scale tests verbal and non-verbal intelligence of adults aged 16 and over.

WISC-R: Wechsler Intelligence Scale for Children – Revised
This scale is given to children ages 6 through 16. It measures general intelligence. Five parts measure verbal abilities and five parts measure non-verbal, or performance abilities. The scores on these two parts are combined to produce a full-scale score.

Achievement Tests

PIAT: Peabody Individual Achievement Test
This test is used to measure general academic achievement in reading mechanics and comprehension, spelling, math, and general knowledge.

WRAT: Wide-Range Achievement Tests
This test evaluates oral reading, spelling, and arithmetic computation. Scores are by grade level for each skill.

SDAT: Stanford Diagnostic Achievement Tests
Assesses math and reading skills. This test also provides instructional objectives and suggestions for teaching.

W-J: Woodcock-Johnson Psychoeducational Battery
Tests of academic achievement and interest measure achievement in reading, math, written language, and general knowledge. These tests also assess the level of academic versus non-academic accomplishments.

343

Index

School Name   Page No.

School Name   # Page No.

School Name   Page No.

About the Authors

Marybeth Kravets is currently the College Consultant at Deerfield High School in Deerfield, Illinois. She has been part of the Counseling Department for 12 years. Prior to joining the staff at Deerfield High School, she taught elementary, junior high, and high school as well as worked in the admissions office at a community college in Michigan. She received her B.A. degree from the University of Michigan, Ann Arbor, Michigan, and her M.A from Wayne State University, Detroit, Michigan. Kravets is a member of Lake County Counselor's Association (LCCA), Illinois Association of College Admissions Counselors (IACAC), National Association of College Admissions Counselors (NACAC), Association On Handicapped Student Service Programs In Post-Secondary Education (AHSSPPE), Illinois Council for Learning Disabilities (ICLD), Council for Learning Disabilities (CLD), American Association of Counseling and Development (AACD), American School Counselor's Association (ASCA), and The College Board. She has served as Vice Chair of the Midwest Region of College Board and has been published in the College Board Journal, June 1990. She is married to Alan Kravets and they have four children.

Imy Falik Wax is a certified counselor, currently in private family practice. She has worked with the adolescent population in social service settings as well as in high schools. She received her B.S. from Mills College of Education, New York City, New York and her M.S. from Hunter College, New York City, New York. She is a member of Association of Children With Learning Disabilities (ACLD), Illinois Association Of Children With Learning Disabilities (IACLD), Association On Handicapped Student Service Programs In Post-Secondary Education (AHSSPPE), American Association Of Counseling and Development (AACD), American School Counselors' Association (ASCA), International Association of Marriage and Family Counselors (IAMFC). She is married to Howard Wax and they have four children, one of whom is learning disabled and was the inspiration for this book.